Phil Stone of Oxford

Phil Stone

OF OXFORD

A Vicarious Life

SUSAN SNELL

The University of Georgia Press

Athens and London

© 1991 by the University of Georgia Press
Athens, Georgia 30602
All rights reserved

Designed by Sandra Strother Hudson
Set in Linotype Walbaum by Tseng Information Systems, Inc.
Printed and bound by Thomson-Shore
The paper in this book meets the guidelines
for permanence and durability of the Committee on
Production Guidelines for Book Longevity of
the Council on Library Resources.

Printed in the United States of America

95 94 93 92 91   C   5 4 3 2

95 94 93 92 91   P   5 4 3 2 1

Library of Congress Cataloging in Publication Data

Snell, Susan.
Phil Stone of Oxford : a vicarious life / Susan Snell.
p. cm.
Includes bibliographical references and index.
ISBN 0-8203-1296-7 (alk. paper)
ISBN 0-8203-1436-6 (pbk.: alk. paper)
1. Faulkner, William, 1897–1962—Friends and associates.
2. Stone, Philip Avery, 1893–1967.
3. Novelists, American—20th century—Biography.
4. Lawyers—United States—Biography.
5. Oxford (Miss.)—Biography.   I. Title.
PS3511.A86Z9727   1991
813'.52—dc20
[B]   90-45958
                                            CIP

British Library Cataloging in Publication Data available

TO EMILY

"Your Riches—taught me—Poverty."

Contents

Acknowledgments

TELLING ANY LIFE, I suppose, evolves into a communal project. I am thankful that in this instance the rituals of remembering, retrieving, and preserving were more powerful than instincts to deny, to hide, and to destroy. I am fortunate, I know, in the persons on whom I have depended. For what they have given, I hope the story that follows and my abiding gratitude offer some recompense. The errors, of course, are my own responsibility. However imperfect the work itself, the collective exercise in which we engaged, I trust, matters more. In trying to recover Phil Stone, perhaps we reaffirmed the value not only of his life but of all life—yes, even our own.

Without Emily W. Stone, pregnant dimensions and much of the substance would be absent from this version of Stone's history. Charles East's fortuitous reappearance as Phil Stone's advocate doubtless insured its publication here. He and Karen Orchard of the University of Georgia Press were patient and sensitive far beyond the bounds of duty. I am also deeply indebted, for spiritual and material support, to Louis D. Rubin, Jr., Nancy C. Michael, and Joseph E. Milosh, Jr.

Stone's family and acquaintances (or their heirs) were both generous and kind: Araminta Stone Johnston, her husband Stephen, their daughters Jennifer and Abigail, Mr. and Mrs. A. S. Scott, Jr., Mr. and Mrs. W. E. Stone V, Evelyn S. Ray, Pauline A. and Philip A. Clark; and Mr. and Mrs. W. M. Reed, Robert J. Farley, D. R. Johnson, W. H. Anderson, Mr. and Mrs. Philip Thornton, Jr., J. D. Thames, Elizabeth Ayers, George and Muriel Rogers, Evans Harrington, Alice James Gatchell, T. H. Freeland III, J. K. Hudson, Jr., Arthur and Zoe Kreutz, Marian D. Chamberlin, W. P. Armstrong, Jr., Calvin S. Brown, Edith B. Douds, Herbert Fant, and others to whom I talked more casually. I thank them all.

For their courtesy in making available to me invaluable documents,

Acknowledgments

I am grateful to the Stones, to the staff of the Humanities Research Center, University of Texas at Austin (Lois B. Garcia in particular), to William Boozer and Louis Daniel Brodsky; but also to Richard Wolf, Cleanth Brooks, officials and librarians at Yale University (for helping my student Michele Lamphiere), at the University of Mississippi, and at Mississippi State University.

Mississippi State assisted the long project through released time and small travel grants. The Department of English for years generously shared its limited secretarial and office resources. Those women who labored with and encouraged me during manuscript preparations added months and years to my life; I count as friends especially those who persevered through the last stages, Tammy D. Bowling (my typist), Joyce Harris, Priscilla Ammerman, Barbara Carver, but also a half dozen others and numerous student workers.

Colleagues on the Mississippi State faculty and elsewhere gave timely advice and support: the late Peyton W. Williams, Jr., Jerry T. Williams, Robert L. Phillips, Jr., Linda Brasher, Matthew Little, Brenda Sartoris, Richard Patteson, Lida K. Barrett, John K. Bettersworth, E. O. Hawkins, Jr., Emilie White, to name only a few; and Christine and Michael Kreyling, Joseph M. Flora, James Seay, Sara D. Davis, Cecille and Douglas Gray, Mab Segrest, Bertram Wyatt-Brown, Alistair M. Duckworth, Thomas L. McHaney, Lewis P. Simpson, the late Carvel Collins, with many others. Special thanks go to Rhoda C. Ellison, with whom I first read Faulkner, and who, over my protests, signed me up for Emily Stone's class in 1966.

Others most dear to me, friends and family alike, long ago grew tired of the very mention of Stone and Faulkner, but had the good sense never to say so. For their tact, for their love, for their steadfastness, whether over months or years, I am deeply grateful.

Portions of this narrative were adapted for articles I previously published: " 'Aristocrat' and 'Commoner': The Professions and Souths of Stark Young and William Faulkner," *Southern Quarterly* 24 (1986): 93–100; "Phil Stone and William Faulkner: The Lawyer and 'The Poet,' " *Mississippi College Law Review* 4 (1984): 169–92; and "William Faulkner, Phil Stone and Katrina Carter: A Biographical Footnote to the Summer of 1914," *Southern Literary Journal* 15 (1983): 76–86. I also made use of Stone materials for the article "Mr. Faulkner: A South-

Acknowledgments

erner's Guide to García Márquez," published in Spanish in the collection *En el punto de mira: Gabriel García Márquez*, edited by Ana María Hernandez (Madrid: Editorial Pliegos, 1985), 315–26.

The debts I owe to the authors or owners of other published and unpublished materials are numerous and are acknowledged, though most inadequately, in the notes following the Afterword.

None of us, thank goodness, has to work alone.

Phil Stone of Oxford

Introduction

IN ST. PETER'S CEMETERY in Oxford, Mississippi, on the high ground overlooking William Faulkner's grave, a modest granite slab is inscribed: "Phil Stone / Born Oxford, Mississippi, February 23, 1893 / Died Jackson, Mississippi, February 20, 1967 / 'Here Is My Earth.'" Among the letters of condolence to Stone's widow that spring in the late 1960s, Yale law alumnus Hubert Starr intoned a quite different epitaph for a life otherwise marked for public oblivion: "William Faulkner is Phil Stone's contribution to American literature," he avowed, "and don't let anybody tell you any different." Herb Starr, a California attorney, was not given to hyperbole; moreover, his long friendship with Stone and Faulkner dated from New Haven in 1918. While there is still ample reason for skepticism in the matter, Faulkner scholars must evaluate afresh the merits of the case, for we have been most premature in relegating Oxford attorney Philip Avery Stone to the marginalia of Yoknapatawpha.

As Phil Stone once noted wryly of his friend William Faulkner, "You can no more stop a professional from writing than you can stop a dope fiend from taking dope." But without Phil Stone, Billy Falkner might well have remained a talented but obscure dabbler, only a portfolio poet, or a provincial raconteur. Stone's tangible contributions to Faulkner's apprenticeship were first documented among the "Burned Papers," remnants from Stone's Faulkner archives recovered from the ashes of the 1940s fire that destroyed the Stone home; manuscript poetry and miscellany there, the nearly complete *Marble Faun* correspondence, and Stone's early New Haven book orders (all now at the University of Texas) certify Phil Stone's indefatigable service at the outset of Faulkner's career. A dozen or more extant volumes from Stone's library—sometimes signed or marked by both men—also testify to their early, substantive literary colloquy.

Introduction

Friends from the summer of 1914, when Phil returned to Mississippi with his first Yale degree, the two young men—Stone, twenty-one, Faulkner, sixteen—embarked upon a singular literary collaboration that was to continue, though often radically transformed, for the rest of their lives. Their marked differences in maturity and intellectual sophistication at the commencement of the friendship initially cast Phil as Mentor to Bill's (fatherless) Telemachus. Stone, tellingly, preferred the comic epithet "wet nurse," which he coined in the 1930s. In truth no label embraces the myriad functions Stone performed for the younger man from that first summer through the 1920s, even as with Faulkner's growth the friends and literary aspirants met more nearly as equals. Phil was tutor, librarian, and purveyor of books during Faulkner's initiation into modern letters; he was first reader, editor, and critic of Faulkner's manuscript verse and early novels. Although ostensibly a practicing country lawyer, he became Faulkner's most visible and zealous champion, acting as agent, publicist, patron—and on occasion bank—for the man called "Count No 'Count," the shame of the Falkner clan.

Looking back, Stone marveled, "I had the gall of Ole Nick in those days." He most assuredly did. Publishers, newspaper and magazine editors, and contemporary authors from E. A. Robinson to T. S. Eliot were alerted to pay attention to young Faulkner of Oxford; he was "a comer," Stone prophesied, for seventeen years. Phil's prescience earned him no laurels then or later. "I am a male Cassandra," he declared, to deafened ears.

After the Second World War, as critic Malcolm Cowley resurrected Yoknapatawpha and the Nobel Academy validated Faulkner's more-than-regional talent, scholars like Carvel Collins and journalists like Robert Coughlan began coming to Oxford to interview the reclusive genius and to savor his milieu. Few accomplished the former mission; their reception at Rowan Oak was often lukewarm at best. Consequently, the critics and journalists grudgingly settled for atmosphere, invariably making their way to Phil Stone's antiquarian law offices just off the square, and thence into the Stones's backyard for bourbon or gin. What they discovered during their time in Mississippi was rather more than an exotic culture; indeed, they had cause to be simultaneously elated and perplexed. Stone's sometimes insistent claims about the years he had spent "fooling with Bill" were in large part confirmed by the papers he exhibited to serious inquirers. At the same time, Phil Stone's smug conceit, perhaps more his transparent envy of his "protégé," surely inclined the visitor to question whether all that he said was gospel truth.

However skeptically they regarded Phil Stone, the first generation of Faulkner scholars assiduously courted their primary witness, besieging him with question after question. If for no other reason, we must acknowledge Stone's long-suffering assistance to Faulkner studies: as archivist and Oxford "stringer"; as one of his friend's first biographers; and, of incalculable value, as biocritical source for scholars the caliber of Carvel Collins, James B. Meriwether, and the late Richard P. Adams.

Faulkner's "mentor," lifelong friend, and witness thus deserves the attention of Faulkner biographers, as they have since the mid-seventies only reluctantly conceded. The extent and complexity of William Faulkner's indebtedness to Phil Stone in the fiction, hitherto generally dismissed to Stone's retrospective vanity, is the much more intriguing and compelling study. Be assured: it is also a speculative undertaking as well. A comprehensive Stone biography, however, provides the leads from which plausible critical theories may—with care—arise.

From my perspective, there is a great irony with regard to Stone's impact upon Faulkner's major work. While so self-consciously engaged as Faulkner's "Muse," as he implies, Phil Stone, almost unwittingly, served American literature more significantly as one of the fictionist's principal character studies—and mirrors. The following pages attest to how thoroughly William Faulkner ransacked Stone's genealogy, life, and contacts for the stories and novels: Phil's great-uncles Amodeus and Theophilus, his first sexual partner Dewey Dell, his roadster Drusilla, his sojourns in the Ivy League, his father's Delta hunts, his friends among the gamblers and prostitutes in Clarksdale and Memphis—only begin the reckoning. The fictional Jefferson's patriarchs derive in part from the formidable, profane old men James Stone (Phil's father) and his idiosyncratic law partner Clarence Sivley. Faulkner's dowagers, spinsters, and other "tough old dames" owe rather a lot to Rosamond Stone (Phil's mother), if not to her Delta kinswomen, who were planters and suffragists long before American women—and by their sweat—earned the vote. Then too, from the first, the Stones' antebellum mansion recurs in Faulkner's architectural details; years later, its destruction by fire seems virtually transcribed into *Go Down, Moses*. Oddly, or perversely, sometimes, as with his General Longstreet encounter, Phil's experiences turn up verbatim as Bill's "autobiography." And on and on. The borrowing was pervasive and continued decades after the men's closest friendship was at an end.

From Faulkner's earliest fiction through *The Reivers* (1961) there was seldom a corner of Stone's life that did not provide the author with copy—for reasons obvious only to those familiar with Stone's history. Remove the anomaly of his relationship with the Nobel laureate and Phil Stone's life becomes a curiously representative specimen: of the Southern "aristocrat"; of "Southern Honor" confronting its twentieth-century crucibles—the rednecks, the Great Depression, James Meredith at Ole Miss (not to mention the emerging modern woman). Granted, Stone's life may now read like regional archetype merely because "omniscient" perspectives on his life—and Faulkner's art—readily lend themselves to revisionist history.

But there is another possibility. Perhaps William Faulkner has conditioned us to regard the particulars of Stone's character and ethos as typically "Southern" because William Faulkner defined "Southern" to us (as to himself) in the guise of Phil Stone. (Stone may embody the regional model too because he so tirelessly refined his own mythology to fit that of a communal Southern mold or ideal.) William Alexander Percy, to name the obvious example, may appear the more stellar representative of the "Faulknerian" or "Southern" character type to which Stone belongs: scions of the planter class, professional men—usually lawyers, sometimes doctors—who more ardently practiced belles lettres and noblesse oblige on the side. But Phil Stone's life, extending into the Earl Warren era, encompasses the whole of the tumultuous, metamorphic period that, as we now realize, recompensed American culture with the "Southern Renascence." Besides, William Faulkner, though an admirer of Will Percy, probably saw the Greenville poet no more than a half dozen times before the latter's death in 1942. The imagery of Phil Stone was daily before him—for almost fifty years.

What compelled Faulkner's attention? Certainly not their common personality traits. Stone was gregarious; Faulkner, taciturn often to the point of muteness. Phil was forward; Bill was self-effacing. Stone was urbane; Faulkner, at ease perhaps only with children, old ladies, and country folk. Phil reveled in farcical pranks, as in the cornucopia of eccentrics divinely apportioned, it seemed, to Lafayette County. In stark contrast, Stone reiterated, the boy with whom he passed their first idle summer was "a most humorless person." Only gradually, Stone said, did they relish together the discomfiture of sanctimony, pomposity, and propriety. Phil Stone's having somehow engendered mirth in the writer now acclaimed as a comic genius naturally invites our incredulity—until we appreciate the societal security, especially its concomitant emotional detachment, from which comic perspectives are born.

Cultural historians and English professors will argue till Doomsday that the nobility of the British Isles did not emigrate en masse to the plantations of the colonial South; "old" families in Richmond and Charleston continue doggedly to protest that *they* know an "aristocrat" when they see one. Likewise, among their kinsmen in Natchez, in the Mississippi Delta, and, yes, in the hill towns of North Mississippi, with any prosperity the landed gentry there too arrogated the class distinctions, if not the name, of "aristocracy."

As with Faulkner's residual racism, we might prefer to believe that an artist of his vision did not succumb to the prevailing class-consciousness of his day. But the circumstantial evidence suggests otherwise. The now hallowed shrine and relics at Rowan Oak fittingly perpetuate the persona even a mature William Faulkner took pains to impart: Squire William arrayed for the hunt in the Cofield portraits, the daunting hauteur of the famous writer while in his cups, and his late removal from Oxford to Mr. Jefferson's university—all betray an insatiable hunger for class ascendancy, one that his association with Phil Stone paradoxically appeased and whetted.

Born too late to observe the career of William C. Falkner, which had marked the zenith of his own family's fortunes, the writer evidently romanticized the "Old Colonel," a multifaceted and controversial businessman, warrior, and author. The patriarch's son, Faulkner's grandfather, J. W. T. Falkner (the "Young Colonel"), like his contemporary and rival Phil Stone's father, in time earned considerable economic and political influence in North Mississippi; but whatever "aristocratic" trappings the Falkners affected, with the subsequent generation the family slipped, disconcertingly, into the middle class. During the writer's childhood and youth, his family bought their groceries first with Murry Falkner's railroad wages, then with revenues from the father's assorted shoestring ventures: a livery stable, a garage, a hardware store, and the like. Only after the eldest son had reached his majority did Murry Falkner become business manager at the adjacent University of Mississippi, undoubtedly through paternal influence at that. William Faulkner may himself have served as prototype for his character "Sarty" Snopes (of "Barn Burning"), as his family too often moved from house to house, finally settling into rental quarters on the university campus.

Moreover, despite Faulkner's later projections of erudition and classicism, namely in his rhetorical, Latinate style and imperious manner, the laureate never formally completed even his secondary public schooling. Yet frequently in his novels and public comments, the writer poignantly laments the once hereditary (or imaginary) prestige and power that he, like his father, either abdicated or was unfit for.

Not coincidentally, during the period in which he was drifting away from school, Faulkner became an intimate in the Stone households and law firm, where—in addition to his further literary education—he could experience at first hand both the wealth and the accoutrement ascribed to Southern "aristocrats." As we shall see, Phil Stone's matrilineal kin laid claim to the requisite pedigree, while his father, mindful of the Stones' mere yeomanry rank, became adept at making money. The elegant 1840s mansion Stone's father purchased when the family moved into Oxford from the Delta only confirmed their pretensions. In a region full of "Colonels" and sometimes a "Major" or two, James Stone, courtesy decreed, was "General" Stone to peers and inferiors alike. As befit the family's status, from boyhood, a precocious, bookish Phil Stone was given a gentleman's education in the classics (in Oxford and New Haven) before he read law at the state university and then again at Yale. In due time he was expected to join the firm of James Stone & Son and to assume the Southern planter class's familial and civic stewardships.

The accidentals of Phil's being the youngest son and his father's remaining vigorous into his seventies occasioned Phil Stone's indulgence with an extended leisure in which to pursue literary interests that had quickened in his years at Yale. Stone knew well the part he was being groomed for, but in the long interval, as he awaited the call to serve, he refined his paternal role models by incorporating into his personality the traditional antebellum dimensions of the Southern gentleman of letters. Phil began effecting that further myth-making at first through cultivation of an older North Mississippi compatriot, the novelist and drama critic Stark Young. After Stone introduced Bill Faulkner to "Mr. Stark" in 1914 or 1915, both younger men paid patrician Stark Young the homage of imitation, in social graces as in their approximation of Young's "artistic" life. In their "Count William" and World War I masquerades, for example, both Stone and Faulkner aspired to Young's sartorial splendor, clumsily affected British accents, and embarked upon Arcadian literary strolls—amid the gnats, mosquitoes, rattlesnakes, and poison ivy of Woodson Ridge. Although Stone would never leave the States, at his urging Bill Faulkner—after the manner of cosmopolitan Stark Young—dutifully undertook the gentleman's walking tour of Europe.

In the patriarchal, anti-intellectual South, Stone's and Faulkner's devotion to Art was permitted as avocation, even forgiven as consuming passion during one's youth; but, as Stark Young and Will Percy also exemplify, Southern poets—even a poet manqué—sooner or later invite suspicions regarding their masculinity. *To say* is not *to do*, as Faulkner's Quentins and Darls, Horaces and Gavins, continually practice self-excoriation. Actions, deeds certify masculine identity. Only "she-men" have to resort to impotent words. Financial reversals culminating in the Depression thwarted Phil Stone's wielding the expected "masculine" power during his prime, ironically just as William Faulkner's most unorthodox Southern profession, of "womanish" words, earned him the means to solidify his upper-class persona—Rowan Oak, Greenfield "farm," and, ultimately, Charlottesville (where he was negotiating for land at the time of his death). From the 1930s Stone's and Faulkner's inverse proportions of debts and money, foreclosures and real estate, disgrace and fame, seem too stark and melodramatic to be true.

In a sense, in life William Faulkner usurped Phil Stone's place in the South's social order. Meanwhile, in the major fiction, the writer's recurring story was the decadent South, the fall of the House of Sartoris, of Compson, not so much, as in his own history, the rise, or restoration, of a proud family. In short, Faulkner's most characteristic narrative became Phil Stone's story, not his own.

Moreover, in Yoknapatawpha Faulkner would otherwise appropriate Stone's personality and profession further to mirror—and sometimes mask—his own personal (usually sexual) and professional insecurities. The "wordmen" of Yoknapatawpha—the Ivy League's Quentin Compson, another "male Cassandra" Darl Bundren, the attorneys Horace Benbow and Gavin Stevens—no doubt primarily manifest their creator, who fashioned them in his own image. But their strong resemblance to an obsessively verbal, fatefully ineffectual Phil Stone does not stop with superficial parallels. In the "motherless" sons Quentin and Darl, for example, Faulkner may have been exorcising his own problematic maternal relationship, but Caroline Compson and Addie Bundren more nearly reflect Rosamond Alston Stone than Maud Butler Falkner. That Phil Stone's mother allegedly withheld her love from him while lavishing it upon her middle son Jim seems to have grievously undermined Stone's self-esteem and power to act—or so he reiterated. Such psychological, if not sexual, impotence, of course, is a trait common to all four of Faulkner's protagonists, but the paralysis that afflicts Quentin and Darl proves more catastrophic than with Faulkner's later personae. So it would be with Phil Stone (as William Faulkner chillingly anticipated and foretold).

In both *The Sound and the Fury* and *As I Lay Dying* Faulkner's configurations of two sons vying for their mother's love (Quentin-Caroline [the elder]-Jason and Darl-Addie-Jewel) implicitly reflect the unstable, volatile dynamics of classic sexual triangles. Two of the three principals, however, commit not betrayal or adultery but incestual infidelity. In Faulkner's own family there seems no parallel for that devastating sibling rivalry. Again, the pattern is quite evident among the family members William Faulkner so long and so closely observed. It takes no Freudian to suggest that Phil's livid jealousy of his brother, especially with his diatribes against his mother, fronted something like his own frustrated Oedipal complex, the "harmless" arrested development, ironically, Phil in retrospect attributed to William Faulkner!

Whatever the psychological causes, during their protracted adolescence together, Stone and Faulkner also came together, as young men will, because women gave them trouble. Oxford assumed that Katrina

Introduction

Carter was destined for Phil Stone, while Bill Faulkner believed he had an understanding with her friend Estelle Oldham. When, for different reasons, neither courtship readily progressed to the altar, Phil and Bill found consolation in the security of masculine companionship. There need not have been—indeed I would seriously doubt there was—any homosexual expression of their deep regard. Nevertheless, what the two men shared, I believe, was a kind of love, perhaps partially and latently eros, so that with one another they opened themselves to betrayal, a vulnerability the unloving are not prey to. In 1918 Stone was gratified that when Estelle Oldham determined to marry someone else, whoever said what or did what (the episode changes with the teller), William Faulkner left Oxford for New Haven and Phil Stone. And over an interval of almost twelve years, literature was the only serious "mistress" either man would have.

At Estelle Oldham's second entrance, in the late 1920s, both men were of an age when matrimony had become societally imperative. Characteristically, Bill was the one first to act. And, confronted by the reality of his marriage to Estelle, Phil Stone was clearly at a loss, a trauma quickly exacerbated by his family's financial collapse. Of course, Stone was thereafter himself "free" to marry—as he did, and apparently for love, in 1935. But from the fateful conjunction of Faulkner's departure and the Stones' ruin, Phil Stone was never to recover, never again, that is, to " 'be' Phil Stone." Over and over, he would tell his wife Emily (whom he met only in the early 1930s): "You've never known me when I was myself."

It seems clear from what follows that around 1930 Stone turned more perilously into the direction that sealed his character and fate. Prompted or driven by some real or imagined childhood need, Stone by his early twenties had come to believe or had discovered that he could certify his human worth only vicariously. He could be a conduit, he thought, but never himself act. For, as he often said of himself, "I can fight a war but I can't fight a battle," and "I'm like an elaborate, intricate piece of machinery which doesn't quite work." The latter statement, like numerous others, Faulkner appropriated for one of his "composite" character doubles, the lawyer-artist manqué Horace Benbow (in *Sanctuary*).

From 1914 through the early 1930s, and after, however, Stone had been alive indeed, through William Faulkner and William Faulkner's art, "their" art, to which Phil contributed incidents, anecdotes, and characters, his whole word and life hoard, in fact. After 1930 or so, for self-validation he reverted to his obsession to win his mother's love, in a quixotic, deadly manner: by assuming his father's $50,000 in debts. If General Stone failed, or faltered, as Rosamond's breadwinner and protector, Phil Stone himself would take on the husbandly role: "Bill," he told Faulkner about that time, "you don't need me any more, and I have to make a living for my old folks." (Had not James Stone at Phil's birth reassured his wife: "He will save us in our old age"?) Before the beloved mother breathes her last, she will turn to us and tell us *we're* the one she has loved and depended on all the while. Sure.

But Phil Stone apparently believed it, even more compulsively after first his two brothers, then his father, died within four terrible years during the middle thirties. At Miss Rosie's deathbed in 1943, he mused aloud, "I'm the only one who stayed with her completely to the end." But the end was not yet. Just as he never settled his father's estate, neither would he ever contract with a stonemason to chisel the date of his mother's death on his parents' tombstone. Closure was impossible until his own death.

But ever mindful of the means by which he had been most "successful" in his frustrated life—from the time of his marriage, Phil Stone also returned again to Art for self-vindication. To prove that the phenomenon of William Faulkner had been no cosmic accident, Stone discovered in the much younger Emily Whitehurst a new surrogate writer. Once again manuscripts went north from James Stone & Sons—for a quarter century—but, alas, this time largely in vain. Then in 1940 Philip Alston Stone, his son and first child, was born into the father's great need. Literate at eighteen months, reading by age three, Philip wrote his first "verse tragedy" at six ("the 'tragedy' was Philip Stone's," a close family friend astutely remarked). At seventeen Philip sold a novel to Knopf, before he matriculated at Harvard in Latin and Greek—and left behind at his premature death in the mid-sixties file after file of manuscripts. As the son had grievously realized, however, for his father it was never enough. The winter after William Faulkner's death, the winter too following the integration riots at Ole Miss, the

Introduction

Honorable Phil Stone was committed to Whitfield, the state mental hospital. It was there that he died, four years later.

Thus, the life of Philip Avery Stone, as William Faulkner intuited long before we could, reads far more like myth than fact, and a particularly Southern, and American, and universal myth at that. Phil Stone sought to validate his life in the stereotypically Western, stereotypically masculine way: 1) by making a name for himself in the world, a legacy (one that became an obsession) imbibed from his beloved Greek literature. Phil so liked to quote his black retainer's telling baby Philip in his bassinet: "Yo' name's gonna be known farther than yo' face!" And 2) by Stone's certifying his worth—and again his masculinity—by means of material wealth, a pursuit that ultimately killed him, like so many others in our culture. In both pursuits, by his own severe assessment, Phil Stone was an abysmal failure. Never mind that his wife Emily and son Philip and daughter Araminta literally adored him. Never mind that he was a great favorite with his young nieces and nephew—and befriended as well as loved, it seems clear, by a grateful William Faulkner.

Paradox was never to quit Phil Stone. Only the writer, who preceded him in death, could and did ensure Phil Stone's immortality. Thanks to Bill Faulkner *and* his lifelong friend, witness, and character study, Phil Stone lives inviolate—and rightly so—as little black marks on good white paper.

We must, then, look more critically at the "definitive" line on Phil Stone and admit that it may take us years, if ever, to read William Faulkner and Phil Stone and their complex use of one another with any hope of or degree of exactitude. And for years after that, we will be debating what, really, Gavin Stevens or Horace Benbow, or Darl Bundren or Quentin Compson, owe to their prototype Phil Stone. In the interim, let us not prematurely give up searching for the elusive "real" lives, lest we forever set, in concrete, lies, not truths.

1

Family

PHIL STONE greatly admired his father, in his professional life seeking to emulate "General" James Stone, whose mistakes in part predestined his tragedy.[1] Of his mother Phil spoke bitterly: "By the time I was five years old, I knew Miss Rosie was a fool and didn't care anything about me."[2] Yet he identified principally with her family, the Alstons, rather than with his father's people. By his maturity Stone had invested the Alston name with virtues traditionally gracing an enlightened, beneficent ruling class. That a man of his breeding, education, and manner inherited prerogatives and obligations reserved to the "aristocracy" was the central concept informing the man whom William Faulkner befriended and observed.

Stone's notions of self-worth did not derive from a close scrutiny of his maternal forebears, but among them were the noble Saxon antecedent, state governor, Confederate officer, Episcopal cleric, and wealthy planter seemingly requisite for an "old" family in the South.[3] He claimed direct relation to South Carolina Governor Joseph Alston, who married Aaron Burr's daughter. But the family peerage, J. A. Groves's *Alstons and Allstons of North and South Carolina*, traces Stone's line instead from a respectable though more obscure pair, Colonel Philip Alston and Mary Drew Temple. From the Carolinas, where the Alstons remain a prominent family, Stone's ancestors followed a common pioneer route, first to Georgia (establishing a branch there recently including another Philip Alston, the American ambassador to Australia during the Carter administration); then, within a decade of the Chickasaw treaties of 1832 and 1834, Phil Stone's great-grandparents, William and Mary Somerville Alston of Telfair County, Georgia, immigrated westward into the former Indian territories of North Mississippi.[4]

Whether or not their Carolina or Georgia relatives succumbed to the sin, the Mississippi progeny of William Alston were steeped in family pride. Pauline Alston Clark, Stone's aunt, was a woman ordinarily with much good sense, but she gave three of her children the family name and became at one time enamored of genealogy—until her discovery of Alston horse thieves in Barbados, at which she lost interest in family trees.[5]

Although he knew few details of the family before his maternal grandparents, Stone quite early imbibed such familial reverence. There were Alston antiques in every room of the Stone house in Oxford, and his mother, Rosamond Alston Stone, was an inveterate family visitor, especially in Phil's childhood. In her parlor too the curious, intelligent child apparently spent hours with leather-bound family albums that enshrined scores of Alston cousins next to the Confederate heroes Stone apotheosized as a boy. Only two of those albums escaped the fire that destroyed the Stone home, but, long before that, Phil Stone had secured a safer repository for other fragments of family history in the chronicles of Yoknapatawpha.

Stone rather liked being told that in countenance and physique he was the virtual double of his maternal grandfather—both men were short and thin with small bones. In reciting the mixed fortunes of Philip Somerville Alston, he seems to have found patience to endure his own intractable circumstance. Born in Georgia in 1831, Philip Alston had been a schoolboy of eleven or twelve years when his father and mother resettled in Wyatt, Mississippi, one of the two earliest communities in Lafayette County. Wyatt lay thirteen miles north of Oxford, on the upper navigable extent of the Tallahatchie River. Briefly a thriving river port, the new town was already slipping toward extinction when the young man began work there as a partner in a dry goods store.[6]

Philip Alston's marriage to Mary Ann Potts in 1852 promised him brighter economic prospects, for her grandfather, though a Methodist circuit rider, by no means "let the ways of God interfere with the ways of Mammon," according to Phil Stone. Soon after the territory had opened, the circuit rider acquired one hundred square miles of land along the Tallahatchie River. Two of Potts's sons, Theophilus and Amodeus, whom the family called Buck and Buddy, cultivated the acres General Stone later retained for his hunting camp.[7]

But it was not for their land that Stone would remember his grandmother's people. "The Potts strain," he said, "was the fatality of those who came after." Stone's father spoke darkly of providential vengeance upon one particularly malevolent Potts, inappropriately a survivor of the Army of Northern Virginia. The soldier had been walking home after Appomattox when, in crossing a branch in Mississippi, he slipped on a log and drowned. The man was a demon, General Stone avowed: "It was God's present to the world that he died." Phil Stone believed that in subsequent generations of his family, one member was mad or demonic because of the Potts blood.

Whether Mary Ann's dowry was a wilderness plantation or a curse, during the marriage mere survival would seem fortune enough. The couple's first child died before his first birthday; their second, at two years. During Mary Ann's third pregnancy, she and her husband lived near her relatives, probably in the neighborhood of Mount Terza Methodist Church, midway between Oxford and Batesville ("Old Panola") in Panola County. On 24 March 1858, eight months after burying their second child, Rosamond Watkins Alston, Phil Stone's mother, was born to the Philip Alstons in Old Panola. By late spring of the next year, Mary Ann was pregnant again, with Rosamond's brother, William Henry. His birth in January 1860 may have involved complications, for within four months of that confinement the mother was dead. Philip Alston would not remarry until after the ensuing war. Meanwhile, his son was suckled by a slave, and both children were entrusted to the care of two unmarried aunts.

Although one family obituary notes only that Alston "served with distinction in the Confederate army,"[8] as a soldier Philip S. Alston attained a position later hallowed by the region's genealogists. Unlike countless pretenders—including William C. Falkner, the novelist's great-grandfather—Alston was in fact a major on the staff of Confederate cavalryman Nathan Bedford Forrest.[9] After the war his horse pistol, saddlebags, and portable writing desk became part of the family's treasures. Thereafter too, Stone's grandfather was to be addressed as

"Major" Alston. But perhaps a generation enduring the privations of war and its aftermath may be forgiven its mythologizing.

While Alston was riding with Forrest, his relatives had become friends with Sara Cooper and her brother,[10] Tennesseans who settled in Panola County during the war. When the young veteran resumed supervision of the family plantations, he began calling upon Sallie Cooper, whom he married shortly before Christmas in 1866. But the first years of his second marriage were also bleak ones for Philip Alston. Whenever later generations inquired about Reconstruction in North Mississippi, those who had lived through it were reluctant to elaborate about those "*terrible* times"; however, Sallie Alston once divulged to her grandchildren that she had sewn white robes for the Ku Klux Klan.[11] Apparently, her husband had had occasion to renew his acquaintance with the Klan's founder, Bedford Forrest. Whatever moral price such experiences exacted of Philip Alston, with the restoration of a planter-dominated social order, a measure of stability and comfort returned to the Alstons and their children—Rosamond, William Henry, Elizabeth Pauline (born in 1870), and Philip S. Alston, Jr. (born in 1875)—during the 1870s.

Phil Stone believed that his mother's "flighty" character had been fixed by her wartime childhood with slaves and the two spinsters, to whom he credited her pronounced hypochondria as well. He once wrote that she "enjoyed bad health all her life and never suffered any pain less than 'agony,' never had a serious illness until she was eighty-three years old, slept with all windows closed, got as little sunshine as possible, lived largely off of molasses and [corn] bread and fatback, said that fruits and vegetables made her sick and when she died from a broken hip at eighty-five she still had half of her own teeth . . . and could read a newspaper without eyeglasses."[12]

Rosamond Alston's girlhood, however, seems stereotypically genteel. To complete her education, Major Alston sent his older daughter away to Memphis to a female seminary.[13] Phil Stone would be incredulous that his mother's record there had earned her an invitation to remain—to teach Greek. More in character, he thought, was her decision to return instead to Major Alston's parlor, where in the late seventies she was entertaining, among others, a young law student named James Stone who, after an extended courtship, finally summoned the courage to propose—by letter. It was a cowardice she never allowed him to forget. On 5 February 1878 Rosamond Watkins Alston and James Bates Stone were married, in a ceremony performed by the Reverend J. W. Bates, for whom both the groom and Batesville had been named. For their first home, Major Alston gave the couple "a suite of parlor furniture": two sofas, two gentlemen's chairs, and six side chairs.

By the time Rosamond's half sister Polly was of courting age, a decade later, the Alstons were living in Memphis, where Major Alston grew wealthy in the feed and grain business with the firm of Webb & Maury,[14] and as a cotton factor. He had sufficient means to send his younger daughter to the New England Conservatory of Music.

After Philip Alston's death in 1893, his widow and her two children decided to return to Mississippi, to Major Alston's plantation near Clarksdale in Coahoma County. There, for almost four decades, Sara Cooper Alston with her "unusual wit" and "happy store of good humor" was in truth mistress of "Casco," the plantation she managed through drought, flood, yellow fever, and five-cent cotton.

Phil Stone spoke of Sallie Alston as "an amazingly efficient woman," and even her fellow planters admitted that she was one of the best "businesswomen" in the Delta. Matriarch as well as breadwinner, she saw her husband's older children often, and she generously assumed the care and education of her stepson's two children when William's wife died in Batesville in 1897.

In 1894 Sallie Alston's daughter Polly became the wife of Walter Clark, a planter who also owned a large brickyard; a year later Clark and Sallie's son Philip were business partners. But soon after her son's marriage, he became gravely ill; and, forced to dissolve the partnership, he moved to the Southwest for his health. Phil Alston would be dead by 1904, at the age of twenty-nine, the family's shock unrelieved by their having foreseen that he would not return home alive.[15]

At first, Sallie Alston's vitality seemed only faintly mirrored in her surviving child. Despite her Boston education, Phil Stone's Aunt Polly Clark appeared to be satisfied with domesticity. Two years after establishing her household, she began a diary, recording her mother's incessant motion, to Oxford, Sardis, Casco, Batesville, Memphis; James Stone's coming over to court; her husband's trip to Chicago for a clay manufacturers' convention, or, during the flood, his vigils at the levee;

the births of sons John Alston and Walter; and Walter's sudden death from diphtheria at age one. By 1899 something closer to Sallie Alston's vigor begins to emerge in Polly's diary. She was attending the Micawber Club on Thursday evenings for cards, pool, and billiards: "I am learning to play pool and like it very much." She and Walter had also marked off a tennis court. Then Belle Kearney of Madison County, president of the Mississippi Woman Suffrage Association,[16] called and later returned to stay at their home when the association held its convention in Clarksdale in April 1899. After the sessions Polly noted, defiantly, "The attendance at the Convention was small but we did well to have one at all."

In the next few years Polly's activity outside the family increased, despite the birth of Pauline Alston Clark in 1905 and Philip Alston Clark in 1911. She collected almost a hundred dollars for the "Old Ladies Home Association," served as secretary-treasurer of the Clarksdale Circle of King's Daughters, who were planning an infirmary, and as corresponding secretary of the Mississippi Suffrage Association went to the national convention in New Orleans. In the 1920s she would be one of the first women to serve in the Mississippi legislature. By the early years of this century she obviously no longer had time for a diary. Aunt Polly—female or no—was an Alston to reckon with. "Sister Rosa," for one, would never be a match for her.

The family into which Rosamond had married was by no means poor, but unlike the Alstons the Stones worked with their hands, or did physical work on their farms. If unable to trace their lineage from a Saxon lord, by the 1890s the family was prominent enough for James Stone's biography to be solicited for "a Record of the Lives of Many of the Most Worthy and Illustrious Families and Individuals" in Mississippi.[17] That history, often in error, states that both sides of Stone's family came from the Kentucky Bluegrass region. Family stories mention Kentucky only to report James Stone's schooling there; they maintain, rather, that the family moved to Mississippi in the 1830s from Washington-Wilkes, Georgia.[18] Phil Stone's paternal great-grandfather, William Evans Stone (1781–1864), an early settler of Panola County, is buried at Eureka Springs, southeast of Batesville, his wife Levenia beside him.[19] According to the biography, James Stone's father, William E. Stone (1823–1888), also born in Kentucky, married there another native,

Elizabeth ("Lizzie") McCoy, and they too came early to Panola County, where he was a successful "agriculturalist" and "a very strong democrat but never . . . himself conspicuous in politics."

Before he settled for the agrarian life, though, Phil Stone's grandfather sought his fortune as a prospector in the Far West. His wife Lizzie was pregnant with their son James when W. E. Stone set out for California, apparently drawn by the gold rush that had begun in the 1840s. Although photographed with cartridge belts crossed on his chest and long knives hanging from his belt, the adventurer, ironically, only ran a profitable general store in the vicinity of Sutter's Mill in that lawless era. On the return trek he staked out a claim in what is now downtown Colorado Springs, where he found silver, or so he said, before returning to Mississippi around 1855 to his wife and the one-year-old child he had never seen.[20]

In his prime a very good farmer, W. E. Stone owned a large plantation two miles west of Batesville still known as the "Old Stone Place." Although he had slaves, no evidence suggests that he enjoyed either the wealth or the cultivated leisure of the more pretentious Delta planter. On the wilderness "plantations" the climate and frontier medicine made it difficult merely to stay alive. Before his son's third birthday, Lizzie Stone was dead, and the young widower had married Mannie Elizabeth Wooten. In December 1857 the couple had a son, the third William Evans Stone, whom they called "Willie."

Motherless from early childhood, as Rosamond Alston was, W. E. Stone's older son James thus was raised from near infancy by a stepmother who, as Phil explained his father's personality, thoroughly spoiled him. If he was spoiled, the circumstances at home and in Mississippi under which he came of age may have contributed as much as a doting stepmother. His father was away again, at least for part of the war. The Batesville Battery, in which W. E. Stone served, was engaged in the defense of Vicksburg. In 1863 Vicksburg fell, and Mannie Stone buried an infant daughter. Just before Christmas in 1869, Willie died, shortly after his twelfth birthday. James Stone, not yet sixteen, thus became an only child. It appeared that he would be a disappointment to his father, perhaps because, as Phil thought, in her grief over the loss of her own children, Mannie Stone gave inordinate attention to her stepson.

Family

Although James was emotionally attached to farming and devoted to the Tallahatchie River bottomland where he had grown up, in the early 1870s his father, following the example of other prosperous Mississippians, sent his son to Kentucky Military Institute, a school near Frankfort administered by the United States Army.[21] Discipline apparently was strict, and the competition keen, for the indulged planter's son soon discovered that he did not like it there at all. After a few months, James Stone was again in Batesville. A former Stone slave once told Phil that the erring son was put at the rear end of a mule and sent to the field—where he plowed that winter, all the next spring, and all the following summer. When KMI opened in the fall, James Stone was only too happy to return. Actually, Stone's purgatory was shorter than a good story could allow, for during 1872 he was in Oxford at the university taking high school work, perhaps remedial courses to prepare for a second attempt at college.[22] Subsequently, James Stone did well at KMI, graduating as a "Second Distinguished Cadet" in 1876.[23] Two friendships that were to be personally and professionally important to him and to his sons date from that school period: with John Sharp Williams, who would serve in the United States Senate, and with Philip Thornton, a wealthy Charleston, Mississippi, planter who joined the hunts at Stone Stop and who befriended Phil and W. E. Stone IV after the family law firm opened a branch in Charleston in 1916.[24]

Soon after graduation from KMI, James Stone enrolled in the law department of the University of Mississippi, "but on account of failing health left school at the end of a few months."[25] At that time Stone, who was six-feet-four, weighed only 121 pounds. His angular frame soon filled out—after his doctor prescribed that he smoke cigarettes. Still, he had not completed his law degree eighteen months later when he and Rosamond were married—Stone was then twenty-three, Miss Rosie nineteen—although one of his law professors, James C. Longstreet, was Stone's best man.[26] He may never have taken his degree; to be admitted to the bar without one was not uncommon in his day. Law school then was a two-year, generally undergraduate, course; and it was not until 1880, after his first son was born, that Stone was admitted to the bar and opened an office in Batesville.[27]

Once James Stone began work, he certainly had no time to dabble in the practice of law (as his son Phil did when the latter returned from law school at Yale only to be full-time gadfly to William Faulkner). In less than four years he and Rosamond had three children—Will (W. E. Stone, born in 1879), James Stone, Jr. (born in 1881), and Mary McCoy, called "Rosebud" (born in 1883). Although Major Alston or his father, or both, were probably helping the young couple, it was essential to Stone's pride that he make money immediately, which he seems to have done, for Miss Rosie had the numbers of cooks, maids, and nurses to which she was accustomed. But to keep her in that fashion by practicing law was not then only a matter of arguing eloquently in the Batesville courthouse. Before the railroads were completed, one had to follow the courts—circuit, chancery, and federal—on horseback or by surrey. Roads to the county seats around Batesville were such that Stone, who preferred horseback anyway, almost never went by surrey. In the early 1880s, although the Delta had had white settlers for half a century, outside the small towns and bordering the plantations, the wilderness, especially at night, was inimical to a man on horseback. Stone's horse had to swim the treacherous swollen rivers, and at night when he made camp he would hear panthers screaming. Fortunately, Stone loved the woods, having been a hunter from boyhood.

The assurance James felt in the wild had been developed on his father's plantation, and naturally he wanted those experiences for his sons. For that reason, perhaps, he agreed with Miss Rosie to send his first son frequently to the Stone grandparents in the Tallahatchie bottom. Will Stone was only a year old when Rosamond discovered that she was pregnant again. Concerned over Will's frailty and burdened with the new baby, she entrusted Will to the care of Mannie and W. E. Stone for over a year on his first visit, and for extended periods throughout his childhood. After Chickasaw Indians who farmed small plots of land near the Stone place persuaded Mannie to feed her grandson bear gravy, his health improved. As a boy Will spent days with the Chickasaws, assimilating lore he may have shared with William Faulkner, whom he came to know through his younger brother Phil. Certainly Faulkner appropriated another of Will's Tallahatchie adventures for his story "Race at Morning." The boy's grandfather was quite deaf, and since the old man loved the hunt, his not being able to hear the hounds proved more than a nuisance. With Will there, however, the planter improvised a remedy: he put the boy in a croker sack hanging from the pommel of his saddle so that when the dogs rushed out of sight into the dense canebrakes or the dark, virgin woods, he could ask, "Which way, boy?" and Will would point, and off they galloped.[28]

The older son was not yet ten when James Stone and his wife suffered a series of traumas that were to effect major changes for them. A month before their fourth child was born, in September 1888, their daughter Rosebud died of diphtheria. They buried the child in a new plot in the Batesville Cemetery, with the epitaph "A Bud on Earth transplanted to the Paradise of God." That December, James Stone's father died, leaving Stone responsible for his stepmother and for the plantation. They were to suffer another loss the following spring when the new baby, Pauline Alston Stone, died at eight months.

In 1890, apparently because the family plantation required his attention, James Stone went into partnership with P. H. Lowrey, a young Batesville attorney whose father, a Confederate major general, had been a friend of W. E. Stone (as in the next generation Perrin Lowrey and Phil Stone would be friends). Lowrey's brother, Dr. B. G. Lowrey, would be Oxford's congressman for many years. The Lowreys, prominent Baptists, until 1920 privately maintained Blue Mountain College in Tippah County. When P. H. Lowrey, the law partner, died in the 1950s, Perrin would write Phil that James Stone and his father "were the last two of the cavaliers." Thus the relationship continued a close one, but because by 1892 the Stones had moved to Oxford, professionally it proved short-lived.[29]

The decision to leave Batesville, abrupt as it may seem, resulted from a well-orchestrated campaign by Rosamond Stone, whose obsession surfaced as the family's Batesville ties were broken: the last of James Stone's family, his stepmother, died in March 1891. There was little doubt that Stone could make more money in Oxford. The federal court for the Northern District met there, and the main line of the Illinois Central Railroad from Chicago to New Orleans then ran through Oxford. Because Stone was local counsel for the railroad at Batesville, he might in time enjoy the same but more profitable position in Oxford (which Stone in fact did inherit from J. W. T. Falkner's firm sometime after 1905).[30] Stone's sons too were fast approaching college age, and the Delta habit of moving a planter's wife into Oxford for the years her children were at the university could be prohibitively expensive. (Moreover, the forty-mile journey to the east by surrey or horse was exhausting and unreliable, even dangerous at times; by rail, with the roadbeds running only north and south, one was forced to travel to Oxford through Tennessee.)[31] Later, Rosamond's frugality on their trips together would greatly embarrass Phil Stone; perhaps the penurious aristocrat simply balked at the idea of handing over good money for her sons' room and board. She was not one to explain herself, but the pressure continued.

Phil's father was more than reluctant to move; personal and professional respect such as he enjoyed in Batesville might not be easily won again. But Miss Rosie was adamant. It was fashionable—and prudent—for Delta families to send women and children into towns in the hills during the spring and summer to escape floods and yellow fever, while the men remained on the plantations with their field hands. After losing two children in the Delta, Rosamond Stone apparently believed Oxford a healthier place to raise a family. At her discovery that she was expecting another child in February, Stone ordered the servants to the attic for the trunks. Major Alston would join them in Oxford to select a new home.

Although James Stone wanted to buy "an ugly old barn of a house" on what now is South Fifth Street in Oxford, Major Alston persuaded him to purchase the antebellum Avant estate on College Hill Street almost a mile northwest of town. Its previous owner, university chancellor Edward Mayes, was the son-in-law of Oxford notable L. Q. C. Lamar (U.S. senator and Supreme Court justice), and Lamar too is said to have briefly resided there. Edward Mayes and his family had left Oxford in December 1891,[32] so that by the time the Stones and Major Alston saw it, the house, vacant for months, was in ill repair. But the mantels were of Italian marble and crystal chandeliers hung downstairs, and a man of Alston's aristocratic taste could envision that with paint and carpentry work the beauty of the house might be easily restored.

The Stones were told that the house was haunted: strange lights shone there; doors inexplicably creaked open; visages materialized behind women sitting at their dressing table mirrors. One morning as James Stone was poised upon a ladder hanging draperies, "he turned to discover a man had silently entered the room and was staring at him. When Stone inquired what he wanted, at first the man refused to answer. Finally, the intruder found his tongue: 'Ain't you skeered to stay in this house with all the hants?' When Mr. Stone replied, 'No,' he said 'Well, I guess you're a lawyer and hants can't harm you,' and turned and strode out."[33]

There were other stories. The one that Phil Stone's son Philip recorded in 1957 for the ninetieth anniversary edition of the *Oxford Eagle* concerns the original owner, Major Tomlin Avant. The younger son of a Virginia gentleman, Avant built the house in the 1840s for his bride, the daughter of a wealthy Lafayette County pioneer.[34] As Philip knew the story from his father, Tomlin Avant had come penniless to the new territory when it opened in the 1830s. On borrowed money, he acquired "acres and acres of land" in Lafayette and Panola counties, including the site for his mansion, which he purchased from Pul-lum-ma-tubby, a Chickasaw, on 19 November 1842.[35] A business acquaintance of Jacob Thompson (later secretary of the interior under Buchanan), Avant bought lumber from Thompson (again on credit) while carpenters were still working on the Thompson house. But twenty-four hours after receiving the last wagonload of building materials, Avant declared himself bankrupt. Thompson, without legal recourse, had to watch helplessly as Avant's slaves raised not only the big house and an overseer's cottage to the west, but also a smaller house with columns to the east, which Avant built in order to have "neighbors worthy of him." Deprived of a fief by primogeniture, the Virginian was determined to live as an aristocrat, financed if need be by "thousands of other people's dollars." Lafayette County blue bloods flocked to his balls and parties, where orchestras brought in from St. Louis, Memphis or New Orleans played for the dancers.[36] Eventually, however, the lawsuits began, and Avant, after losing the showplace, moved into his overseer's cottage, where he died owing thousands to the more respectable gentry of North Mississippi.

During the Civil War and Reconstruction, Federal troops were quartered in the house, a period from which, when the Stones moved in, there was a single reminder: two windowpanes in the upstairs hall engraved with a diamond: "M. M. Grant, 1866."[37] Chancellor Mayes had left behind in that hall a more visible sign of his residence. The hall itself, always a dark place, for Miss Rosie invariably ordered the shutters closed, ran for fifty feet down the middle of the second story. At one end, at the front of the house, which faced south, "a tall door opened upon a shallow . . . balcony" graced with a wrought-iron balustrade, as in the Sartoris mansion: "On either side of this door [too] was a narrow window set with leaded panes of vari-colored glass."[38] Along the east wall, between the two doors leading off into upstairs bedrooms, there were floor-to-ceiling bookcases, and along the same wall, between the front bedroom door and the balcony door, there was a plantation desk, with an enclosed glass bookshelf. These shelves were lined with hundreds of leather-bound books, which, for some reason, Mayes had abandoned.

Not surprisingly for a family interested in law and politics, the Mayes books were mostly histories—of the South, of the war (there was Jefferson Davis's history of the Confederacy, but every library in the South had one of those)—and books on philosophy, and some poetry. A handful were inscribed by Davis, one or two by Alexander Stephens, and quite a few by L. Q. C. Lamar, including a first edition of Swinburne's *Laus Veneris* (1866). As a sickly child, Phil Stone spent months abed imbibing from those books the South's fables about itself—apologias he would never question, as William Faulkner later recorded.

Part of the South's mythology derived from its planter culture, and the Stones' town estate was to be a plantation in miniature. The family eventually owned fifteen hundred acres adjacent to the house, including the "Old Kendall Place," the pasture in the rear, which had once belonged to Maud Falkner's relatives. At some point James Stone seems to have sold the Panola County land that he and his wife had inherited, except for the fifteen hundred acres where the men hunted, but whether he did so in 1892 in order to buy the Oxford property is unclear. Perhaps he kept it all. Phil often accused his father of an inordinate possessiveness about land. During their oil speculation in the 1950s, Phil Stone complained to a Jackson partner that another of their business associates "acts about [oil leases] just like my daddy did about a piece of land, afraid to sell it like it was the only piece of land in the world."[39]

Whether he retained plantation deeds or not, the virtually self-sustaining operation James Stone set up at "Stone Lodge," as the *Oxford Eagle* called it,[40] reflected the scale of his continuing plantation ethos.

Family

Each winter in the smokehouse in the backyard, spareribs from three or four Duroc hogs were packed in salt, and hams, shoulders, sides of bacon, and yards of pork sausages were swung from the rafters above. By summer's end the huge barn beyond was redolent with curing hay. From a two-acre garden plot servants harvested salad greens, "new" potatoes, carrots, onions, and assorted peas and beans in summer; in August turnips and other greens were sown for the winter garden. Years later, with only Miss Rosie, Phil, and the servants to feed, James Stone still planted six rows of beans the length of the garden. Farm tenants worked the garden behind his pair of "strapping" mules, which he stabled in the back lot with Bob, his Tennessee walker, and Glendolyn, his wife's surrey mare. The sires of his dairy herd, imported from the Isle of Jersey, were kept in the nearby "bull house."

Because Stone had retained a wholesaler's license from his Delta commissary, he still ordered barrels of oysters from the coast and cases of sardines, boneless herring, and salad dressing from Massachusetts; and to his supply of homemade apple cider he added cases of bourbon and casks of Budweiser and Blue Ribbon beer. Such extravagant tendencies were evident in his finances too; the family said that General Stone "always made a lot of money, spent a lot of money, and borrowed a lot of money," habits at which his son Phil was amused. But something of James Stone's temperament rubbed off on his youngest son, so that all his life Phil Stone was to be financially and emotionally at odds with life "off the plantation."

James Stone continued to play another planter role after the move to Oxford. Like Major Alston, Stone kept a staff of black retainers, some from the ranks of his tenants, to work the garden, tend the stock, build the fires, cook the meals, and nurse the children. One sharecropper regularly provided a mess of squirrels to be fried for breakfast. "Preacher," Green Liggin, and his wife Anna served the Stones for forty years. The Liggins and another couple lived in the two servants' houses west of the driveway, screened from the house by a large red oak and three elm trees. Phil Stone charged that his father fostered incompetence in the other blacks he kept about "doing nothing." Over Phil's protests, even in his seventies General Stone continued to walk behind the barn to catch and saddle his white stallion himself, while loafing on the back steps sat half a dozen men who worked for him.

Phil Stone of Oxford

Having been raised to do physical work himself, James Stone may have been reluctant to delegate menial tasks, although in general he did adopt the Southern aristocrat's paternalism toward his black retainers. Stone was certainly familiar with a white man's social obligations to blacks he employed. Before Christmas each year he went to B. J. Semmes's in Memphis to buy a $2.50 bottle of Yannissee Rye for Jim Kuykendall, an old Panola County slave, and two or three others who knew to expect more than a salutation in reply to their "Christmas gift, General Stone."

Stone himself drank more than a Christmas toddy, surely, as the cases of beer and liquor and the cider attest. In late summer after the Oxford move, the Oxford *Globe* reported that "Mr. James Stone, one of our prominent and reliable lawyers, after spending several weeks at Iuka Springs, has returned home much improved in health." The paper had noted in July that Stone had been recently ill. The major illnesses the family recall were his "toots," his periodic fits of drinking. Such bouts may have sent him to Iuka Springs; perhaps they were also behind his occasional visits to Allison's Wells, near Jackson, which the *Eagle* mentioned in the early 1900s. When he did drink, his wife could do nothing with him; if it appeared that the spell would be prolonged, she sent for Sallie Alston, who could handle Jim Stone as well as she ran her plantation.[41]

Although professionally very much a success in Oxford, Stone may have been too old at thirty-eight to adapt emotionally to leaving home. His son Phil would feel a similar bond with his native Oxford; in his prime, even when away on short trips, Phil Stone felt compelled to return home before dark. The father could find solace in a bottle, or in his annual escapes to the Delta woods. For the son, the years at Whitfield, the state mental hospital, would be unrelieved exile. In one of the more chilling conjunctions of life and art, Phil Stone would later share in Jackson the "cage" of Faulkner's character Darl Bundren, a Southerner with a similar obsession: "How often have I lain beneath rain on a strange roof, thinking of home."[42] The psychological impotence of Phil Stone and Darl Bundren, moreover, can be traced to a common source.

2

Childhood

PHILIP AVERY STONE, the fifth and last Stone child, was born in Oxford, in the house with the "hants," on 23 February 1893. Rosamond Stone later confessed that she had thought herself "through with child-bearing" after Pauline's birth in 1888, and that she did not want to have Phil. Her younger surviving child, Jim, was almost twelve when Phil was born. James Stone, according to custom, entered his son's name and date of birth in the family Bible, having chosen the middle name Avery after his friend a Memphis attorney; but it was Rosamond who had given the boy her father's first name, perhaps as her penance, for Stone believed his mother never to have cared for him. There were only three persons, he said, whom she ever loved: Major Alston, her son Jim, and her grandson Philip. One night as a small boy Phil Stone heard his parents' raised voices from the parlor below and went to the top of the stairs to listen. His mother was lamenting the injustices of a woman her age having to rear another child. "He will be our Joseph," James Stone argued. "He will save us in our old age."[1] In his father's steadfast defense of him, Stone was later to discover a reason for being.

The number and seriousness of Phil's childhood illnesses, however, would have taxed a much younger woman than Rosamond Stone. In the terms of the day, Phil contracted "brain fever," "typhoid pneumonia," "typhoid fever," and "pneumonia," all before his tenth birthday. He remembered having to learn to walk three times, for almost a third of his childhood was spent in bed, as Stone wrote in his short Whitfield autobiography.[2] Once, when his fever had subsided, "he crawled out of bed, tried to walk and fell, full length, on the floor." His mother "screamed that Phil was crippled for life and would never walk again." After days of determined crawling, however, his legs again would bear his weight. Twice the family expected him to die. During one crisis, in the winter of his eighth year, the two physicians who had attended him daily told the Stones there was nothing further to be done; the boy "could not live until dawn." "His father was crushed," Phil wrote; he never doubted his father's love. But, as he bitterly recalled, "his mother pushed back and forth on the foot of the big four poster bed and cried again and again: 'My baby is going to die, my baby is going to die.' " The "baby," however, "rose on the pillow still awake, and calmly said: 'I'm *not* going to die; I'm going to live until I'm an *old* man.' "

Stone was incensed at her self-indulgent hysteria. He remembered it vividly, even at Whitfield. He believed that her wails had so enraged him that he had found the energy to keep fighting for breath, although each one was "like a knife sticking in him." He "refused to let himself go to sleep, fought to stay awake," until his fever finally broke at dawn. Dr. P. W. Rowland's bill, dated 1 October 1901, lists a hundred visits to Phil Stone between April and June (at $2.00 a visit) and fifty visits between July and September (at $1.50 a visit).[3]

Forbidden physical outlets available to other children his age, Phil turned early to words. He began to read in his third year. Perhaps his seventeen-year-old brother Will encouraged him, for Will was always a gentle man, and one especially kind to children, as Phil would be.[4] Among the volumes left upstairs by Chancellor Mayes, he found sets of boys' books, including a series of the G. A. Henty adventure tales. Miss Rosie was disturbed at his reading such "trash," but James Stone characteristically countermanded her: "Let him alone; let him read 'em." It was not long before Phil, reading more extensively in Mayes's library, became enamored of the Civil War histories.

In his months of convalescence, not content just to read about the war, Stone also worked out elaborate war games, which he played alone. On a circle of cardboard cut from a suitbox, he printed a variety of moves for shotgun-shell infantrymen and the "cavalry," "cannon," and "supply wagons" he pilfered from the Stone kitchen and tackroom: Advance two miles. Lose a company. Retreat across the river. Surrender.

After each spin of a sewing needle, Phil recorded the moves in a note-book, so that when he was well again and it was warm enough that even his mother had no objections, he transported his soldiers outside to replay the maneuvers in the Stone pasture. Such games were a chief diversion from the time he was four or five until his health allowed him to enter school for the first time at the age of ten.

The summer that Phil was five, men to whom his father talked around the square were vaguely uneasy about rumors from Beat Four. At Taylor's Station, eight miles south, fifteen persons had a suspicious fever. News from Orwood, a hamlet with two or three stores and a post office near the Panola County line, was even more disturbing: forty cases of fever were reported there. As yet, few in Oxford were seri-ously concerned; there had been no deaths in either place. But C. L. Sivley, James Stone's colleague (and soon his partner), was taking no chances. Because he had some experience with yellow fever, he real-ized that nothing was more dangerous than to treat those cases lightly. "Realizing how difficult it would be to get away if it spread to Oxford, I left at once and propose to stay away until it has been stamped out of the district," Sivley told a reporter on the Louisville *Courier-Journal* (9 September 1898), which noted in its society column that Sivley and his mother were "stopping at the Galt house." It would be a miracle, he said, if Oxford escaped the yellow fever.

Shortly thereafter business in Oxford did come to a halt as other white citizens in near panic evacuated the town.[5] On a day early in the progress of that "greatest epidemic," the Stones and a trainload of their townsmen followed Sivley to Kentucky. Boarding the train at dawn, they left in a hurry, Miss Rosie wrapping Phil in his father's old dressing gown. It was to be a hot, tension-filled day. Some passengers tried to get off along the route in Mississippi and Tennessee, only to be greeted at each stop by men with shotguns, so great was the fear of contagion. Finally they were allowed to detrain at a town in Kentucky unscathed by the disease, but even there they were told to move on. Late that afternoon the exhausted refugees boarded an omnibus for Princeton, Kentucky, where they would wait out the epidemic.[6]

The Stones and their closest friends in Oxford escaped the disease, and with cool weather the community returned to normal. At the turn of the century, routine for James Stone meant supervising his Delta farms and timberland and practicing law with Julian C. Wilson from an upstairs office at the northwest corner of the courthouse square. Wilson was associated with Stone until September 1903, when he was appointed a chancery court judge after James C. Longstreet's resignation.[7]

It was not unusual for James Stone to lose partners to the bench. Earlier, it seems, he had been associated with Sam C. Cook of Clarksdale, who became a Mississippi Supreme Court justice.[8] Stone's personal ambitions never lay in that direction, or even in amassing a fortune by practicing law. If he had wanted more money, his greatest opportunity came when the Illinois Central Railroad invited him to transfer to Chicago as one of their principal attorneys, but his roots in Mississippi were too deep and he persuaded Clarence Sivley, his partner, to accept the position. Sivley, who replaced Wilson,[9] was James Stone's most colorful associate. Because they were both aggressive, commanding men, they made a very successful pair.

After coming to Oxford to attend law school, Sivley had remained there to practice in an office adjacent to Stone and Wilson;[10] thus he and James Stone had known one another for some time. Sivley was married to Minnie Bowles Clopton, a niece of Mrs. Bem Price, whose husband was president of the Bank of Oxford,[11] and the Sivleys were eventually to inherit Ammadelle, the Price mansion on North Street, still an Oxford showplace.

After they became partners, Sivley and Stone bought the law office on Jackson Avenue just off the square, from which Stones were to practice law for sixty years.[12] Built before the Civil War, since 1861 the building has housed only lawyers. Behind its eighteen-inch brick walls, Nathan Bedford Forrest had founded the Mississippi chapter of the Ku Klux Klan, General Stone told Phil. L. Q. C. Lamar had practiced law there, Stone said, and Judge James C. Longstreet. Even with renovations made later, the exterior has remained virtually unchanged since the turn of the century, when the small, turretlike "sun room" was added.[13]

Stone and Sivley had the interior redecorated in 1905, and on the canvas ceiling Will Stone supervised the painting of a large floral border enclosing (Masonic?) symbols and the facsimile signatures of former tenants and Stone's legal associates, which has been retained to the present.[14] Still in the office yard too is the white stone called the "upping block," used by Phil's father when he mounted his stallion Bob. The block originally belonged to the "old Methodist church" across the street from the office.[15] In the thirties a black man named Mulberry, who had been a United States marshal during Reconstruction, was the office "janitor"—and groom.[16] Twice each day Mulberry caught Bob from the office pasture and brought him around to the upping block where Stone mounted to go home to dinner or supper.

James Stone, with his military school bearing, his height, his snow-white hair, and dark blue eyes, was awesome on the big Tennessee walker.[17] Mrs. Sivley, the first to call him "General," was not the only one to think that he resembled a general riding his white horse. Estelle Patton, a Stone stenographer, would remark his "who-in-the-hell-are-you" look. It exasperated opposing attorneys that, because he looked important, he could cow both witness and jury. One lawyer became so frustrated that he complained to the bench: "Your Honor, I could win this case, but I can't win it against that affidavit countenance of Jim Stone."[18] Stone won his cases as much with a look of innocence as by intimidation; Phil's contemporary Robert J. Farley remembers that in court James Stone "looked like a saint and spoke like a Baptist preacher."

But juries who believed in a gentle Jim Stone must have lived far back in the county, for half the town witnessed his fury almost every Sabbath. General Stone and Mr. Sivley habitually scheduled their "secret" conferences when everyone else was in church. Nevertheless, to ensure their privacy, General Stone would send for the secretary, to station her near the door as their front line of defense: "By God, don't you let anybody in here; we're going to have a private conference." And Mr. Sivley: "For Christ's sake, don't you let a goddamn son of a bitch in this place; we don't want *anybody* to know we're here." Both sentiments were delivered in booming voices; they were furious men, both of them, and deaf too, to make matters worse. The secretary would reply with great diffidence, "Yessir, yessir," and tiptoe out as they began, "You goddamn white-headed son of a bitch . . ." A half hour later their neighbors were forced to send over a delegation from the Methodist church to "ask the General and Mr. Sivley to stop cussin' so loud, so we can have Sunday School over here."

Rosamond Stone may have commissioned the reluctant messengers, for twice each Sunday her horse Glendolyn was hitched in the church-yard across the street. Rosamond and Sallie Murry Falkner, William Faulkner's grandmother, were said to run the Methodist church. Both were active in the Home Missionary Society. In October 1902 their "circle" convened en masse for a Sunday afternoon Children's Rally during the Women's Christian Temperance Union convention in Oxford. The local group had been the first WCTU chapter in the state.[19] Rosamond Stone certainly was involved, because of her husband's drinking and because her niece Irma Alston with other children presented "well-rendered and appropriate" "recitations" that afternoon.

Rosamond's public image as a champion of Christian morality had not been hurt when, for several years, she assumed from Sallie Alston the care of her brother's daughter.[20] The *Eagle* often noted the parties Rosamond gave for Irma Alston at Stone Lodge. But the public image was a facade. As Phil Stone, who was three years younger than his cousin, commented later, "I would certainly hate to meet my Maker with what Miss Rosie had on her conscience about the way she treated her orphan niece." Phil remembered his mother humiliating Irma by continually reminding her whose bread she was eating. When they were grown, he was relieved that Irma's husband was well-to-do and protective of her, hoping that with him Irma might forget the unhappiness she had known as a child. Rosamond Stone seems to have been generous and unselfish only with her middle son Jim.

Miss Rosie's social activities were not confined to church functions, however. For one thing, she was prominent in the Browning Club. Oxford society women generally joined either the Browning Club or the Woman's Book Club, but never both; the Browning chapter claimed that their club had been founded a few days before the otherwise identical Woman's Book Club (in the 1890s), which gave Miss Rosie and her friends no little satisfaction; but Emily Stone, who made the mistake of not consulting her mother-in-law before joining the rival club, heard that it was the Woman's Book Club that was older. The two factions were never quite sure and argued the point for years.

Once it was Miss Rosie's turn to be hostess. Whether she thought so or not, her family was quite aware that she knew nothing about cooking; in eighty-five years she managed never to cook a meal. Yet

Childhood

a dozen times each morning she trotted back to the kitchen to direct preparations for the Stones' dinner—her cook must have been able to recognize Rosamond's quick, light step in her sleep: "Anna, have you put on the turnip greens yet? Anna, have you made up the biscuits?" When the Browning Club was invited to her home, Rosamond in ignorance ordered the sandwiches made a day or two before. That afternoon, although the soggy sandwiches were largely untouched, the women stayed until dark, which was unheard of, and, as they left, exclaimed to Rosamond how much they hated to go home, for it had been the best meeting they remembered.

When General Stone rode in from town, a few surreys were still hitched in the drive. The kitchen was several yards behind the house proper, so that when, after looking in the icebox, Stone boomed out, "What in the name of God has happened to my cider?" the ladies lingering in the parlor did not hear him. General Stone did not keep his apple orchard and fifteen-foot cider press for refreshments at the Browning Club. Besides, the hard cider in the icebox had been laced with bourbon.

Besides rarely staying at home, Rosamond Stone seldom stayed even in town. In 1903 and 1904 the newspaper was hard-pressed to have a society column without her. Most frequently, she, always with Phil in tow, visited Alstons, but her travels were often more distant than to Batesville, Memphis, or Clarksdale. She and Rosa Johnson, from the Browning Club, and Phil, of course, traveled "in the west" with friends from Memphis during "the entire heated season" of 1902. Some summers, after short trips to Allison's Wells, she and her son would wait for cool weather in Mississippi at Holland, Michigan, on Lake Michigan's eastern shore. (The Falkners went to Alma, in central Michigan.) For shorter excursions Rosamond and Phil, like the Falkners, went to Biloxi.[21] Expenses were reduced to room and board and souvenirs, for the family of General Stone, an attorney for the Illinois Central, were never without railroad passes.

Because of her tight purse, Phil seldom enjoyed his trips with his mother, but during their Western vacation, in the summer after his pneumonia crisis, Phil's health had so much improved that the nine-year-old could relish a mischievous adventure. When Miss Rosie went upstairs after lunch for her nap, she left Phil in the lobby reading a book, but he preferred, it seems, to climb Pike's Peak. Hours later, to his dismay, close to sundown, although the hotel resembled a toy down in the valley, he found that he was not even a third of the way up. Forced to quit, he returned to the resort long after dark to be greeted by hysterical women. Stone enjoyed more success with less effort when he again tried the summit by burro—this time with a hotel guide and his mother's permission.

Stone's greatest thrill as a child came one summer, probably in 1900, when he and his mother left Holland, Michigan, as the summer places closed there and went back to Chicago to stay as usual on the South Side until the hot weather broke in Mississippi.[22] That September they were at the Hyde Park Hotel. To the child who had spent a third of his life in bed reading Civil War histories, "people like Lee, Jackson, Longstreet, and Stuart were just demigods," Phil said. "That such heroes existed in the flesh" was inconceivable. But there in the lobby where Miss Rosie "rocked and gabbled" sat General James Longstreet "with his flowing white beard." Longstreet's second wife and a daughter by a former marriage were there with him. Phil, "entranced," stood by his mother's chair "and stared at him by the hour."

"Philip," Miss Rosie said when she sensed her son's fascination, "don't you bother General Longstreet now."

"No'm," he promised. "I won't."

But the old man soon noticed the boy, and they began to walk together in the afternoon. Phil asked incessantly about the war, and Longstreet told him "what we did and what the Yankees did," sometimes showing Phil with his cane where he had sent his troops and why. "But all the time there was a question I burned to ask him," Phil told his wife. "It was a matter which, though I did not know it, had been a raging controversy since the day it happened." Later, as they were walking back to the hotel one afternoon, Phil said, "I finally got up courage to tell him that I wanted to ask him a question if it would not make him angry." Longstreet "smiled indulgently and said that of course it would not make him angry," so Phil plunged: "Is it true, General, that we lost the battle of Gettysburg because you disobeyed Lee's orders and did not support Pickett's charge?" "The old General's face turned purple," Phil remembered. "He threw down my hand he was holding, shouted a thunderous No! and strode angrily away." After that, if they saw one another in the lobby, Longstreet ignored the boy. "He sat there like iron," Stone said. They never spoke again.

When Phil Stone returned from his summer travels to begin school for the first time in 1903, his brothers were still engaged in the initiation rite known as "finding oneself." His older brother Will, now more often called by his baseball nickname "Jack," had taken a degree from Ole Miss in 1901, but two years elapsed before he decided to follow his father in a legal career. Between visits with college friends and trips to New Orleans, Jack played billiards with Jim Stone upstairs at home or walked over to the campus to advise his brothers in Delta Kappa Epsilon. On occasion, he did accompany General Stone to courts around the circuit.[23] But his father, never known for his patience, must have decreed that eighteen months of idleness were enough, for in December 1902 the *Eagle* congratulated Jack Stone on the "good fortune" of his appointment as notary public.

But Jack Stone was never really lazy. Continuing as notary for the firm, he taught himself shorthand to work as a court recorder when, the next fall, he entered a bachelor of laws program at the university.[24] Stone received his LL.B. in 1905 and was admitted to the bar in the same year. At first he practiced law at Sardis, but in 1907, two years after Clarence Sivley left for Chicago, he returned to Oxford to join his father in forming James Stone & Son.[25] That arrangement assuredly suited General Stone, but Jack's—and later Phil's—success only made life more difficult for Jim Stone, Jr.

By 1903 Jim Stone, continually in hot water with General Stone, had bypassed college for a time, and from September into the next summer he held a "position" in Okolona, Mississippi,[26] the first of several interests he would pursue. After that, he tried his hand at law school, entering the university in October 1904, but taking only a few courses for the next two years. Meanwhile, according to his niece, he played football and baseball for Ole Miss.[27] Jim Stone, like his brothers, could be very charming; he seems to have enjoyed an easy good humor. He was more popular in town and at the university than either Jack or Phil, but because he never became a lawyer, part of the family's life blood was forever alien to him.

Deciding that he had no talent for the law, Jim went down to Greenwood to learn the cotton business. There he courted Martha Pillow

Greene, called "Matsy," whom he married in December 1909. Jim Stone would become adept at cotton grading. By December 1911, however, he was district manager for the Continental Casualty Company. If not a lawyer in the family tradition, Jim was a Stone in matters of finance: in days of prosperity the male members of the family spent money unconsciously; in days of hardship still they were reluctant to forego social pleasures and the servants deemed essential to home life. Like them, Jim had little sense about money, and soon found himself badly in debt; but he would not, or dared not, request assistance from his father. His situation was so desperate by the end of 1911 that his wife secretly appealed to General Stone for help.[28]

Matsy Stone complained of Jim's drinking, of their overdue bills from doctors, druggists, and the grocer, and of his squandering much of his salary on membership in a local fraternal organization, the Eagles Club—"no one but the toughest of men belong to it." To her remonstrances, Jim protested that he was attempting to emulate his father: women, he lectured, were "men's inferiors," "only made to raise babies . . . not to butt in to men's affairs." General Stone "never told Mother anything . . . and went off on the train" at his pleasure. In those ways, perhaps, Jim compensated for the vacuum he felt in his father's regard. The April before, he had confessed how he felt to General Stone: "Now I know Father, that I have never given you any pleasure, as you say, and I also realize that I do not in any way stand as high in your affection as the other two boys, but that now I cannot help."[29]

In spite of his chauvinistic pronouncements, Jim Stone, his brother Phil thought, was Rosamond's child, and the rapport of mother and middle son would gall Phil Stone. Although in 1903 Miss Rosie wrote Polly on the back of a photograph that she was teased for favoring Jack, "Pet, this is he, in whom 'they say,' my heart is centered," a half-century later Phil would vehemently deny it: "The handwriting [is] your grandmother Stone['s]," he told his son. "But it isn't true. 'Jimmie' was her whole heart."[30] Phil believed his father "generous but never just" and thought General Stone hard even on Jack. Yet it always irritated him that his father gave Jim considerable financial support, especially after his marriage. (Phil himself would not be self-supporting until he was almost thirty.)

Whenever General Stone tightened the purse strings trying to slow

Jim's extravagances, Jim would appeal surreptitiously to Miss Rosie, who never failed him, according to the disaffected son. Phil suspected that she had even sold or pawned her wedding ring to rescue Jim's family in one late crisis. Jim Stone, Phil told Faulkner critic Carvel Collins, was one of the prototypes for Jason Compson, but Phil Stone's problematic maternal relationship may have furnished other materials for *The Sound and the Fury*.[31] The animosity, however, was not all Phil Stone's. After the deaths of his father and two brothers in the 1930s, both his brothers' families believed that Phil somehow swindled them out of the Stone "fortune," a fortune in notes at the time of General Stone's death. But that vicious sibling rivalry would not surface until years later.

In the autumn of 1903, Phil Stone was finally enrolled in Oxford's Graded School. As he joined the other ten-year-olds in the fourth grade, of more immediate concern were the restrictions imposed on him by his medical history. Although his father had proclaimed that a boy who "had lived through two prophesied deaths should be able to go to grammar school," his mother kept cautioning Phil that he was "not strong like the other boys"; in August before school opened, she had taken him for one last bath in Iuka's mineral springs.[32] General Stone, moreover, so far had resisted Phil's campaign to accompany the men on the November hunts, almost certainly because of Miss Rosie's fears. And even though the boy had one friend in the neighborhood, Stone's invalidism and frequent travels resulted in his playing with few contemporaries, except at church and the usual birthday parties, until he went to school. His academic debut did not go well, as might be expected of a child who had been reading voraciously for years and who conversed almost exclusively with adults over forty. Early in his first day, when the teacher sent him to the board, the other children laughed at him because he printed his work. Never having been taught script, he had learned to print from his books.

Stone's social development was not seriously retarded by his late entry into school, however. He confessed to his wife that he believed young people of that day were better than he and his friends had been when they were "coming up," and his reference was not to the time when he had to talk his way out of getting caught, with some boys, in a neighbor's peach orchard. There was a girl up the railroad tracks named Dewey Dell, he claimed, who had introduced Stone and his friends to sex when he was ten—in Stone's first year of grammar school.

Not being privy to such boasts, General Stone was still concerned about his son's frail health. In March after Phil's eleventh birthday, his father placed orders with the Royal Forest Beagle Kennels in Pennsylvania and with W. M. Stebbins of the Hastings National Bank of Michigan for two pairs of English beagles, for which he paid thirty-four dollars. The dogs arrived by rail in April, and James Stone registered one pair with the American Kennel Club under the names Lady Inex and Clarence Sivley. Phil later wrote his son Philip of his father's unorthodox physical therapy:

> They would not let me have a gun that soon and I used to hunt rabbits with these little dogs. These dogs were not very fast although they could trail very well. Every afternoon about time for me to come home from school they would go down to the corner of the yard where the big house was and sit like stair steps and watch up the street for me. Almost every Saturday and almost every other afternoon I would go over on the farm and hunt rabbits with them. I would run right along with them, up hill and down hill, through the briar patches and right across the creeks. Three or four years of this toughened me so that I have not had a serious sickness since I got those dogs when I was eleven years old. Of course, your grandfather Stone bought them for that purpose.[33]

Friends had taught him to look for steel taps lost from trains along the tracks down the hill from the house. The boys pounded those taps onto the ends of sticks for weapons. When his beagles flushed a rabbit, Phil aimed the steel end ahead of the small target and threw the tapstick with all his might. Sometimes, he said, "I'd hit one." His outing "one cold January day" would furnish William Faulkner's initial setting for *Intruder in the Dust*. That morning, Stone wrote, he followed Lady Inex and Clarence Sivley and the others "right through a branch, breaking the ice at every step." Soaked and thoroughly chilled, he set out for "Aunt" Mag's cabin nearby; her family were tenants at the Stone farm on the edge of Oxford. The woman dried the boy's clothes and cooked him fried eggs and a "hoecake over the ashes in the fireplace," the best meal of his life, he said. But when he returned home, his mother "had a fit":

"You're going to kill yourself," Miss Rosie said. "You just can't go out with those dogs any more, and that's all there is to it."

But General Stone calmed her. "Let the boy alone, I tell you. Let him alone."[34]

In 1905, when he was twelve, despite his new stamina, Phil apparently was still left behind when his father and the other men made their November hunt.[35] Nevertheless, after starting school, Phil spent more time with his father than with Miss Rosie, once or twice accompanying him on business trips to Chicago. One afternoon after the day's conferences there, General Stone decided that his son ought to see a museum. The rest of the afternoon was a blur to Phil, but he would remember vaguely one painting, by Renoir or another of the Impressionists, of peonies or a similar flower. What had italicized the trip in Stone's memory, to his astonishment even then, was that his father became enthralled by the painting and kept returning every day they were there to study it. The experience would always baffle Phil, although the incident may offer an ironic note on the father.

Stone's blindness to the connection is odd, for it seems clear that his father's behavior is directly linked to the family's most damaging discord. Phil's brother Jim as a boy had exhibited some artistic talent, which General Stone loudly and persistently ridiculed as effeminate; Rosamond, however, praised Jim's tapestries and displayed her son's "Cavalier" in the parlor.[36] The reverberations from James Stone's ignorant cruelty would not cease even after both men died in 1936, for Phil Stone seems never to have understood his mother's championship of Jim as in part reaction to her husband's rejection of his second son. But for a few hours in a Chicago museum, perhaps the country lawyer was himself allured by the beautiful. Back in Mississippi, he had more practical concerns to attend to.

General Stone was solidly established in Oxford by the time Phil was twelve. In 1904 he had been elected vice-president of the Bank of Oxford.[37] Stone and Sivley had impressive new offices and a thriving practice. On his plantations Stone was importing new breeds of animals and experimenting with crop diversification.[38] Miss Rosie's standard of living would have made any Delta planter's wife envious. There was no reason that his precocious youngest son should not have the best education available—in Oxford.

In 1905, when three veteran educators announced that they had secured the campus of the old Union Female College on South Eighth Street for a "training school for boys," the Stones made inquiries and enrolled Phil, after only two years in grammar school, in the first class as a day student.[39] President J. R. Preston was the only member of the faculty of five with a master's degree. All were graduates of Mississippi colleges. The school was loosely affiliated with the state university—students had access to the campus library—and Ole Miss faculty members lectured there as well. Evidently the school was initially well endowed and warmly received by Oxford's "aristocrats." The reception hall was richly decorated with palms and Oriental rugs. Oxford's businessmen advertised in its bulletins: the Bank of Oxford, Neilson's, James Stone & Son, Falkner Transfer Company–Coal Dealers, Dr. A. A. Young, and others. Of the maximum enrollment of seventy or eighty students, approximately fifteen were graduated each year (including a few women).[40]

University Training School hoped to develop "practical school men" and promised drill in fundamentals and discipline in order to "lay broad and deep the foundations for Christian Scholarship and for the development of Christian character." All courses of study included biblical instruction; church attendance was compulsory. Students were required to wear a military uniform and the "corps" was to be run according to rules modified from those at West Point. The *U.T.S. Announcement* for 1907–1908 informed parents that the "vigorous" physical training "often transforms a youth of delicate physique from a weakling into an erect, robust, broad-shouldered boy, with full chest, elastic step, and manly carriage." Phil Stone, who was small and had a trick knee, thus posed a challenge for J. W. Conger, the commandant. "What a martinet he was!" Phil recalled grimly. As a day student, who rode his pony back and forth,[41] however, Stone probably missed much of Conger's regimen.

In his four years at UTS Phil Stone read a conventional nineteenth-century blend of literature and history also meant to inculcate a vigorous manliness in the adolescent mind. *Julius Caesar, Macbeth, Richard III*, and *Coriolanus* were the selections from Shakespeare. Sea adventures were commonplace. History too was made palatable as tales of adventure. Stone read Dickens's *History of England* and ancient history in the textbook series *The Story of the Greeks, The Story of the Aeneid*, and *The Story of the Teutonic Tribes*. A UTS student was decorously confined to the amours of Miles Standish, Uncas, and, worse, Ichabod

Crane. *David Copperfield, Silas Marner,* and the placid *Vicar of Wake-field* were also required books; and Bryant, Poe, and Hawthorne were among the required American authors. For the record, despite Stone's 1924 protests of having forgotten, not stolen Hawthorne's title,[42] he did read Hawthorne's *The Marble Faun* at University Training School.

An English student also developed his grammar, vocabulary, and prose style in weekly themes, letters, stories, and "business forms." General Stone, it seems, regularly perused his son's compositions, even imposing Phil's *Silas Marner* essay on his law partner Clarence Sivley. A mind capable of such an analysis, Sivley tactfully responded, was "a phenomenally good mind!"

In those years too the boy apparently became something of a student of poetry. At school Stone was drilled in analysis, parsing, and probably scansion of "involved poetical passages," which served him well during the Faulkner apprenticeship—if not in his own verse. Although no English Romantic poets were included on UTS reading lists, Phil owned an 1896 edition of *Poems by John Keats* in which he scribbled school assignments. There in the margin below Keats's "Isabella; or the Pot of Basil," a youthful hand also composed or copied perhaps the single extant Stone poem:

> Twilight just after the sun has sunk and
> The trees stand out in leafy arabesque
> The eve-born crickets' whirring news of night,
> The Lord of day has settled down to rest
> Beneath a saffron-o'erlaid robe of blue,
> And high-zenithed clouds of waning silver rose
> Are lingering, pilgrim like, toward a shrine—
> Of one lone star low-trembling in the west.[43]

It is obvious that Stone returned to the Keats volume repeatedly later, and the sound devices and imagery of his poem echo those of his *Oxford Magazine* prose, but the faulty meter and rhyme, and the handwriting, suggest a much earlier date than that of his Faulkner friendship. Phil's inspiration too might well have been stanza three of Keats's ode "To Autumn."

In the best Romantic tradition, the nature poet avoided science classes at the "Prep School," and suffered in his two-and-a-half years of math under drillmaster Conger. As a four-year-old Stone had astonished his older brother's friends by "connecting the numerical day of the month with the day of the week, past, present, or future," a variation of a trick with which as an adult he often amused his niece.[44] But the formal study of mathematics was inevitably his bane. Geometry, he swore, he could not learn at all, so he memorized the theorems.

Stone had far more confidence in his facility for languages. He spoke most respectfully of his first Latin teacher, who gave him a thorough grounding in the subject, he thought. He read the *Viri Romae*, then Caesar, Cicero, and Virgil. But at fourteen Stone discovered Greek, his passion for the next sixty years. Later he would sound off about the exactitude of the language in which some verbs have twenty or more endings carrying variants on the meaning.[45] Stone performed well in his two years of grammar drills, prose compositions, and written and sight translations of Xenophon's *Anabasis*. His marks for one year were "98 98 98," according to another note he made in his Keats book.

The school fielded baseball, football, basketball, and tennis teams, and, surprisingly, Phil Stone was photographed with the 1909 tennis club. His teammate there is Jim Kyle Hudson, who had been on the WCTU program with Phil's cousin Irma Alston. In 1909 Hudson's school "recitations" earned him the Declamation medal. Stone too had more academic than athletic ability. He and Hudson competed each year for the J. E. Neilson medal for scholarship. Stone won it in 1907 and Hudson in 1908, but in their senior year both lost to another student. Because Stone was not exactly overladen with school prizes, one can only wonder whether he was pleased or embarrassed by an item appearing in the *U.T.S. Announcement* the year after his graduation: "Mrs. James Stone of Oxford, has founded a medal in honor of her son, Phil A. Stone, a graduate of the Training School, hereafter to be awarded to the Junior speaker."

During his son's early schooling General Stone, like his father "never . . . himself conspicuous in politics,"[46] nonetheless took an active interest in promoting the ambitions of members of his class who did run for public office. In 1904 he had served with Stark Young's father and three others as managers in "a white primary for the election of town officials."[47] Generally James Stone worked behind the scenes, and from an early age his son absorbed endless yarns of the social revolution in Mississippi that would subsequently give the literary world the character Flem Snopes. One skirmish in the class struggle between patrician and plebeian had been waged in the political races of 1907. In the 1950s, when Stone ran across the year's election issue of the *Oxford Eagle* among his father's papers, he wrote for his son Philip a commentary on the qualified successes of the "aristocrats."[48]

In the governor's race General Stone had supported Charles Scott, a "high class man" from the Delta, but after Scott's defeat in the first primary Stone backed E. F. Noel over Earl Brewer to thwart an unscrupulous faction from gaining the statehouse. On the day of the second primary, fourteen-year-old Phil Stone stood in the courthouse yard begging people to vote for Noel, who emerged the winner.

The Senate race the same year set the controversial former governor James Kimble Vardaman against General Stone's boyhood friend John Sharp Williams. Lafayette County voted heavily for Vardaman, but in the state returns Williams beat Vardaman by 648 votes. The Vardaman campaign had been based solely on racial hatred, according to Stone, with the candidate vowing to amend the Fourteenth Amendment and to repeal the Fifteenth. "Of course your grandfather Stone and all of our folks were for Williams," Stone assured Philip. "We were never for Vardaman." Implicit in his note is that the same could not be said of the Falkners, who, for reasons of their own, apparently had gone over to the "rednecks."[49]

Not only was William Faulkner's grandfather pro-Vardaman; J. W. T. Falkner had actually taken into his law firm the "rascal" Lee M. Russell, who was elected to the legislature in that 1907 balloting. The absurdities with which the Falkners justified the awkward alliance greatly amused Phil Stone: "The story goes that when Russell was Lieutenant Governor (to which office he was elected in 1915 when Bilbo was elected Governor for the first time) he went down one Sunday afternoon to pay a call on Colonel J. W. T. Falkner, that Colonel Falkner came to the door and asked him what he wanted, that Russell replied that he had come to pay a visit, that Colonel Falkner told him that their relations were business and political and not social and slammed the door in his face."

"This sounds just like the Falkners," Stone added. Russell, governor himself in 1920, left office "in disgrace," Phil continued, "because of a suit filed against him in the Federal court here by a woman named Frances Birkhead who sued him for seduction. She lost her suit but she killed Russell politically." Phil's son would hang the plot of his novel on that scandal.

Phil Stone must have had an inside look at state government about the same time that he became absorbed in Mississippi political intrigue. General Stone, who seems never to have thought that Phil might not make a lawyer, arranged for his son to work one summer as a page for James Greer McGowen, a state legislator from Water Valley.[50] There are no anecdotes from that experience, but the relationship proved mutually beneficial. McGowen later participated in two milestones in Stone's career, as chancellor of the Third District, introducing Phil to the court when he was officially admitted to the bar in 1919 and administering the oath of office when Stone became president of the Mississippi Bar in 1948. Phil, in turn, convinced McGowen in 1925 to run for the state supreme court, where he served with distinction.

In the summer of 1908 General Stone and Minnie Sivley, who was visiting at Ammadelle, joined forces in an intrigue of their own. Rosamond Stone, as usual, was away for the summer, and Phil had gone with her. He was fifteen that year and somewhat infatuated with Mrs. Sivley, who in her thirties as in her old age was a very pretty woman. Her driver spent weeks that summer in the Stone kitchen with "Preacher" and Anna Liggin while Mrs. Sivley rushed about the empty house itself taking elaborate notes. Later Mrs. Sivley's carriage might be seen hitched outside the Stone law firm. In late July, General Stone caught the train to Memphis for his appointment at the DuVal-Barnum Company, "Importers of Fine Wall Hangings, Decorative Novelties, Wall Papers, Interior Decoration, Fresco Painting." At the end of their meeting, DuVal had agreed to paint, paper, and decorate the entire house—both front halls and staircase, the parlor, the dining room, the six bedrooms, the two baths, the two pantries, and the back halls—and all work was "to be executed in a first class and workmanlike manner . . . guaranteed artistic in every detail." The bill came to twelve hundred dollars.[51] Stone and Minnie Sivley were quite pleased with themselves, but they had only begun. Before the decorators arrived, the Italian marble mantels were removed for the cabinet mantels stylish then and the chandeliers discarded for electrical fixtures resembling gaslights. The single improvement they made in the general despoliation was both expensive and unnecessary. The original wide pine flooring was replaced with oak parquet in which a border surrounded a Greek design.

To complete the transformation, General Stone got his men off the back steps long enough to grade the front yard to a gentle slope with mules and scrapers. Perhaps originally terraced, the lawn had long eroded into red clay gullies.

At the end of the summer, Preacher Liggin drove General Stone down to Stone's Crossing, a few hundred yards below the house, where Illinois Central trains sometimes stopped for the family, even though it was less than a half mile to the Oxford depot. Preacher was remarking how surprised and pleased Mrs. Stone would be over the changes. But on the return trip, when the surrey breasted the hill, Rosamond shrieked, "What's happened to my jonquils!" and began to cry. Liggin and Phil were dumbfounded, but Phil's father grasped his mistake at once: "God A'mighty, goddamn it to hell, I forgot all about the goddamn flowers." The Mayes family had had bulbs planted up and down the long front walk, and the mules and scrapers had scattered them over the yard. For days Rosamond Stone bewailed the wasteland; her comments on the house were not recorded. Phil Stone concluded, not for the first time, that she was the most ungrateful person he had ever known.

But the next spring, in February before Phil's sixteenth birthday, Miss Rosie's bulbs began coming up all over the front slope—first, daffodils and narcissus, then, about the middle of March, "sweet yellows," a tiny, old-fashioned jonquil. In time there were thousands of flowers, so many that the grass was never cut until June commencement. After the "sweet yellows" came flags, Dutch irises, and then gladiolus; by that time the University of Mississippi had graduated another class.[52] The next fall freshman Phil Stone would begin his college career.

3

The Hunt and College

DURING Phil Stone's late adolescence and early manhood, General Stone wielded no little power in Lafayette County. In 1908, upon the death of D. T. Carter, James Stone became president of the Bank of Oxford, a landmark on the southwest side of the square since 1872. Not long after Phil's father assumed responsibility for the institution with its $85,000 in capital,[1] J. W. T. Falkner, William Faulkner's grandfather, with $30,000 chartered the First National Bank of Oxford on the west side of North Street at the square. It was said in town, as Joseph Blotner discovered, "that a kind of rivalry existed between the two men, although both families were on good terms and Mrs. Stone and Maud Falkner were particular friends."[2] (In fact, it was "Old Lady Falkner," as Phil called Bill's grandmother, who was Miss Rosie's friend.)

However, banker Stone, still at heart a planter, was preoccupied with other matters than a Falkner rival. In an attempt to stimulate the area's moribund two-crop economy, he mounted an energetic personal campaign for crop diversification and other innovative agricultural techniques almost a generation before their adoption.[3] Transfixed by his dark blue eyes, a dirt farmer could only submit to "that affidavit countenance of Jim Stone": Yes, the county did have the most godforsaken land he'd ever seen; gullies were eating into all his fields; it had been years since he'd made any real money; yes, sir, if he didn't want to be in the poorhouse in a few years, he'd better plant something besides cotton. Maybe he'd buy some hogs too.

The Hunt and College

Among the more intelligent yeomanry, Stone made grateful converts. One family heirloom is a gold umbrella head inscribed "To James Stone: From the farmers of Lafayette County." Yet the poverty or ignorance of the others with whom he argued often had tragicomic results. After importing his two Jersey bulls (at an exorbitant price of $1,750), General Stone gave several registered calves to 4-H boys in the county—who fattened the purebred dairy stock and "butchered [it] for meat."

Had the gentleman farmer himself succeeded with his experiments, perhaps more of his financial customers would have followed his lead; but stray dogs decimated his flock of sheep, and the Angora goats he purchased to fight the dogs delighted instead in ravaging the nearby university campus, or, subsequently, "promenading along the top" of their expensive new "hog wire fence." When Stone's dairyman peddled milk from his Jersey herd around Oxford, Phil contended, General Stone "was bound to have lost a dollar and a quarter on all he sold," for he was far too impatient to allow any one scheme sufficient time to mature. As soon as his prizewinning Durocs became profitable, his son prophesied, "Now Dad's going to get rid of 'em; he just ain't willing to make money out of farming for hell," and within a year, General Stone did find some excuse to sell them.[4]

James Stone was more politic in another phase of his agricultural extension program. Because the local Board of Supervisors refused each year to allocate money to hire a professional county agent, Stone, the bank, and Mrs. Delle Price (the widow of former president Bem Price) provided the requisite amount. In the meantime Stone saw to it that the farmers' wives became conversant with modern agriculture. After the ratification of the Nineteenth Amendment, his new allies promptly turned out the shortsighted incumbents; thereafter, the Board of Supervisors budgeted funds for an agent's salary.

Phil's father was accomplished in masculine charm. On Valentine's Day in 1916, when a Sumner woman appealed to him for her favorite charity, she received a reply in verse:

> Dear Mrs. Rowland:
> You ask a penny for each year of my life,
> My gift would be less, but for the troubles I've borne,
> For each Calendar year, I've lived two or more;

My troubles are those of a man who marries;
So this little purse a hundred pennies carries.

There was one major compartment of his life, however, into which
no woman ever intruded. Each November, literally until the day of his
death, General Stone put aside his civic duties, left his marital troubles
at Stone Lodge, and went into the Delta to hunt. His son might think
it easier to get drunk at home, and consider a stag party "the dullest thing in the world" (Phil said that he liked the "shimmer" women
added to an occasion), but James Stone loved the fellowship of men in
the woods. A hunter since childhood, when he moved to Oxford he had
wasted no time in organizing an annual expedition back to the Tallahatchie in Panola County. Two months before Phil was born, the *Globe*
reported that "Stone, Temple, Gallegly, and Morrow, all of Oxford, returned from a bear hunt in the bottoms last week."[5] Because it was not
simply hunting but the logistics of a hunt that engaged James Stone,
very likely he was a moving force in the Tallahatchie Hunting and
Fishing Club, which spent a day on the river in late November 1902
"enjoying the sports of the season."[6]

General Stone's hunts always assumed massive proportions, and not
just to the boy who stayed home either. During preparations for the
annual event, according to his granddaughter Evelyn Stone, "it was
bedlam around the big house. My Grandmother, and all of the black
help, would be going in circles, while Big-Daddy, the 'Boss,' would be
giving orders." As an adult, Phil Stone would observe the manic confu-
sion with silent amusement: "When Dad is getting off on one of these
trips, it's like the fast train leaving New York City."[7] But it would have
been impossible for the boy to feign such indifference. He was desperate to go. But he did not have his stand in the canebrakes, he told his
wife, until he was ten.[8] It seems more likely that Phil Stone did not
graduate from rabbits to bears—except in his imagination—until after
his thirteenth birthday.[9]

Finally the fall came when the boy was allowed to accompany the
men. Several days before the hunters started, Phil watched "Short
John," Uncle Ad Jones,[10] and the other servants set out for the bottoms southwest of Oxford with the dogs and horses, and the wagons
loaded with sacks of flour, sides of bacon, and cases of whiskey and

ammunition. Phil followed later with his father and one or both of his brothers, the Oxford hunters—Van Tankersley, Bud Waller—and, for comic relief, Culley Archibald, who never ventured out of sight of General Stone's whiskey box.[11] When the hunters converged upon the designated site from Oxford, Batesville, and Charleston, the advance party would already have raised the tents, dug the "barbecue pits, and cut hacks or wide paths through the cane which grew sometimes as thick as a man's wrist and closer than the hairs on a dog's back." The machetes had sliced the cane "low enough so that a running horse would not disembowel himself, but high enough to impede a bear."[12]

"Old Reel Foot" haunted another camp,[13] but there were sufficient bear in the canebrakes in the low places to have a hunter on his stand at first light. As the novice, Phil drew the poorest stand, and he and Jack Stone for the first few mornings huddled in grim silence when the dogs drove the game down the hacks to the intersections where Van Tankersley or Bud Waller waited. In the excitement a boy might forget, run down to see the kill, and be mistaken for a bear himself. But, at last, to the relief of both brothers, General Stone was convinced that Phil would "indeed stand," and Jack left Phil "to wait alone for what he never even hoped would happen."[14]

Luck presented the boy his opportunity in fact on one of his first hunts. Not long after sunrise one morning Phil was already stiff from waiting—and cold and nervous. Twice he had been sure a bear was coming his way and worried again whether a mere shotgun could stop the animal; all the men, he knew, had rifles. For the moment, however, he relaxed; the dogs, as Phil could hear, had lost the trail. Only then did he realize how much his shoulders ached from carrying the gun. But all at once the voices changed; the dogs were coming toward him. "General Stone called [to] Phil to climb back on his white mustang pony and not to try to shoot for fear the bear, possibly wounded . . . might be infuriated and attack."[15] As Phil only half listened, instantaneously, it seemed, the animal loomed before him: " 'Then I was shaking all over. I was a fool, but I didn't know it. I didn't know anything. I lifted my gun and let him have both barrels. Then I opened my eyes. He was lumbering and he came toward me, and he fell. I was just lucky, that's all. The gun had no business to kill him. Nobody had so much as dreamed that I'd even get a shot to begin with, and they were horrified that I had tried. If the bullet [?] hadn't hit his heart (he was angling away from me), he'd have torn me to pieces. But I wasn't thinking about that.' " [16]

Hearing the gunfire and the cries of his son, General Stone broke his own rule and galloped to Phil's stand, shouting for him to stay on his mustang because the wounded bear "might be vicious with pain." But Phil, seemingly unhurt, was only yelling, "I killed a bear! Daddy, Daddy, I killed a bear!" [17] The young hunter, of course, was met with skepticism. When at Phil's insistence General Stone urged his horse into the canebrake, "there sat the panting dogs and there lay the small three hundred pound black bear, completely dead. The horns were blown [to assemble the rest of their party] and the hunters . . . got off their horses, cut open the belly of the dead bear, rubbed their hands in the blood," [18] and smeared the boy's face with it, "as they always do with your first bear," Phil said. "I wanted never to wash it off any more." [19]

Until that moment, the youngster had been content just to be there— to be shaken awake in the gray November chill when the man came to get General Stone's keys to the whiskey for the hunters' predawn drink. If the humid air was not warming up for a winter rain, and the tales, the poker, and the drinking had abated at a reasonable hour the night before, the camp convened for breakfast in fine spirits. One of the hunters would slip Uncle Ad a forbidden second or third whiskey, and "he would flip the batter cakes or the eggs a yard or more in the air (causing the men to laugh, and the Negroes sitting lax on a log . . . [to] say, 'Sho, now. Will you look at that-air.') Then he would make them land as softly as flowers back in the spider (frying pan) he held in his long thin yellow hand." [20] After the single breakfast drink, the liquor was locked up until nightfall, when they might all get drunk with impunity, but on General Stone's hunts, "if a man insisted on bringing his own [liquor]," Phil said, "he would be invited to go home."

James Stone, nevertheless, made an exception for Culley Archibald, who, according to legend, "stayed drunk for thirty years." Culley, almost as old as General Stone, went on the hunts for decades, but if he ever hunted no one caught him at it. Once the hunts moved to Stone Stop, Culley rarely set foot outside the hunting "lodge," where Charlie Watts kept him company. Watts, an "old red-neck," "wasn't much," according to Phil, but General Stone allowed him to stay at the camp during the year as a caretaker of sorts.

The Hunt and College

In Phil's youth the men hunted on "Section 14" land, acreage that Miss Rosie had inherited from Major Alston.[21] Even before the large Northern lumber companies began cutting timber out of the Delta, General Stone and Clarence Sivley were buying up standing timber and large tracts there as investments. Phil would say that while farming was no more than an expensive hobby for General Stone, he was an expert at timber. Phil believed his father to have made as much money from that as from the practice of law. Stone and Sivley acquired one stand of virgin timber in the southern corner of Panola and Quitman counties close to where the Tallahatchie and the Yocona rivers converge, in what was called the "Big Bottom."[22] Another name for the spot was the "Big Eddy," because there the river looped around in a deep, narrow curve.[23] John Cullen claims that virgin forests stretched over five thousand acres there with trees so tall that "a two-hundred-pound bear would jump into a wood-pecker's hole at the pursuit of dogs."[24] According to Phil's nephew, the bottom was almost impenetrable jungle, even in winter. The Batesville and Southwestern Railroad ran a spur into the tract to bring the timber out, and as a courtesy to Stone and Sivley, who were prominent railroad attorneys, made a flag stop near the camp that became known as Stone Stop.[25]

Paul J. Rainey, the Pennsylvania multimillionaire and Mississippi's most illustrious hunter, would inevitably hear of General Stone's hunts.[26] While his father had exercised power as a coal baron, Rainey cared only for the hunt—lions in Africa, tigers in India, ducks in Louisiana. His dogs were famous among international sportsmen, and he showed them each year at the United States Field Trials at Grand Junction, Tennessee, fifty miles from Oxford.[27] Early in the century Rainey met there a New Albany doctor who introduced him "to the hills and valleys of north Mississippi." The land very much appealed to the hunter, and Rainey began accumulating deeds for a game preserve around a tiny hamlet called Cotton Plant, which he soon owned. In time much of Tippah and Union counties belonged to him. His first purchase had been the homestead and farm of one H. M. Ratliff in January 1904, and he spared no expense in improving the property. The Ratliff place was soon a twenty-room mansion, complete with heated indoor swimming pool. Moreover, Rainey would insist that Cotton Plant and the area around it join the twentieth century. He built his own power plant, a private railroad siding for his private car, and the Rainey Hotel in New Albany, for which he imported a French chef.

Phil Stone and his father may have been introduced to Rainey when they bought a puppy from his Tippah Kennels sometime between late 1908 and late 1911. Their dog's sire, Tom Bigbee, and its littermate, White Man, valued at a thousand dollars, were Rainey's pride, the ideal brace of "gentleman's shooting dogs." However it came about, Rainey joined the Stone bear hunts for several years, probably during those seasons when he was in Mississippi between 1908 and the time he left for France to drive his own ambulance during the First World War. After Stone and Sivley bought the land at Stone Stop, Rainey had a clubhouse built for the hunters there.[28] His own "lodge" in Cotton Plant was a bit eccentric—he had built his mansion onto the small Ratliff home—but there was a kind of elegant rusticity to its tiled baths, trophy room, sunken gardens, and goldfish ponds. The "lodge" or "clubhouse" at Stone Stop could have been mistaken for a sharecropper's shack.

Although Phil, John Cullen, and Philip Thornton's son all remembered Rainey hunting with the Stones, no stories survive about him at Stone Stop.[29] Perhaps coincidentally, one Rainey anecdote, however, anticipates that of Faulkner's Uncle Ash in *Go Down, Moses*, though its setting is a safari instead of a bear hunt. The story recounts the six-hour hunting career of the Swede who drove the chuckwagon and did the cooking for Rainey's African hunts. For years he had pestered Rainey to be allowed to join the lion hunts. Finally one morning Rainey told him to grab his old shotgun, saddle up the chuckwagon mule, and come along. What the Swede did not know was that the hunters surrounded the lion on horseback and got him to charge one of the horses; only then would the others shoot. Of course, the lion headed straight for the Swede's mule, both Swede and mule were "scared out of their wits," and the cook never mentioned hunting to Rainey again.

Late in 1910 his manager at the Tippah Kennels sold off the last of the more than thirty dogs in order to accompany Rainey on one of his hunting expeditions. They were to be gone two years, most of that time in Kenya where he had another plantation and game reserve.[30] As usual Rainey took along a large party, and that time he invited seventeen-year-old Phil to accompany the group. Phil, of course, was "crazy to go," but General Stone and Miss Rosie insisted that college was more important, so Rainey went to Africa without Phil Stone.[31] Rainey would return to Mississippi after the war, but by then the bears were gone from Stone Stop.[32] He was en route to India by way of Capetown, to hunt tigers, when he collapsed and died at sea at the age of forty-six.

By the time of his Faulkner friendship, during the years Phil was in law school at Ole Miss, Phil Stone had given up hunting. "Because by then," he said, "I'd seen the deer."[33] When he was sixteen, he told his wife Emily, he was out by himself in the highlands (the Delta highlands, "which ain't very high"). All his life Stone rhapsodized about the woods there. Oaks and gum trees stood almost a hundred feet apart, their branches meeting in a canopy high overhead, through which a November sun cast only a dim, golden light. Nothing green grew on the forest floor, piled with generations of brown leaves. That open high ground was the home of the deer, which depend upon speed for their protection. Phil told a hundred times what happened that afternoon: "Right there where I'd been looking all the time, or I thought I had, suddenly there stood a big buck. His head was down and he had a tremendous spread of antlers."[34] As Phil raised his gun, the buck lifted his head: "I don't know whether he heard me or smelled me or just sensed death somehow. I looked at him and he looked at me and there was in his eyes a desperation beyond despair. He knew he was gone." Phil "soundlessly" lowered his gun, and the buck "whirled" and bounded off.

After William Faulkner and Stone were friends, Bill asked Phil to take him on the November hunts, because Phil talked so often about them and because Bill "thought so much of General Stone." The friends went together a few times; Faulkner hunted with General Stone for "ten years or longer,"[35] but Phil soon ceased to go. After his experience with the deer, he said, "I didn't want to handle a gun" or to hunt anymore. "I couldn't give an animal life, and I can't take it away."

Phil had seen the deer when he was sixteen. Earlier in the autumn of 1909, when Faulkner was in the sixth grade, Phil Stone walked over to the Ole Miss campus, paid a ten-dollar matriculation fee, and registered for Latin, Greek, English, and mathematics.[36] Twenty-six of the 131 students in the class of 1913 were from Oxford, only three from out of state, none from north of the Mason-Dixon line. A "certificate of good moral character" was required for admission if a student was "not personally known to members of the faculty." Most were. University Training School graduates at Ole Miss numbered almost thirty: Charlie Patterson from the Delta, W. B. McMahon, George Hightower, three of the Rowlands, a Carter, a Neilson, and Jim Kyle Hudson, Phil's good friend and rival.

Not even a stranger could have gotten lost on the small campus west of Oxford. Besides a new residence hall for women, a library, a chapel, and the antebellum Lyceum, the only buildings were Taylor, McCain, and Gordon Halls, a dormitory for men, and a few faculty and student homes.[37] The university offered instruction in six departments: Science, Literature, and the Arts; Law; Engineering; Education; Medicine; and Pharmacy. The faculty of the provincial university, numbering just over fifty, included eighteen M.D.'s and six LL.D.'s, but only six Ph.D.'s (although all instructors were addressed as "Doctor").

Four years later, when Stone received his degree, his associates on the 1913 *Ole Miss* staff would write of him: "Our courtly gentleman from Oxford town has never been seen in any situation or condition however trying, in which he failed to display the most beautiful of manners. Nor, in this case, is manners all the man, for the University records show four years of brilliant grades for Phil, and he has likewise found time to leave his mark among the boys and in society." Although he failed a quarter of freshman math, his grades at Ole Miss were most often *A*'s; Stone was awarded his first bachelor's degree "with distinction."

One might say that Stone majored in languages, for he took two years of college Latin, four of Greek, three of French, and, in his senior year, intermediate German. After his sophomore year, his fourth year of Greek, he abandoned Latin, exasperated by what he called its "clumsiness." The myriad inflections of ancient Greek, by contrast, "taught one absolute accuracy," a verbal precision Stone believed invaluable in his later courtroom rhetoric.[38] For three of the four years Phil was the student of Canadian Alfred William Milden, a Johns Hopkins Ph.D. who had come to Mississippi in 1910 after a decade at Emory and Henry. Stone deeply respected Milden's scholarship, but his "cherubic innocence" was a subject for ridicule to Phil's younger friend Edith Brown, according to Stone. Her class relished Milden's leaping up and down the room in imitation of the Greek dances.

Edith's father was never accused of such innocence. The gossip around campus was that Calvin S. Brown, M.S., D.Sc., Ph.D., was an atheist. Brown invited further speculation by his habit of walking the university grounds with his head cocked back, as if in a trance.[39] Dr. Brown's credentials were more impressive than those of other faculty members, and he had studied two years abroad, at Paris and Leipzig universities and in Spain and Italy too. Phil Stone took four courses in French and German under him, and made A's in three of the four.

But in the main Phil found the Ole Miss faculty unremarkable. Perhaps because the small town and its contiguous university were so dependent upon one another for society, an Oxford student like Stone knew too well the men whose lectures he attended. Quite often they were also his brothers' former professors or his parents' friends, if not the fathers, uncles, or brothers-in-law of his own companions. Except for minor eccentricities, exorcised through ridicule in the town's anecdotes, the academics seem to have afforded little intellectual variety or color to Oxford's prevailing conservative tone.

One university family with whom Stone was variously connected were the Somervilles, who enjoyed a special status in Oxford because of their impeccable credentials. The mother was "a Vassar," the town said reverently, and the father, dean of the law department in Stone's freshman year, bore the illustrious name with which Stone himself claimed relation, through his great-grandmother Mary Somerville Alston. The two youngest Somerville girls—Ella, his contemporary, and Nina, who was four years younger—were among Stone's closest friends in his youth. The sisters were well liked within Oxford's college set, although rarely invited to go out, apparently because neither was particularly attractive. Nevertheless, for a time Phil Stone escorted Nina Somerville to university dances, a "courtship" rather short on romance, according to his later vain account of it to his wife: "Phil used to say that one of the things he liked to do was to take out a girl who was *not* popular. . . . This was his principle. He said the ones who are pretty and popular are not nearly so 'rewarding' as those who are not. So he made it his business in a number of instances to court them and make them popular." No doubt Stone congratulated himself when sixteen-year-old Nina was chosen maid of honor for the 1913 junior class prom, but later she surprised even Phil by marrying the successful Oxford surgeon John Culley.

It may have been through "Ellaville" and "Ninaville," as Phil called the Somerville women, that he first became acquainted with a serious writer. He had, of course, known Stark Young, the son of Oxford physician Dr. A. A. Young, "since boyhood," but the eleven years between them checked any initial rapport. By the time Phil entered Ole Miss, Young had published a volume of poems and a verse play, had lived for a time in New York, and had traveled abroad.[40] Young was never formally Phil's teacher, having left the university's English faculty to teach drama at Texas before Phil enrolled at Ole Miss. As General Longstreet had made manifest Phil's Confederate demigods, Stark Young initially embodied for Stone literature incarnate. For "it was Stark Young," he said, "who opened my mind."

If Stone found intellectual stimulation outside the university, he discovered how to be young with his peers. Of course, there were a few serious students among the party crowd, but, in Faulkner's phrase, "high-hearted dullness"[41] was socially more acceptable. By his senior year Phil had developed the subterfuge under which he maintained his popularity. That year, besides Greek, French, and English, he elected to take second-year German for no credit, under Dr. Calvin Brown, from whom he expected A's. It was the eleventh hour for the math deficiency and his curriculum required two hours of freshman chemistry, another stumbling block that he had postponed. Stone decided to attempt the chemistry in two quarters instead of three, and although he must have spent hours memorizing for both courses, he projected an air of nonchalance before his freshmen classmates.

He made, that time, a gentleman's C in math and two B's in chemistry, but to Mack Reed, who took chemistry with Phil, it was a different scenario: at examination time, almost as soon as the professor finished writing the questions on the board, Phil handed in his paper. Astonished, the professor picked up Phil's blue book and read it. "This young man knows everything there is to know about this course," he declared. Mack and the other freshmen were impressed. Mack labored two and a half hours on his paper and barely passed.[42]

In his undergraduate years at the University of Mississippi, Stone belonged to the French Club and, as a junior, Sigma Upsilon (the Scribblers' Club), "an organization for the promotion of the literary spirit in the university." Even before he went off to Yale for the first time, his avocation was well known. Stone, class poet, was literary editor of the 1913 *Ole Miss*, under Thomas Mayo, the Scribblers' secretary. The club's most distinguished officer, however, was Phil's DKE brother John W. Kyle, Rhodes Scholar and "Best Student" of 1913. All those young men certainly wrote poems or stories, but poetry and prose published in extant issues of the *University of Mississippi Magazine* usually are either anonymous or signed with pseudonyms. Stone, it seems, was never a member of the senior debating societies that published the monthly while he was an undergraduate,[43] and although he did write some poetry in his youth—which he later admitted only to his wife[44]— there seems no way to determine whether he submitted poems to the magazine. Probably he did not.

The most published student in campus publications in those days was Phil's classmate Arthur Palmer Hudson, later an eminent folklorist at the University of North Carolina. In 1910 Hudson and Stone had entered a university tennis tournament together, but in the first round they lost to Anderson and Pound, the subsequent champions, 6–0, 6–0.

Obviously literature ranked far behind sports as a campus enthusiasm, but that was not the case with state politics, and the fireworks had started early in the 1911 campaign. Phil, Jack, and General Stone, as usual, entered the lists against the scoundrels running for office, but the results were more than disheartening this time. William Alexander Percy's father, Senator Leroy Percy, the incumbent, had been campaigning vigorously since 1910, according to historian John K. Bettersworth. At a Fourth of July rally, stung by the epithets of a pro-Vardaman crowd, Percy had called his hecklers "cattle" and "rednecks." Senator Percy would have done better to have kept his temper, for, as Bettersworth continues, "Promptly the Vardamanites accepted the names and made political capital of them. Henceforth, the supporters of Vardaman wore red neckties; and when Bilbo later succeeded to Vardaman's throne, the red necktie became his trademark."[45]

Vardaman went to the Senate; Earl Brewer, whom the Stones had helped to defeat in 1907, won the governor's chair without opposition; Theodore G. Bilbo, Vardaman's protégé, became lieutenant governor, and the "rascal" Lee Russell, a member of the state senate. The New Orleans *Picayune*, as Joseph Blotner notes, observed aptly that Mississippians, in electing a new generation to public office, "were putting the foot down firmly on all that remains of the old aristocracy."[46]

Jim Stone, Phil's brother, at times could villify the "bottom rail" with the best of the aristocrats: "You can't be subtle with these rednecks," he blustered. "You got to slap them in the face with a buzzard gut."[47] But Jim did not endear himself to General Stone or to his brothers when he became a Bilbo supporter, a treason even Faulkner's grandfather was never guilty of.[48]

When, a month later, Phil Stone began his junior year, he may not have realized how quickly Ole Miss would feel the effects of Lee Russell and a Vardaman legislature, although Jack Stone must have remembered the fury of Russell's revenge on the Greeks in 1902 after Russell had been first blackballed and then publicly humiliated by an Ole Miss fraternity.[49] Jack would not have abandoned his fraternity brothers in the crisis over the new regulations imposed then to satisfy Russell's ire. A loyal Deke, he had held every office in the fraternity and had gone twice as a delegate to its national conventions.[50] But that furor had all blown over a decade before, or so they must have thought. Russell, however, could hardly have had his bags unpacked in Jackson before he introduced a measure to outlaw fraternities at the state university; by the end of February in 1912, he had successfully steered it through both houses, despite petitions signed by twenty-six of the faculty and most of Oxford's business community stating that Russell's charges of gross immorality among fraternity men were obviously untrue.[51]

Phil Stone, following Jack's example, had pledged Delta Kappa Epsilon. But by Phil's senior year, fraternities by law did not exist; only graduating seniors and their *Fratres in Urbe* were given a place in the 1913 *Ole Miss*. Chi chapter, chartered in 1850, for a while was forced underground.

Although there continued to be a great deal of resentment toward Lee Russell among the students, they soon found ways to circumvent— and to flout—him. Football distracted them during the first term, but by the winter quarter, to fill the social vacuum left by the demise of the Greeks, Phil, Jim Kyle Hudson, John Kyle, Cornell Franklin, and sixteen other seniors formed the Red and Blue Club. The group labored to construct a reputation for dissoluteness, as in an event recorded—or, more likely, fabricated—by the *Mississippian* in March:

> In spite of the nipping wind, the square was circled, and, joined by Phil Stone, who gave a graphic representation of the winning of the Vanderbilt cup, said cup being strikingly like a whiskey bottle, the entire party entered the Opera House, where a matinee dance was in progress. The management kindly stopped the dancing to make way for The Red and Blue grand march, which was led by Bobby Burnes, who furnished the respectability for the whole crowd, and Thomas Mayo, his debutante fiancee. After this the initiates mingled with the dancers for a short while, and then returned rather disheveled to the campus, to talk over an affair which was certainly a pleasant lightening of the usual mid-term monotony.[52]

Later that spring Phil Stone posed for the club's yearbook photograph with a pint whiskey bottle in one hand and a garden watering can marked "liquor dealer" at his feet.

With so few coeds on campus, university men often invited women from town to the more decorous college socials. Estelle Oldham, whose father was Oxford's federal clerk, became sponsor to "The Outlaws," another, smaller dancing club for which Phil's classmate Cornell Franklin served as chairman. (Franklin would be Estelle's first husband.) Stone himself had recently summoned his gallantry to court Katrina Carter, whose late father had been president of the Bank of Oxford. In 1913 both women, friends from childhood, were applying to prestigious girls' schools in the upper South. Oldham was soon accepted at Mary Baldwin College; Carter, at Fairmont Seminary.

As Stone's Mississippi collegiate career drew to a close, he began contemplating further schooling in the Northeast, even though academic matters were hardly his most pressing concern. In the spring quarter of his senior year he registered for a leisurely schedule: English, French, and German on Monday, Wednesday, and Friday mornings, Greek for an hour on Tuesdays and Thursdays. From the record it would appear that diligent studying was in progress those long spring afternoons, for his grades averaged 95. Stone confessed, to the contrary, that his schedule had been designed to leave "ample time for poker," a skill that when perfected would stand with Greek as the foundation of his education, as he later maintained with the utmost seriousness.[53] If Greek teaches

one "absolute accuracy," poker, he reiterated, "teaches one people."
Asserting always that the "poker face" was a myth, Phil believed that
every man inevitably reveals what he thinks. Crediting his own success
in the courtroom to a long and careful "watch" of witnesses, attorneys,
and jurists, by the end of his career he claimed to be able "to read
about two dozen lawyers in Mississippi who unconsciously give their
thoughts away." The art derived from the game "which, his opponents
said, he handled brilliantly." Poker would be a regular Stone pastime
for the next fourteen years.

Liquor and guns might not mix, but playing poker and drinking
whiskey were complementary occupations. General Stone certainly
thought so. And since Stone children and grandchildren were raised
finishing the "heel-taps" of his toddies,[54] Phil was no stranger to whiskey even before he went on the hunts. In college he began to drink
heavily, regularly consuming a quart of bourbon a day for almost a year.
At a more abstemious stage he recounted how the liquor had affected
him: "I got very white," he remembered, "and was *exceedingly* polite."

A few weeks after commencement, apparently because Stone felt that
he ought to help finance the postgraduate year in New Haven he was
proposing to his father, he joined several other college students working
in a new state highway construction program. Sweating out the previous night's liquor under a hot Mississippi sun for a dollar a day did
not reform him, however. At summer's end Phil had fifty-seven dollars
saved for Yale, but the alcohol was beginning to scare him. Twice he
had passed out before he even realized he was intoxicated. He vowed
"to throw one more drunk" and then to have nothing more to do with
whiskey, but it would be almost six months before he could bring his
drinking under control.

In Mississippi, as elsewhere in the South, fathers who could afford
it customarily sent their sons to Eastern schools. One of those who
convinced General Stone of the benefits for a Southerner of the Ivy
League experience was Walter P. Armstrong, an ambitious young lawyer from Coffeeville. Armstrong had grown up savoring the adventures
of Frank Merriwell, the "wholesome" Yale sports hero of over two hundred novels. In part because of those books, as Armstrong admitted in
his maturity, he had decided to go to Yale, and he urged Phil to follow
his example.[55]

In Stone's freshman year at Ole Miss the Dramatic Club had lampooned the Ivy League in the comedy "At Yale," but while laughing at naive, affected Dick Seeley, class of 1905, some students may privately have shared Faulkner character Dawson Fairchild's associations with the Eastern universities: " 'I guess there is a time in the life of every young American of the class that wants to go to college or accepts the inevitability of education, when he wants to go to Yale or Harvard. Maybe that's the value of Yale and Harvard to our American life: a kind of illusion of an intellectual nirvana that makes the ones that can't go there work like hell where they do go, so as not to show up so poorly alongside of the ones that can go there.' "[56]

Although Stone went to the Yale Law School also, he was well aware of the greater prestige in having an undergraduate degree from Yale and was always glad that he had gone. He knew that the experience had given him a perspective on the world he would never have had otherwise. It was not uncommon then for a student to transfer to another college in his senior year. Both Yale and Ole Miss made provision for such arrangements. With Phil's grades and liberal arts degree, he probably had only to apply to be admitted as a Yale senior. The entrance committee accepted forty-two credit hours from Ole Miss—everything, apparently, except his senior-level courses.

In the autumn of 1913 Stone, John Kyle, and Katrina Carter arranged to go East together on the train.[57] Kyle, the Rhodes Scholar in Phil's Ole Miss class, was probably en route to England. Katrina, Stone's then serious romantic interest, was entering the freshman class at Fairmont, the girls' school in Washington, D.C. On the train the Mississippians were in high good humor (Katrina, especially, had a contagious vivacity) and attracted the attention of passenger Eugene Strode, an Alabamian, who joined them for the rest of the journey. Strode was "mad to be an actor," and, worried that his nose was unflattering, he talked of having plastic surgery. Katrina listened in sympathy, commenting that one of the younger girls she had met at Fairmont in the spring shared his dreams for the theater, acted "every moment of the working day," and struck dramatic poses whenever she had an audience. Subsequently, Eugene Strode managed only a short tenure as an underling in a New York Shakespearean troupe, and from his brief stage career, only a carefully cultivated Oxford accent, a noticeably deepened baritone voice, and a new name—Hudson Strode—would survive.[58] In the fifties, after Strode became a successful creative writing professor at the University of Alabama, he and Phil Stone held marathon discussions whenever they met at the annual Southern Literary Festivals.

Stone later confessed to his wife that only when he went to Yale did he find out that there were "other smart boys in the world." He was shocked to learn that native intelligence alone did not bring academic acclaim, as it had done at Ole Miss. Despite his three years under Dr. Calvin Brown, at Yale he discovered that he was failing French, realized his predicament, and had to apply himself in the third-year course for Yale freshmen.[59] After an embarrassing 1.65 in first-semester French, he made a rather spectacular recovery by spring, raising his average to 2.75. Yet Stone was never fluent in the language, and read his Balzac and most of the Symbolists in translation. He would speak only Anglicized French words.

Stone was more interested in English and Greek literature, and his program seemed arranged to take advantage of his opportunities in the year at Yale. He made "a rapid reading of all the authentic plays" of Shakespeare in an intermediate senior course under Charlton M. Lewis. With special permission he enrolled too in the more advanced class English Lyrical Poetry, with Edward Bliss Reed. That course followed, "in the main, reading outlined in the instructor's *English Lyrical Poetry*, beginning with *Deor's Lament* and ending with the lyrics of Noyes." Another volume he purchased for the class became a cornerstone in his library and in his tutelage of Faulkner: Arthur Quiller Couch's *The Oxford Book of Verse: 1250–1900* (Oxford: Clarendon Press, 1912).

It was Stone's good fortune at Yale to study with two of the college's legends: William Lyon Phelps, "who taught a course called 'Tennyson and Browning,' popularly known as 'T. & B.' "; and Horatio M. Reynolds, with whom Phil studied the Athenian dramatists. In the twenties and thirties Phelps wrote the widely respected "As You Like It" column in *Scribner's*. As a teacher, amid recitations and discussions of "Tennyson as poet and artist, and . . . Browning as an interpreter of life," Billy Phelps enlivened "T. & B." with yarns his students would remember into the 1970s.[60] The respect that Phelps inspired derived from more than narrative skill. With a sometimes volatile student body—the "Hyperion Theater riot" followed one Harvard victory—Phelps persisted in championing unpopular political views, as 1915 alumnus John Donald Robb illustrates in an incident involving the English professor and Hudson ("Boz") Hawley, a friend of Phil Stone:

> One night somebody got out in the middle of the Old Campus with a bass drum. Because we were all condemned to our studies in our rooms after dinner, all that was needed was an excuse to bring us out. So, preceded by the drummer, we marched to the front of old Osborn Hall . . . [where] the headline address was made by a fellow named Boz Holly [sic]. Boz hit the proper keynote because there had just been a confrontation between the United States and Mexico, and President Huerta of Mexico and Woodrow Wilson were on the brink of war.
>
> So Boz Holly called on the boys to knock the hurt out of Huerta. That started an off-campus parade, and we all marched over to the home of William Lyon Phelps. . . . Nobody realized that this was just a student prank, and I suppose that we seemed quite a menacing mob. But Billy Phelps came out on the balcony and with great courage said: "Gentlemen, go home and go to bed. I'm a pacifist. I don't believe in war and you're provoking it and you ought to behave yourselves." [61]

Phil Stone, who may have slept through the "riot," earned his highest grade, a 3.35, under Phelps, who taught at Yale until 1933.

In his seventh consecutive year of Greek, Phil read Aeschylus, Sophocles, Euripides, and Aristophanes with Yale's famous "Limpy" Reynolds. George Wilson Pierson, the Yale historian, describes Horatio M. Reynolds as the "perfect, complete gentleman":

> His was a special appeal. For more than twenty years he had been charming his students into reading outside of class. In the eighties he had got Billy Phelps to read Grote's *History of Greek* every night from ten to eleven. In the early 1900's athletes were known to read Greek on the train. When Reynolds found a student floundering, he wouldn't take advantage. "Perhaps I can handle that for you," he would say—and from that moment he might do all the translating to the end of the hour. The College allowed half-cuts or "dry-cuts" for those confessing unpreparedness in advance. But when Reynolds had planned to do all the translating himself, he would say to an applicant like Emerson Tuttle '14, "I don't believe I should take a cut today, Mr. Tuttle, not today, Mr. Tuttle." [62]

Later, hearing of a scornful account of Reynolds in the *New Republic*, Stone grew outraged at the heresy. Even at Whitfield, half a century later, Phil Stone was able to recite long passages from the Greek dramatists he had studied with Horatio Reynolds.

Stone's program at Yale may have required that he add to his spring schedule a course in biblical literature, but the "Social Teachings of Jesus and the Prophets" would have held some interest for him. He was never the Bible-reading churchgoer that his mother was, and he was a young man when he became disdainful of Methodist evangelicalism, but he believed in God and he had high ethical standards. After his marriage in 1935 Stone was active in St. Peter's Episcopal Church; and during his marriage, if not from childhood, he said his prayers nightly before retiring. In New Haven, Stone attended the compulsory morning prayers and Sunday worship in Battell Chapel, but his 1953 letter to "Mel" Price, a Yale classmate then on the *New Yorker* staff, suggests how little religion outside the classroom occupied their minds in 1913–14: "By the way, I am a member of the vestry in our church. I wonder if you and Boz Hawley have yet approached such a degree of sanctification?"[63] Hawley was Mel Price's roommate at New Haven; both were Connecticut Yankees.

Phil Stone had gone to New Haven determined not to drink. He decided that to his new friends he would pretend he had never tasted alcohol. He felt that if he could abstain until Christmas, then perhaps "he could drink occasionally and quit on one drink." But his resolution was shaken immediately by an unexpected homesickness. Hawley and Price were yet distant, and twice, to his disgust, Stone found himself drunk. Gradually he developed a stratagem for those times when he "walked the streets of New Haven craving a drink." He would go to the saloon of the Taft Hotel or to the Bishop Hotel across the street, order a drink at the bar, pay for it, "smell it a good while, taste the whiskey with his tongue several times, put the whiskey glass down," and walk out "the saloon door to the street," muttering to himself: "Damn you, John Barleycorn! You may beat me tomorrow but I have beaten you today." In the autobiography he claims that "there was no more failing" and that he abstained for the next twelve years, "until he knew he could taste whiskey without trouble."[64]

With the private war, and his grades at first so weak, Stone spent more time at his books than in the cultivation of friendships during his first year in the East (unless his friendship with Byrne Hackett dates from that period). All Yale men were required to live in college-approved dormitories,[65] but as one of twelve in his class with a degree already, Phil was permitted to live in rooms at 35 High Street, about two hundred feet from campus. He ate in Commons, nevertheless, and after a while met his classmates in the residence halls. He had not heard from Mel Price, however, for almost forty years when Price saw Stone on television in the 1953 *Omnibus* documentary on Faulkner. In 1958 another member of the class of 1914, Henry Tetlow II of Philadelphia, who lived down the hall from Price and Hawley, resumed a correspondence with Stone after a lapse of twenty years.[66] Phil's Yale ties thus were more to the institution than to persons he knew there only in 1913–14. Over the years he wrote a dozen letters to the *Yale Alumni Weekly* or to his class representative and acquaintance Henry W. Hobson, the Episcopal bishop of Ohio. In addition, in February 1947 Stone gave the Beinecke Library two typescript poems, "Don Manuel" and "Orpheus," from the Faulkner papers in his possession.[67]

By Christmas 1913 his homesickness was acute. Although his railroad pass was still good, Stone was always concerned that he was spending too much of his father's money, and Yale was by no means cheap: by 1920 tuition alone was three hundred dollars; room rent in the dorms, another three hundred (Phil's rooms in town were probably higher); board cost almost four hundred dollars.[68] General Stone, however, reiterated that he had spent far more money getting Jim Stone out of trouble than he could ever spend on Phil's education and urged him to come home as planned for the holidays. In fact, the Stones, not accustomed to having their youngest son gone even for the night, were as eager to see him as he was to see them at Christmas. Thus Phil, with a lighter heart, boarded the train at Yale Station for the trip to New York, where most of his classmates departed, and headed south.

An incident during his trip home would turn up later in *The Sound and the Fury*. Soon after his train crossed into Virginia, it stopped unexpectedly in the country and Phil walked out on the platform for some air. There at a crossing sat a black man on a mule. "Hey, Uncle!" Phil hailed the man, and they began to pass the time of day.

"Where you stays?" the man wanted to know.

"I've been in New Haven," Stone replied, relishing the man's Southern accent.

"You sho' don't sound like New Haven," he said, and Phil explained that he was on his way back home to Mississippi.

"Mississippi! I've got an aunt living somewhere in Mississippi."

So Phil issued an invitation: "Why don't you come down to see her?"

"I believe I will," the man chuckled. "You ain't got room there, is you?"

The conductor was climbing back on the train, so Phil wished the Virginian a Merry Christmas and flipped him a quarter. The Yale man was close to tears. He knew, he said, that he had come home.[69]

In Oxford among his friends Stone discovered that an Ivy Leaguer was "prince of the realm."[70] He did the rounds of the holiday parties with Katrina Carter and talked incessantly about books and writers, and the plays and concerts he had attended. William Butler Yeats was to come to Yale in the spring, he told Katrina. He described for Jim Kyle Hudson the new Deke house under construction at Yale, where their fraternity had been chartered, and the colossal Yale Bowl, which would seat over seventy thousand spectators when completed in 1914.[71] Yet Stone had found in New Haven only confirmation for their suspicions about Yankees. Southerners, he assured them, were much less "rigid" than Northerners. One could easily see the differences in the tactics each had used in the Civil War. The Yankees employed "massiveness," their chief weapon; the Southerners, on the other hand, were "more improvisory"—the cavalry, for example, constantly in motion, adjusting to the needs of a situation.

Emily Stone claims that after three years in New Haven those ideas had only solidified, that Phil had a "mind-set" about Northerners, namely, that they were "rigid," which, as Mrs. Stone thinks, seems "pure projection." But Phil was convinced that one had to be arrogant with Yankees, especially with "the Ivy League people."[72]

With such prejudices Phil Stone was somewhat reluctant to return to Yale after New Year's, especially since he returned to face first-semester exams; but New Haven's factories did not look so depressing under a blanket of snow. Stone began to feel a part of the class of 1914 in the spring, as serious matters gave way to "roller skating, top spinning, and going bareheaded," the senior's "coveted privileges," according to one alumni publication—although Phil used most of his time to better advantage. With conscientious effort, by the end of the year he had raised his semester average from 2.56 to 3.02, and still he found time to indulge his taste for books outside the classroom, browsing among the "best current literature" in the twenty-thousand volumes in Chittenden Hall and in bookstores in town.[73]

It is not clear exactly how or when Stone first met Edmond Byrne Hackett, but it may be that their friendship began during the 1913–14 term and that Hackett, who also had a love for books, was the one from whom Phil's literary imagination caught fire. By the time he returned South, after June commencement, his zeal in the cause of letters was impossible to resist. As Ella Somerville told Blotner, Faulkner was not the only one to find himself set upon by the convert: " 'Have you read this?' [Phil] would ask excitedly. 'You must read that,' he would say. 'I'll lend you my copy.' "[74] Stone knew Hackett better later, after Hackett and six others in December 1915 incorporated the Brick Row Print and Book Shop, which Stone frequented between 1916 and 1918 (and with whom he had a sizeable account in the twenties).[75] Their mutual interests may have brought them together, or Stark Young may have had a hand in it; if so, the Stone-Hackett friendship probably dates from the time Stone was in law school.

In Stark Young's correspondence with student poet Howard Phelps Putnam, Yale, 1916, one November 1915 letter is addressed to Putnam at the Elizabethan Club, of which Byrne Hackett was also a member.[76] But Young perhaps knew Hackett through Young's association with the *New Republic*, where Hackett's brother was a member of the editorial board. In 1922 Stark Young would replace Francis Hackett as the magazine's associate editor.[77]

If Stone knew Byrne Hackett in 1913 or 1914, he may have been invited to tea or to lectures at the Elizabethan Club. In the spring of 1914 George Lyman Kittredge and Alfred Noyes were the chief attractions, and on 23 April the men celebrated the 350th anniversary of Shakespeare's birth: "Professor Phelps to read Shakespeare's sonnets at [the] club at 4 precisely."[78]

According to the Alumni Advisory Board's *Life at Yale* (1920), the Elizabethan Club convened in a beautiful old home with a valuable collection of rare books, especially of Shakespeare and other Elizabethans. "The founding of this club in 1911, and the subsequent establishment of the Brick Row Print and Book Shop [in 1915], gave an impetus to book collecting as a sort of student avocation, and the literary discussions of students and Faculty in the daily afternoon gatherings and evening meetings of the Elizabethan Club, many of the latter informally addressed by outstanding contemporary men of letters, have made possible to many a student a new interest in things literary and artistic." [79]

That was indeed the case with Phil Stone (even if he benefited from the club at second hand, through Hackett). Although Phil watched his money carefully, in his years at Yale he began to buy first editions of the poetry of Eliot, Pound, Robinson, and Masefield, as investments, because, as he said, "I knew they were comers." He was right, but by the time he could have realized his investment, most of those volumes had been lost in the fire that destroyed the Stone home.

Again, perhaps, with Hackett, Phil discovered another interest while in New Haven. Accustomed to the fare at the Opera House in Oxford, like other young men sensitive to the arts, he was intoxicated by his first encounter with real music in concerts at the Shubert Theater and in Sprague Memorial Hall. In orchestral music his tastes ran to Mozart primarily. He had a weakness for violin sonatas and concertos. Bach, he said tellingly, reminded him of a problem in algebra. But Stone's first love was the vocalist, especially a soprano like Rosa Ponselle, or the coloratura Amelita Galli-Curci, whom he adored. (When Phil returned to New Haven for law school, he and Bill Faulkner purchased balcony seats in April 1918 when the well-known Irish tenor John McCormack appeared in concert at Yale.) [80] General Stone had given him an expensive Victrola for Christmas, and in New Haven he began to assemble what was to become a rather extensive record collection.

It must have been during 1913–14 that Phil heard Enrico Caruso, the legendary operatic tenor. Stone was enchanted with the tenor's exquisite voice, but equally charmed that Caruso was so obviously having a "glorious" time. From the first note, the Italians in the balcony were in ecstasy: "Bravo," "Bravo," "Bravo." All the while, as Phil remembered, "Caruso stood up there and just *sang* and looked up at the Italians as if to say, 'Ain't it grand, boys; ain't it grand!'" When the concert was over, encore after encore would not satisfy them; cheers brought him back again and again.

Even that night would be eclipsed, for Phil Stone, by a night in March 1914. The Yale *Daily News* ran the announcement: "Tonight, under the auspices of the Yale Dramatic Association, William Butler Yeats will lecture in Lampson Lyceum on the subject of 'Theatre and Beauty.' Mr. Yeats has been, and is yet, the literary spirit behind the Celtic artistic renaissance. In his lecture tonight, Mr. Yeats tells of his ideas and ideals with regard to the theatre, the value of which has been so well known by the success of his own venture with the Abbey Theatre. Prices for the ground floor will be one dollar, and for the balcony, fifty cents."[81]

It was Yeats's third American tour. The Stone anecdotes place him again in America in the spring of 1918, when Bill Faulkner shared Phil's rooms on York Street for a few months, but it appears that after 1914 Yeats did not return until 1920, when he came for the first time with his wife.[82] Besides the temptation of a more striking anecdote, Phil's juxtaposition of the two distinct experiences may betray how seldom he could conceive of Faulkner as separate from himself, or absent from his life.

In any case, as Emily Stone knew the anecdote from Phil, Stone *and* Faulkner had heard Yeats make a public address, and they were both very much taken with him. Phil was intrigued by the exaggerated way in which Yeats read, which was "practically incantatory," he said, and as early recordings substantiate, and Stone would try to reproduce it: "Come awayyy, come awayyy."[83] According to the story, Yeats was on campus for several days and Phil and Bill by chance saw him again as they were walking down a corridor in a classroom building. A door there was open and Yeats was inside. In awe of the great man, they stopped to listen. Yeats had with him a "bunch" of what Phil Stone called "old schoolteachers," and he was having the women recite in concert with him, very slowly and dramatically: "WE ARE THE OXEN."[84] Phil and Bill exchanged a look and then sprinted down the hall to get away before they burst out laughing, because, as both had realized at once, Phil said, "They sho' God *were* oxen."

At home in Mississippi the "heated season" was well advanced by the time the class of 1914 queued up for spring commencement in New Haven in mid-June. After his faltering start, Phil Stone had made a good record at Yale, good enough to graduate cum laude in a class numbering almost three hundred students.[85] In the *Banner and Pot Pourri* the facsimile of Stone's signature is half an inch high, the *P* and the *l* fat and tall, the cross to the *t* sweeping the length of his surname. He signed his name, even on official documents now, as *Phil Stone*, in emulation of his father, who had dropped his middle name because, like Phil, he preferred the spondee, *James* or *Jim Stone*. In Phil's senior portrait, one of the last taken before his hair begins noticeably to thin, a dominant feature of the quite handsome, erect, and seemingly self-assured twenty-one-year-old is his eyes—large, dark, and direct. The annual staff learned that Phil Stone expected to become a lawyer and that he hoped either to attend the University of Mississippi Law School or return to Yale to study law.

As Phil packed box after box with books and records to send ahead to the station, not even he could have guessed that for the next seventeen years—if not for the rest of his life—the reality most central to Phil Stone would be one William Faulkner; nor that by the last quarter of the twentieth century the boy he remembered vaguely from church and around the square would be named, with William Butler Yeats, in the pantheon of great writers of the century.

4

Phil and Bill

HISTORIANS FREQUENTLY REMARK a singular euphoria in memoirs from the idyllic summer of 1914, especially in Great Britain. Rumors of a European war were heard, of course, in America that summer, but in the Western Hemisphere battle lines had been drawn only in Mexico, where in the spring the villainies of dictator Victoriano Huerta had welded together the unlikely allies Venustiano Carranza, Álvaro Obregón, Pancho Villa, Emiliano Zapata—and President Woodrow Wilson. But at Yale, for example, a young man called upon Wilson "to knock the hurt out of Huerta" with the same conviction a cheerleader mustered calling for the damnation of Cornell.

In Mississippi in the summer of 1914 men went quietly about their business, only a few suspecting that within four years sixty thousand of them would be in uniform. At twenty-one, Phil Stone, now twice a B.A., apparently was also content to let the future take care of itself that June. Everyone assumed that he would follow General Stone and Jack into the law. He knew nothing else and probably considered no other career. He needed to go to law school in Mississippi if he intended to practice there, his father maintained. For all his misgivings about the North, however, Phil had vague notions of returning to New Haven. But there was no hurry. For a while longer James Stone & Son could do without the inconspicuous *s* that would be added to mark his entry into the firm.

At night, playing blackjack with his father or listening to the clink of Miss Rosie's keys as she locked up her silver and china, Phil Stone might have imagined himself arrested in childhood. But when the couple went to bed and he climbed the stairs to his own room, the new books and magazines piled everywhere—in the corner, on the mantel, on his long law table—affirmed the reality of his months in New Haven. Swinburne and Yeats, Eliot and Pound inflamed his imagination in quite a different way from the Confederate heroes of his youth. Here was a significant purpose, if not a secret vocation. Stone "smoked a match" on his Dunhill pipe and listened to Caruso and Geraldine Farrar's duet from *Faust* before settling down to his reading. One could see the light from his bedroom long into the night.

Stone already received Harriet Monroe's *Poetry: A Magazine of Verse*, and with a thoroughness duplicated in his book orders in the twenties, he subscribed, as he said later, to the little magazines and to other journals championing modern letters as they appeared. Always a hoarder, he stacked and tied complete volumes of the old issues and stored them in the walk-in closet off his bedroom. When the house burned, the Stones lost not only Faulkner poetry manuscripts, but also, as they listed in an insurance inventory, files for "numbers of years" of *Poetry*, the *New Republic*, the *Double Dealer*, as well as "others now quite rare." Only Stone's August 1924 issue of *Poetry* is extant. In October 1961, in a letter to Richard P. Adams, professor of English at Tulane University, Stone reported "having called Bill's attention to" early poems and essays by T. S. Eliot in his copies of *Poetry*, the *Little Review*, the *Egoist*, and the *Dial*.[1]

Phil was never one to keep quiet about his discoveries, and although few were as zealous as he, he found a sympathetic ear in the Somerville girls and others of his Oxford contemporaries, and an even better forum if Stark Young made his customary visit to Dr. Young that year. Phil did put in an appearance at the law office during the summer, not for work, but because 1013 Jackson Avenue, just off the square, served as a convenient rendezvous for his friends, home too now from college. At those gatherings he expected, of course, to see Katrina Carter, or "Sister" as he called her, for whose benefit Stone soon convened his first literary tutorial.

Mary Katrina Carter, two years younger than Phil, belonged to one of the oldest and wealthiest families in town,[2] but one "newly rich" to gentility like the Stones who had made their money before "The War." Her father, D. T. Carter, had preceded General Stone as president of the Bank of Oxford. In 1914 Katrina and her widowed mother lived in the Carter home on North Street (now North Lamar), a classic Greek Revival structure before her family added the verandas. Minnie Wohlleben Carter, a blacksmith's daughter, called the house Shirley, after her husband's ancestral home on the James River in Virginia; but the family's money, according to local gossip, was Wohlleben money. The blacksmith's five surviving daughters together owned well over half the town square.

Outlandish tales are told in Oxford about those eccentric matrons. On social occasions fifteen minutes of their breathless monologues might silence even Phil Stone. It was folly to cross them, especially the imperious Mrs. Neilson (whose husband owned Oxford's department store). Dinner invitations to her table could not be declined; furthermore, if her guests did not themselves make a prompt departure, Annabelle Neilson would dismiss them: "Well, you've been here long enough; ya'll go." Most Oxford citizens kept a respectful distance from the viragoes, a distance, though, close enough to observe their daily, inexplicable feuds. One summer afternoon Belle Neilson, sitting in the back seat, was being driven out North Street by a black chauffeur for her afternoon ride. As the big touring car neared the Carter home, Mrs. Neilson, catching sight of her sister on the front porch, scrambled down into the foot of the limousine, whispering up to the chauffeur, "Drive *fast*! I can't *stand* for Minnie Carter to see me!"

However he heard the story of Mrs. Carter's father, the gossip that Stone knew—and Faulkner used later in *Mosquitoes* and *Requiem for a Nun*—is summarized in John Cullen's *Old Times in the Faulkner Country:*

> In *Requiem for a Nun* Faulkner describes "a German private, a blacksmith, a deserter from a Pennsylvania regiment, who appeared in the summer of '64, riding a mule, with (so the tale told later, when his family of daughters had become matriarchs and grandmothers of the town's new aristocracy) for saddle-blanket sheaf on sheaf of virgin and uncut United States banknotes. . . ." This is an old story. The German was old Bully Wohleben (we pronounce it Woolubun), who was with Forrest's regiment. They captured a Federal payroll somewhere between here and Memphis,

and old Bully made saddle-blankets out of uncut bills. He brought three horse loads of those Federal banknotes home. He said nothing, quietly ran his blacksmith shop, and bought a lot of land in Texas and . . . Oklahoma. . . . Then when his daughters married, he set all his sons-in-law up in business. When he was an old man, he still ran his blacksmith shop. One of his daughters owned a bedspread made of ten-dollar bills that were never cut apart until a few years ago. When one of old Bully's grandsons died in Oklahoma, his estate was valued at thirty-eight million dollars.[5]

Unlike William Faulkner, whose borrowings at times border on transcription, Cullen is always constrained to embellish a story, but there is a measure of truth even in his account. Katrina's grandfather Herman Wohlleben, a "thorough-going, hard-headed German" who emigrated from the Munich area in the 1840s, was owner of a blacksmith shop on the square, veteran of Oxford's Thompson Cavalry, father-in-law to five prosperous businessmen (some of whose descendants did live in Oklahoma)—and, by 1898, vice-president of Oxford's Merchants and Farmers Bank.[4] Whether the Federal banknotes story was true or not, members of General Stone's generation "condemned the family as being nouveau riche because they made their money after the war and because they made it by stealing from the Confederacy." As a soldier, Wohlleben was morally bound to have delivered the Federal money over to his superiors. The moral issue did not stop General Stone from trading at Neilson's, however. Nor did it stop Phil Stone from falling in love with the blacksmith's granddaughter. But to give a girl books or take her to a dance was one thing; getting married was far from Phil's mind, he protested.

Matchmakers had been at work on the other bachelor Stone while Phil was still in New Haven. Donald G. Ross, at his wife's suggestion, had invited his friend Jack Stone down for a weekend in Grenada in order to meet Myrtle Lewis, from Pascagoula, a classmate of Allie Ross at Belhaven College. Given Jack's long evasion of Oxford's mothers and daughters, the conspirators were remarkably successful; by 1914 elaborate plans were underway for a June wedding. The Stones were probably taken somewhat by surprise, for at thirty-four Jack had seemed a permanent fixture at home and in the office. The couple were married in Pascagoula a week after Phil's graduation. For a wedding present, General Stone bought Jack and Myrtle a zoo of farm animals: two pigs,

Phil and Bill

two cows, a rooster, some hens, a beagle, and a fox terrier—everything, he thought, no home should be without.[5]

Propping his feet up in the sun room at the office or sipping lemonade on the Carters' porch, Phil Stone, while describing the Pascagoula affair for the girls, kept assuring the company at large that he had no such plans. He felt about women "as [Sewanee professor] Ab Martin did about giraffes": " 'I like to look at them,' he said, 'but I never wanted to own one.' "

When Jack Stone moved out, he left behind a set of the works of Balzac on the mantel above the fireplace. Phil had seen the books before, but that summer, or the next, he casually picked one up and, captivated, began to read Balzac in earnest. Thereafter, he proselytized for the French novelist. As late as the thirties, Stone insisted that his wife read Balzac, explaining, "I used to get *furious* with Balzac because I would think that the characters were going to react one way, and they did something different, usually the opposite. I would throw the book across the room in outrage because he'd outsmarted me; I saw that Balzac was right and I was wrong." Stone and Faulkner read them all, and Bess Storer, a friend in the twenties, later told Alabama professor O. B. Emerson that the three of them read much of Balzac aloud together.[6]

Most of Stone's friends, meanwhile, were really more interested in the latest dances or the nearest bootlegger than in Balzac or T. S. Eliot, but since Phil enjoyed W. C. Handy as well as Caruso, the occasional summer dances on the Carter veranda or upstairs at Ammadelle across the street were a welcome diversion—except for the temptation posed when Mrs. Carter or Mrs. Price was satisfied that the last female was under her father's roof and the young men were left to their own devices. Like Gowan Stevens, Stone's friends most often finished the evening with corn whiskey, and Stone still did not trust himself with alcohol. As his autobiography puts it, "All the young men with whom Phil had moved before all drank and Phil was then not interested in drinking." Ironically, it was William Faulkner's sobriety that at first made their friendship possible. Subsequently, as the autobiography continues, Phil "ran across young William Faulkner whom he learned to know as a possible writer, they talked day and night of writing and the summer was very pleasant."

Katrina Carter had been telling Stone for months that "he ought to know this little Falkner boy who writes; he's always telling stories." But at first Katrina's suitor was not interested in Billy Faulkner (or Falkner, as he then spelled it), nearly five years his junior. Stone only half listened to Katrina's tale of seeing Faulkner delegate a chore to younger boys who did his work in order to hear his yarns. Phil knew him, of course, for Miss Rosie and Faulkner's grandmother "ran the Methodist church" and General Stone and the "Young Colonel" owned rival banks, but it was Katrina who actually brought the two men together.

Before Christmas in 1913, Faulkner's father had bought the M. P. Bishop home[7] in what Oxford residents now call the "V," just north of Ammadelle and the Carter place, where North Street veers sharply to the east and Sivley Street to the west. The next summer, home from Fairmont, Katrina was alarmed one night to hear gunshots from the Falkner house. Her mother sent a man up to inquire, but it was only Billy Faulkner sitting in bed shooting rats as they ran across the floor.[8]

When he walked past Ammadelle on his way to the square that summer, Faulkner often heard animated chatter from the Carters' side porch swing. Recognizing one voice as Estelle Oldham's, he slowed his pace and "casually" crossed the street in order to be invited to join the girls, entertaining Katrina and Stelle in return with impromptu stories.[9] Faulkner might be available for mixed doubles later, when Phil and Florrie Friedman, who lived near the Carters, came up for tennis, which they played in Katrina's side yard.[10] More probably, because Faulkner did not know Stone, or at least very well, he observed silently from the veranda.

Robert Farley, another younger, occasional tennis player at the Carters', likewise shared Faulkner's hopeless infatuation with an "older woman." Farley was an ardent admirer of Katrina Carter. Like Estelle, she had "rather deep-set eyes," and both girls had distinctive, engaging laughs, from the throat, not a man's laugh, but a full-voiced laugh instead of a girlish giggle.[11] Katrina's short hair was brown, with highlights of red, and, photographed leaning against a car with Estelle or perched on a fence with a group of picnickers, or alone against a background of leaves and sunlight, she appears a young woman very much alive and, as Farley recalled after sixty years, beautiful indeed.

Katrina may have been somewhat relieved when Phil Stone and Bill

Phil and Bill

Faulkner began to spend time together, not because she did not enjoy Stone's company but because with a more receptive audience Phil was less likely than before to discover whether she actually read the books on aesthetics and volumes of modern poetry that came from him as presents for birthdays and Christmas. Always impressed by Stone's erudition, and having written poems herself, she listened with interest, though her tastes ran more to Old South romances. Katrina never understood later why Faulkner wrote about the lower classes.[12]

Very reticent then—as Katrina certainly was not—Faulkner was an ideal complement for Phil Stone during the first wave of Stone's discovery of himself. Phil's words poured out—his mind intricate, agile, lucid. Not only the ideas but the emotional phenomenon must have engaged the boy, himself by temperament—so he seemed to Phil—a listener, an observer, a collector of shiny bits of glass. But, as Faulkner in time seems to have concluded, and even Stone may have realized at last, to act as a conduit was to become essential for Phil Stone. As he often said of himself, "I can fight a war but I can't fight a battle," and "I'm like an elaborate intricate piece of machinery which doesn't quite work."[13] Somehow it was impossible for Stone to act: later he allowed General Stone's law practice to dwindle away, although he worked nights and weekends; he never settled his father's estate; his mother's tombstone still lacks the date of her death; bills were paid at the eleventh hour, if at all; the big case, subdivision profits, an oil strike, never were effected in time or to his satisfaction. Instead, he was compelled to talk and talk and talk, and to discover, not a voice, but an ear.

William Faulkner, of course, was not merely an instrument for Phil Stone, but the initial, necessary passivity of a shaper of words may be betrayed in Faulkner's own comment about that summer: "At the age of sixteen, I discovered Swinburne. Or rather, Swinburne discovered me."[14] Although Phil would allow others to say he had discovered Faulkner, Faulkner credited Sherwood Anderson, not Stone, with that find, apparently not out of ingratitude for Phil's early support but because, with Anderson, William Faulkner discovered himself. So it was with Phil's epiphany: with Billy Faulkner, Phil Stone found Phil Stone. And because Phil indeed "discovered" William Faulkner in the summer of 1914, Stone lives now—paradoxically—as words in books.

Phil Stone of Oxford

The friendship began simply enough, yet probably with a degree of seriousness for Stone only when it became clear that he would not return to New Haven in the fall; or, as he phrased it, "In 1914 General Stone kept Phil at home to attend the Mississippi Law School."[15] Reminiscing of those earliest years on the occasion of the 1949 Nobel Prize, Stone wrote that Faulkner "was painting some then, and was faintly interested in writing verse. I gave him books to read—Swinburne, Keats and a number of the moderns, such as Conrad Aiken and the Imagists in verse and Sherwood Anderson in prose."[16] One afternoon that summer he must have shown the boy Lamar's inscribed first edition of Swinburne's *Laus Veneris* (1866) from Mayes's library. Swinburne, "one of the best," Stone wrote Richard P. Adams a month before Faulkner's death, "is simply out of style." Of the "particular Swinburne poems" that Faulkner admired, Phil then could remember only "the one about the coming of spring: 'The hounds of spring on winter's traces' or something like that. It was probably *Atalanta in Calydon* as much as anything else."[17] Stone told Faulkner that Swinburne had carried the oral resources of the language to their limits, that poets thereafter "had to break the mold and start all over again."[18]

A second major reading assignment for Faulkner in those years was John Keats. In "Verse Old and Nascent: A Pilgrimage" (1925) Faulkner professed that although at first he read Keats (and Shelley) unmoved, later he found in the odes "the spiritual beauty which the moderns strive vainly for with trickery."[19] Phil had owned the Athenaeum Press's *Poems by John Keats* (1896) as early as his junior year at University Training School. In a hand obviously closer to Faulkner's than to his own, "Phill Stone" first indicates his ownership; in the back of the book are two of the "large flowing signature[s]" of the Yale College period; another "three signings" evidently correspond with the date "on the free front endpaper, '3/24/19.'"[20] Unlike his pupil, who seems rarely to have done so, Stone characteristically scribbled multiple arrows, underlinings, and brief comments in the book as he read. He might not endorse Faulkner's now-famous remark that "the 'Ode on a Grecian Urn' is worth any number of old ladies," but he observed in the margin beside the poem: "Beautiful in suggestiveness."

Stone and Faulkner read the Imagists, Swinburne's radical successors, perhaps in the little magazines in 1914, and the following year Stone acquired a first edition of Amy Lowell's *Some Imagist Poets* (1915).[21] Pound, by his own choice, was absent from the volume, but Lowell invited contributions from Richard Aldington, F. S. Flint, and D. H. Lawrence to accompany her own poems and those of fellow Americans Hilda Doolittle and John Gould Fletcher.[22] The volume suffered so much wear in Stone's "circulating library" and from its owner, who underlined and annotated it extensively, that in time it had to be rebound. Faulkner seems to have hand-lettered the new titles, but the binding appears to have been the work of a professional, perhaps one at the Brick Row.[23] Although diligent to follow the poetry of their time, the two men, however, were not blindly avid modernists. Faulkner's college reviews later are often sharply critical of contemporary verse. How often the new poets disappointed Phil Stone is more than evident in his marginal invectives: on Marianne Moore, "My God! Can she really take herself seriously?"; on an e. e. cummings imitator, "Printing never could make poetry"; on Marsden Hartley, "*Why*, oh *why!* don't these damn fools spend a little time learning to write?"[24]

Also among the poets Stone and Faulkner read was A. E. Housman, whose talents outstripped that of the avant-garde, they thought. Stone said that he pointed out to Bill the subtle effects of that poet's masses of monosyllabic and disyllabic words.[25] The incantatory nature of Yeats's poems, Swinburne's orchestration, Housman's monosyllables together suggest that it was the music of poetry and the means by which those effects were derived that most fascinated Phil Stone.

Phil approved as the young man began in his own verse to experiment with those techniques. Faulkner's talent, Stone reiterated, was obvious, but as yet William Faulkner clearly knew little of the tradition in which he wished to practice. Stone's conceptions of the artist and his vocation were more definite, although still subject to revision from his reading. Unlike the dilettante, who rarely ventures into the maze of literary theory, Stone found the abstractions and generalizations there riveting. It was not unusual for his attention to wander from a line or poem before him to muse over some principle underlying Great Art. He may have done his close, independent reading of Benedetto Croce's influential *Aesthetic As Science of Expression and General Linguistic* as a college student, for he owned a first edition of Douglas Ainslie's translation (London, 1909).[26] In March 1917 he would mark up Clive Bell's *Art*.[27]

The foundations of Stone's aesthetics, however, were established by his reading of the minor American aesthetician Willard Huntington Wright, an associate of Mencken on the *Smart Set* (1913–14). Phil was so taken with Wright's pronouncements in *The Creative Will: Studies in the Philosophy and Syntax of Aesthetics* (New York, 1916) that he ordered another copy of the ponderous volume for Faulkner's twentieth birthday.[28] In the 1930s Stone objected strongly to Louis Cochran's "serious omission" of *The Creative Will* in the draft of Cochran's article on Faulkner that Stone had asked to read, "because the aesthetic theories set forth in that book, strained through my own mind, constitutes [sic] one of the most important influences in Bill's whole literary career." If Faulkner critics "would simply read Wright's book," he told Cochran, "they would see what he is driving at from a literary standpoint."[29] Two decades later, in an embittered gesture, Stone asked Faulkner to return the Wright gift—ostensibly to replace Stone's copy burned nine years before. To excuse the repossession, Phil wrote inside, "I gave this book to Bill but I don't think he ever read any of it." The diction and premises of Faulkner's 1920s reviews suggest otherwise, but the argument is really beside the point.

In the years he spent in Stone's company, Faulkner could not have escaped Willard Huntington Wright, who impressed upon Phil Stone that Art is Craft, a requisite literary perspective, to be sure, but one by no means universal at the time. Wright believed "*complete order*" to be the germ of "all deep and significant expression"; hence, the artist must discern and assimilate "the principles of aesthetic form and organisation," a process requiring years of solitary toil along "a tortuous and vicissitudinous road" of study and experimentation. "Creation and analysis are one," said Wright, noting the incessant revisions of a Beethoven, a Balzac, or a Cezanne, men whose art derived from "exact knowledge" rather than an "impulsive" moment.[30]

Artistic fallacies and excuses were epidemic in literary communities, " 'quarters' in which the shallow iconoclasts, the failures and the imitators congregate for the purpose of exchanging their ineffectual ideas and of consoling one another for their poverty of mind." According to

Wright, "the truly great and progressive artist is the one who, after he has absorbed and mastered all the learning which has preceded him, can create new forms in line with that evolution." Poetry, "the chief, as well as the most highly developed, aesthetic occupation of Americans," presented a special challenge, particularly in its present condition, as Wright saw it. Because Swinburne had "carried the rhymed lyric to its highest point of development," according to Wright and his disciple Stone, poetry awaited its next evolutionary surge, the genre presently floundering, poverty-stricken, inept, the most influential of the innovators, the Imagists, writing from principles not of poetry, but of prose.[31] Where was the new poet to master such a challenge? The education of apprentice William Faulkner was to proceed as though Phil Stone believed his young friend might actually redirect the course of modern poetry.

The seriousness with which Stone and Faulkner entertained their lofty ambitions must often have seemed absurd to outsiders. Judged by Wright's strict standards, Parnassus was a sparsely populated hamlet. But to Phil and Bill, there seemed no reason, granted years of hard work, that Faulkner would not make one of that select company. That the young men were themselves proud of their audacity is evident in one of Stone's comments in his *Marble Faun* preface: "On one of our long walks through the hills, I remarked that I thought the main trouble with Amy Lowell and her gang of drum-beaters was their eternal damned self-consciousness, that they always had one eye on the ball and the other eye on the grandstand. To which the author of these poems replied that his personal trouble as a poet seemed to be that he had one eye on the ball and the other eye on Babe Ruth."[32]

Not surprisingly, Phil conducted such discussions as he walked. Unlike Bill's grandfather, who bought John Buffaloe's homemade contraption before 1909,[33] General Stone always professed an abhorrence of automobiles, and only after Phil earned his own money practicing law and bought "Drusilla" did he travel very much by car. Even when he owned an automobile, it was his habit to walk to his office twice a day for as long as he practiced law. Carvel Collins was told that Phil and Bill often traversed "twelve or fifteen miles . . . on a Sunday" in the twenties, when automobiles were readily available.[34]

In any season, the favorite haunts of Stone and Faulkner were the slopes of Woodson Ridge, the highland extending north of Oxford from Highway 30 almost to Abbeville. Folk history has it that North Mississippi had been settled from the northeast ridge by ridge—Pontotoc Ridge, Woodson Ridge, and so on.[35] In 1934, when Phil Stone wrote on Faulkner for the *Oxford Magazine*, the highland still appeared untouched by time:

> From any part of Oxford it is only a little walk to numerous places where one can find the unspoiled golden peace of legendary days and where the sound of mankind's so-called progress comes only dreamlike and from afar. There are dim and shadowy groves of silver-white beeches where springs gurgle out from the foot of the hill and sunlight spills dimly through the trees and there is no company but the birds. There are soft carpeted pine hills white with dogwood in the spring. There are rows on serried rows of far hills, blue and purple and lavender and lilac in the sun, hills upon which you can look day after day and year after year and never find light and shadow and color exactly the same.
>
> In the summer there is the shade of aged trees, in the fall there is a riot of brilliant gold and orange and crimson and russet brown where ever you turn and in the winter, occasionally, there are the dark green pines burdened with snow. It is a country with very little grandeur in the scenery but with infinite variety.[36]

In the beech or pine groves of Woodson Ridge the men talked of aesthetics, the Greeks, the Civil War, and Mississippi politics. Little did Stone and Faulkner realize that first summer and fall what nemeses Theodore Bilbo and Lee Russell would continue to be; they were more concerned then with the fall of the house of Cadmus than with the rise of the redneck. Stone said that his young friend was intrigued by the sound of classical Greek and that he often recited for Faulkner what he called "Oedipus' lament," from *Oedipus Tyrannus*, the speech after Oedipus "had found out the truth about himself" and put out his own eyes. In 1957 Carvel Collins was curious whether Faulkner had ever asked for a translation, to which Stone replied that "although 25 or 30 years ago it may be that I did translate some Greek to Bill in some conversations . . . so far as I know he never asked me for any."[37] While recording a conversation about his Faulkner relationship as part of his therapy at Whitfield in the 1960s, Phil startled his wife one afternoon when he suddenly began "*Eo, eo, stumna prossedor,*" quoting verbatim the long passage from Sophocles, as he must have done fifty years before on Woodson Ridge.

In the fall of 1914 Stone once more enrolled at the University, this time as a law student. In his two years of legal training in Mississippi, academic affairs clearly diminished into a minor consideration. Phil would not submit photographs to Mack Reed's 1916 *Ole Miss* because of his balding head, but the phrase Reed's staff assigned him accurately reflects the tenor of the period: "Phil Stone, LL.B. 'Still treads upon the heels of pleasure.'" One friend from Stone's undergraduate days, Wall Doxey (later a Mississippi congressman), had paid his way through Ole Miss playing poker. Unable to plead economic necessity, Phil Stone had to fabricate another excuse for the two years he spent playing poker. With his nocturnal pastime, Phil acknowledged later, if "I hadn't made such good grades, they would have thrown me out of the university." (In 1914–15 Stone's grades averaged 92.8; in 1915–16 his average slipped to 88.6.) There was no challenge to it, Phil said; at Ole Miss one simply read the law books and gave back the answers. At Yale, by contrast, one's entire resources were engaged in parrying the thrusts of an attacking law professor.

At that time the Mississippi law faculty consisted of three men rather short on advanced degrees, whose experiences in private practice had been supplemented by a miscellaneous assortment of minor legislative or judicial posts within the state. Leonard Jerome Farley, Bob's father, was dean of the law department and instructor for junior law; Duke M. Kimbrough was professor of senior law; and in 1915 Judge Tom C. Kimbrough served as acting professor of senior law. Attorneys from town also occasionally lectured in the old Geology Building that housed the small law school.[38]

Phil Stone spent far more stimulating hours with the farmers and storekeepers from out in the county with whom he played his nightly poker. Those "old-country-boy" card players, all older than he, not only played very shrewdly but maintained during a hand a low-keyed, incisive repartee that kept Stone and his college companions "sore from laughter." Men like Lamar Russell, Stone said, could have starred on vaudeville stages in the East. Phil also played with the Woodwards. During campaign speeches in his race for chancery clerk one year, "Uncle Willy" Woodward probably lost some votes by his disconcerting habit of loudly snapping his tiny black bow tie. Having known those men was one reason Stone later persuaded Faulkner not to go North when Faulkner was convinced that he must in order to write professionally. No chauvinist, Phil Stone; he told Faulkner that "there are more characters per capita in Lafayette County than you'll find in all of New York City."

Over the dozen years that Phil played poker regularly, graduating in time to the professional gamblers in Clarksdale and Memphis, he relished, as with literature, its technical aspects and loved to theorize about the game and the persons who played it. He had already memorized the odds for various hands and understood complex strategy for both draw and stud poker; still he deliberately bet in an unorthodox manner to keep his opponents off guard. He studied the players and tried to see how their minds worked and played to that instinct rather than to the cards he held. Phil learned too how much easier it was "to win money from an expert than from an amateur." While the expert will fold when the odds are against him, the amateur's betting is erratic, and thus unpredictable.

Years later Stone could recount any number of hands he had played —"how remarkable some of them were," he thought, especially with the gamblers. Although those stories proved ephemeral, among the several pages devoted to poker in the autobiography Stone penciled at Whitfield, he haltingly reconstructs "one of the nights in 1916" when, after winning $150, he "was preparing to go home early." A friend of Phil's had had a consistent run of bad luck that evening, "in a very short time [losing] every bet he was in and [becoming] so disgusted" that he vowed to quit the game after his losses totaled over $250.

"Let me play my $150," Phil offered. "If I win you [can] get whatever I win and [I will] keep my own money. If I lose . . . you can pay me back . . . when you are not pressed for money." Drawing up his friend's chair, Stone returned to the table with a stake of "$150. in checks." His principal opponent that night was Paul H. Bowdre, the secretary of his senior law class, who was in the Blackstone Club with Stone too. Although Bowdre also shared Stone's taste for expensive clothes, their friendship had developed out of their mutual respect for the other's skill at cards: "Phil said [Bowdre] was an expert poker player and Bowdre said the same thing of Phil."

Eight men placed the dollar ante in the pot; the dealer shuffled; the man to his right cut the deck; and the "$500. winner" dealt each man five cards. The first five men refused to bet, but "Bowdre opened the pot for $8.00," and Phil raised him twenty. "Strangely Bowdre called Phil's bet," and raised him eighty more. "This bet Phil simply called." With the third man's bets (who evidently withdrew early), in a matter of minutes, Phil had only "$1.25" left in front of him. Bowdre requested cards in the first round but none in the second, and although Phil "had a jack and no pairs whatever . . . he refused to draw any cards." When Phil would not bet in the next round, Bowdre "did not raise." At that juncture, Stone analyzed the situation: "The actions of Bowdre indicated that he had a pat hand, probably a small straight . . . and Phil's way of playing his hand indicated that Phil had a pat hand of a flush or a three pat hand . . . or [a full house], each of which would be above the straight held by Bowdre." On the next round, "Bowdre checked the bet, and immediately Phil bet the last $1.25 he had." Bowdre, "thinking Phil had a larger pat hand and considering Phil . . . a careful player," refused to meet that last bet, and thus Phil won for his friend more than $200, because "Bowdre would not call Phil's $1.25."

Another of the hands that Stone frequently retold found its way into "Was" in *Go Down, Moses*, where Amodeus McCaslin and Tomey's Turl join forces to vanquish Hubert Beauchamp at cards.[39]

At school Phil Stone preferred to avoid competition, confident of his place among the "bright boys" of his class.[40] During Moot Court in 1915, class poet Phil Stone was murdered "in cold blood" by John Cutrer; a law brief presumably was not required of a corpse. Many of his campus activities were even more adolescent, founding a Bachelor's Club, or allowing Hudson and others in Senior Law to shave his nearly bald head in the ritual freshmen shearing on Lee's birthday.[41] It was bad form to take law school too seriously.

D. R. Johnson, from Batesville, the president of Stone's senior class, studied his way through law school, and later graduate courses, while employed as the university's postmaster. (His successor at the post office would be William Faulkner.) During the Depression both Stone and Johnson were reduced to accepting legal hackwork on the Sardis Reservoir project. But, more incongruously, the Batesville attorney teased in law school as a "plodder" was the man to whom Phil Stone handed over his entangled finances in the late fifties, as Johnson says, "putting more confidence in me than I wanted."[42] No gambler would have wagered on such an outcome in 1916.

Even after acquiring law degrees, few of Stone's set, however, went to work immediately. Jim Kyle Hudson, who finished school three years before Stone, was actually slower than he to practice seriously. For six or eight months, Hudson went "prospecting" in the mountains of Honduras on the excuse that he was going into the mahogany business, a statement that fooled no one. His friends knew that he was only "having a lot of fun and doing some hunting." Back in Mississippi, he practiced law in Clarksdale briefly.[43]

More often, Jim Kyle Hudson was in Oxford, where just before and after the war Hudson, Stone, and William Faulkner usually practiced idleness together. (Faulkner's addressing his friends by their surnames, according to Robert Farley, was one of his British affectations.)[44] From January 1916 Faulkner, the youngest of the trio, was the only one gainfully employed—as a bookkeeper of sorts in his grandfather's bank, a post he endured only with the aid of the Young Colonel's liquor, he said.[45] Immediately after work he would accost Bob Farley on the street. "Have you seen Stone?" he would ask, or "Is Hudson up at the Carters'?"

Because Phil had abjured not just whiskey but hunting too, only Hudson and Faulkner now went on the hunts, sometimes with General Stone, but several times for three or four weeks out to the Tallahatchie and up into the wilds in boats. Sleeping in tents, waited on by black servants, the men hunted and fished all day and drank and played poker all night. Those pots sometimes ran to sizeable amounts. Once or twice, Hudson "made a killing up there," he later told his son. Coming home, apparently by way of Memphis, he bought a car and hired a chauffeur to drive him back to Oxford. Hudson's vacation might be extended for weeks: "I'd just have fun until I ran out of money, when I'd sell the car, fire the chauffeur, and go back to practicing law." In Stone's circle, one was assured of bed and board at home long after formal schooling had ended; the rare parental remonstrance was merely cherished for its humor. After the Murry Falkners moved into the old Delta Psi house on campus around 1920, the men were in a marathon poker game in the corner tower room there late one night when they were suddenly interrupted by an angry Presbyterian father: "Jim Kyle, Jim Kyle, I know you're in there playing cards. Now come on out and go home!"[46]

Whenever Stark Young returned to town for summer visits with his father between 1914 and 1925, Phil Stone and William Faulkner generally left their poker games or the perennial college crowd at Chilton's soda fountain to spend the afternoon with him. Young sometimes rented a room for his writing above New's Drugstore; in other years Stone and Faulkner were invited to Dr. A. A. Young's. Although they would call it friendship, in retrospect the relationship that evolved among Stone, Faulkner, and Young would scarcely merit that label. The Mississippians shared a preoccupation with literature and the South, but in the broadest sense, for their definitions of both were often sharply at odds. Perhaps the personalities, the successes, the tastes—and the ages—of the three men were too disparate, or their egos too sensitive, ever to eliminate the friction that seemed inevitable to their encounters. In 1938, piqued at an allusion in the *New Republic* to Sherwood Anderson's "discovery" of Faulkner, Young devoted a few editorial paragraphs—"for the sake of the record"—ostensibly to give credit to Phil Stone, "who constantly worked, in person and in correspondence, for the promotion of a man he believed in." But the editorial allowed him also to document Stark Young's early contacts with the writer (whom his *New Republic* colleague Malcolm Cowley was to rediscover): "I used every summer to go for a short visit to my father in Oxford, Mississippi. I used also to see there always a friend of mine, Phil Stone, something younger than I was [Young was over eleven years Phil's senior] and older than William Faulkner, about whom he often spoke, and whom he soon brought to our house. I already knew the family of course. That was about 1914. Later on I used to see Bill Faulkner and read the manuscripts that his friend had praised and pushed so."[47]

In the article that Stone wrote when Faulkner won the Nobel Prize, he neglected to mention Stark Young among those in Oxford who had believed in the beginning writer. Obviously stung by the omission (for which Stone publicly apologized), Young fired off a letter to the *Oxford Eagle* reiterating his early support and recounting his part in Faulkner's propitious introduction to Sherwood Anderson in the 1920s. Acknowledging that some might suspect his Faulkner "interest" in the general acclaim (even though he had known of Faulkner's talent for "thirty years"), Young tried—too hard—to deflect that suspicion with an *ad populum* appeal:

> I am anxious to have this long belief on my part known in Oxford; since it is only natural that there will be some people, some of them friends of both of us, who may wonder why I as an Oxford man and a fellow writer should never have shown an interest or admiration for William Faulkner. I am already touching on this point in certain New York quarters; on numerous occasions various critics and authors have said to me as taken for granted that of course I did not care for Faulkner. I have always tried to convince them how mistaken they are, though I have never seen my way exactly to telling them in my opinion Bill has more of the real thing in his little finger than all these New York writers put together.[48]

In *The Pavilion*, Young's 1951 memoir, he remembered other details of his "fortnight" summer visits to Oxford. Faulkner "was writing poems and would bring me a notebook of them, I can still see it lying in a parlor table drawer. It is so long ago that I cannot recall the poems now," he continued, "only that they strove for great intensity of feeling." The extent of Young's involvement early in the Faulkner career would remain a sensitive subject for Phil Stone too. In 1962 an academic infuriated Stone by suggesting that Young had introduced *him* to Faulkner: That's "ridiculous," Stone replied. "I was still fooling with Bill long before I took him over to meet Mr. Stark Young. Mr. Young was teaching at the University of Texas or at Amherst at the time and when he came by one summer to see his father I took Bill to see him."[49]

Stone said that it was Stark Young who had "opened" his mind, yet the reservations with which the adult Phil Stone later greeted Young's major enthusiasms evidently displeased so opinionated a mentor. Young was enthralled by the talented Italian actress Eleonora Duse, whom he met at Amherst: "In Duse of all artists people most felt the thing they most respond to in all living, an infinity of tragic wonder and tenderness." He could be equally effusive about the plays and poetry of her lover Gabriele D'Annunzio, of whom he became enamored perhaps as early as his 1907 trip to Italy.[50] One afternoon when Young mentioned D'Annunzio to Bill and Phil in his "office" above the square, the younger men began to make fun of the Italian dramatist and politician. Silent only a moment, Young broke in, saying, "Oh, but you know, he still has quite a following," at which point Faulkner and Stone burst out laughing. There was a stony silence that time, and they soon made an excuse to leave. Clearly exaggerating, Phil said afterwards that "Mr. Stark never did care for us any more."

To Phil Stone in the mid-teens, however, Stark Young connoted belles lettres. Already Young was a published poet, dramatist, translator, and scholar. During 1914 he had written a novel. The young man from Como, Mississippi, not yet thirty-five, in only a decade had moved from instructor at a local military school to a chair at Amherst, having certified himself as cosmopolitan too with five tours on the Continent. In 1915 Young was asked to teach summer school at Dartmouth, where he met Phelps Putnam, Yale '16, his correspondent for the next fifteen years. The contact may have facilitated Phil Stone's second sojourn in New Haven, for the young poet figured in a minor way then in what university historians call Yale's "Literary Renaissance." [51]

When Stark Young returned to Oxford from the East on a short visit in September 1915,[52] perhaps he reported the "Renaissance" in progress to alumnus Phil Stone. In any case, there was no question of Stone's transferring in 1915. After satisfying his father with a Mississippi law degree the next year, Phil was once again free to indulge his literary avocation in a congenial setting while becoming a proper student of the law. In the fall of 1916 he bid William Faulkner adieu and returned to New Haven.

5

New Haven and the Great War

ON FORMAL OCCASIONS in New Haven, "orators were able to point with pride to Yale's college presidents, ministers, doctors, lawyers, and even foresters and lexicographers, but it was very difficult to say much about Yale's literary men," according to Brooks Mather Kelley. Difficult, that is, until the seeds sown by the humanist Henry A. Beers and cultivated by William L. Phelps, Charlton M. Lewis, Edward B. Reed, C. B. Tinker, and John M. Berden began to bear fruit. As historian George Wilson Pierson puts it, "Once Sparta to Harvard's Athens—so lately the champion gladiator—pragmatist, activist, philistine Yale College . . . [suddenly found itself] a center for belles lettres: the home of poets and a nest of singing birds." Between 1909 and 1920 "for the first time since the days of the Connecticut Wits, the College could laugh at its literary detractors":

> Instructors of all ages were publishing more voluminously and in better style than ever before. In 1908 the Yale University Press had been started. Three years later the *Yale Review* was reorganized as a literary quarterly. Simultaneously the new Elizabethan Club began bringing students and faculty together for companionship and discussion of their literary enthusiasms. Most gratifying and astonishing of all, the undergraduates were scribbling as never before, scribbling and play-acting and composing and reviewing and—best of all—being published.[1]

The young professors who inspired student writers in the lecture halls at Yale were not above risking their own money in the service of literature at the same time. After the Brick Row Print and Book Shop opened for business in December 1915, three recent alumni additions to the English faculty sat with Vice-President Byrne Hackett on its board of directors: the "brilliant and sensitive" Professor Chauncey Brewster Tinker, '99; the precocious Assistant Professor Samuel B. Hemingway, '04, who had prepared variorum editions of Chaucer as an undergraduate; and the "mercurial" Instructor Lawrence Mason, also from the class of 1904. Mason, the book shop's president in 1918, won notoriety on campus by flunking those he did not like and by scheduling a fifteen-minute interval during his exams at the bar in the Hotel Taft.[2]

Archibald MacLeish had taken his degree at Yale in 1915. But the fervor for all things literary, according to Pierson, actually intensified just before the Great War.[3]

Normally in the three-year law course at Yale, the first year was devoted to Contracts, Criminal Law, Pleading, Property I, and Torts; but the entrance committee allowed Phil Stone a year's credit on his work in Mississippi and required only that he take Corbin's Contracts of the regular freshman curriculum.[4] Stone was at once impressed by the quality of instruction. Arthur Linton Corbin and Walter Wheeler Cook, his Trusts professor that year, were identified for special praise when Stone joined the law school's defenders in a controversy raging in the 1927 *Alumni Weekly*. But by the end of his first year, during the pressure-filled exam week of 1917, sleeping five hours a night, as he wrote his mother that Sunday, Phil was not eager to run the gauntlet set up by Corbin and Cook, and his professors for Evidence and "Con. of Laws." Those finals looked to be "the fiercest I ever lay my eyes upon." "I can't help but smile," he wrote, with a show of bravado, "at the thought of the University of Mississippi Law School, and nothing would give me greater pleasure than to put the professors down there up against one of these exams. I'm pretty tired of them as I have been studying like I never studied before in all my life, but they will soon be over, thank the Lord!"

The one examination he did take with ease in his first year was John Wurts's "Federal Practice," which he had written the day before: It "was so easy that I didn't do so well as I would have done if it had been harder but I did all right, of course. It was too ridiculously easy to do any other way."[5] But Stone had not yet adapted to the competition, it seems. When the grades were mailed that summer, he had B's in U.S. Practice and Contracts, C's in Evidence and the "Con. of Laws" course, and a 69 in Trusts. Grades appear to have been given less uniformly in law than in Yale College, and class rank apparently mattered more than any standard scale.

Having to read heavy case loads in his textbooks curtailed Stone's cultivation of things literary, but not seriously. He continued to follow modern poetry, reading Amy Lowell's "Patterns" and Wallace Stevens's "Peter Quince at the Clavier" in William Stanley Braithwaite's *Anthology of Magazine Verse for 1915*, a book he wrote his name in on 13 November 1916.[6]

The European war was a much more powerful distraction. Soon after he had taken rooms at 120 York Street, Phil walked a block down to the Brick Row Print and Book Shop, at 104 High, in his old neighborhood, to look up Byrne Hackett "and the boys"—Arthur Head and J. Al DeLacey—whose conversations now were more often about "the beastly Hun" than of meter and metaphor. With England's bookmen at war since 1914, the used book trade had been paralyzed and European publishing was at a standstill. The Brick Row directors, thus, had been at an economic disadvantage since the incorporation late in 1915; they could anticipate only sleepless nights if the chaos spread across the Atlantic. The literary community as a whole had been tossed about in the controversy over the war mounting since the previous spring. William Lyon Phelps was quoted in the newspapers as having said that "to spit on the flag was not so bad as to fight for it." Even with the correction the *Alumni Weekly* ran—Phelps "had actually said, 'If a foreigner should spit on our flag that would not disgrace us so much as if we dyed our flag with American blood to avenge the insult' "—President Arthur Twining Hadley, anything but a pacifist himself, drew sharp criticism defending Phelps in the name of academic freedom.[7]

War fever soon swept the campus. First the Aero Club joined the Navy, then the Motor Boat Patrol. In only a short period Captain Robert M. Danforth of the United States Army reported to Hadley that Yale's ROTC "was at least a year ahead of other colleges," and that the Corps was being given "artillery training by no means inferior to that . . . at West Point." In April, Walter Camp, the popular Yale coach, "proposed a Senior Service Corps for overage men."[8]

Just as the Kaiser's submarines converted the last of the lukewarm pacifists, antiwar activist David Starr Jordan agreed to come to Yale "to plead for peace," whereupon Jordan and William Lyon Phelps, his sponsor, were deluged with hate mail. In class on the morning of Jordan's speech, Phelps appealed to Yale's sense of fairness; "the honor of Yale" was at stake. That night, when by prearrangement two front rows of uniformed undergraduates filed into the hall just as the lecture was to begin, Professor Phelps "stepped to the lectern and raised his hand. Then he intoned: *Nos morituri te salutamus.* It went over," one of Phelps's students recorded. "The crowd gave him a hell of a hand. Then he introduced Jordan and the meeting was on." During the lecture "the students behaved 'magnificently,'" according to Pierson. Only when Jordan had finished did they swing "out to parade behind the band, as it marched away playing patriotic airs." Everyone in New Haven had been there; Lampson was so crowded that the meeting had to be adjourned to the larger Woolsey Hall.[9]

Full of respect for his former professor, Phil Stone, older than the undergraduates and worried about the financial burden he had imposed on his father when he committed himself to a second law degree, would have been given much to think about that night. He may well have wished for Woodson Ridge, if he took a roundabout way home, leaving Woolsey behind him as he walked out to the Old Observatory. From Prospect Hill that evening in early spring, the town's streetlights were "obscured by smoke from Winchester's, working overtime"—just a week before the declaration of war—"on munitions for England."[10] In early 1917 Stone had marked up Rebecca West's *Henry James* (1916) and Clive Bell's *Art* with his usual hieroglyphics.[11] But the sanctuary of Stone's private studies in narrative and aesthetic theories could no longer forestall the incursion of reality.

Congress declared war over spring vacation, and the campus underwent a metamorphosis. Like poets Rupert Brooke and Wilfrid Owen, Edward Bliss Reed, with whom Stone had surveyed the English lyricists in 1914, quickly donned a uniform and began to drill two faculty batteries. The University Emergency Council organized "early morning calisthenics," daily drill from four to six, and an hour's "evening instruction" for "everyone who desired it and was physically fit." Chapel was "abbreviated"; classes, "speeded up." The undergraduates were hopeful that the "somehow irrelevant" June examinations would be abandoned; however, at the Law School, in Hendrie Hall, not even Zeppelins over Battell Chapel would have stopped the yearly trials designed by Cook and Corbin, or even by William Howard Taft, Kent Professor of Law, who, foreseeing American involvement earlier that year, had argued for "compulsory training."

As commencement neared, more and more men left to enlist, although the administration now waged an intensive campaign to keep the student body intact. But with the droves of departing students and the economic uncertainty generated by America's entry into the war, prices soared. The administration was faced suddenly with a quarter-million-dollar deficit.[12]

Phil Stone too became short of funds, and in the middle of exams let his parents know, none too subtly, that a Bank of Oxford check would be welcome. Surprisingly, like his brother Jim, he appealed to his mother rather than to General Stone:

> I'm afraid I'm going to have [to have] another installment of money, though I'm hoping and praying that I won't. Expenses have been so much more than we could foresee on account of everything being so high. I have been talking to several of the fellows who have been working their way through for I wanted to get some points from them in regard to cutting down expenses; but they have the same story to tell and seem to be spending about the same as it has cost me. . . .
>
> Don't bother Dad about it unless it becomes necessary. I feel a little disheartened about this year . . . [although] it has done me more good than any one year of my whole life. . . . I'm going to do my class bit with the money I was counting on using for Commencement spending money, (Each class is going to buy some Liberty Bonds as a unit, also) but I don't need any money to waste in foolishness. . . . I don't need any clothes except some sox and a pair of shoes and a hat for which I'm very thankful. . . . I can't see any sense in buying a new suit when I'm only going to be at home a couple of months probably. . . .
>
> I intend to come back and get my degree if I ever get the chance, but I certainly hope that I get a Commission and can save enough money to put myself through that year. I not only don't like to be dependent, but I am tired of being a millstone around poor Dad's neck; it looks like a man

ought to at least take the burden of himself of [sic] his father by the time
he gets to be twenty four years old. If I don't save the money some way by
the time I get to come back, I think I shall get one of the University jobs
and work my way through. I have cost Dad such an awful lot of money in
my lifetime and as yet there is nothing at all to show for it. . . .

. . . I suppose the strain of exams have [sic] gotten on my nerves, as I
rarely let anything at all worry me. . . .

Your Baby Boy.[13]

The "sons of Yale" raised $500,000 that year, keeping the univer-
sity in the black.[14] Stone too probably received extra commencement
money. Yet if his college epistle seems merely the stereotypical one, the
composition in retrospect is most sinister. As early as 1917, Phil Stone's
adult tactics of apology and helplessness were already set—irrevers-
ibly. Except for his talk of Liberty Bonds and a commission, the letter
could have been written at any time after 1930—to his creditors; to the
bursars at Hotchkiss and Harvard, where his son's accounts too were
continually in arrears; to the Internal Revenue Service, with whom he
rarely filed a return on time; or to political friends, begging for a salaried government job. Phil Stone might manage words with a certain
facility, and be expert at dates, poker, and law briefs, but money was
as intelligible to him as "Oedipus' lament" would have been around
Oxford's courthouse square.

In America's first months in the war, however, inflation and defi-
cits were hardly the most unsettling issues in Phil Stone's future. On
18 May 1917 the Selective Service Act was given final congressional
approval. Under its provisions, "all male persons between the ages of
twenty-one and thirty" were subject to the registration set by Wilson
for the fifth of June.[15] Although an ardent patriot, Phil Stone had no
desire to go to France as a common soldier. To his relief, his draft
number was apparently far down the master list drawn after the first
registration, and following commencement he intensified his pursuit
of a commission.

No details survive of that first campaign, but in light of subsequent
ones it is not hard to imagine the zeal with which Stone pulled strings.
Because his father's friend Senator John Sharp Williams, never more
popular in the state, also enjoyed a long, "close friendship" with the
president,[16] it is curious that Stone failed to get his bars in the sum-

mer of 1917. One explanation may be that General Stone, meanwhile, at Miss Rosie's prompting, was lobbying to ensure that his son get his degree. Weeks passed as the letters passed back and forth between Oxford and Washington. Although the Army had long since decided how best to employ Phil Stone, only in late autumn, after he was again enrolled in school, were their actions clear to him.

Phil had received a rather vague letter from Major General Enoch H. Crowder, the judge advocate general, who was in charge of the draft.[17] When Stone completed a questionnaire mailed from his local board, he had referred them to Crowder's letter. In the meantime, as he had promised his father, he had discussed his bewildering official correspondence with William Howard Taft, his Constitutional Law professor, who was "very kind about the matter." Taft "thought [that] the appointment [mentioned in the Crowder letter] was allright [sic]," Stone reported to his father, "but [said] that he knew so little about such things that he would rather I didn't trust entirely to his judgment." Taft had given Stone his card with a note for his brother Henry Taft, who reviewed questions of draft status in New York, and advised that Stone write him. Before he could do so, Stone received his draft card from Oxford; finally he was able to decipher the military and legal jargon of Crowder's letter. At midterm, in 1918, he reconstructed for his mother the process that had officially sent him back to Yale "in the Judge-Advocate General's reserve":

> I got a letter from Dad yesterday and see that he is mixed up on my draft classification. There are five classes and class V. is the last class to be called. Division D. of class V. embraces those who are either in actual service or in reserve; so when I filled out my questionnaire and referred them to the letter I got from General Crowder in regard to the appointment in the Judge-Advocate General's reserve. [sic] I got back my classification card saying that I had been put in class V. Division D. It simply means that my letter from General Crowder was an appointment in the Judge-Advocate General's reserve. So I will probably be able to finish out the year allright.[18]

Rosamond Stone probably cried a few tears of relief. Until the next summer, however, her son would have to make accommodations with his bruised pride.

Stone mailed Taft's card to Miss Rosie as a keepsake. The former president had written his brother that "Phil Stone is one of my best students in the Law School. He has a question of his own under the draft act. Help him out. WHT." In January 1944, in a note Stone made for his son Philip on the letter enclosing the card, Phil either mistakenly juxtaposed two different encounters or embellished that single contact: "Chief Justice (ex-President) Taft . . . was recommending me to his brother, Henry Taft, for a position in the latter's law office in New York." It was a claim Phil made elsewhere; he had been tempted to accept, Stone recalled, but the spell of Oxford and of his father had been stronger. It is clear, however, that Stone made no attempt to alter or destroy the seemingly contradictory evidence.

Still expecting a commission during his summer vacation at home in 1917, however, Phil Stone had awaited his call to service with impatience, although diplomatically understating his excitement to Miss Rosie—and to Bill Faulkner, who at nineteen could not enlist without his parents' permission.[19] To pass the interminable summer, on weekends the two friends sometimes escaped parental constraints by excursions into the Delta. They often caught a ride over to Charleston, where Phil's older brother had opened a branch of the family law firm in early 1916. Jack and Myrtle had a pleasant home on East Main Street where Phil and Bill always found congenial company—and free food and drink. But Jack Stone was as frustrated as Bill Faulkner. Overage for military service, he was tireless in war work, promoting Liberty Loans, War Savings Stamps, and Red Cross drives throughout Tallahatchie County.[20] Over lunch and dinner, the three men indulged themselves with fantasies of military command. Before leaving, remembering that it might be years before he saw Charleston again, Phil walked over to say good-bye to Phil Thornton and his son. His sentimental gesture was not fully understood, however. Having seen Stone to the door, Mr. Thornton grumbled about Phil's Eastern mannerisms and of his "coming home wearing those Oxford clothes." Stone's sophistication had dazzled the younger Thornton, though he had sense enough to keep his opinions to himself. "I like Phil Stone," his father continued, unreproved, "but don't like any man to put his arm around me."[21]

At the depot in Charleston, Stone and Faulkner bought train tickets for Clarksdale, though not to call on Aunt Polly Clark and her mother, who formed the remnant of respectability for the boom town.

Like the gamblers lured from Memphis by the smell of money, Stone
planned to invest a night winning cash off the free-spending, newly-
rich Delta planters. In Clarksdale, Stone played his poker at Reno's
Cafe or another such establishment in the red light district across the
tracks. "The Poet," as Faulkner was to be called by Stone's gambling
associates, received special permission from proprietor Reno De Vaux
to "railbird," that is, to observe everyone's hand from inside the bar
separating the table from spectators possibly in league with a cheating
gambler. In the brothels later Faulkner would talk downstairs with the
girls. At Curry Ellis's party about that time, he was introduced to Eula
Dorothy Wilcox, one of Reno's friends, who owned "her own beauty
parlor" in Clarksdale.[22]

If Stone had won any money, he and Faulkner might take the morning train to Memphis to do some shopping. Phil might be looking for
a new hat; covering up his bald head was becoming an obsession. In
a few years his friends would say that one saw him without a hat only
in court. Phil dressed with care, in spite of his sometimes small clothes
budget. Unlike General Stone, who bought his suits off the rack at
Neilson's, he usually assembled his wardrobe at Phil A. Halle's in the
Exchange Building in Memphis, "Importing Haberdashers, Clothiers,
Booterers, Hatters, and Shirtmakers to at least 85% of the well dressed
College Men in the Entire South." Over the past year and a half, Bill
Faulkner too had spent his bank wages on clothes at Halle's.[23]

For Phil, having to return to New Haven in civilian dress in September, however, was not only a disappointment but an embarrassment.
Every letter coming from Mississippi reported on another Ole Miss
friend in war service. D. I. Sultan, Jr., Katrina Carter's cousin, had recently attained the rank of lieutenant colonel; in January 1918 he would
be "selected for duty on the General Staff" in Washington. John Kyle
and Mack Reed were in training as artillery officers. Another member
of Phil's class, Cornell Franklin, had entered service in Honolulu in
late August and by December had been commissioned judge advocate
general in the Hawaii National Guard with the rank of major. Even the
usually idle Jim Kyle Hudson would become a soldier. After he enlisted
at Fort Myer, Virginia, in December 1917, Hudson was assigned to the
Quartermaster Corps in Camp Travis, Texas.[24]

Phil Stone should have noticed the curiosity of Hudson's traveling to Virginia to enlist, for he knew another Oxonian to be in Washington, D.C., that autumn, the young woman to whom Stone apparently at some point proposed marriage. In the summer of 1917 Katrina Carter had bedeviled her mother until she signed false affidavits swearing that Katrina was of an age suitable for canteen work with the YMCA. Although Mrs. Carter made periodic trips north to check on her—in New York Stark Young took them to dinner at the Astor Hotel—the subterfuge secured Katrina a job in the capital and then in New York until the Armistice.[25] When Stone inscribed Thomas Hardy's *A Laodicean: A Story of To-day* (1881) for Katrina's birthday, he had teased her about the perjury: "7/30/17 / To Sister on her 2(?)(?)!?1st / birthday."[26] Phil may not have realized that he was being replaced in Katrina's affections. But, as he said, he felt no sense of proprietorship with regard to women; those birthday and Christmas gifts, with loans from his library, were to continue for seven more years.

Katrina was not the only woman Stone knew who had volunteered her time to the war effort. At home Ella Somerville became "instructress" to the University Red Cross, and Nina too wore the white nurse's uniform with its distinctive cap with stiff, wide wings.[27]

By Christmas 1917, then especially, Phil Stone and William Faulkner felt themselves to be pariahs. When fall classes had opened in New Haven, a slim majority of the students were still civilians—but over a thousand had not returned. Those who had were stung by Captain Edward Reed's November pronouncement that the "intellectual leaders among the students are just where they ought to be—in France or making ready to go there."[28] It was difficult to keep one's mind on books. To compensate for his embarrassment, Phil Stone took an overload. Whereas in 1916 he had registered for nineteen hours, in 1917–18 he enrolled in eleven courses totaling the thirty-four hours he needed to graduate. A normal senior load was twenty. Stone's grades, accordingly, were mixed: from a 55 in Henry Wesley Dunn's Office Practice to *A*'s in Taft's Constitutional Law and in a course called Private Corporations. (Taft, he charged, despite their rapport, was a "terrible teacher—dull as hell.") He had been especially worried about Art Corbin's Suretyship: "Every minute counts for Corbin's exams are always hard," he wrote to Oxford at midterm. Four days before the test he was glued to his chair typing "Suretyship notes for review."[29] In spite of everything, he made only a 66. Somewhat misleadingly, Stone later told his wife that he had ranked number five in his graduating class. Without other grades for comparison, one might be tempted to doubt him, except that the war class of 1918 numbered only twenty students.

As at Ole Miss, Phil participated in few legal extracurricular activities. But at Yale he was elected to what he called "Corbey Court," a chapter of Phi Delta Phi. Two law classmates of Stone with whom he later kept in touch were Karl Nickerson Llewellyn, from Brooklyn, and Hubert Starr, from Los Angeles. Both were more stellar students than Phil Stone. In 1917 second-year Llewellyn, a member of the Law School Society, became an editor on the law journal. The next year, although only a special student, Herb Starr also made the Yale law review. Two of the Samuel J. Elder Prizes went to Llewellyn and Starr in 1918.[30] Stone was closer to Herb Starr than to Karl Llewellyn, but he later followed the latter's enviable career as a distinguished legal scholar.

Outside the classroom Stone continued to be drawn more often to literary discussions than to arguments about abstruse points of law. Byrne Hackett was probably responsible for his introduction to Carl Purington Rollins, Harvard class of 1900, printer for the Yale University Press for fifty years. While Rollins knew little contemporary literature—his tastes, Rollins once wrote Stone, were those of "an elderly mid-Victorian"—in his company Phil read and admired the lineaments of a bibliophile, a more attractive role model to Phil Stone than stolid William Howard Taft.[31]

Some of Stone's friends were not connected with the university. Six years later, Stone and Faulkner asked that *Marble Faun* announcements be mailed to three men addressed in care of the New Haven city schools: Professor Paul Moody, George Hutchinson, and S. B. Smith.[32] Perhaps those acquaintances also rented from the two "old maid sisters" who ran Stone's rooming house at 120 York Street. With Joe Biglin, a blue-collar workman from Denver, Phil Stone would frequent Longley's, or savor bowls of the exceptional Irish stew at Mory's. "Swaggering" down the streets of New Haven with his friend the impeccably dressed Mississippian, Joe, with the wonder of a child, would whistle, "*Geez*, look at all them trees, right here in the middle of town."

New Haven and the Great War

Joe Biglin had come east for the money in the war industries. He did manual labor at the Winchester Repeating Arms Company.

When Stone explained his draft status to Miss Rosie in the winter of 1918, the war in France still seemed distant: "I got through the exams allright as I told Dad, and I have had some glorious slleep [sic] since then. I didn't get up till ten this morning, and Ray Noon, 'Smitty', and I had a very nice breakfast of our own getting. It was of Ray's getting really, he is the official chef. I was counting on several nice days of rest but I found out yesterday that it was all a mirage; the Law School opens Monday. I have two classes to-morrow and I have to get them up pretty soon." Yet among Stone's associates, few careers were not being disrupted in the last year of the war:

> Dr. Drushell [relative of a Sardis attorney] has left the University to take a position with some chemical company which pays him a great deal more and the family have gone South. Jack Berry, one of his students who roomed here, left for New York this afternoon, where he is going to work for the Barrett Chemical Co. A classmate of mine, Bill Huff [Wilbert James Huff, '14], is working at the same place. I hated to see Jack go because he is a very nice fellow, but he was doing his work for his degree under Prof. Drushell and Jack thought that he would himself be drafted for chemical work pretty soon.[33]

At Christmas, Phil had come home to a despondent William Faulkner—sick of his banking job, exasperated at the parents who refused him permission to enlist "until he was of age."[34] But there was something more. Bill would not discuss it, but as Katrina must have told Stone, in the spring apparently Estelle Oldham was going to marry Phil's Ole Miss classmate Cornell Franklin, then a successful lawyer in Honolulu. Neither Phil nor Katrina could quite believe it, for both were certain that Estelle and Bill had loved one another since they were children. To Katrina, if not Bill, Stone may have allowed himself the pleasure of sounding off on just what he thought about Estelle's treatment of his friend. Clearly she was "not worth a damn to anybody and never would be, but that she always had lived off the fat of the land and always would." Later he calmed down, but Phil Stone ("born suspicious," his mother said) never quite trusted Estelle Oldham. After she and Faulkner were married in 1929, Stelle and Phil were very cordial to one another,[35] but both the Faulkners probably sensed Stone's misgivings and, in some measure, resented them.

Stone, interestingly, never refers to the matter in his autobiography:

> While still in Yale Law School Phil sent in his name for military service, was rejected and was informed from Washington, with several more classmates in the Yale Law School that they had been set aside for the lawyer's work in the army and would be called for action later.
>
> So Phil went on but at this time England had at New Haven recruiters . . . [who] could get [them] . . . [in] service at once in Europe. . . . [The] agency in New Haven . . . [was] conducted by two Canadians, one injured in the Princess Pats and another injured in the Black Watch. When Phil came home Christmas 1917 he told Bill about this and they schemed to ship Bill to the Canadian Air Force.
>
> In the spring of 1918 they manipulated for Bill to come up to New Haven early in April and Phil got him a job.

That account differs from the version *Life* reporter Robert Coughlan and Estelle Faulkner gave to biographer Joseph Blotner. While researching his 1953 Faulkner article, Coughlan talked to Stone extensively, but at a time when Phil, not at all conscious of any jealousy on his part, deeply resented what he called Faulkner's "Nobelitis in the head." Bill's refusal to cooperate with Coughlan only confirmed Stone's opinion. The loyalty of friendship was thus undermined, and Phil told Coughlan that he had invited Bill to New Haven in order to prevent his eloping with Estelle, for he was convinced that such a marriage "would spell the end of Falkner as a writer." He did ask that Coughlan not use the information (as later he tried to tone down the article with regard to Faulkner's drinking and his relationship with his father).[36]

In their interviews with Blotner, Coughlan and Estelle Faulkner both claimed that in 1918 Stone had intervened even more directly: "He called Maud Falkner from New Haven and told her that Billy had tried to enlist because Estelle was going to marry Cornell Franklin. For all Stone knew he might now turn elsewhere and try to enlist again." At the same time, Stone suggested the New Haven visit, telling Bill's mother, as Blotner says, that her son "could get away from Oxford, get a job or not as he chose, and have an opportunity to think things through." The alternative seemed better than Faulkner's "doing something impulsive that he might later regret." It seems strange that Faulkner, after the family caucus Blotner describes, went meekly off to the very friend who had alerted his family to the possibility of what Blotner calls his "desperate gambit"—an elopement.[37] At any rate, thus began three months of Stone and Faulkner's most high-hearted association.

Unlike Faulkner, Phil had always had a room to himself and was thoroughly unprepared for the give-and-take of sharing close quarters. Fastidious about his own carefully pressed suits, Stone was horrified that Bill, "on going to bed . . . would throw his suit all crumpled on the floor." The next morning, gathering up his case books and notes for class, Stone was dumbfounded at the ritual in progress in the sitting room: "On waking," Faulkner would lift the suit from the floor, straighten it, brush it, straighten it again, and put it on. It was "immaculate." On the other hand, Stone said, Faulkner "adored anything in leather," and "when he removed his shoes he would patiently spend an hour getting off every speck" and "then place the shoes very, very carefully"—on top of Phil's sitting room table.

Coming in late one night after Bill was in bed reading, the host had had enough. Stone took one look at the clothes piled on the floor and another at the polished shoes on the table: "Bill you [can] sleep here in my sitting room for nothing, you can . . . [throw your clothes] on the floor for nothing, but I will be damned if you think you are going to put those shining shoes on the only table I have in my living room." Faulkner, without a word, "gently lifted the shoes and put them on the floor." Two nights later, the shoes were back, where they stayed, "until both he and Phil went home in late June."[38]

With Joe Biglin's assistance, Faulkner was hired as a "ledger clerk" at Winchester Arms, where he reported for work on Wednesday, the tenth of April.[39] Until he resigned in mid-June, according to Stone, Faulkner "did very little but read," and "was paid quite well for sitting where he could be seen." Munitions, Stone explained, were manufactured on a cost-plus basis. The manufacturers "didn't care how much money they spent; the more they spent, the more profits they made." Winchester was offering time-and-a-half for overtime, for which Bill often volunteered. Most of that overtime, his friend said, Faulkner improved with stacks of books and magazines carted off from Phil's apartment.[40]

What money the Mississippians had they spent freely. In June the Bursar's Office would withhold Stone's degree until he settled his account; they had to borrow train fare home. Their principal objective was to get to the front, but in the meantime they might see Charlie Chaplin in *A Dog's Life* at Poli's Palace, or Pauline Frederick in *Mme. Jealousy* at the Olympia. George M. Cohan and other celebrities performed "Out There" for a local Red Cross benefit. Byrne Hackett probably accompanied the two young men to hear tenor John McCormack; or, on other evenings, when they could afford it, they might all go to the Shubert for grand opera, or to hear the Letz Quartet play Beethoven, Haydn, and Schumann—despite the then rampant anti-German sentiment. (During the war the professor of German at Yale taught mathematics.) [41]

Student poets such as Stephen Vincent Benét, class of 1918, often read from their works at informal sessions. Lectures at the Elizabethan Club as before might be open to nonmembers. And if William Butler Yeats made no return engagement, Stone and Faulkner still could hear Alfred Noyes recite "The Barrel Organ" and other poems. Less than a week after Noyes's recitation, John Masefield was at Yale to address a Sprague Memorial audience on poetry and war.[42] Stone and Faulkner were probably in that audience too.

Meanwhile, their own poetry discussions were continuing. Printer Carl Rollins—"closely cropped brown hair . . . thick-lensed glasses . . . brown goatee," as Phil later jogged Faulkner's memory—often joined the younger men in Stone's rooms "for bull sessions." Herb Starr of the law school was also a student of literature. One night at York Street, Rollins, Starr, Faulkner, Stone, and "the uncurbed Westerner" Joe Biglin were all crammed into Phil's sitting room. Faulkner and Rollins were absorbed in a discussion of Swinburne, frequently illustrating with long quotations as they talked. As one Swinburne line died away in a respectful silence, Joe Biglin suddenly "jumped up and said that Bill and that 'black headed fellow', meaning Arthur Head," would "sit around Longley's and drink coffee and spout that stuff and pull one another's hair and hold one another's hands" by the hour. In the wake of Biglin's breathless announcement there was "a dead silence"—until "Herb Starr roared," as Phil reminded Rollins in 1959. In his letter to Faulkner, however, Stone added, "You might remember that Mr. Rollins looked like somebody had shot him." But before Rollins had even begun to collect himself, Joe, out of his element, "swaggered out" the door, saying, "I think I'll go and shoot a little pool."[43]

By then Faulkner and Stone had approached the Canadian veterans at the New Haven recruiting station.[44] As Phil described it later, "If you wanted to volunteer they promised to get you to the front in thirty days and no questions asked. All you had to do was to say you were Canadian." Stone and Faulkner practiced Canadian English for "more than a month," but because they never mastered "rolling" their "r's," their accent was "too much even for a Canadian recruiting officer who was all too ready to believe anything you told him—so [they] decided to be Englishmen."

Sitting at their table in Commons was a British soldier named Reed, whose patriotism had been stymied in a manner similar to Phil's. Reed had been a chemist in Peking when his country went to war, and hungry to fight, he had volunteered, only to have the government send him to Yale to study more chemistry. With little urging the Englishman agreed to tutor the Mississippians. Phil claimed that he and Faulkner "got to be pretty good": "He had us saying 'bēēn' for *been* and 'Eye-syyy' and such things and he gave us his sister's mailing address for it to be ours. Then we made us up an Anglican clergyman whom we named the Reverend Edward Twimberly-Thorndyke recommending us as 'God-fearing, Christian young gentlemen.' We addressed [the letter] to the recruiter in New Haven, mailed it to the sister in London, and asked her to drop it in a box there. She did." As Blotner notes, they were acting under the assumption that an old RFC directive was still in force requiring that recruits "bear the ear-marks of a gentleman."[45] Phil Stone, who never learned to handle a screwdriver, was dead to join the artillery; Bill Faulkner dreamed of being a flier.

Their ruse apparently worked in their initial contact with the Canadians, but Stone, after several weeks' vacation following graduation, was still supposed to report for duty at the Judge-Advocate General's Department in Washington, where a major's rank and a desk job awaited him. Something more had to be done. While Stone wrestled with exams, however, Faulkner was free to enlist. He took the train down to New York, and on 14 June at Lord Wellesley's recruiting station on Fifth Avenue was accepted for training as a pilot with the Royal

Air Force—Canada. Back in New Haven the following day, he resigned his job at the munitions plant.[46] Stone's degree was being held up by his delinquent account, and while Bill sat on his suitcase, Stone moved about the administrative offices talking his way out of the snarl. Finally, on 19 June, Yale voted Phil Stone his second law degree, and they were free to go home.

Stone and Faulkner left from New York, where friends saw them off. With the financial tangle over the degree and their train tickets more than they expected, they had to borrow sixty dollars from those friends to get home. Even then they did not have enough cash to travel by Pullman or to eat in the diner. Soon they were starving and slipped into the diner anyway. At their second meal, however, the young men were hardly settled before the conductor caught sight of them. "May I see your tickets?" he asked, exchanging glances with the waiter who had recognized the freeloaders. Their explanations did not satisfy him, and he escorted them to their seats. As the door closed behind him, nonetheless, they were on their way back to the diner. That time, they were taken up by a trio of drunken businessmen, and when the conductor reappeared and ordered them out, one of those men said that he would buy their dinner, setting the pattern for the rest of the trip. At the sight of the conductor, one salesman would sing out, "I'll pay this time," and at the next meal, another, "Put this one on my check." The conductor went off grumbling: "Goddamn, I thought railroading was easy." Over the stop in Charlottesville, the conductor got off the train and walked up and down the platform rather than attempt to cope with such rascals.

At Grand Junction, Tennessee, the train was late, and Stone and Faulkner missed their southbound Illinois Central. There were several slow freights that ran through Oxford on their way south, but they preferred passage home on a through freight. Phil sent a telegram to his father, the Illinois Central attorney, to wire the engineer to stop for them at Grand Junction. As they waited all day for that train, they were beginning to miss their generous companions. Walking around the wretched little town with ninety cents in their pockets, all they could afford to eat was ice cream, on which they spent their last change. The freight train did stop for them, but they had to walk half a mile back to the caboose, lugging two big suitcases.

New Haven and the Great War

On the way to Oxford Phil began negotiating with a black railroad worker to persuade the engineer to deposit them at the Stone house, as Illinois Central trains did for General Stone. Although the locomotive pulled on into the depot, the caboose on the long train did come to rest near Stone Lodge, where Stone and Faulkner jumped off yelling back to the black man that they would pay him a dollar to get their suitcases to the office.

When she heard what Phil was about to do, Miss Rosie donned sack-cloth and ashes. But with Bill's help, Stone was determined to escape sitting at a desk in Washington, D.C. They used Faulkner's key to get into the First National Bank one night, stole Eddie Avent's notary public seal, and forged their names "to enough documents to have put us in Leavenworth for the rest of our lives, swearing that we were Englishmen," Phil remembered. The extra documents would do Faulkner no harm when he reported at Toronto, and might cement Stone's own success. Less than three weeks later, Phil saw Bill off at the depot.[47] The two friends shook hands and Faulkner wished him a successful enlistment. As the train pulled out, neither had any idea that Stone would have no trouble in delivering his customary Christmas volume— that year George Moore's *Lewis Seymour and Some Women* (1917)— for both would be civilians by Christmas.[48]

In another three weeks it was Phil's turn to be seen off. On the first of August the *Eagle* reported that Phil Stone "left a few days ago for the recruiting station in New York City where he expects to join the field artillery."[49] That time, sleeping in the Pullman and eating in the diner, Phil spent money extravagantly. As he selected an expensive entree from the menu, a man's shadow fell across his table. "I'm a train-riding . . ." the voice said. "Do you own the train?" It was their conductor.

The plan Stone and Faulkner had honed so carefully almost worked, according to the story. Stone was accepted in the British Army and was ordered to entrain for Halifax, Nova Scotia. At Grand Central Station, afraid that he was late, he inquired of a short, very black British soldier, "What time does this train leave?" The Bermudan replied in a decidedly British accent, "I cyn't say, sir; really, for the life of me, I cyn't say," and hurried off. Phil was shaken. He had forgotten and lapsed into Mississippi English.

Just after he handed his papers to the guard at the gate, he turned white—his draft card! In later years in that part of the story, Phil Stone became the criminal in the detective story foiled by the simplest, most ironic detail. As a student in the legal reserve, he prevaricated, his classification was an *F;* "the classification for a friendly alien in this country," he said, was an *E.* "All I had to do was to make one little mark at the bottom of the F to make me the friendly alien I was supposed to be; with all the lying and forging I had done that would have been easy. But I thought about it a moment too late—just after I'd handed over my papers." Actually, his classification was "Class V. Division D." and that of an enlisted "subject or citizen of [a] cobelligerent country," "Class V. Division K." (A friendly "resident alien" drew an *F* and class *E* was reserved for an "alien enemy.") [50] But Stone's version made a better story. When the guard saw the draft card, Phil tried to explain the irregularity as just a clerical error, but he made no headway with the M.P. As Phil told it, "He knew all the time, I think, that it was a put up job, and he wasn't going to be a party to anything that didn't have the records straight, so he bundled up all my papers, saying he was *sure* I was right but maybe I ought to go back and get it all straightened out and *then* come back."

Not satisfied that the man would not report him, Stone, definitely alarmed now, gave it up and got in touch with his father, who, as a lawyer, knew at once that Phil was in trouble. General Stone sent Phil back to Washington to see Senator John Sharp Williams. As a last resort, he suggested that his son talk to Colonel D. I. Sultan at the Pentagon. On 2 August 1918 Stone wired his mother from the Congress Hall Hotel: "SENATOR WILLIAMS OUT OF TOWN AM GOING TO SEE COL SULTAN TODAY AND [TORN] HOT BUT AM GOING TO KEEP ON UNTIL I GET IN." In a telegram to his father dated 2–3 August 1918 Phil reported: "SAW COL SULTAN AND PROVOST MARSHALL PLEASE HAVE LOCAL BOARD WIRE ME PARTICULAR DIVISION OF CLASS FIVE IN WHICH I AM PUT AND PERMISSION TO GET PHYSICAL EXAMINATION HERE IF I CAN GET INTO CLASS A [I.A.] ONE CAN GET SENT TO FIELD ARTILLERY TRAINING SCHOOL IMMEDIATELY." Dan Sultan, Wohlleben grandson, Ole Miss graduate, and "celebrated lineman" at West Point, was then a colonel on the General Staff.[51] Phil told Sultan that he wished to join the American Tank Corps, but in the epilogue to the enlistment stories, provided only in his 1963 autobiography, Stone says that "Col. Sultan got him in the field artillery . . . got him quartered and ordered him to report. In a few days the war was over and Phil went home to Oxford." Perhaps his papers languished for weeks in wire baskets at the Pentagon. Because the bulk of the Army's World War I records were destroyed in a warehouse fire, the military is unable either to confirm or to deny whether Phil Stone was actually inducted into the service. The circumstantial evidence suggests how eagerly he pursued that end. That his incessant plotting and influence-peddling ultimately stymied rather than effected his goal seems the more probable, and characteristic, outcome. At any rate, during that interval Phil Stone passed one milestone not recorded in any Army file: he completed Henry James's *The Golden Bowl*, on Saturday, 24 August 1918.[52]

In Canada in the interim William Faulkner was spinning his own fictions. Stone and Faulkner corresponded over those months, but Stone was seldom the recipient of the more spectacular fabrications and delighted in puncturing some of them later, as when he wrote critic Glenn O. Carey in 1950 that he knew Bill had never flown as he claimed, because "in the R.A.F. only a commissioned officer could be a combat pilot." "All this stuff about his war service and injuries is just a romantic tale that Bill cooked up sometime when he was half drunk and had a gullible audience," Stone said. "No doubt Bill Faulkner had told this tale so often that he has come to believe it himself."[53]

It had been fun, all the lying and scheming and forging, but the strategic retreat into anecdote manifests the disappointment of two children. The great event of their youth, which wiped out "the last literate generation" in Britain and marked irrevocably Faulkner's colleagues in literature, had passed them by. In Yoknapatawpha the adolescent summer of 1914 would continue, although William Faulkner limped around Oxford and New Orleans and Phil Stone refined his tales of their military chicanery. Stone was always embarrassed that he had not seen active service. In Oxford the prevailing joke was that Stone had done his best "not to get into the army."[54] In the thirties, when Congress passed the Soldiers' Bonus Bill, Mack Reed, who had been an artillery lieutenant, refused the stipend, declaring that it had been an honor to serve his country and that he wanted no material reward. At the time the Stones were so desperate for money that his wife inquired whether Stone intended to claim his bonus. No, he replied, with a curious expression on his face. He believed as Mack did, he said, and turned away.

Just before Christmas in 1918, Stone and Faulkner were in the university post office when Bill got a letter from Canada enclosing "his pip, his wings and his commission," Stone said.[55] It was over.

6

The Lawyer and the Poet

WITH THE GREAT WAR BEHIND THEM, and no patrons forthcoming to set them up in the practice of literature, twenty-five-year-old Phil Stone and twenty-one-year-old William Faulkner returned like errant boys to their fathers' houses late in 1918. But their former dependency was to undergo at least cosmetic changes in the new year. Their parents, heretofore patient and indulgent, now must have put aside the *Commercial Appeal* at breakfast or sat upon the foot of their beds at night, to discuss "the future." Faulkner, having no desire to resume his banking "career," evaded the pressure by deciding to enter the university in the fall;[1] in the meantime he would work at odd jobs around Oxford for spending money. Phil, on the other hand, already had four degrees; not even he could have mentioned school to his father again. Besides, Stone had gotten "his legal fill of the law" at New Haven, he said.[2] It was time at last to practice his profession. Faulkner later rather enjoyed teasing Stone about his inglorious debut in the family firm in 1919: Horace Benbow, says one of the characters in *Flags in the Dust*, "has spent so much time being educated that he never has learned anything."[3] But it was true. As he began the practice of law, Stone discovered that he really knew nothing about trying a lawsuit; nor had he reckoned on his panic at the prospect of a courtroom speech. A quarter-century of Rosamond Stone's admonitions, he rationalized, had seriously undermined his confidence.[4]

Paradoxically, talkative Phil Stone was not by natural disposition an

advocate, as his father was. His wife thinks that Stone, having repudi-
ated his mother, yet unsure of his own powers, tried to make himself
over in the image of his father, but that he failed, for he was actually "of a judicial temperament" (Phil always told her that the state
Supreme Court was "his" court).[5] Lawyers who had heard both Stones
in court disagreed somewhat with that appraisal, and in their evaluations of Phil's success before judge and jury. Like many others, Robert
Farley, one of a family of lawyers, and W. H. Anderson, chancellor of
the Third Judicial District, spoke of Phil's father as an excellent trial
attorney.[6] It was Farley who remembered the outburst over Jim Stone's
"affidavit countenance." (He commented too on the son's courtesy to
the elderly man in court, where Stone always accompanied his father
whether associated with the case or not.) But, according to Farley, while
General Stone enjoyed the "best practice in the area"—the railroad
and utilities accounts—Phil Stone, never much of a trial lawyer, was
indifferent to "ordinary country practice," only challenged by cases
involving a "novel point of law." The younger Stone deserved his reputation as an appellate attorney, Farley said, for he knew the law and
conscientiously constructed a case, but he was really more "a student
of law than a practitioner."

Judge Anderson, before whom Stone often argued, believed Phil
more suited to teach the law, but thought his performance in court
nevertheless "above average." Stone was a perfectionist, he said, in preparing his briefs, and tenacious in support of a client. Phil's courtroom
personality came across as genuinely warm and friendly, but Anderson questioned whether he would have been successful in the judiciary,
both because of his tendency to make up his mind too quickly and because he lacked patience with the common man. Witnesses in Anderson's court had too often turned to the bench in puzzlement over Phil's
wording of a question.

Law students, however, especially after he was state bar association president, sought Stone out just to talk to him, Jack's daughter
Allie Jean remembers. Her husband, Soule Scott, and his friends found
Stone's advice very practical: for example, that "to cultivate the clerks
and bailiffs" and other court attaches might profit a young lawyer more
than a high academic rank. Laymen like Mack Reed, seeing Stone
in action in federal court in his prime, came away convinced of his

"brilliance": "If a point of law arose, I could close my eyes and ears and know for a certainty that Phil would graciously and deferentially supply the answer to the judge, citing case after case."[7] Such poise was not a natural endowment; in the first of his forty-three years in court, Stone was shy and nervous. His relish for arcane appellate contests was also an acquired taste; it would be over ten years before he settled down in earnest to practice the law.

In the winter of 1915, men at the hunting camp at Stone Stop had told General Stone that the Northern lumber companies moving then in force into the Delta were looking for competent local counsels and suggested that he take advantage of the lucrative fees such business afforded. Because Charleston was fifty miles to the southwest, General Stone later told a timber executive on the telephone only that he would recommend an attorney for him. Talking it over with his sons, he must have had second thoughts about turning the man down, whereupon Phil suggested, "For God's sake, send Jack!" It was not a bad idea. By January 1916 the firm had opened its Charleston branch.[8]

General Stone, as Phil often remarked, "was generous but never just," and until that decision had somewhat stifled his even-tempered junior associate. Phil could sense Jack's humiliation whenever, too often, their volatile father "bawled him out in front of clients." The newest attorney with the firm enjoyed an easier relationship with General Stone, because, as Phil explained it, "I stood up to him." Perhaps James Stone, a man of sixty-five by the time Phil entered the firm, had simply mellowed. Despite his father's preferential treatment of his youngest son, when the oldest died suddenly in 1932 General Stone recorded Jack's name and the date in the family Bible—with a private epitaph: "Dearest of all. Dad." And it was Jack, not Phil, the older lawyers said, who inherited General Stone's instincts in the courtroom.

In his short career in the timber boom town W. E. Stone IV gained a solid reputation in corporate law as counsel for two banks, two railroads, Railway Express, the telegraph and telephone companies, a chemical company, and the Memphis-based Columbia Mutual Life Assurance Society, where he also sat on the board of directors.[9] When Jack Stone went to Charleston in 1916, Lamb-Fish Lumber Company was the town's principal employer. In 1919 its plant in Charleston was said to be "the largest hardwood mill in the world."[10] But soon that company (and others) had clear-cut the oaks and sweetgums for miles in every direction. The big saws first ran half a day, then only twice a week. When Lamb-Fish filed for bankruptcy, the courts appointed Jack Stone one of the receivers to liquidate the company's assets.[11] Ominously, by 1925 Stone represented Turner-Farber-Love, Lamb-Fish's successor, a company based in Leland, Mississippi, sixty miles deeper into the Delta.

During the halcyon days at Lamb-Fish, Phil Stone was officially introduced to the bar at the Charleston courthouse by Chancellor McGowen, for whom he had been a page as a boy. Phil would practice there with his brother more or less for the next three years, taking a room with Jack and his wife on East Main Street.[12] When Phil moved over, in the late spring of 1919, Charleston—today a sleepy little town with fewer than three thousand persons—had no doubts about its future. The Charleston Development Club was active, and its president, W. B. Burke, had every reason to be optimistic. Burke had flourished for thirteen years as vice-president and general manager of the Lamb-Fish mill. By 1907 Lamb-Fish owned a hundred thousand acres of virgin forest, which it would strip and sell to farmers for cultivation. On 6 September 1919 Burke and "lumber magnate" Garrett E. Lamb, of Clinton, Iowa, the president of Lamb-Fish, joined Burke to celebrate the opening of a half-million-dollar wood products factory. The plant would require "over 20,000 cords a year" and employ two hundred men "in the wood camps and the factory." It was designed so that the company could double its output without enlarging the original physical plant.[13]

In addition to other executive positions, Garrett Lamb was president of the Southern Ball Clay Company, in which the Stones and their friends the Thorntons also held stock. An enterprising geologist had discovered large deposits of a clay peculiar to the region used during the First World War for ballast and in paint and face powder.[14]

Laborers at Lamb-Fish and Southern Ball Clay lived on "Tin Row" and "Silk Stocking Row" and the like in company-built Milltown east of the Yazoo and Mississippi Valley tracks separating it from Charleston's main residential area and north across Main Street from the mill. There had been no place in Charleston to put up visiting buyers when the management arrived, so Lamb-Fish also built the Lafisco, a private two-story stucco hotel. Phil, Jack, Myrtle, and their older children often went there for supper. Lamb-Fish executives and the Delta aristocracy played golf on the company's nine-hole course behind Milltown.[15] Early in his career Phil Stone spent more time there and on what Florrie Friedman's father called the university's "golfing pasture" than in either branch of James Stone & Sons. "A client would be coming in the front door and I'd be going out the back—with my clubs," Stone said, "so I had to quit."

In their first months at home, Faulkner, although he too played golf, was somewhat more committed to his "career." As he reminisced six years later in "Verse Old and Nascent: A Pilgrimage," "When the co-ordinated chaos of the war was replaced by the unco-ordinated chaos of peace I took seriously to reading verse." While Jack showed Phil Stone how the student of law becomes a practitioner, Bill apprenticed himself to the English poets. Phil was not one to take instruction humbly. Insulted as a boy when forced to share a stand with Jack on his first hunt, he was now sensitive to any sign of condescension from his mild-mannered, patient older brother.

Faulkner describes himself as a more willing student: "I believe I came as near as possible to approaching poetry with an unprejudiced mind. I was subject to the usual proselyting of an older person, but the strings were pulled so casually as scarcely to influence my point of view. I had no opinions at that time, the opinions I later formed were all factitious and were discarded. I approached Poetry unawed, as if to say; 'Now, let's see what you have.' Having used verse, I would now allow verse to use me if it could."[16] Both apprentices, however, soon registered their first successes.

Stone's came in *Ruffin vs. Black*, a lawsuit that went all the way to the state Supreme Court. Into the thirties Stone retained printed copies of the briefs he filed for that case in Jackson. In the suit he was an associate of a Memphis attorney, but the linchpin of their case had been discovered by Stone, and not through brilliance but through "sheer drudgery," as he admitted. The suit turned on a single canceled check, and on the floor of the back room in the office sat the junior associate, from dawn to dusk, going through thousands of old drafts. But Stone had found the pertinent check that sweltering summer, and the victorious attorneys split a sizeable fee—Phil's first.

Faulkner in the meantime had not been idle either. Although it would be five years before he mailed the manuscript of his first book to a Boston publisher, Faulkner later dated the composition of the *Marble Faun* poems as April, May, and June, 1919. In those first months home he also completed a poem that he may have first conceived as a cadet in Toronto. At any rate, Faulkner was soon reading "L'Apres-Midi d'un Faune" to Phil Stone, who, as with other Faulkner manuscripts of the period, gave it to the firm's secretary to type. One copy she "typed on the back of a sheet of stationery marked 'The First National Bank of Oxford, Oxford, Miss., J. W. T. Falkner, Pres.' "[17] (Someone, Faulkner perhaps, had scruples about James Stone & Sons supplying typist, typewriter, and paper. They rarely made such distinctions later.)

By that time, according to Stone in 1959, he and Faulkner were already veterans of the Oxford–New York mail traffic, but so far Bill's poems had all been returned "post haste." Stark Young's appearances in *New Republic* may have encouraged them to try that publication, but with Young busily preparing for an autumn trip abroad, it seems unlikely that he had a direct hand in their success.[18] Faulkner submitted "L'Apres-Midi d'un Faune" to the magazine in the summer of 1919. To their astonishment, *New Republic* not only took the poem but, as Phil said, even more remarkably, "paid fifteen whole dollars for it." When the check arrived and the poem appeared in the August 6 issue, he continued, "Bill and I felt like the lucky country boy at his first crap game: How long has this been going on?" Thereafter they besieged the *New Republic* with poems, but with no further success. Before returning the office stenographer to General Stone, in their disappointment the two men concocted a revenge. From Phil's copy of the *Oxford Book of English Verse* (1912), they selected John Clare's "Lines from a Northampton Asylum," because "very few people seem to know it," and "without title and without Bill signing the poem," they submitted a copy to the magazine that now scorned to publish Faulkner's poems. "Our plan," said Stone, "was to have *The New Republic* accept it and publish it and then secretly to notify *The New York Times* of the affair and let the dull *Times* rib the smarty *New Republic*."

Forty years later Phil would still wonder whether one of the editors had recognized it or whether the poetry editor, now familiar with Faulkner's work, thought him incapable of so fine a poem. It had been

returned to them without comment. Determined at least to be credited with a good joke, they then abandoned all subtlety and "copied
off" "Kubla Khan," and sat back and waited for a reply. They were
not to be disappointed. One of the editors wrote: "We like your poem,
Mr. Coleridge, but we don't think it gets anywhere much."[19]

In the fall of 1919 Faulkner, minus a high school diploma, was accepted as a special student at the University of Mississippi—upon the
recommendation of Stark Young, according to Maud Brown.[20] Faulkner once told Emily Stone that he "never graduated from anything,"
that when his grammar school commencement was in progress he and
two or three other boys were hidden in the school basement: "We
thought graduation was for sissies." After he quit school altogether,
the family had "tried to make a banker out of him," according to Phil
Stone, but "even the hard-headed Falkners soon gave that up." Now,
for a year and two months, William Faulkner would be a student at
Ole Miss. Estelle, Katrina, and Ninaville no longer decorated for Cotil-
lion Club dances, nor did Stone and Hudson any longer participate
in the freshmen shearing. As before, however, Faulkner would make
only rare appearances at the college dances, to stand in a corner "like
a bump on a log" and watch as the boys hovered around a favorite
coed, as once they had clustered around Estelle. On a weekend visit
to Charleston, one of Stone's new friends, a Memphis girl, had related
how her friends often stayed at home when they learned Estelle Oldham was in town for a dance, for all the men flocked to her. Faulkner
apparently spent much of his time reading, sketching, and submitting
poems to the *Mississippian*, the campus newspaper. By the weekend he
must have been relieved when Phil's insatiable homesickness brought
him back to Oxford.

Indeed, during the three years that Stone lived in Charleston, he
must have spent a third of that time at home or en route between the
two towns. Covering the fifty miles by train usually meant traveling
a zigzag route of twice that distance. Consequently, as soon as Stone
made his first fees, he bought an automobile, a Ford coupé with white
wire wheels. He called his new car "Drusilla."[21] After that, when court
adjourned he was free to start for Oxford. Once he had passed the
Lamb-Fish mill and factory, he was out in the country on a dirt road.
Beyond Oakland the car climbed Yocona Ridge, in the descents pick-

ing up a little speed. Then Water Valley, and northeast for a few miles, finally due north, past the narrow little cow path to the bootlegger's dogtrot house seven miles out; past the black "Sanctified" church; then it was South Street and the square and his father's stallion grazing in the lot behind the office.

After supper, Bill Faulkner would cut through the university woods to General Stone's, often finding Phil and his father on the veranda smoking and reviewing the week's case loads. Soon the old man would rise, flip his cigarette over the intertwined crape myrtle and rosebush at the porch's edges, and go upstairs to bed. Then Phil would hear "Cathay" or "Landing in Luck" or the other poems and stories Faulkner was writing then for the *Mississippian*.[22]

In December 1919 Phil took off work in mid-week to return home for an SAE initiation at General Stone's dairy farm. His brother Jim, who supervised "Hill Crest Dairy," had invited the fraternity to the farm for the annual ceremony. Though Jim Stone was then in his late thirties, he offered his friendship to every class at the university and was often seen in student company at the fountain at Chilton's Drugstore or in the stands during football and baseball season. Phil Stone was a loyal Deke, but Jim had invited him to the SAE hazing because the fraternity had issued a bid to Bill Faulkner. That evening Phil may have arrived early, in time to see Jim's daughters Mary and "Gena," as he called five-year-old Evelyn Stone, before they went to bed. As usual, he would slip each child a nickel or a dime for an Eskimo Pie. Eight-year-old Mary Stone had been a faithful correspondent while he was in New Haven, and Phil frequently drove by for the girls for ice cream and Sunday afternoon rides to Water Valley. Whenever the children were in town with their mother, as Evelyn Stone recalls, they would "silently almost pray . . . [to] see Uncle on the street." After Phil tucked the girls in and kissed them goodnight, he rejoined the fraternity brothers assembled—illegally, thanks to Lee Russell—to test the commitment of their new pledges. Stone, seeing Faulkner and entering into the spirit of the occasion, shook his head, saying, "I don't believe this boy will ever stand this initiation. Dave [Callahan, another initiate] might pass it, but I don't think Bill ever will." But the trials were soon over, and Faulkner—belatedly—became a Greek.[23]

Because of his fraternity dues Faulkner may have been temporarily embarrassed for funds at Christmas; Stone dropped off his customary striped tie or book, but it was not until New Year's Day, apparently, that Bill reciprocated—with the first of his hand-lettered poetry booklets of the 1920s, *The Lilacs*. That one, with the reversed s's characteristic of *Marionettes* and *Mayday*, Faulkner bound in red velvet. In addition to his poems, there were also two illustrations in the volume: in the back a small nude in black and white, and on page four the rare Faulkner watercolor, of a female figure. What remains legible of the dedication to Stone, dated "Jan. 1 1920," mostly the French *"quand il fait Sombre,"* [24] may owe something to a poetic offering of A. E. Housman's persona Terence: "It should do good to heart and head / When your soul is in my soul's stead; / And I will friend you, if I may, / In a dark and cloudy day" ("Terence, This Is Stupid Stuff," lines 54–57).

While Faulkner's college French might be competent, he was having trouble with Horace Bishop's British literature survey. Stark Young could be nostalgic later about Bishop's ponderously dignified manner, but Faulkner, like Stone, must have found it trying. With a *D* at mid-year Faulkner dropped the course and turned more of his attention to French literature.[25] Stone said later that Bill read many of the Symbolists in books he owned, "some in the original but most in translation," and acknowledged those writers to have had "some influence" on Faulkner's verse.[26] Phil had given Katrina Carter the Gertrude Hall translation of Paul Verlaine's poems as early as September 1917. While Stone and Carter were reading Siegfried Sassoon's *Picture-Show* in March 1920,[27] Faulkner was engaged that spring in writing four Verlaine translations for the university newspaper. Publishing imitation-decadent poetry, carrying his handkerchief in his coat sleeve in the British manner, and sporting a cane from time to time (along with a mustache) Faulkner deliberately provoked, it seems, a circle of campus satirists eager to deflate his affectations. They called him "The Count" and parodied his "French" verse.[28]

Stone rarely mentions that spate of abuse, but when David Cohn later asked that he write about how Oxford's "proletariat" had reacted to Faulkner, he remembered the mock-title and noted that "they don't think of William Faulkner at all unless they happen to see him. They don't read his books, they don't read books at all very often. . . . When they think of him they think of him with respect, respect for the fact that he is articulate enough to write a whole book and for the fact that he has made money." By contrast, the educated classes, Stone continued, had greeted the black sheep of the Falkner family with "polite, derisive smiles."[29] He and Faulkner had had too little encouragement in the early days to be able to stomach the lionizers and autograph seekers. The poetry war raging in 1920 in the *Mississippian*—of all places—was only their first taste of disdain. The attacks may have seemed too silly for Phil's anger, but Bill apparently withdrew further behind a facade of arrogance.

That autumn the Charleston office of James Stone & Sons was absorbed, it seems, in one of the periodic spurts of activity peculiar to country law practice at the opening of the various courts. With Phil working, for once, Faulkner talked books with Ben Wasson, a college student from Greenville. According to Blotner, the literature regularly distributed from Phil's library to Bill and to Ella Somerville, and at times to Wasson, now was going also to Lucy Somerville, a Delta cousin of the Oxford Somervilles. It was Lucy's idea to start a book review column for the campus newspaper, to which Faulkner contributed then and later. She and Wasson also persuaded Faulkner to join the Marionettes, an amateur drama group they organized that year. Ella Somerville was a sometime director for the company, and Katrina Carter, the troupe seamstress. William Faulkner, the property man on one production, evidently entertained the idea of becoming the resident playwright. Stone later praised Eugene O'Neill to Faulkner as "one man who comes pretty near having genius." Yet the only Faulkner play surviving from that period bears little resemblance to any major contemporary American drama.[30]

What *The Marionettes* does recall, in an often "showy and self-conscious display," according to Faulkner scholar Noel E. Polk, is the six years of Faulkner's "omnivorous and catholic" reading, particularly in the poetry of the French Symbolists. The reading of course took place in Phil Stone's library. The author lettered, illustrated, and bound as many as six copies of the one-act, though the Ole Miss drama group never staged it. One of the surviving copies (until the 1950s) belonged to Katrina Carter; sheets from the play were found in the ashes of the Stone home.[31]

In the autumn of 1920, Faulkner's second year at Ole Miss, he quietly withdrew from the university.[32] He had had little patience with the literature taught by the professors at the school and seemingly preferred to return to the poets themselves. If Faulkner needed a library, he could remove everything but the front seat and load Phil's books and his own into "Drusilla" and find a tree or two under which to read. That June Stone had bought Alfred Kreymborg's anthology of new verse *Others for 1919* and Putnam's edition of *Georgian Poetry, 1918–1919*,[33] two volumes Faulkner may have stashed in the coupé. If he needed a tutor, Phil was prepared to advise what to read next or to point out when "too much Housman" crept into Faulkner verse, and to propose exercises such as the ones during the time when they "were enamoured of Housman" and Phil asked Bill to attempt poems entirely in monosyllables. (Sheets from a set of manuscript poems sold to a collector in the sixties have figures such as "180–30" at the bottom. Those numbers, as Emily Stone suggests, were apparently the syllable counts Phil made to gauge the success of such experiments.)[34] Ben Wasson, Katrina, and the Somervilles were more stimulating companions than the persons with whom Faulkner had shared classes and newspaper space. And, as always, Phil Stone was usually available for golf, walks, a ride to Clarksdale or Memphis, or, in the absence of housepainting jobs, an occasional loan.

One of Stone and Faulkner's friends in Oxford when they were young was "Doc" Lott, the son of Calvin Lott, a dignified black man who worked as a servant for university chancellors "for a generation or two." The gossip in Oxford was that Calvin Lott was the illegitimate son of "a real Virginia gentleman" on the faculty, perhaps because of his aristocratic bearing; his son "Doc" had no such manner. The younger Lott found a job in a barbershop in Memphis shining shoes, where he was working when the Eighteenth Amendment became law in January 1920. During Prohibition, barbershops were often outlets for bootleggers, and the shoeshine men frequently peddled whiskey themselves. Although Doc was only a messenger for a Tennessee bootlegger, the Treasury men arrested him anyway, and a Republican judge, Phil said, gave him ninety days in a jail north of Memphis. Calvin Lott, outdone with his son, went to the university chancellor for sympathy: "*How many times have I told Doc not to sell whiskey to strangers!*" When Faulkner and Stone heard about Lott's conviction, they sent him ten packages of cigarettes a week. Furthermore, Phil got on the phone to Walter Chandler, a friend of his in the Crump administration, and Doc, soon paroled, came home to Oxford.

Contacts among the races in small towns in Mississippi were quite common and, superficially at least, free from tension. Men like Stone or Faulkner no doubt thought themselves blind to the color of a person's skin, but the details of their stories belie them. Another black family the Stones knew well were the Boleses. They too were of mixed blood. Cliff Boles operated a shoe repair shop in Charleston, and Rob owned a similar shop in Oxford across the alley from the law office; James Stone & Sons represented both businesses.[35] Among the older families it was common knowledge that Rob Boles (1878–1959), son of Maggie Boles (according to his obituary),[36] was a cousin of William Faulkner "on the wrong side of the blanket." He was "a most superior person," according to Emily Stone, "more filled with dignity and self-possession and gentleness than almost anyone I have ever known."

Boles was "unquestionably the prototype for Lucas Beauchamp," she thinks. Like his brother, he could easily have passed for a white man. One time when a new Ole Miss student mistakenly addressed him as "sir," as the story goes, Boles corrected her, in a typically low reply: "I am a Negro." Robert Boles had started out in Oxford in 1893 with only a leather apron and a hammer, but because of the exceptional quality of his work and because, unlike Lucas Beauchamp, he knew his place in white society, he maintained a sound business there for over sixty years.

It may be that the constant reminder of Rob Boles's white skin and the artist's gift for empathy developed in William Faulkner opinions on the question of race that his family and few of his friends were ever able to share. The Stones, like Faulkner, generally practiced a version of the familiar Southern paternalism toward blacks. Freeman's Town lay east of the Stone property on the western edge of Oxford. As was appropriate for members of their class in that society before the late fifties and early sixties, the Stones scorned the white "trash" that some-times harassed the black community there (as later they would refer to one racist governor only as "that shyster lawyer"). When Phil Stone abruptly adopted the language of bigotry in the 1950s, no one noticed that Stone's paranoia about "Yankees and niggers" was the earliest, and the clearest, symptom of his advancing arteriosclerosis. Ironically, his madness was thoroughly camouflaged within the region's epidemic racism.

In the 1920s, besides handling the legal affairs of the Boles men, the Stone attorneys also represented the local Chinese. Phil Stone helped Hom Wo, the Oxford laundryman down on Depot Street, to become a U.S. citizen. The Chinese in Charleston (as in the Delta generally) were more numerous. Jack Stone frequently worked on their naturalization papers, and for fee the Chinese gave Myrtle bolts of silk and shawls and scarves. One paid his bill with a mahjongg set.[37]

As for the other minority in an area dominated by Baptists and Methodists, Phil Stone always claimed that anti-Semitism did not exist in the South, pointing out to Carvel Collins, for example, the assimilation of both generations of Friedmans in Oxford society. Florrie Friedman's father and uncle, Russian emigrants, ran prosperous clothing stores. Florrie Friedman and Katrina Carter were as close as sisters as long as his mother lived, says Jim Hudson. Yet General Stone's law partner, Julian Wilson, a Jew, had changed his name in order to ensure his success in private practice. Phil's nephew Jack Stone would think that the father of his friend Freddie Friedman *owned* Freedman's Town, perhaps only as a child confuses words—or perhaps because he had heard a racist joke on the square that he failed to understand.[38]

By November 1920, with Bill out of school permanently and Phil practicing law only periodically in Charleston and the other county seats around, the young men began spending days away from Oxford, with newer acquaintances. Faulkner was already a frequent visitor to Charleston, where Jack and Myrtle Stone occasionally put him up for the night.[39] Through Phil, Bill soon met Katherine Lawless, the Memphis woman who had commented on Estelle Oldham's popularity at dances among her social set. During 1919 and 1920, when Stone knew her in Charleston, Katherine was a county Home Demonstration agent, with an office in the Tallahatchie County courthouse. Until he met her, Stone had been miserable in that, to him, "countriest of country towns." The two, who were lifelong friends, "never really had any dates, but they would talk very confidentially and say very frank things to one another" during their Charleston years, Phil said later. She was "a big woman," a brunette, very intelligent, and "full of sparkling vitality." Stone and Faulkner became "devoted to" Katherine Lawless and gave her the nickname "Sunshine."

Although Faulkner rarely missed an expedition into the country-side with Phil and Katherine, in only a short time there was another, more compelling attraction in Charleston—the Stone stenographer, "a very pretty little girl," according to Phil, named Gertrude Stegbauer. "Bill fancied he was in love with her," Stone said, but the three of them (Katherine Lawless had moved away) went together to dances be-cause Bill refused to escort her by himself. When she first knew them, Gertrude told Stone she was sure that *he* would give up the law and make a writer. Faulkner had broken his habitual silence to disagree: "No, Stone doesn't write; he's too busy living to write." Years later, Stone still thought the remark "a shrewd saying by Bill." The Faulkner-Stegbauer courtship was a most platonic affair, as John Faulkner inti-mates in *My Brother Bill:*

> There was a girl there—I think she was Mr. Jack's secretary—who fell for Bill. He used to take her presents and every Christmas she would send him some handkerchiefs. The top one or two in the box would have his initials worked in them, but the rest would be blank. She always sent half a dozen and never did get his initials worked in all six of them. Bill used to begin worrying to Mother, several weeks before Christmas, about the girl laboring over his initials. And sure enough, when Christmas came there would come the box of handkerchiefs.
>
> Bill made a book of poems for her. The book had a dozen pages in it, hand lettered, and a design sketched in it around the edges. He got a piece of purple leather and bound the volume. When he showed it to me I liked it so much I did one for my girl too.[40]

Bill Faulkner and Gertrude Stegbauer were rarely alone together. It was as if, after Estelle, Bill preferred a Marietta of "fancy" to a young woman of flesh and blood. Something happened to remind Faulkner that she too was human after all, as he confided to Phil, and the in-fatuation, in an instant, was destroyed.[41] Nevertheless, in 1924 a copy of *The Marble Faun* presumably went to Miss Gertrude Stegbauer, living then in Memphis, and Stone knew her married name and address as late as 1963.

Stone and Faulkner were often bored in quiet little Charleston, and

"Drusilla" was soon on the road to Memphis or Clarksdale every weekend. Either place afforded them contacts with the highest and the lowest social classes in the South, and they seem to have been as comfortable with one as with the other. Anglo-Saxon society in Memphis was dominated by former Mississippi families, like the Alstons, who had moved there in the eighties and nineties, a migration that continued into the twentieth century. "Boss Crump," the colorful Mayor E. H. Crump, for example, was from Holly Springs. After five years in Chicago, Clarence Sivley had also settled in Memphis, where in 1915 he founded the firm of Sivley, Evans & McCadden. In Chicago the Sivleys had joined the University and South Shore country clubs. In Memphis they were popular society figures in both the Tennessee and Memphis country clubs. Perhaps because their only child had died as an infant,[42] the Sivleys always relished the company of young people. Katrina Carter, according to her son, had once been invited to Chicago in the private railroad car the Illinois Central kept in Oxford for the Sivleys. Later the dances at Ammadelle were simply moved to Memphis.

Perhaps through the Sivleys, Katrina and then Stone and Faulkner met the R. P. Lake family, originally from Grenada, Mississippi. Richard Pinckney Lake, a sixteen-year-old Confederate cavalry lieutenant under Major Alston, had been a politician and railroad executive after the war, but it was as general agent for the Equitable Life Assurance Society for Mississippi and Tennessee that he made his fortune and became "a leading figure in business and social circles."[43] Robert and Donelson Lake, two of his sons, were in business with their father. Stone, Faulkner, and Katrina knew the Lake sisters somewhat better, especially Estelle, Dorothy, and Alice. The young women were avid hostesses, and the elegant garden and walks of their home on South McLean in Memphis were often filled with couples from April to November.[44] One of the Lake house parties had taken place soon after Faulkner's poem appeared in the *New Republic*. Still euphoric when he wrote Estelle Lake a thank-you note, Faulkner apologized for his "eccentricities" by enclosing a drawing "which, when I have become famous, will doubtless be quite valuable."[45]

Estelle ran the lending library for the Nineteenth Century Club, the women's club on Union Avenue where Memphis society women still

read, swim, and play tennis.[46] Dorothy Lake married a French noble-
man, August Brabant, whom she had met during the war when he was
in Memphis buying cotton cellulose for munitions. Phil Stone remembered Dorothy as hostess one night swooping down on him in outrage
when she spied Stone and a girl lying in a hammock in the garden.
Ignoring his defense that one could hardly manage any "foolishness" in
a hammock, Dorothy handed him his hat and walked him to the door.
Although Stone's manners generally assured him more graceful exits,
the Lake sisters were probably well aware that Phil and Bill seldom
returned straightaway to their rooms at the Peabody Hotel. Decorum
required that no one mention it, but after leaving the ladies at South
McLean the men, in search of quite different company, often stopped
off for a beer in the city's red light district.

Memphis had ceased to be a "pure" town as early as 1830, when a
tavern operator opened its first brothel.[47] For "a city of churches," as it
is often called, the river port was also blatantly "wicked": "If whiskey
ran ankle deep in Memphis and each frontdoor had a dipper tied to it,
you could not get drunker quicker than you can in Memphis now," pronounced an evangelist in 1893. "The only difference between Memphis
and hell is that Memphis has a river running alongside it," observed a
St. Louis visitor in 1907. "They make more moonshine liquor on Presidents Island and in remote sections of Shelby County in a day than the
wildcatters of Hardin, Davidson and Morgan counties do in a week," a
revenue agent reported in 1923. "THE FAMOUS SHUTDOWN order came on
April 23, 1940 and it came as rather a shock to the girls and madams,
several of whom said they had just paid their poll taxes and made their
political contributions," wrote a *Commercial Appeal* reporter in 1969.
A century of periodic crackdowns and reform politicians notwithstanding, prostitution, gambling, liquor, and murder were as ubiquitous in
Memphis as cotton in the Delta. Only Federal pressure in 1940 persuaded Crump to order his police commissioner to the cleanup work
from which he emerged as "Holy Joe" Boyle. "Mr. Crump don't 'low
no easy riders here" took thirty years to become fact.

In the early twenties the Memphis "tenderloin" was situated on Main
Street south of Linden Avenue, other brothels "were scattered along
Third, Fourth and Mulberry," and the "more solidly established places,
like the famous Stanley Club," were on Gayoso Street. Some of the

gamblers with whom Stone played poker either owned or pimped for the brothels, and it was through men like Lee Brown and Reno De Vaux that Stone and Faulkner became acquainted with the prostitutes, Phil said. The door of the two-story brownstone at which they rang on the night of the Lake party was probably opened by Mary Sharon, the Memphis madam of whom Stone so often spoke. To Phil, the idea that prostitutes are exotic-looking women was "absurd." "They look like middle-aged Baptist Sunday School teachers," he quipped. Mary Sharon had emigrated from Sweden at the age of sixteen, a number of years before. When Stone knew her, her hat was "full of plumes," and she was "fat and flamboyant."

Another woman with a special status in the hierarchy of that sub-culture was Dorothy Ware (her professional name), one of Mary's girls; sometime earlier she had become the mistress of Lee Brown, the Clarksdale gambler whom Phil knew, and no longer went to bed with anyone else. Her status had been won in part by a not inconsiderable physical courage. As a girl Dorothy had scandalized her family by be-coming "tied up with" a city man. When her father and brothers swore to kill her lover if the affair continued, Dorothy had left the moun-tains of North Alabama—on foot—for Memphis. She never saw her family again. Bill Faulkner was especially fond of Dorothy and often went to Clarksdale alone to see her. Faulkner and Lee Brown soon became friends as well. Whenever Stone and Brown began a night's play, the gambler did not neglect his younger guest. "Don't take Bill off," he would tell Dorothy. So the two sat a few feet away and talked, or someone might bring out a guitar and, with a few beers, they all would sing.

In Memphis on other nights Faulkner remained in the parlor down-stairs drinking beer and "carrying on foolishness" with Mary Sharon and her girls. Playfully, Mary tried to talk him into going upstairs with her. Another of the girls, who was saving her money to go out west, also propositioned him, but Bill replied, "No, thank you, ma'am; I'm on my vacation." The younger prostitute, a "sweet, lean, country girl," looked at him blankly: "Where are you going to take your vacation?" One afternoon, when Stone, Faulkner, Major Oldham, and a third law-yer were waiting in Memphis to catch a train, the lawyer invited them to Mary's for a beer. Before going upstairs with a woman, their host began coarsely to tease the youngest member of the party, asking the prostitutes if they had ever "had a good time with little Billy." Faulkner did not create a scene, but Stone, quite aware how much "Bill resented his small size," knew the effort he made to keep his temper.

The poker skills Phil Stone had polished on Lafayette County players in college he now regularly employed in the hotel rooms, supper clubs, brothels, and surburban gambling houses with professionals. Another of the men with whom he played was Bob Berryman, a man the Memphis papers "variously referred to as the 'czar of Memphis night life' and a 'sportsman about town'—the latter when he donated $1,000 to a Christmas charity fund." In 1927, the year Phil Stone kept books on his winnings and subsequently renounced the game, the police discovered "a thriving Monte Carlo" run by Berryman in the Gehring Hotel at 84 Union, "in the heart of downtown." Nevertheless, only two years later Berryman reportedly invested a hundred thousand dollars in the Silver Slipper, "a plush nightclub on Macon Road just outside the city limits." "On opening night," newspaper columnists gossiped, "the '400' of Memphis society were among the 450 guests 'lucky enough to get reservations.'" None of those accounts mentioned Berryman's occupation. But at the Silver Slipper there were dice and roulette; and a few months after "several Memphians lost $4,000 to $6,000 apiece there," the owner paid a five-hundred dollar fine and did thirty days at the Penal Farm.

Poker in "fancy" places like the Silver Slipper was rigidly restricted by the professional gamblers' code, according to Phil Stone. The gamblers were quite particular about who played, assuredly; they insisted that the table be protected by the "rail"; and they were scrupulously honest about paying their debts—or a man got no cards. Flashy diamonds and stickpins protected the professionals through a momentary run of bad luck. Phil Stone was fascinated by everything about them. While those men often "won or lost ten or fifteen thousand dollars" in a day, Stone left the table whenever his winnings or losses totaled five hundred. Even though, as he said, "they knew he would not be money to them," the gamblers liked him and respected his skill.[48] Three gaming establishments in Memphis had even asked Stone to play for the house, he said, pleased at the compliment.

When the big games moved down to Clarksdale, Stone joined the

The Lawyer and the Poet

inner circle there too, although he was playing with strangers one night when some of his Delta companions grew suspicious at his winning pot after pot. The house broke in twenty-three decks of cards to see whether Stone had marked them, as the dealer also became persuaded that Phil was "too lucky." Yet Stone's run of luck continued—until he "broke up the game," a source of wonder in the "New World" bawdy district for months.

In the New World, where W. C. Handy lived in the early 1900s and black musicians played and sang the blues,[49] there were seven or eight whorehouses across the Greenwood, Clarksdale, and Memphis tracks, and a number of places such as Reno's Cafe. Dorothy Ware supervised one house there under the protection of "her man" Lee Brown, Phil's friend. The couple, in some respects, anticipate Faulkner's Reba Rivers and Mr. Binford in *Sanctuary*. The sexual fidelity of the former lady of the night, as befit her new status, was sacrosanct. Thus Dorothy was deeply hurt one night when Stone, and then Faulkner, managing straight faces, teased her, asking that she go to bed with them. As Stone recalled, "She was not to them a prostitute but a friend, and she was embarrassed." Dorothy Ware and Lee Brown had a rather stormy relationship, chiefly because of the times Brown often spent drunk or asleep "for several weeks." On such occasions, after he did not come home for twenty-four hours, Dot would drag all his suits out of the closet and throw them on the doorstep. After he sobered up, he knew, however, that Dorothy would exact only an innocuous, if unpleasant, penance: "*Get* your clothes and come on home."

Phil Stone alleged that he had later lost interest in cards and described the experiment that had convinced him to give up poker. Having thought then that he might make a career of his aptitude for cards, for the twelve months of 1927 he kept books on his expenses—gas, his car, lodging, food—the number of nights he played, and the amounts won or lost. Stone checked and rechecked his arithmetic, knowing his weakness with numbers; but the figures showed a net profit per day of over two dollars. Taking that into consideration, he reasoned further that the hours were bad and the "working conditions" debilitating; therefore, he concluded, despite his talent and experience, he could make a better life for himself practicing law. Thereafter poker ceased to be a major pastime.[50]

After they were married, Phil often told Emily Stone, "You've never known me when I was myself." By 1935, the vitality of the teens and twenties was somehow sapped, he felt. With Faulkner, Hudson, Katrina, "Sunshine," Dorothy, Brown, and soon with "the Bunch," his whole being was given free play. One of the quickening agents, of course, was that he had money then, which he spent as capriciously as any "Delta blade." In February 1922, for example, Lee Brown and Phil Stone were settling accounts for a recent Clarksdale "party"; the six or seven friends had spent fifty-five dollars in "supplies," "including the one at the Hotel," plus fifty dollars in cash. Brown was afraid that Stone would "stand" the bill himself. When he sent the check, Stone assured him that, no, "the other fellows are going to pay their share." Before that party bill was paid, however, hearing that Stone and his "friend" were coming over, Brown, "T. B.," and Reno were lining up another: "The Party is on," Lee wrote. "So be sure and don't disappoint us. . . . Dorothy said you don't owe her anything. But be sure and come over and bring the Poet." The lawyer and the poet did not make that gathering, but another was in the works for early March, when Phil had court in Sumner. Promising to wire Brown at Reno's Cafe, Stone sent his regards to them all, "especially Dorothy." [51]

But it was not only money that Stone missed by 1935. Like Merton Densher in *The Wings of the Dove:* "He suggested above all, however, that wondrous state of youth in which the elements, the metals more or less precious, are so in fusion and fermentation that the question of the final stamp, the pressure that fixes the value, must wait for comparative coolness." [52] Although Phil Stone probably did not recognize the signs, economic and societal changes were already afoot that would send North Mississippi and the world into the Great Depression, sound the death knell for men like General Stone, the last of the "cavaliers"— and fix the character of the last thirty-six years of Phil's life.

When the Lamb-Fish Lumber Company went into bankruptcy, the court appointed Jack Stone and Frank Kelly, a Chicago attorney, to act as receivers. It was a lengthy assignment, and both Phil Stone and Faulkner (but especially the latter) accompanied those officials on business trips. In spite of Faulkner's later claim to Malcolm Cowley that he was "friend," "drinking companion," "assistant," and "sometimes a secretary" to one of the receivers, Stone said Faulkner was never actually in their employ, but that he was "a voluntary companion for Frank Kelly . . . and Bill and Frank drank whiskey together." Faulkner told Cowley too that "he was about to go to Cuba as an interpreter" on Lamb-Fish business when Stark Young invited him to New York. Faulkner added other details in the semiautobiographical article that he wrote for *Holiday* magazine: "His official capacity was that of interpreter, since he had a little French and the defuncting company had European connections. But no interpreting was ever done, since the entourage did not go to Europe but moved instead into a single floor of a Memphis hotel, where all—including the interpreter—had the privilege of signing chits for food and theater tickets and even the bootleg whisky." [53] That fiction seems closest to the truth.

The Lamb-Fish money was so plentiful that while the case was in progress even the drinking companion lived extravagantly. But Jack Stone, like his father, had always been a money-maker—as well as a spendthrift. Jack traveled to Chicago, especially, a great deal anyway. Whenever he returned, fur coats, barrels of Haviland china or crystal came with him—for Myrtle, whom he always treated royally. (According to Jack's youngest daughter, "When we were babies, he kept us so Mother could sleep late. When we woke up at five-thirty or six, he took us in his arms to the coffee shop on the courthouse square and got a spoon and fed us coffee while he talked to the men.") As the big fees continued to pour in, Jack and Myrtle Stone bought a summer house in Pascagoula and employed a chauffeur, cooks, and nurses; they were planning a trip to Chicago for the World's Fair at the time of his death. [54]

It is worth noting that Jack Stone earned larger fees from liquidating companies than in his other specialty, setting up new corporations. [55] William L. Giles, writing about the decade in the Bicentennial *History of Mississippi*, calls the period "Boom, bust, and boll weevils," and argues that in Mississippi the Depression actually began in 1920. Just after the Armistice, the Delta especially had been "more prosperous than at any time since the beginning of the Civil War." In expectation of "dollar cotton" by July, the planters had held their 1919 cotton crops, and prices rose to 38.5 cents a pound in April 1920. But after April, the market collapsed; a price of 13.7 cents was recorded, then "a low of 9.8 cents in April 1921." (By 1931 the price of lint had fallen even further, to 6.16 cents).[56] Numerous others joined Lamb-Fish executives in bankruptcy proceedings. There was a clock ticking away for the Stones too. Jack, General Stone, and then Jim would die in the middle of the debacle, leaving Myrtle, Phil, and Matsy to try to reconstruct their lives. Only Myrtle Stone would be equal to the challenge.

In Oxford in 1921 General Stone began putting pressure on Phil to return home. With his sons in Charleston, James Stone, sixty-five in 1919, had practiced alone only an interval before inviting Lemuel E. Oldham, his vice-president at the Bank of Oxford, to join the firm. Early in 1919, "Major" Oldham, subsequently William Faulkner's father-in-law, had resigned his federal clerkship, after sixteen years, to practice law. One of the accounts Oldham brought with him was that of the Kosciusko & Southeastern Railroad.[57] (When Estelle's father operated a coal yard and icehouse later, Phil Stone was always much amused at the glass on the Major's office door, with its gilded lettering "The Old-ham Interests.") Lem Oldham was "the original Republican in this part of Mississippi," Stone said. His daughter Dorothy, a "black-and-tan" Republican, later was a delegate to the National Convention. Thus, the Oldhams can hardly be described as popular in Oxford. Neverthe-less, the firm letterhead, contrary to legal precedent, soon read "James Stone, Oldham, Stone & Stone." "It sounds like a dern gravel pit," de-clared Phil's friend Herb Fant, a Sardis attorney. Whether he planned it that way or not, it was a shrewd alliance for General Stone.

Major Oldham seems to have liked Phil Stone and Bill Faulkner, but it was he, and perhaps not inadvertently, who shortly curtailed their visits to Mary Sharon's and the New World. In the spring of 1921 Old-ham, a "Harding man," was appointed United States attorney for the Northern District. Soon after his confirmation, he recommended to the attorney general that Phil Stone be appointed his assistant, and by autumn Phil had the salaried position. Stone's brother Jack had been assistant district attorney from 1907 to 1914; by 1923 Phil, evidently as fond of being federal prosecutor as Faulkner was of being postmaster, returned the post to his brother.[58]

Faulkner in the meantime managed a brief trip east before Major Oldham forced respectability on him. Since quitting the university, Faulkner had used his father's house as a base, and Stone as a bank; when not with Stone or in Clarksdale, he was writing, or developing "his strong wrists," said Stone, playing golf, habits he supported by looking after the university course and selling soft drinks. When Stone was short of money, Bill painted an occasional house, fired boilers, or hung wallpaper. As a result, "Count William," as the university students had called him, had become "Count No Count" to the men around the square. He was an embarrassment to the family.

One summer day Faulkner's Uncle John, Stone said, "was standing in front of the First National Bank on the street corner hanging onto the mailbox (his favorite podium), and cussin' Bill to a group of men standing there: 'that damn Billy is not worth a Mississippi goddamn—and never will be. Won't hold a job; won't try; won't do anything! He's a Falkner and I hate to say it about my own nephew, but, hell, there's a black sheep in everybody's family and Billy's ours. Not worth a cent.'" Stone had come up during the tail end of the oratory and, quite aware of the discrepancy between the talents of the nephew and the "judge" who knew no law, countered in deliberate politeness: "No, sir, Judge Falkner, you're wrong about Bill. I'll make you a prediction. There'll be people coming to Oxford on account of Bill who would never have heard of the place except for Bill and what he writes." "Ah, hell!" John Falkner said, walking off, "that goddamn tripe Billy writes!" At other times Phil's remarks that Faulkner "was a writer of ability and would one day be more famous than Stark Young," may have underscored Murry Falkner's suspicions of Stone's negative influence on his exasperating son.[59]

At the same time, Oxford's senior writer, Stark Young, smothering in academe, resigned his chair at Amherst on the strength of an offer to join the editorial board of *Theatre Arts Magazine* and a hint of a position at the *New Republic* in 1922. After a summer in Italy and Sicily, he would move into the basement of Elizabeth Prall's brownstone at 51 Charlton Street in New York City. Soon after his return from Europe, Young had made a short trip home where he saw Stone and Faulkner. As he wrote in *The Pavilion*, "It seemed to me more and more futile that anyone so remarkable as . . . [Faulkner] should be thus bruised and wasted, and so I proposed that he should come to New York. I promised that my friend Elizabeth Prall [sister of his friend and traveling companion David Prall], who directed an important bookstore, could give him a job there to tide him over till he could settle into something that suited him better, and meanwhile he was more than welcome to stay with me."

Later, Stone told Carvel Collins that Faulkner had decided to make the trip "partly in order to be nearer publishers who might accept his poetry."[60] Whether that was Stone's advice or Young's, or Faulkner's own idea, is not clear; nor is it clear whether the trip itself was Stone's suggestion, as he later claimed.[61] At another time, when Faulkner felt that living in Greenwich Village could be stimulating, Stone argued against it, first noting the disparate per capita ratio of "characters" in Lafayette County and Manhattan. "In the second place," he said, "you'll get up there and *talk* out your writing and not write." More respectful of Stark Young in 1921 than later, and perhaps not yet so much distrustful of "literary people," Phil may in fact have suggested the temporary change of scenery. But almost immediately he began lobbying efforts that would bring Bill home, reluctantly, after less than two months.

With a hundred-dollar stake from house-painting jobs, Faulkner bought his ticket for New York but arrived only to discover that Young would not be at home for a week. Faulkner may even have gone up before Young completely moved in, sometime after 10 October. In that interval, apparently, for several weeks he "spent . . . a second and rather poignant sojourn at New Haven," according to Carvel Collins, "writing seriously and trying to place what he wrote with publishers, but . . . also . . . trying seriously to improve his graphic skills, especially with pencil and colored crayon." He supplemented the forty dollars left after his fare by washing dishes in a Greek restaurant in order to eat. When Young returned, he made good his promise to recommend Faulkner to Miss Prall, manager of the Doubleday Doran Bookstore in the "carriage driveway" of Lord & Taylor on Fifth Avenue at 43rd Street. She hired him for the pre-Christmas rush.[62]

Hardly a month had passed when Stone heard that there was another political appointment in the offing in Mississippi. His former classmate D. R. Johnson, university postmaster since 1914, had decided to resign in November to open a law practice in Panola County. Unlike poker, the job in such a small post office promised easy hours, comfortable working conditions, and enough quiet that a poet might even manage reading and writing on the job. The fifteen-hundred-dollar salary also

The Lawyer and the Poet

surpassed Doubleday's eleven dollars a week. To Stone the position was made to order for Bill Faulkner. Phil took the matter up with his partner and patron, and Major Oldham arranged for Faulkner to become temporary postmaster with the understanding that if Bill went through the motions of the civil service exam and other red tape, the job would be his on a permanent basis.

When the conspirators notified Faulkner, however, he wired back, "NO THANKS." But Stone kept after him, and after a fight Bill, disappointed in New York anyway, capitulated and returned home. On Saturday, 10 December 1921, Faulkner was in Oxford taking the civil service exam with W. B. Potts and army veteran Evern Jones. Despite the results, the temporary appointee would stay on in the federal employ for almost three years, years to Faulkner of sheer misery. To Stone, however, it was a matter of practical necessity for his talented friend, and, later, a source of some of the best stories in Faulkner biography: "I forced Bill to take the job over his own inclination and refusal. He made the damndest postmaster the world has ever seen."[63]

Although Oldham and Stone believed the matter wrapped up, during the generally routine Senate confirmation the next spring, Mississippi Senator Pat Harrison stalled briefly while he weighed the relative political advantages of choosing between two "friends," or, as he explained it to Stone in May, sometimes the "requests of friends collide and in that event one must exercise his best judgment." Lieutenant Evern Jones, like Senator Harrison from Greene County, not only had made the highest civil service score, but during the political campaign of 1918 he had persuaded his regiment to vote their absentee ballots for Harrison rather than for James K. Vardaman. The senator was also "very close" to Jones's family.

Until Phil's letter, Harrison was not aware that Faulkner too was his "friend"; what Harrison did know was that "some members" of the Falkner clan were "opposed to me politically," or at least "friendly to those men who are unfriendly politically to me." "I naturally hesitated," Harrison wrote, "and wanted to know why [Jones] was side-tracked for Faulkner." Soon after Stone's letter, however, the senator "requested the Committee having the matter in charge to report out the nomination of Falkner and he has since been confirmed," for which "you and Lem Oldham can take the credit," as he wrote Phil. Harrison,

Senate nursemaid to much of the New Deal legislation, did lose the game of politics a few times—his bitterest loss when he was defeated by one vote for Roosevelt's majority leader—with Senator Theodore Bilbo, his Mississippi colleague, voting against him.[64] However, in this case, opting for the continuing support of James Stone, Oldham, Stone & Stone, Harrison found it expedient to support a Republican and a suspected Vardamanite. As he wrote Phil Stone, "I have always tried to deal openly and on the square. It is the only safe road for one in public life to travel."[65]

Harrison must not have been aware of the extent to which the Stone influence was already being eroded. On 12 January 1922 the front page of the *Eagle* announced General Stone's resignation as president of the Bank of Oxford. Two years before, James Stone had been as surprised as everyone else in town when his rival J. W. T. Falkner had walked into the Bank of Oxford swinging a pair of tin buckets as if he were coming to put out a fire. For once, George Knight, the head cashier, had been at a loss for words. "The Colonel," he said, recovering somewhat in Stone's office, "the Colonel wants to open an account." General Stone had issued expletives appropriate for the occasion and sent Knight back out front to help Abe Linker sort the currency, coins, papers, and notes of his late competitor, for deposit into the vaults across from the First National Bank—where J. A. Parks now sat in the president's chair. Economic conditions since that coup d'etat were not to be glossed over by newspaper hyperbole to the effect that in 1921 the Bank of Oxford, the "oldest and strongest" Lafayette County bank, enjoyed "one of the most prosperous years in its long and successful history." Seven banks in Mississippi had closed since Colonel Falkner's ouster.

There were additional factors involved in General Stone's "wish to be relieved of the active management of the Bank" besides his desire for more time to "devote . . . to his law practice." Soon after the 1914 Mississippi banking law was enacted, establishing a state banking department, a guaranty fund, and regulations about reserve requirements and incorporation, the Bank of Oxford had challenged the new law in court, hoping "to enjoin the state bank examiners from interfering with its stockholders and directors in administering its internal affairs and seeking to recover the money it had paid for support of the banking department." James Stone & Son, representing the bank, lost the case before the state Supreme Court in 1916 and again on appeal to the U.S. Supreme Court in 1919. With his executive powers thus constricted, the sixty-seven-year-old Stone might just as well turn over crop loans and foreclosures to a younger man, albeit one who would respect "his sage advice and financial acumen" as he stayed on as major stockholder and bank attorney. Although the board and the stockholders sought to dissuade him, "finally, though very reluctantly," they accepted his resignation. It was some comfort to James Stone that, unlike those at Falkner's old bank, the directors of his bank were all "gentlemen."[66]

It was apparently within days of his resignation that General Stone summoned his youngest son home permanently, but Phil was only too happy to comply. In one of the earliest letters of the extant Brick Row correspondence, Al DeLacey is curious about his friend's sudden change of address: "What does your return to Oxford signify? Hope it means you have made enough money in your short term as assistant prosecuting attorney to retire for life and buy all the books you want." In reality, his father's decision to turn management of the bank over to others, in conjunction with other events, would within a decade force Phil's virtual retirement, not from the law, but from literature.[67]

7

The Marble Faun

UPON HIS RETURN to Oxford from Charleston, Phil's immediate responsibility was to cheer up both the aging father now sitting with time on his hands in the sun room at the office and the morose young poet serving time at the university post office. Each was quite capable of turning to the bottle in his despair. James Stone had too much energy to sit for long, however, and he soon became absorbed again in practicing law, in part out of necessity—his son certainly was not tending to the Oxford business with any diligence. Ebullient in spirits from being home (and from having a steady flow of cash), Phil Stone seems once again to have been engaged primarily in a feverish literary promotion.

When Stone wrote Faulkner that he "expect[ed] to come over home to stay sometime between the fifteenth and the 19th" of January 1922, the two were already making plans to publish some of Faulkner's work in "pamphlets." They probably had in mind not hand-lettered booklets like *The Lilacs*, but gatherings of typed poems that Faulkner would bind and title, like *A Vision in Spring*, a gift he had presented to Estelle Franklin upon her visit to Oxford the previous summer. The new Faulkner publication was to be heralded by an anonymous letter to the *Commercial Appeal*, presumably with Phil Stone's prediction that the time was then ripe for Southern letters and that there was a young writer from Oxford whose work would put the region at the forefront of modern literature. The men had seen H. L. Mencken's "The Sahara of the

Bozart," probably in *Prejudices: Second Series* (1920), and had been excited when the *Double Dealer* began publication in January 1921 as if rising to meet the Mencken challenge.[1]

It was becoming fashionable now for educated Southerners to berate the Philistines: one Sunday in early January, Stone noted a *Commercial Appeal* editorial "entitled 'Lip Service to Art' a criticism of the people of Memphis for their failure to attend a certain series of concerts and a number of Shakespearean plays." This glimmer of cultural awareness offered "the golden opportunity" for Phil's letter, as he wrote Van Kincannon, an Ole Miss friend then in New York to find a publisher for his own poetry manuscript.

The next step in Stone's plan was for "Skeet" Kincannon to follow Phil's letter to the *Commercial Appeal* with a review of Faulkner's work for the Memphis paper. In return, Stone and Faulkner promised "to do a little log rolling" when Kincannon's book appeared. Phil thought that he "could get the book reviewed in the Double Dealer of New Orleans and the New Republic," if Van wished. Stark Young was their *New Republic* contact, of course, and Phil and Bill "sometime ago" had met John McClure of the *Double Dealer* staff, who had been "favorably impressed with some verse of Mr. Faulkner."

On 18 February 1922 Stone returned to the scheme when he wrote Al DeLacey at the Brick Row: "Bill is getting along fine and is turning out some very good stuff. I took him over to Clarksdale last week and gave him a party. I think he had the time of his life. I have a friend there who is a professional gambler, and he got us two quarts of Johnnie Walker. After that, it was almost impossible to keep up with him. We are going to get his pamphlets out very soon—as soon, in fact, as I overcome my inertia sufficiently to write an open letter to the Memphis papers." Perhaps the pamphlets were to be the "Mississippi Poems" Stone sketched out again on a title page in 1924, and Stone's regional propaganda was to be supplemented by publicity circulated from the New Haven bookshop.[2]

The campaigns of Phil Stone were usually studied and undaunted affairs, and it may have been with ulterior motives that he initiated another literary contact in early spring 1922. He received a reply from 28 West 8th Street, New York, in a letter dated 7 March 1922:

Dear Mr. Stone,

Let me thank you for the poem by Swinburne—which I do not remember, though I must have seen it—and for your interesting comment. I should have said Swinburne, if only for the line, "All the sting and all the stain of long delight—." On the other hand I "see what you mean" and thank you for your courtesy. I am glad to infer from your note that you and your friend have found something in my work that you remember.

Yours very sincerely,

E. A. Robinson[3]

Stone's correspondent, whose *Collected Poems* (1921) was awarded the Pulitzer Prize for poetry in 1922, was well represented among the first editions of Stone's select, private collection of "comers." (Two copies of one volume in Phil's library were autographed by Edwin Arlington Robinson.) Stone was undoubtedly flattered that a major poet had found his remarks of interest; yet the exchange effected, it seems, no more tangible issue.

Indeed the design to introduce poet Faulkner to the world of letters in 1922 would not mature. Probably Phil merely procrastinated further with his *Commercial Appeal* letter, and the two men confronted at last the realities attendant to their impressing a working legal secretary into the tedious reproduction of even a dozen "pamphlets," much less the small edition their grandiose publicity implied. At any rate, in the spring of 1922 poetry alone was no longer sufficient enchantment for Stone and Faulkner, because they had begun tentatively to explore, with their friend Bess Storer, the dimensions of prose.

During the beginning of Faulkner's closest association with younger Oxford friends called "the Bunch," in 1921, and especially in the spring of 1922, Edith Brown implies, it was Ben Wasson then who most encouraged Bill to write poetry: "Phil, however, was interested in seeing Bill write down the stories which he could tell aloud so well." In either genre, she contends, "To say that Phil 'encouraged' Bill, as so many biographers do, is gross understatement. He cajoled, browbeat, and swore at him; he threatened and pleaded; encouragement came later."[4] After reading only promising Faulkner poetry (and two or three manuscript plays) over the last eight years, a man versed in poker odds could easily have thought it time his friend broaden his range (as, three decades later, with Phil's approval his student Emily Stone turned from fiction to drama). That Stone's advice to Faulkner also was to write "stories" lends support to the claim Phil made later to more than one incredulous Faulkner scholar—that it was fiction he had wanted Bill to write all along.

There can be little doubt that by 1922 the art of fiction had become for Stone and Faulkner a conscious pursuit. In Phil's extant Brick Row orders for that year—twice remarked on in New Haven for being unusually "generous"—fiction outnumbers verse by more than two to one. His requests generally are for current novels, like F. Scott Fitzgerald's *The Beautiful and Damned*, D. H. Lawrence's *Aaron's Rod*, and Aldous Huxley's *Crome Yellow* (among others whose titles are now obscure). One of the March orders, however, was for Melville's *Moby-Dick*. Perhaps more telling is that Percy Lubbock's *The Craft of Fiction* was also charged to Stone's account that month. In addition, there was a curious nonfiction miscellany among the 1922 orders: Max Stirner, *The Ego and His Own*; Walter Lippmann, *Public Opinion*; H. L. Mencken, *The American Language*; historian James H. Robinson's *The Mind in the Making*; and Louis Berman's *The Glands Regulating Personality*. Moreover, Stone bought seven volumes of the Loeb Classical Library in 1922.[5]

Whatever else such selections indicate, these inferences appear sound: if there were now a conscious decision by the two men that Faulkner write fiction, they planned to go about it scientifically. The human heart must be dissected for character motivation, hence the new psychology books. If one were to sell fiction rationally, it was a good idea to be exhaustively familiar with what publishers buy; thus in fiction especially the orders read like the year's trade lists. To facilitate that survey, it was also useful to write reviews for publication whenever possible. There might be some money and recognition in it, and writing reviews forced one to weigh the strengths and weaknesses of his contemporaries and competitors. Faulkner was a veteran college reviewer of poetry and even drama, but in his final appearance in Lucy Somerville's "Books and Things," in December 1922, he reviewed three Joseph Hergesheimer novels that are listed among Stone's Brick Row orders.[6]

As for the classics on those lists, from Yale contacts, from their acquaintance (at least) with the *Double Dealer* circle in New Orleans, and from their reading in the little magazines, Stone and Faulkner, Phil implied later, had begun early to scent the modern fascination with ancient myth and to note the increasing cultivation of mythic allusion as a powerful literary device. According to his widow, Stone at one time owned a one-volume edition of Sir James G. Frazer's *The Golden Bough* (1922); he and Faulkner had at least heard of Freud and Jung; they would read *The Waste Land* in the *Dial* in November 1922, and James Joyce as soon as they could get the books (not before 1924, it seems).

They may have read excerpts from *Ulysses* as early as the serialization in the *Little Review* beginning in March 1918. Before they saw the complete novel, however, Stone read T. S. Eliot's "Ulysses, Order, and Myth" in the *Dial* for November 1923 and apparently took note there of a passage he pointed out later to R. P. Adams: "In using the myth, in manipulating a continuous parallel between contemporaneity and antiquity, Mr. Joyce is pursuing a method which others must pursue after him. . . . It is a way of controlling, of ordering, or giving a shape and a significance to the immense panorama of futility and anarchy which is contemporary history. . . . Psychology . . . ethnology, and *The Golden Bough* make possible what was impossible even a few years ago. Instead of narrative method, we may now use the mythical method." Eliot's idea would quickly become dogma to Phil Stone; anyone who subsequently attempted fiction, he intoned, "must go to school to Joyce." [7]

Even before John McClure at the *Double Dealer* published "Portrait" (June 1922), Faulkner's second poem in a professional journal, the writer had himself begun to experiment with fiction. "Landing in Luck," his first published story, had appeared in the campus newspaper almost two years earlier. Vastly dissimilar to the poems of the period in tone, diction, and content, its analogues are the apochryphal war stories with which Faulkner had diverted acquaintances and strangers. More recently, other aviation fictions, along with Far Eastern touches perhaps borrowed from the experiences of Cornell and Estelle Franklin, apparently supplied the raw materials for "Love," a draft of a melodramatic story the writer set in 1921.

Faulkner would tell bibliographer James Meriwether that another work, "Moonlight," written sometime between 1919 and 1921, was "about the first short story I ever wrote." The sexual anxiety of that story's two young "sophisticates," who resort to corn whiskey to assist their dalliance with prostitutes and the virginal Cecily; the small-town settings of drugstore fountain, courthouse lawn, and dark verandas— in such details William Faulkner is clearly beginning to mine the Mississippi world he shared with Phil Stone.

Early in 1922, however, the apprentice undertook a more ambitious project, in the ambiguous plane between poetry and prose. On 10 March 1922 the *Mississippian* published "The Hill" by William Faulkner, a short prose sketch of a day laborer poised for an instant on a hill crest at sunset. The style may owe something to Amy Lowell's attempts at "polyphonic prose," but the central figure whose inarticulate impressions Faulkner tries to render concretely seems one with the enigmatic silhouette inspiring E. A. Robinson's dark pentameter ruminations in "The Man Against the Sky." Later that March, Phil Stone submitted a Faulkner story to John McClure at the *Double Dealer.*[8]

Although in 1922 the Stone law firm employed another stenographer ("k"), some of Faulkner's early stories may have been typed by Bessie Storer, a young woman who worked for Major Oldham and Stone in the U.S. attorney's office at the Oxford post office. Stone was always respectful of Storer's intelligence, and apparently she carried her weight in Phil's ongoing literary colloquium. Instead of joining Stone's lending library, Bess opened her own account with the Brick Row bookstore, and ordered Bill's first novel in 1926 from his publishers. O. B. Emerson, a friend of Bess at the time of her death in 1956, says that she frequently spoke of Stone and Faulkner, "always glowingly" of Stone, "sometimes critical[ly] of Falkner." Yet for thirty years Bess Storer carefully preserved some items she had retrieved one afternoon from a trash can: "a sketch of a cowboy on a bucking bronco, a figure of an old man, and several heads," signed and dated by Faulkner on 3 June 1922.[9]

It was probably in the same year that the trio—Stone, Faulkner, and Storer—instigated their nightly reading of Phil's earlier discovery Balzac's *La Comédie humaine.* W. H. Wright's *Creative Will* had persuaded Phil Stone to view the French novelist as the master of fiction— and to regard the proper reading of Balzac as a significant aesthetic test: "It is only the able literary craftsman who consciously and analytically traces every word and phrase and device of a book who can read Balzac, for instance, over and over again with increasing pleasure." Such a reader, Wright implied, would discern in Balzac "the colossal literary architect," whose designs were not the "simple block form of composition" illustrated in literature by the prosaic structure "'theme with variation.'" Instead, Balzac sometimes (like Conrad in *Youth* and *Victory*) achieved the "higher" and "more complex type of composition" Wright denoted as "rhythmic order," i.e., organic design. Its effect was of "an eternal becoming, like life itself":

> . . . Balzac, a profound philosopher, follows the methods of nature and lets the effect result from a bringing together of fundamental causes and life forces. Balzac creates first a terrain with an environmental climate; and the creatures which *spring from this soil*, and which are *a part of it*, create certain unescapable conditions, social, economic, and intellectual. Furthermore, the generations of characters that follow are, in turn, the inevitable offsprings of this later *soil*, fashioned by all that preceded them. [italics mine] [10]

At the conclusion of their Balzac seminar Faulkner and Bess Storer would have been prepared to stand an examination on *The Creative Will*, for Phil apparently invoked Wright's concepts as often as he plagiarized the critic's words. A half-century before Stone chose as his epitaph "Here is my Earth," Phil was preaching, in art as in life, the determinism of "soil." The *Marble Faun* poems, like their author, Stone's preface would insist, had "roots in this soil as surely and inevitably as . . . a tree"; behind that stylized literary landscape, Phil Stone claimed to see "a man steeped in the soil of his native land." Ironically, other extant external clues to Faulkner's indoctrination in W. H. Wright on fiction date from later, embittered periods when Phil Stone employed Wright as touchstone no longer to instruct or praise but to criticize his onetime pupil. In a 1931 letter to Louis Cochran, Phil would allege, incongruously, that his "present discouragement" over his friend's career stemmed from his skepticism about whether Faulkner's "having his roots in this soil" would "ever be articulate in prose." (Stone held steadfastly to the idea that in poetry Faulkner's creations did bespeak "this part of him," advising Cochran to examine the forthcoming *Green Bough* to confirm Stone's 1924 preface.) [11]

Far more obvious, in retrospect, is that behind the "rhythmic order" of Yoknapatawpha stand Faulkner instructors Balzac, Wright, and Phil

Stone. But Phil later could not, or would not, see it. Instead, he would choose to believe, as he wrote Malcolm Cowley in 1945, "that Faulkner apparently lacks any comprehensive sense of design."[12]

There was another feature of Faulkner's work that drew Stone's criticism in a 1931 letter to Yale printer Carl Rollins: "The most unpromising thing of all to me, however, is that [Faulkner] seems to completely lack that richness and exuberance that invariably goes with the highest type of genius in Balzac, Shakespeare, Fielding, Goethe, etc. I am heartily in favor of the modern style of spareness and economy of treatment but Bill seems to me like he has to use up every chip and shaving in everything he produces. There is none of that sense of plenty which produces enough crums [sic] left over to feed a mob."[13] The surviving manuscripts and the variant printed versions of any single Faulkner work provide overwhelming evidence of how often the frugal writer did indeed rework and revise, recycling the chips and shavings—even the timbers—of his lathe. For that and other reasons, it is often rank speculation to date his early compositions, especially the unpublished fiction of the early twenties.

But there are tantalizing traces. Circumstantial evidence suggests that in 1922 and 1923 the poet assayed his talents in a much longer narrative form.

In the summer of 1922 Phil Stone thought wistfully of a return to New England. Al DeLacey had promised him tennis, golf, and a place to stay in New Haven. Stone did order tickets for the annual Harvard–Yale game that autumn, but business grew so negligible over the summer that, caught by September in a familiar "dry spell," he stopped ordering books from Brick Row "until my account is again on the right side of the ledger." Unable to afford a trip East, Stone mailed the football tickets to his young Alston cousin Polly Clark, a student at Westover School in Middlebury. But in November, worrying that his alumni tickets might not be transferable, Stone asked DeLacey to make sure Polly could use them without embarrassment. As it turned out, Polly's school refused her permission to attend and she passed the tickets on to a teacher, who got to see Harvard beat Yale once again. But what is significant in the fuss over the football tickets is that the seventeen-year-old was well acquainted with William Faulkner from his having gone to Clarksdale so often with Stone "for court." And when she wrote thanking Phil for the tickets, she inquired too about Faulkner's work: "How is Bill getting along with his novel and his book of poetry?" The date is 7 December 1922.[14]

Within six months Faulkner would offer his revised poems to a publisher, but the scant literary remains from 1923 offer no clue to the fate of his other writing. Perhaps the fiction in progress with which Polly Clark was acquainted was one of the two novels Faulkner later confessed to having destroyed. At any rate, there seems nothing else to suggest that Stone's and Faulkner's interest in fiction was waning. For Christmas 1923 the writer gave his friend Aldous Huxley's *Antic Hay* (1923) and James Branch Cabell's *Jurgen: A Comedy of Justice* (1919). Faulkner apparently had acquired his own copy of the latter earlier the same year. Moreover, Faulkner may have bought his first Sherwood Anderson book then, for among the Rowan Oak volumes is a first edition of *Horses and Men: Tales, Long and Short, from Our American Life* (1923).[15]

Had poet-novelist Faulkner lived among Greenwich Village or French Quarter literati in 1922 and 1923, the envious, the jealous, and the admiring there later might have reminisced in detail of the manuscripts of those years. But the papers over which Faulkner toiled in private did not enthrall the young persons in whose company he and Phil Stone spent most of their leisure in the early twenties. "Nothing is more fatal to the creation of a living and growing art than the dead hand of culture," Stone argued in his 1934 Faulkner essay; and Oxford, Mississippi, university or no, was remarkably innocent of culture, according to Phil Stone, its citizens "quite wisely living life instead of talking about life or writing about life or reading much about it."[16]

When the experiments faltered or his writing grew stale, for example, Faulkner amused himself by directing the elaborate "paper chases" with the faculty children that Calvin Brown describes in *William Faulkner of Oxford;* shortly thereafter he became scoutmaster for the Oxford troop. Faulkner even persuaded sedentary Phil Stone to join one afternoon of "hare and hounds": "It nearly killed him," Brown says. "It was probably the first time Phil had been off a sidewalk in ten years. After that, Phil confined his association with the youth of Oxford to something more in his line—taking a group of girls considerably younger than he (including my sister Edith) to the drugstore for sodas and milk shakes."[17]

Actually both " 'older men,' " in Edith's words, "adopted" the half-dozen girls of Edith Brown's "Bunch" and their male contemporaries, for whom Stone's coupé and law office became virtually communal property. When Edith was to be a bridesmaid in a Delta wedding, Phil Stone and Bill Faulkner convened planning sessions to coordinate the usual details. Flowers, telegrams, Special Delivery "love letters," and long distance telephone calls always were to accompany the *"femme fatales* who . . . left desolation behind in Oxford's male population by even brief absence." To further impress the men from Sardis or Holly Springs whom their Oxford girls fancied, Phil staged front-porch scenes in which, as the visiting suitor watched from the swing, Stone roared up to the curb, brakes squealing, slammed the door, and strode up the front walk to the girl's porch. The gist of the impassioned (male) and tearful (female) dialogue was that the girl must renounce her new beau or break off forever with Stone. Reluctantly, of course, she chose the stranger, who now knew himself to be "hot stuff," Stone said.

Looking back, Edith Brown Douds recognized a rare "kindness and perception" in the seriousness with which Stone and Faulkner had undertaken those productions. The younger boys had often tired of the office plotting. " 'Sister Edith don't need all that help,' said one of them crossly. 'Everybody needs all the help he can get,' replied Bill."[18]

During their courtship in the mid-teens, when Katrina Carter left Stone to cool his heels in the parlor well past the hour appointed for their dates, once or twice Phil had walked out on her. More disinterested now, and perhaps suspecting that Edith at least was somewhat infatuated with him, Phil adopted with the young women the avuncular, beneficent persona he assumed with his brothers' children. The intrinsic comedy of the bachelor's gallant drugstore "assignations," however, did not escape the town—or William Faulkner, who would exploit it in Gavin Stevens's "avuncular" concern for Linda Snopes.[19] Stone delighted in "campaigns," moreover, and in devising tactics whereby his "sisters" vanquished their social rivals, he may have been sublimating his own social—and sexual—insecurities. It was not the last time that Stone's ego would feed upon vicarious satisfactions.

Perhaps only Faulkner was aware that in the same period Stone was himself carrying on a relationship by mail with a young Memphis woman. Over four years, including the Four Seas negotiations, and extending into 1926, Marian Davis received personal letters, Faulkner manuscript poems, two copies of *The Marble Faun*, and letters of introduction to Byrne Hackett and Stark Young in New York—all without ever meeting either Phil Stone or William Faulkner. As it happened, the acquaintance was otherwise typical, as Marian Davis Chamberlin explains: "Honestly—it seems *so* silly—but I never in my life laid eyes on Phil Stone—nor William Faulkner either—though Phil & I carried on a rather voluminous correspondence. His father was my father's lawyer down in Oxford—for at the time my daddy was operating some lumber mills at Taylor and, having no son, he decided I should know about his business—and be of help to him also when I was home from school (Jr. college) & then Art School."

At first merely amanuenses for General Stone and for Marian's father, Henry Jefferson Davis, the two soon were exchanging opinions and talking books. Stone would write her "about this young friend of his who was showing great promise as a writer," and enclose "poems by Faulkner for me to read and comment on."[20]

Although she has forgotten the incident, at the height of their correspondence, when she went to New York to buy for a Memphis "specialty shop," Davis intimated to Phil her ambition of "going on the stage." On a subsequent trip East in July 1926 she carried the letters from Stone to Young and Hackett. Phil asked Mr. Stark to "put her in touch" with persons in the Theater Guild and told him that "if you will help her I shall appreciate it as much as a favor to me personally." Stone thought that Byrne Hackett's brother Francis might have theater contacts as well. Ten days later, however, Stone wrote Marian Davis at the Gotham Hotel that he had just learned Young was in Europe and that Hackett had written that he knew few stage people after all. Perhaps after the evaporation of his "contacts," Phil had qualms about ever meeting her face to face. In 1977, in conversations with book collectors, Mrs. Chamberlin would advise them to sit down before she related the denouement of her story: "I burned up a hatbox full of Faulkner manuscripts & typescripts—with hand written notes—and Phil's letters—when I was clearing out a closet before getting married in 1928."[21]

In sharp contrast, the friendship that Stone renewed with William
McNeil Reed in the summer of 1923 and the subsequent affection of
Bill Faulkner, Phil Stone, and Mack Reed had almost nothing to do
with the written word.[22] When the Ole Miss alumnus first returned to
Oxford from Chickasaw County in July 1923, he worked as a pharma-
cist at the Gathright Drug Store on the north side of the square. Reed's
future partner Byron Gathright, the owner's son, and Branham Hume,
an associate of the Bunch, ran the soda fountain at the drugstore. In
1923 and 1924 Phil Stone often drank a Coke there after work before
setting off with Bill Faulkner "on one of their long walks," Reed recalls.
But the link among the three men was otherwise forged.

The recent loss of a brother who wanted to be a writer kindled Mack
Reed's empathy for Stone and Faulkner's literary preoccupation.[23] The
work, however, was really as foreign to Reed as the speakeasies and
brothels where the pair spent their leisure. Yet, completely free of the
intolerance so often accompanying the naturally good men of fun-
damental faith, Mack Reed loved and supported Phil Stone and Bill
Faulkner—without judging them.

The services Mack rendered Bill Faulkner were as unpretentious
as the man himself: a small loan before the Liveright contract (when
Faulkner, for collateral, left his gold piece, in its drawstring velvet
pouch); the New York papers and the *Saturday Evening Post*s that Bill
read sprawled on the floor in front of the store's magazine rack; the
Faulkner manuscripts that Reed packaged, "only a few times," he insisted, to mail to the publishers. In the forties and fifties the writer's
morning ritual in Oxford usually included a short visit with Reed at the
pharmacy after one with Stone at the post office.

But Mack Reed's employment in the "public domain" at Gathright-
Reed—and his instinctive diplomacy—designated him for further,
often annoying Faulkner service, as "forwarding agent" for the professors, book collectors, and celebrity-seekers who in time descended
upon Oxford. Some wished to know about Faulkner's drinking, or
Faulkner's women, at which point Mack Reed changed the subject.
Serious students he referred to Stone or to Maud Falkner, "after first
telephoning them," for additional screening. Only once would the two
friends quarrel, though predictably as a result of Mack's precarious
literary duties. After a reporter had divulged some item of Faulkner

biography, "Bill came in [to Gathright-Reed] with fire in his eyes. 'You *talk* too much!'" he lashed out. "'Well, maybe I *listen* too much!'" Reed fired back. The man who "only needed to be fitted for wings to fly up to Heaven," according to Phil Stone, also could stand his ground, even with a bullying Faulkner.

As junior members of Oxford's professional community, Stone and Reed were frequently engaged in civic affairs, from which Faulkner's singular occupation usually excused him. During an early political campaign involving Bill's uncle, the Falkners persuaded Mack to accompany the J. W. T. Falkner entourage to Pontotoc and Okolona to introduce the candidate to his friends there. Stone, Bill Faulkner, and Reed rode down in John Falkner's Model T together, but as Reed politely collared the first constituent and the talk turned to politics, Bill wandered off, watching the spectacle of the streets with "those intense eyes," according to Reed. Highways around Oxford were so impossible in the twenties that Stone and Reed worked together too on a $600,000 bond issue, which they accomplished only by "great effort," squeezing a modicum of support for the gravel roads from the Holly Springs highway commissioner, whose concern for his district stopped at the Marshall County line.

Although Stone admitted that to quote oneself is a mark "of intellectual petrification," he reiterated ad infinitum that "there had been only three persons who believed in Faulkner all those years": one was Maud Falkner, and the others were himself and Mack Reed. "Mack," Stone said, "deserves the most credit of all. Bill's mother believed in him because he was her son. I believed in him because I knew he could write. It was perfectly obvious; I was betting on a sure thing. But Mack," he said, "doesn't know anything about writing; he just did for Bill out of the goodness of his heart." [24]

By 1923 Faulkner and Stone were thinking more and more seriously of publishing a book of Faulkner poems. The choice of a publisher may have been determined by an order placed by Phil Stone. In March 1922 the Brick Row had charged Stone for almost twenty books. The classics accounted for one third of those; another third were for contemporary fiction; however, four of the orders were for volumes of poetry: *Hymen* by H. D., Elinor Wylie's *Nets to Catch the Wind* (which Stone was especially eager to get), Swinburne's *Poems* (which may have been a gift for Bess Storer or Marian Davis), and William Carlos Williams's *Sour Grapes.* Williams's new poems had been issued by the Four Seas Publishing Company of Boston, former publishers of Conrad Aiken, H.D., and Mencken, as well as the Yale poet Stephen Vincent Benét. On 20 June 1923, Faulkner himself mailed a manuscript called "Orpheus and Other Poems" to Four Seas.[25]

Five months went by. Stone and Faulkner grew perplexed whether the delay spelled success or a failure so complete that they were not to receive even the usual printed rejection slip. In November Faulkner wrote them again. Apparently, the university postmaster had somehow mishandled his own mail, for he never received the June letter Four Seas appended to their 13 November reply. It was satisfaction and disappointment all at once. Although he recognized Faulkner's indebtedness to Housman, "and one or two other poets perhaps," the publishers' reader, "RES," observed further, to their delight: "You certainly have a flexible poetic method of your own." Ordinarily, the reader said, Four Seas would be happy to take such a book. The rest of the letter, however, was disheartening. The poetry budget of the Boston firm was overextended, and they could offer Faulkner only the arrangement that he and Stone accepted the next year, that Faulkner "stand solely the manufacturing cost of the first edition," with author's royalties per copy of that printing as "the return of [his] original investment." Any further editions would be financed by the publisher.

There was nothing to decide. Faulkner wrote back on 23 November: "As I have no money, I cannot very well guarantee the initial cost of publishing this mss.; besides, on re-reading some of the things, I see they aren't particularly significant. And one may obtain no end of poor verse at *a dollar and twenty-five cents* per volume [italics mine]." Stone's slang phrase for small amounts of money and even more their usual practice suggest joint authorship of the initial Four Seas correspondence, which, unlike their 1924 letters, for some reason was not filed at the Stone office.[26]

Over the winter the author and his mentor kept returning to the Four Seas proposition. Neither relished the idea of having Bill's poems published by a vanity press. But the suitbox lid on which they recorded the submission and rejection dates of Faulkner's poems, and now his stories, was an oracle the men could hardly ignore. Phil was resentful that Stark Young had done nothing to bring Faulkner's work to the attention of a publisher. They seemed already to have tried everything else. At the same time, both were financially strapped. No longer assistant district attorney, Phil had to depend for income on the rare client who did not prefer the legendary Jim Stone to plead his case. Bill might be frugal, but thrift was neither a Stone nor an Alston trait. Staying away from Clarksdale and Memphis only made them restless, but when he did play poker, Stone, now too eager for a big pot, may have overplayed his cards. They walked—more frequently in silence. They spent time with the Bunch, or drove out to collect Jim Stone's children for a Sunday afternoon excursion.

Finally, deeming it essential that Faulkner "get some recognition" if they were to continue, Stone and Faulkner agreed to approach Four Seas anyway; Stone would raise the publication costs somehow. The poetry might attract critical attention, they decided, and the cycle of eclogues Faulkner had composed in 1919 formed a congruous manuscript of suitable length.[27] As Phil explained in 1962, "*The Marble Faun* was one poem. In fact it was about the one-tenth of about a hundred poems. We were just trying to get something published and I had to pay for it myself, but actually it turned out that Bill and I both made money on it later as a piece worth preserving."[28]

Under the office letterhead on 13 May 1924, Phil Stone wrote Four Seas: "We have a manuscript of poems by a young man whom I consider to have a great deal of talent." Acknowledging the risk to a publisher "of an unknown man," but also citing Four Seas' reputation for being "especially considerate of contemporary poets," Stone inquired whether they might publish the poems if he "personally put up publication costs in advance." Uncharacteristically, there was no mention of Stark Young or the *New Republic* or the *Double Dealer*; Stone requested only the "publishing price."

The publisher's representative thought such an arrangement "quite probable," but asked first for the manuscript, which Stone and Faulkner mailed on 24 May, Stone a little concerned that Four Seas not "take any steps whatever" before he knew exactly what his financial investment would be. Phil was not all caution in that second letter, however: "Of course, every young writer has a debt of gratitude to his first publisher and I think you will be making a wise move by publishing this stuff both from a financial and artistic standpoint because Faulkner has in preparation some stuff much better than this." The manuscript they mailed to Boston was entitled *The Marble Faun*. Faulkner had "read some Hawthorne," Stone wrote critic William Van O'Connor in 1955, but not "a great deal." But "the title had nothing to do with Hawthorne . . ." Phil said. "I know because I am the man that put this title on it."[29]

The publisher's report on the manuscript contained perfunctory criticism of the "excellent piece of work" with its "many striking and beautiful couplets"; but readers at Four Seas served Mammon, not the Muse. A first edition of a thousand copies would cost Stone about four hundred dollars, "EID" informed them, rehearsing the terms. And should "the contracts . . . be made out to you or to the author"? he inquired in some puzzlement.[30]

Stone may have won or lost five hundred dollars in a night's work at the New World, but a country law practice was usually quiet in the summer and without other patrons Stone was somewhat reluctant to undertake the project. Perhaps he tried to interest others in the venture, someone like Marian Davis or her father, for example, who might more easily have raised the sum. Persons like Bess Storer or Ella Somerville, Stone knew, were sympathetic, but too poor or too uncertain in the deepening recession to invest more than the price of a single copy. At any rate, he stalled almost a fortnight before answering Four Seas' 13 June letter: "Just at present neither the author nor myself are in a position to put up the $400.00 necessary for manufacturing costs. I think we shall be in a short time and would suggest that meanwhile you send up contracts so that we may go over the matter."[31]

When the forms arrived in Oxford in early July, presumably the author and his attorney perused them together (although for the next month Faulkner, not Stone, would handle the correspondence). Based on a retail price of $1.50 per copy, the author was to get a royalty of 30 percent, according to Blotner, or $.45 per volume sold. Almost the entire first edition would have to be sold before their investment could be returned. Art Corbin's student instructed Faulkner to inquire about one loophole concerning the contingency of the author's buying the book plates, which could have cost them another four hundred dollars. Four Seas agreed to the change, and an initial publication date was set "not later than November 1, 1924." Before Stone returned to the correspondence, on 20 August, the contracts and the initial two hundred dollars were sent to Boston, with Faulkner's first dedication, to Maud Falkner.[32]

In late August 1924 postmaster Faulkner took his annual leave with the Boy Scouts encamped at Hedleston Lake—without bothering to answer Four Seas' letter of 6 August or to comply with its numerous, tedious requests.[33] His nonchalance may have been a mask for disappointment; to be published in a vanity press, at his friend's expense, could not have pleased a proud William Faulkner. Meanwhile, attorney Stone, clearly nettled by Faulkner's irresponsibility, resumed the correspondence and its chores in some pique: "Mr. Falkner is not so very keen at attending to business and I shall probably have to handle most of the business matters connected with his part of the publication of this check [sic]." Stone's impatience with Faulkner was only exacerbated by his own disillusionment over Faulkner's first publisher, for Phil's cynical "check" allusion apparently was no slip. Nevertheless, Phil Stone would make the most of their small opportunity. In his most solicitous tone he promised prompt delivery of the publicity Four Seas had requested of Faulkner. He would himself compose not a "biographical sketch" but "a short preface," and a paragraph "describing the book" (perhaps for use as a blurb). Publicity lists would be mailed by the first of September. The poet had balked at the publisher's request for publicity shots, for "Mr. Falkner is not keen on photography and flatly refuses to put out any money on photographs," Phil explained. Mr. Stone, however, could "handle this part of it all right"; those too would be in the mail soon.[34]

In "Faulkner Gets Started," Emily Whitehurst Stone records Phil's success at manipulating a camera-shy Faulkner into sitting for a photograph:

> "We went up to Memphis to have it made," Phil said. "See there where Bill's collar is open? We wanted him to look like a romantic poet—you know, like Byron with his thrown-back head and flowing tie. Except we couldn't put on him a tie like that."
>
> . . . I did not tell Phil, for I did not wish to hurt his feelings, but that open collar did not look Byronesque to me. It looked just like what it was— the collar of a scrawny young man who had ridden eighty miles to Mem-

phis through the dust of graveled roads and his own sweat with his tie on (in those days young men did not go to Memphis with open collars; they wore ties), and then had jerked it off and had his picture made with all the sweat and dust still in the hot collar.[35]

But while the now compliant author mailed his photographs and requisite biographical note, his patron promised Four Seas a preface— but found time only for more publicity suggestions. By 10 September the publishers were compelled to wire Phil Stone: "PREFACE NOT RECEIVED AFRAID CANT PUBLISH BOOK NOV. 1 AS PROMISED FAULKNER." It would be a week before Stone wired back: "HAVE BEEN OUT OF TOWN AND ENGAGED IN COURT PREFACE WILL GET OFF TO YOU MONDAY NEXT YOUR LETTER TO FAULKNER TRIFLE OBSCURE BUT HE TELLS ME TO AUTHORIZE YOU TO USE ANY FACTS REAL OR IMAGINARY THAT YOU DESIRE TO USE IN THE BOOK OR ADVERTISING MATTER."[36]

The opening of fall court, in truth, generally necessitated Phil's closer attention to business, yet "Case No. 133733-C," to which postal inspector Mark Webster referred in his letter of 2 September 1924, unexpectedly provided the firm's junior associate with a new law client. "There were three typed pages of complaints, completely deadpan and serious about all the things Bill had done," Stone later marveled. William Faulkner was instructed to answer "seven different categories of charges," or the postmaster would be assumed guilty as charged. The former federal prosecutor knew that the government would have no trouble proving its case. There were already a score of post office anecdotes in Stone archives. His wife later merely catalogued the repertoire: "[Faulkner] would not put up the mail; he would not get up to wait on persons at the window. He made the life of a complaining mail sorter on the train a thing of misery. He left the stamp money outside and put the jug of whiskey in the safe. He spent his days with his feet on the table so he could be comfortable while he read the magazines that came in."

When "action was imminent," Emily Stone continues, "Phil called Senator Pat Harrison, a family friend, to stop it." Harrison's political sense told him not to mention Lieutenant Evern Jones, his original choice for university postmaster: " 'What in hell am I going to do, Phil? Why don't you let us go on and fire him?' " " 'He needs the money,' " Phil replied, candidly. " 'He's going to quit pretty soon anyway,' " and he explained about *The Marble Faun*. At Stone's urging, Harrison apparently effected a compromise. Faulkner would continue his odious duties through October 1924, when he was allowed to resign.[37]

With that episode as background, as well as ten years of intimacy with the person, Stone said later, "who, at times and in some small ways, is the most aggravating damned human being the Lord ever put on this earth,"[38] Phil Stone finally got around to the preface he sent Four Seas on the day before Faulkner's twenty-seventh birthday.

"These are primarily the poems of youth," Stone began (half a year himself from thirty-two), and, thinking back to the spring after the Armistice, "They have youth's sheer joy at being alive in the sun and youth's sudden, vague, unreasoned sadness over nothing at all." But Phil also sensed in the poems, as in their author, "the defects of youth— youth's impatience, unsophistication and immaturity." (At other times, he thought that it was not youth at all, but Bill's "Falkner" blood coming through.) Stone's belief in Faulkner's talent was absolute, but so were his expectations. The note recurring in the preface is one of "promise," or "possibilities," "a hint of a coming muscularity of wrist and eye," or a talent that "will grow, will leave these things behind, will finally bring forth a flower that could have grown in no garden but his own."[39]

The private conversations over the manuscripts are lost, but the public words Stone employed in his letters and anecdotes are always of that stamp, continually "almost" or "not quite," "will be" or "could be." Stone seemed never to admit that to write a single word is in some measure to compromise. Anecdotes, like drama or music, may always await an ideal performance; print freezes, at least in part, a poem or a novel. Stone would write Stark Young of the artist's inevitable depression following his incarnation of the ideal,[40] yet that disappointment must really belong more to Maecenus than to Horace. The writer has as counterweight the exaltation of breathing life into nothingness, giving shape to chaos. In the 1930s Stone, more candidly than he realized, revealed how inseparable his ego was from that of his instrument William Faulkner: "If I have to write what good is Bill to me?"[41] But if he had written more than a handful of poems in early youth, his praise might lack the inevitable qualification.

Nevertheless, there was much to admire in *The Marble Faun*. Stone saw in the poems "an unusual feeling for words and the music of words, a love of soft vowels, an instinct for color and rhythm." The poet, he said, was "a man of varied outdoor experience, of wide reading, of quick humor . . . [and] of rigid self-honesty." Yet, more important to Stone, the poet was "a Southerner by every instinct, and, more than that, a Mississippian." According to Stone's prejudices, that identity preserved him from the innate rigidity of Yankees: Faulkner was a man "of the usual Southern alertness and flexibility of imagination." After all, the provincial was the way into the universal, Stone believed, paraphrasing George Moore, and remembering his Wright ("Balzac creates first a terrain"). Stone, a Southern contemporary of the lost generation, but untouched by the slaughter in the trenches, derived his values from the past, not the present, century: "All that is needed—granted the original talent—is work and unflinching honesty." [42]

With the preface completed, Stone was free to turn again to promotional schemes. As he and Faulkner set to work compiling publicity lists, Phil instructed Four Seas to attach subscription blanks to their book notices, which were to be complemented by and coordinated with personal letters from the indefatigable publicists. Stone could leave nothing to chance: "Be sure to state on the notice that Faulkner is a Mississippian and it might be a good idea to add that the book has a preface written by me." [43]

The letters now regularly crossed in the mail. Page proofs and copy were already en route to Oxford. The publishers were willing either to go to press at once or to run another set of proofs after the author's corrections. Stone need not worry; order blanks on book circulars were de rigueur at Four Seas, the publishers wrote on 29 September, tempering the rebuke with compliments on Phil's "very interesting and effective" preface: "We are glad to have it in the book." On the same day, Stone and Faulkner returned the proofs by registered mail, with their own compliments, for the "very few mistakes" in what the novices judged "an unusually good job first proof." [44]

In their page of suggestions—to be implemented only if there were no charge—the two men argued first for more distinctive breaks between poems and fewer lines per page (twenty, they thought). Faulkner suggested too that the book be "bound in very pale green boards" with "straw colored label[s]" for the front and spine. Stone's instinctual preservation of artifacts may have inspired Faulkner's "very anxious" request for the binding of the first proofs as "his personal copy." But Phil's tone became didactic as he insisted upon the hyphens and accents that Four Seas had omitted in the proofs: "You can see the difference between frothed and froth-ed, between hushed and hush-ed. Please note these grave accents very carefully." As he concluded, Stone added, more casually, that the second two hundred dollars would be sent by the author "either today or tomorrow."[45]

The accommodating press had accepted the changes, which would be "carefully incorporated" in a new set of proofs. The book's "binding boards" were already a light green; Four Seas liked the idea of "buff colored labels." The new proofs were shipped 6 October, the same day the publishers acknowledged receipt of Faulkner's check. Meanwhile, the publicity department at James Stone, Oldham, Stone & Stone "had to work Sunday morning" to compile "one-fourth of the list of names we have" and approximately "ten per cent" of the final sales list. That list Stone promised to supplement daily. Phil was also to "attend to getting reviews of the book" in the periodicals they listed. When he mailed another compilation on 13 October, Stone reported that the re-vised proofs "have been corrected by me," and that "Mr. Faulkner was to look over them and return them to you today." "I shall see that this is done," he promised. Stone and Faulkner had the proofs back to Bos-ton in record time; Four Seas acknowledged their safe arrival on the sixteenth.[46]

The seven legal-sized pages of names for book circulars now at-tached to the 13 October letter apparently incorporate Stone's first two mailings. In one group, probably the first, Major and Mrs. L. E. Oldham head the 110 Oxford listings, which include the two men's friends and relatives; the remaining dowagers and old maids among the Oxford gentility; doctors, ministers, judges, and professors; members of the Browning and Twentieth Century clubs; and businessmen on the square, such as Elton Frazier, who agreed to take a hundred books on consignment at The Variety Store.[47] The second largest group of poten-tial buyers were from Charleston, where Jack and Myrtle's names begin the survey of Stone's friends and acquaintances, including "Chief Bag-well"—Carl Bagwell—who had played on the Ole Miss football team and who was now superintendent of schools in Charleston, and "Miss Inex Barnes," who long before may unwittingly have shared her Christian name with a Stone beagle. There were a dozen or so names from Sumner, Mississippi, the other county seat of Tallahatchie County, and almost thirty names from Clarksdale, among them Sallie Cooper Alston and Pauline Clark; Stark Young's half sister, Mrs. Gerald Fitzgerald; Stone's classmates; and even former Governor Brewer.

From the additional page listing bookstores and periodicals, four of Byrne Hackett's stores were to be notified; books were to be sent to the *Commercial Appeal*, the *Eagle*, the *New Republic* (c/o Stark Young), the *Dial*, *Poetry*, the New York *Evening Post*, the *Measure*, the *Double Dealer*, and the New Orleans *Times-Picayune* (the last two c/o John McClure). The Lord & Taylor bookstore, Frank Shay's Bookshop, The Sunwise Turn, and Brentano's in New York should be mailed "publicity stuff" with a "cut on placard" for Faulkner's old employer, if possible. Announcements were also to be sent to the *Fugitive* in Nashville, the Jackson papers (not omitting the *Woman Voter*, an organ that suffragist Polly Alston Clark probably supported), and seven newspapers in the northern half of the state.

People from Batesville and the three towns north of there on the Illinois Central line and from the principal Delta towns, mostly those in law or state politics, make up two-thirds of what appears to be a second mailing, which ends with thirty-one names from Jackson—hardly less than a registry of government officials, from Governor Henry Whitfield to the state and federal prohibition agents.[48]

After completing that lengthy assignment, Stone took advantage of a short break in the Four Seas correspondence to announce the forthcoming publication to the *Yale Alumni Weekly*. He reiterated the qualifications and praise of his preface: "While this book has the usual defects of all first books, I have great faith in this young man's ability and believe he will some day produce something very fine indeed." Noting that the author was a "personal friend" and that he himself had "written the preface," Stone added, in words suggesting a political appeal or a speech sponsoring a fraternity rushee, "This poet is my personal property and I urge all my friends and classmates to buy his book." (In the same tone, the partisan Democrat also mentioned that he was Lafayette County president of the Davis-Bryan Victory Club.)[49]

Even when the Stone secretary called in sick (delaying the completion of more mailing lists), Phil could not be checked for long. On

19 October he sat down to type two recent Faulkner poems and another letter of advice for Four Seas. Stone said he was quite impressed by one of the new poems, probably "Mississippi Hills: My Epitaph": "I think the epitaph shows traces of something very much like genius in its restrained and passionate sincerity and especially in its simplicity." Only 22 of its 132 words were "not monosyllables," none were "of more than two syllables," and not more than three words departed from "ordinary conversation by ordinary people." (Monosyllables were also preponderant in the second poem, he noted.) Stone's plans were to quote from the epitaph in his local newspaper announcements and perhaps on "large placards" printed and distributed in the area. He encouraged Four Seas to exploit the poem in their "broadside," as long as Faulkner retained legal rights to the verse. Stone's excitement over Faulkner's newest work was such that he returned to the poems in a handwritten postscript: "Notice the improvement in technical accomplishment over 'The Marble Faun.'"

A second, embryonic strategem mentioned in the letter also involved new Faulkner compositions, two articles they hoped to sell to the *New Republic* or the *Double Dealer.* In yet another scheme he advanced, Stone enclosed a note in longhand for duplication on Four Seas circulars. "It will be of no value unless you can reproduce the handwriting as it is," he advised. While the "vulgarity" of the appeal might "offend a few," he believed the gimmick would stimulate interest among most of those targeted for direct mail. (The Oxford publicists, it seems, had tabled their original idea of personal letters until they measured the success of the first assault.) In the note Stone had written:

> Dear friends:—
>   I'm spending about fifty dollars of my own money and days and days and days of my time simply to help a Mississippi poet and to help advertise Mississippi and put it on the map artistically. Won't you help just a little by pinning a money order to the enclosed subscription blank and mailing it off AT ONCE?
>
>   Phil Stone

Stone was asked to recopy the appeal, more legibly, on different paper, but the publishers, with unqualified enthusiasm, moved to implement all of his ideas, at the same time requesting copies of his local publicity.[50]

The Marble Faun

On 5 November, after Stone's return from a business trip to St. Louis and Chicago,[51] eight legal-sized pages were mailed to the publicity department at Four Seas. If informed of sales, Stone wrote in the accompanying letter, he could "keep after" the persons who did not take the first bait. A new copy of his "Dear friends" letter went north with that packet: "It would not do for this appeal to be too legible; if it was my friends might suspect that it was not my handwriting." He enclosed too the Faulkner articles and copies of the letters submitting them to the magazines, giving the Boston publisher first refusal in their latest plan, to finance "two or three years" in Europe for Faulkner. The poet was about to "enter into a contract with some publication to supply them with weekly articles . . . [of] literary merit . . . as good as any of their kind." Stone and Faulkner were "also contemplating" signing a contract to collect those published articles in a book, all rights to which they were willing to sell now, "for $250.00 cash, the contract to be executed at once." The "male Cassandra" prophcsicd that Faulkner would not "remain unknown long"; his apprenticeship was already in its tenth year, and Phil Stone, "better . . . than anyone else," was in a position "to realize at just what point he has now arrived."

Stone gave Four Seas until "6:00 P. M. on November 15th next" to reply. Because Faulkner was set to embark on 1 December, they were beginning to be concerned about the delayed publication of the first volume: "Please hurry the book forward as much as possible because we don't want the enthusiasm we have aroused to die down before the book comes out." At the bottom of his second, single-spaced page, Stone added that with a campaign similar to the one in progress, "we can easily sell the second book." "We are going to oversell 'The Marble Faun,'" he concluded confidently.[52]

In the second mailing list, which begins with Calvin Lott and forty-six others connected with the university, Stone and Faulkner more frequently add names of mere acquaintances, like those of three postal inspectors, to the friends listed in almost fifty Mississippi towns. The last two pages extend the coverage to neighboring states—almost forty members of the legal and business community in Memphis, the Sherwood Andersons in New Orleans, and SAE's at Tulane. With their Yale friends, the two Mississippians managed almost thirty Yankees who might be interested in *The Marble Faun*, the Frank Kellys in Chicago, for example, the "First Assistant Postmaster General" and Chief Justice William Howard Taft in Washington, and a few Westerners as well. Third from the bottom appears the most distant potential buyer, Mrs. Cornell Franklin, Box 952, Shanghai. Evidently neither Stone nor Faulkner had any idea that Estelle Oldham Franklin would be coming home early in December.[53]

In their reply the publishers took pains not to alienate their new associates, while explaining that they "would hardly feel justified in contracting for Mr. Faulkner's next book at present," hoping that they might be considered after the travel essays appeared serially. There was another disappointment in the 10 November Four Seas letter: the late preface and second proofs had pushed the publication date back to 1 December.[54]

Miss Rosie must have seen her son only at an occasional meal that late autumn. General Stone practiced alone in Oxford. He had no partner; he employed no secretary. Faulkner seems to have been stimulated in all the excitement to write a folder full of new poems. Phil Stone, to whom any opportunity was significant, was now working after hours, it seems, not only to launch the career of William Faulkner but also to underwrite his friend's trip abroad. He mailed "an Armistice Day Poem" to the *Atlantic Monthly* on 13 November, mentioning to the editors the coming book at Four Seas and *Atlantic* contributor Stark Young. Stone provided a paragraph of analysis as well: "Don't be deceived by the apparent simplicity of this thing. It is written by a man who has gone all the way through the new verse movement and learned tricks from all of them. The work he is doing just now is simple just because he has come out on the other side." That night before walking home, Stone wired Boston: "BOOK NOT YET RECEIVED HOLDING UP PUBLICITY AND SELLING PLANS RELEASE WIRE AT ONCE WHEN WE CAN EXPECT BOOK."[55]

Sunday's *Commercial Appeal* carried an initial announcement of the publication; that Monday, 17 November, Stone used the excuse of requesting two hundred circulars to badger Four Seas again. It would be another three weeks before he heard from the publisher. Faulkner had already executed papers assigning Stone his power of attorney, but Phil very likely exaggerated in implying that Faulkner's foot was on the gangplank. When they could stand it no longer, Stone wired Boston again on 9 December, repeating the negative consequences of delay and requesting an immediate reply. It came the same day: "BOOK JUST READY. CAN SHIP AT ONCE."[56]

Stone mailed off a twenty-five-dollar check for twenty-five copies, and, expecting Faulkner's author's copies on every train for a week, they virtually camped out at the depot. On 16 December Faulkner was forced to dip into his travel funds. "IF YOU HAVE NOT SHIPPED MY TEN FREE COPIES MARBLE FAUN AND IF CAN BE SHIPPED FOR GODS SAKE SHIP THEM AT ONCE AS THIS IS HOLDING UP MY SAILING EVERY DAY," he wired.[57]

On Friday, 19 December 1924, Phil Stone apparently hosted an impromptu autograph party at the Stone law offices on Jackson Avenue. General Stone offered his congratulations. Faulkner's agent and stenographer chatted with the friends who dropped in while it must have been the author now who sat behind a desk, signing Stone's copies and the gifts to his family and closest friends. If one of those was inscribed to Phil Stone himself, it initiated a ritual observed as long as Faulkner lived.[58] Ella and Nina Somerville, Bess Storer, and Katrina Carter all received books inscribed by Faulkner on 19 December. The Alstons may have been at Sister Rosa's for the holidays, for Bill also inscribed books that day for "Cousin Polly," Mrs. Clark, and Sallie Cooper Alston.[59]

Because Major Oldham and General Stone had dissolved their partnership by mutual agreement sometime the previous autumn, Faulkner—conveniently—would have had to leave the office to deliver one copy to be inscribed that Friday for Lemuel and Lida Oldham. Estelle Franklin and her two children, surely he knew, had returned to her parents' home a few weeks before.[60]

Faulkner and Estelle may have seen one another again at the local Christmas parties or dances. Phil and Bill drifted together to watch, or to talk politely to the old ladies about Faulkner's book or his coming trip abroad, although some of the girls in the Bunch cast eyes in their direction most of the evening. The surprise of the season was that Katrina Carter and Jim Kyle Hudson were to be married in late January. Mayor Bob Farley and Nina Culley wondered how Phil was taking the news. For the first time in months, Phil Stone and Faulkner had reason to forget about *The Marble Faun*.

8

Distant Company

THE LAST LETTER from Phil Stone to Four Seas in 1924 had conveyed assurances. Enclosing fifty dollars to cover their recent *Marble Faun* shipment, Phil explained that with the Christmas holidays he and Faulkner were yet "to really get into the sale of the book," which Stone could turn to only after Faulkner's departure for Europe. Nonetheless, Stone reported having "sold fifty copies here without the slightest effort," confident that he could "easily dispose of 500 copies in Mississippi between now and the first of April." Almost a week passed, with sales in Oxford averaging five books daily. Undaunted by any suspicion that *The Marble Faun* could not be placed in every literate household in the county, Stone ordered fifty additional copies, inquiring too about bookstore sales. In the meantime, Faulkner, leaving money from his First National account with Phil Stone, wrote a last check to the Boy Scouts of America. Then he bought a train ticket to New Orleans for 4 January.[1]

With a supply of *Marble Faun*s in the baggage car, Stone and Faulkner took the southbound train together that Sunday night. The next morning they checked into "a hotel on the south side of Lafayette Square," the small park in the central business district a few blocks uptown from the French Quarter. On the north, or lake, side of the square, trolley cars rattling up St. Charles Avenue to Tulane University passed in front of Gallier Hall, New Orleans's municipal offices then. The Post Office was on Camp Street, the southern, or river, border.

Distant Company

To the east, the Times-Picayune Building occupied an entire block. Stone and Faulkner had found rooms at the Lafayette Hotel, the newer of the two hotels on the street across the park from the newspaper. Frequently embarrassed as a boy by his mother's niggardly tips to bell-hops and waiters, Stone nevertheless was accustomed to more lavish accommodations than what Elizabeth Anderson would remember as a "funny little hotel with rickety rooms that opened onto a ramshackle courtyard." On other trips to New Orleans he stayed at the Monteleone, a hotel slightly less opulent than the Roosevelt, but with his bank account depleted by poetry investments, Stone was not at all reluctant to match Faulkner's frugality, and the hotel was convenient to the *Times-Picayune* and to the offices of the *Double Dealer* on Baronne, the street behind Gallier Hall.[2]

The moment they were settled, Stone and Faulkner walked across to the newspaper to see literary editor John McClure about Faulkner's yet unsold travel articles. (Sometime before, George Healy, the paper's Ole Miss stringer—and future editor—had urged McClure to consider Faulkner material for his Sunday book section.)[3] McClure's first words came as a shock: neither the newspaper nor the *Double Dealer*, where he was also editor, had received review copies of *The Marble Faun* from Four Seas. Stone had probably counted on the psychological advantage of the book preceding them to New Orleans. But McClure accepted one of Stone's copies and promised reviews in the two publications as soon as possible.[4] The editor also apparently agreed to read the two (or more?) sample articles that Faulkner had brought with him and to pass them on to his friend Roark Bradford, another member of the staff. The *Times-Picayune* might consider not a contract but an informal publishing relationship. McClure's seemingly genuine interest in Faulkner's most recent work elated the Mississippians, who then tried to implement a second phase of their New Orleans campaign. They got the address of the Sherwood Andersons (in the upper Pontalba Building on Jackson Square), probably from McClure—only to learn that the writer was out of town lecturing. Nevertheless, Faulkner called Mrs. Anderson, who evidently invited them over for drinks.

Back in September 1922, Sherwood Anderson, already separated from his second wife, had met Elizabeth Prall at the Lord & Taylor bookstore where Faulkner had worked late in 1921. "Like many authors," William Spratling remarked, "the young Sherwood, browsing in book stores, liked to be recognized." "They married and came to New Orleans," Spratling continued, omitting the two-year delay. Actually, Stark Young had shared Thanksgiving dinner with the couple in New York in 1922. The next summer, trying to negotiate a Nevada divorce, Anderson had written Young in Italy to find a ring for Elizabeth Prall. At last the divorce had come through, and in the fall of 1924 Sherwood and Elizabeth were married and living in New Orleans, where Anderson reigned—"our Royal Personage," said Hamilton Basso—among the writers and would-be writers of the *Double Dealer* circle.[5]

During the autumn that Stone and Faulkner were caught up in publishing *The Marble Faun*, Young's play *The Saint* was produced, to poor reviews, and about the same time D. W. Huebsch published Anderson's *A Story Teller's Story*, a work that elicited high praise from Young in his letters to the Andersons in November and December 1924. But Huebsch could not compete with the money Horace Liveright began offering "most of the better writers of the time," and the following spring Anderson reluctantly switched to Boni & Liveright for *Dark Laughter*. In June 1925 he wrote a few lines for the cover of Young's play, in Stark Young's first book with Horace Liveright.[6] Among those three friends, at least in their published letters, there is no mention then of William Faulkner, a rather startling omission in light of subsequent claims.

Faulkner, nevertheless, knew Sherwood Anderson's work. Although the single extant Stone order for Anderson's fiction would be placed in 1927, Stone wrote in his Nobel reminiscence that Sherwood Anderson was the modern prose writer he had recommended to Bill in the early days. Anderson's *Winesburg, Ohio* (1919) had given the Midwesterner his widest audience, and Stone may have also seen his work in the magazines. Faulkner at some point bought not only *Horses and Men* (1923), but also a December 1925 reissue of *Dark Laughter*. Ben Wasson told Carvel Collins of Faulkner's "great admiration" for the stories and of his ranking Anderson's "I'm a Fool" with Conrad's *Heart of Darkness* as his favorites within the genre. Wasson claimed also to have initiated Faulkner's calling on Elizabeth Anderson in late 1924 in order to meet her husband. Free from his postal duties by November, Faulkner acted on Wasson's suggestion, says Collins, with Anderson appropriating their introduction for his sketch "A Meeting South."[7] Yet as late as 5 November 1924 Faulkner and Stone had given only the *Double Dealer* as address for the Andersons' *Marble Faun* circular, although they sent notices to three of Faulkner's SAE brothers at Tulane, where Faulkner may well have bunked during a previous New Orleans visit.

There is no explicit reference in the Stone papers to a Faulkner-Anderson meeting in 1924. Only at the end of March 1925, when Faulkner returned home for a visit, did Stone write Four Seas of Faulkner's being "the original" for "A Meeting South" in the *Dial* for April. The papers are also silent about Phil's opinion of Anderson's work, until a 1927 letter submitting Faulkner's reply to a *New Republic* essay on Anderson: "While I think part of it [the published analysis] is accurate I think the two great troubles with Anderson are mere garrulity and a lack of a sense of humor."[8]

One of Stone's pervasive claims about his relationship with Faulkner was that the boy of sixteen he had met in 1914 "was a very humorless person." "If I ever taught Bill anything," Phil reiterated, "it was a sense of humor." Faulkner in "Verse Old and Nascent" likewise confessed to a "youthful morbidity." (By the time of their maturity, however, it was impossible for an outsider like Emily Stone to distinguish between the humor of the two friends, which was overridingly "sardonic.") Ideas about humor that Stone shared if not originated evidently lay behind some of the less flattering remarks that Faulkner would make regarding Anderson in his controversial essay on the older writer published in April 1925 in the Dallas *Morning News*. There he frequently echoed other Stone phrases as well, especially of the *Marble Faun* preface:

I do not mean to imply that Mr. Anderson has no sense of humor. He has, he has always had. But only recently has he got any of it into his stories, without deliberately writing a story with a humorous intent. I wonder sometimes if this is not due to the fact that he didn't have leisure to write until long after these people had come to be in his mind; that he had cherished them until his perspective was slightly awry. Just as we cherish those whom we love; we sometimes find them ridiculous, but never humorous. The ridiculous indicates a sense of superiority, but to find something partaking of an eternal sardonic humor in our cherished ones is slightly discomforting.[9]

Stone did not belittle Anderson's importance for Faulkner, however. As he wrote Glenn O. Carey in 1950, "With all the efforts we
made, I was not able to get Faulkner published and Sherwood Anderson was." Closer to the New Orleans period, Stone acknowledged to
Louis Cochran "the magnitude of Bill's debt" to Anderson, although
remarking that Faulkner "owes Stark Young a big debt also." [10]

At any rate, the two young men were never in doubt about their regard for Elizabeth Anderson. In 1965 Joseph Blotner talked with her
about their January visit forty years before: "She welcomed them," he
wrote, "and then they asked her to go out with them. Bill was his usual
quiet, courtly self. Phil was very gallant and commanding. The two men
had planned some sightseeing, and Phil insisted that Miss Elizabeth
must go with them. . . . [F]or three days they saw much of each other.
It was very gay, and to Elizabeth Anderson it later seemed as though
they had laughed for days."

Elizabeth Anderson returned to the "light-hearted interlude of talk
and laughter" in her 1969 memoir:

> At night, we would roar around town, seeing crowds of people, exploring
> murky bistros along Bourbon Street, and sometimes going to a movie the-
> ater that catered only to colored people. The theater was located on Ram-
> part Street, which was a marvelous place of shops, cafes, nightclubs and
> open markets. Here the famous Negro bands originated, which played at
> funerals and led the parade at carnival time. The movies that were shown
> in the theater were always Westerns and always dreadful. . . . It was a hor-
> rible, stuffy place, but we sat in the balcony, joking about the good guys
> and the bad guys and laughing ourselves to a point of near nausea. One
> night the two Bills, Spratling and Faulkner, and a few other young writers
> held a footrace over the rooftops of the Quarter.[11]

Stone and Faulkner also spent some hours with John McClure and
the *Double Dealer* crowd at the loft on Baronne, for Stone was drawn
to McClure, although like W. H. Wright he was suspicious of literary cliques. Much later, in 1954, Stone reminded Carvel Collins of his
bias in explaining that it "is not at all safe to assume that Bill read
Freud" during his contact with those young men: "The truth is that
the literary group in New Orleans, with the exception of Spratlin [sic]
and Sherwood Anderson wer [sic] to Bill a comedy group and he paid
very little attention to anything they said. In fact I had for years, as

Distant Company

I have told you, warned him against 'literary people.' " But to Stone, McClure was no dilettante. Looking back, Phil would remember sadly "the tragedy of John McClure, a poet who could 'almost' write." As James K. Feibleman recalled in "Literary New Orleans Between World Wars," Knopf had published the Oklahoman's first poetry manuscript in 1918, but refused the second, thereby destroying the "sweet, sensitive man" who spent most of his life behind the *Times-Picayune* copydesk. His friends—H. L. Mencken for one—urged him to submit his poems to the Eastern publishers again. Feibleman said he persuaded William Alexander Percy to promise to accept the second volume for the Yale Series of Younger Poets, but McClure refused Feibleman's help. "It would be using influence," he said.[12]

Stone and Faulkner were together in New Orleans for nearly a week; and in the wake of the post office imbroglio and the pain of seeing Estelle again, Faulkner warmed to the conviviality of Miss Elizabeth and her friends and felt a kinship different from his link with Stone in the company of fellow writers. Soon after their arrival, the Mississippians had canvassed the piers and warehouses inquiring about Atlantic freighters, and Faulkner had "registered with a shipping office for passage to Europe as soon as it was available," says Collins. But now he wanted to stay at least until Sherwood Anderson's return. Phil, meanwhile, had literally exhausted his bank account (although their experience of New Orleans cuisine was confined to the creations of the Andersons' cook). Luckily, Stone had his railroad pass for the trip home. Bill Faulkner, with less expensive habits, in time of need could revert to the bohemianism of his brief Greenwich Village stay. Until Anderson came home, Elizabeth Anderson offered Faulkner the spare room in the apartment where she and her husband's son Robert were living.[15] Bill estimated that he could live on a dollar a day in the Quarter, a budget easily maintained if, as they hoped, the *Times-Picayune* took some of his work. If that prospect failed, he was not above washing dishes. But unless he too rolled up his sleeves, Phil Stone could stay no longer, returning, reluctantly, to the hills of North Mississippi, to promote *The Marble Faun*, to see after his "old folks," and, least appealing of all, to earn a few legal fees.

Exhausted from the trip and the pace of the days in New Orleans, Phil did not resume his dictation until Tuesday, 13 January 1925, when he wrote Four Seas complaining about McClure's review copies. A letter from Monte Cooper, the "Maiden Lady Critic" who edited the *Commercial Appeal* book pages, had been on his desk when he walked in. The favorable review she had promised in November was also being delayed by Four Seas' lethargic mailroom. Stone was outdone: "Now it does look to us like you might hurry these out. If you will just do your part we are going to sell this whole first edition . . . and possibly do better than that."[14]

The publishers replied that at Stone's request they were mailing out review copies, but the delay had been intentional. With the book's late publication, it had missed the Christmas trade, and Four Seas was waiting to announce it with the spring list. They promised Stone an extra copy to replace the one he had given McClure and, to placate him further, offered six free copies for local reviews. Stone forwarded that letter to Faulkner in New Orleans for his suggestions.[15]

On the first Monday of his return Stone attended to some necessary banking embarrassments. He wrote the First National Bank a check to cover Faulkner's New Year's Boy Scouts payment. It did not take Four Seas' note on 10 January to remind him that his own account was also overdrawn. They were very polite, were sure there was some mistake, despite the return of his twenty-five-dollar check marked "Insufficient funds," which they were redepositing that day.[16]

In the same week, Phil's name was conspicuously absent from the guest list of a bachelors' party given by David Carter at the Tea Room for a "number of the friends" of Jim Kyle Hudson. Dr. John Culley, the toastmaster, Bob Farley, and L. C. Andrews, Hudson's law partner of the last year, were among the after-dinner speakers. When the groom rose to respond to the words of his friends, according to the *Eagle*, he "assured all present of his absolute self possession, notwithstanding . . . that several times during the evening he was observed to be very nervous and apprehensive of something, which was said to have been fear of retaliation on the part of a guest present, Mr. Will Lewis."[17] Subsequently a partner at Neilson's, at the time Will Lewis was a store clerk.

The "retaliation," however, came from an unknown quarter later that month, only hours before the marriage of the "popular couple." On the morning of the wedding, a small fire broke out in the First Presbyterian

Church. A volunteer brigade quickly extinguished the flames, but, as in any small town, Oxford's citizens had poured into the streets at the first alarm. As they drifted back to the courthouse in groups of threes and fours, they were startled to see Phil Stone running through the square, hollering, "*I* didn't do it; *I* didn't do it." Stone was making a joke of it, but for several years the Hudsons would be ill at ease with him, uncertain how their old friend felt about them. The bride was twenty-nine, the groom thirty. They had waited to marry, Katrina claimed, because they "were having too much fun!" The wedding and reception at Shirley made the front page of the *Eagle* the following Thursday, by which time the Hudsons were off by train "for points north." Directly under that story was a filler: "Phil Stone spent a few days in New Orleans recently." [18] To the square, Katrina Carter was eternally "Phil Stone's tragedy."

The newspaper that a quarter of a century later devoted front-page columns and most of section two to the Nobel Prize winner gave five column inches on an inside page to a belated announcement of *The Marble Faun* in the issue featuring the "Delightful Dinner Party." Although full of purple prose, the article had been merely reprinted from an earlier notice in the *Mississippian*, concluding, "The author's friends will await with much interest a second book book [sic] from his hand." The editors of the January–February issue of the *Double Dealer*, who published three Faulkner works, had also heard of a forthcoming new volume of poetry, "The Greening Bough." Phil said, much later, that most of the poems for the volume published in 1933 as *A Green Bough* were written as "an exercise" during 1925. "The different poems are supposed to have had a different point of view but, generally, more like *The Shropshire Lad* [sic]" than *The Marble Faun*. The published volume "was never intended to be one poem," he explained. [19]

If the notices in Oxford and New Orleans offered some support to the poet now at work on a second collection, favorable critical attention from Memphis continued to elude William Faulkner. In a *Double Dealer* essay, he had employed an analogy that he often used for shock value: "Surely, if there are two professions in which there should be no professional jealousy, they are prostitution and literature." [20] Faulkner's resorting to the analogy in his first conversation with Monte Cooper would ensure their relationship could only deteriorate. Miss Cooper,

who, Stone said, "fancied herself the arbiter of Memphis literary culture generally," invited Stone and Faulkner in 1924 or 1925 to one of
her parties. "Bill said he wasn't going," Stone recalled, but he had insisted: "You damn sure *are* going; *both* of us are going up there and see
if we can't sell some of these books; we want to get our money back."
They did go, but Faulkner volunteered few words before his buxom
hostess "spied him" alone in a corner of the crowded room, and "sailed
across the room like a frigate."

"You're Mr. Faulkner, aren't you?" she opened.

"Yes, ma'am," Bill said.

"Well, Mr. Faulkner, have you read so-and-so?"

"No'm," Faulkner replied.

"Oh, well," said Miss Cooper, taken aback. "What about so-and-so.
Have you read that?"

"No'm."

"Surely . . ."

"No, ma'am," Bill repeated.

So she said, "Well, Mr. Faulkner, I've been told that you were one of
our coming young Southern writers. You mean to say you haven't read
any of these people?"

"Madam," he said, "did you ever hear of a whore sleeping with a
man for fun?"

Phil Stone would not easily contain the damage of that remark.

By the end of January, the *Times-Picayune* had bought five Faulkner
sketches for twenty (or twenty-five) dollars,[21] and the *Double Dealer* was
about to accept the three works; Faulkner obviously would not leave
for Europe for some time. Stone mailed Monte Cooper two dollars for
Faulkner, probably for a subscription to the *Commercial Appeal*. She
had gotten her review copy "at last," she wrote Stone in February from
a North Carolina resort. "I shall read it here, and write something about
it, perhaps for the issue of February 15th."[22]

But McClure's 29 January *Times-Picayune* review would precede
Monte Cooper's by over two months. McClure, who was Phil's age,
generally agreed with Stone's *Marble Faun* preface. The first book's
"deficiencies" were those of "youth": "Immaturity is almost the only
indictment which can be brought against the work." John McClure also
affirmed Stone's habitual prophecy: "Those who wish to keep in touch

with the development of Southern poetry will do well to acquire *The Marble Faun* and the new book when it appears. One day they may be glad to have recognized a fine poet at his first appearance." [23]

Between the publication of *The Marble Faun* and Phil and Bill's departure for New Orleans, Stone had scheduled a protesting author to wholesale autographing sessions at the office. If he were to sell out the edition, Stone intended for Faulkner, as well as Four Seas, to do his part; the ploy of having him inscribe many of the books in advance had become a standard sales technique. Of the surviving copies, seven date from that interval: two on Christmas Eve; one in "Dec. 1924"; Postal Inspector Webster's the day after Christmas; and Lee Baggett's the next day. On New Year's Eve "P. A. Stone" autographed a copy to a family friend and Bank of Oxford director; Faulkner inscribed it on 2 January. Another copy that Faulkner signed on Christmas Eve, "P. Stone" autographed and presumably presented to the Honorable P. B. Furr, J.P., on 6 January. Of course, the technique sometimes backfired, "leaving the two promoters with an inscribed book on their hands," as Carvel Collins has written.

Now Faulkner also inscribed copies for new friends in the Quarter; for example, one book signed on 12 February went to Anita Loos, the author of *Gentlemen Prefer Blondes*, whom Faulkner met in New Orleans. At home Stone continued to push the inscribed copies and to handle Faulkner's expenses.[24]

In late February, planning then to embark for Europe in March, Faulkner came home to see his family, bringing with him some of *A Green Bough* for the Stone stenographer or Bess Storer to type. One of the "Philomel" burned fragments, published in 1933 as "The Raven bleak and Philomel . . . ," is dated 26 February 1925 in Oxford, Mississippi. Also in Faulkner's suitcase that day may have been the drawings Faulkner had promised student George Healy for the *Scream*, a magazine of campus humor to which friends such as Stark Young had agreed to contribute. A notice about the magazine in the *Commercial Appeal* listed Phil Stone among Ole Miss's alumni "literary lights," his "preface to 'The Marble Faun' [having] created nationwide comment," according to the newspaper. (Healy, who owned as many as four copies of *The Marble Faun* at one time, would have known better.)[25] By the time Healy had filed that story with his Memphis paper, Faulkner was back in New Orleans—but not before further alienating Monte Cooper (although he may have reserved the insult until after her *Marble Faun* review).

In 1931 Stone wrote Louis Cochran of the mishap: "Before Bill had made his reputation he was in Memphis and Miss Cooper invited him to lunch, probably a literary one, and Bill accepted. When the time came for lunch Bill was getting drunk with his friend Reneau De Vaux [sic], well-known Memphis Gambler and road-house proprietor and now proprietor of the Club Seville near Memphis. Bill simply did not go to the lunch and Miss Cooper has never forgiven him for it and never mentions his work in her column if she can help it. It is most amusing." [26]

Back home, before Faulkner caught the train to New Orleans, Phil and Anna Liggin carefully packed a bouquet of narcissus from the front lawn in layers of wet newspaper in a box for Elizabeth Anderson. Faulkner, as Phil told Carvel Collins, especially liked the flower. Otherwise, Stone said, Benjy "would have been carrying an Easter lily." According to Sherwood Anderson, who saw him on that March 1925 visit, Faulkner had other baggage too: "some six to eight half gallon jars of moon liquor . . . stowed in the pockets of the big coat" [27]—perhaps Reno's "Bon voyage." It was Prohibition, and Mississippi had been the first state to ratify the Eighteenth Amendment, but in Memphis and Vicksburg, on the Mississippi Gulf Coast, and assuredly in New Orleans there were open bars with signs out front when revenue agents were at full strength.

This time in New Orleans Faulkner postponed his voyage once again and moved in with artist William Spratling, a member of McClure's circle who was teaching in the Tulane School of Architecture. By seven each morning, Spratling said, "Bill would already be out on the little balcony over the garden tapping away on his portable, an invariable glass of alcohol-and-water at hand." Even when Faulkner's mother got no letter, Stone usually heard from him, but there had been no word for almost three weeks when Phil sent off a wire: "WHATS THE MATTER DO YOU HAVE A MISTRESS." The reply was affirmative: "YES AND SHES 3000 WORDS LONG." A letter soon followed. On 31 March 1925 Stone passed along the news to Four Seas: "Mr. Faulkner is in New Orleans at present and is writing some very good stuff in verse. He is also writing a novel and he and Sherwood Anderson are writing a novel together."[28]

Drawing from both his war stories and the story of Cecily in "Moonlight," Faulkner by the end of March was well into his "second" novel, which he called *Mayday* (later *Soldiers' Pay*), a work set in Charlestown, Georgia, and the mannered landscape of *The Marble Faun*. According to Joseph Blotner, Anderson was reading the manuscript and encouraging the younger writer to employ his native material. Yet at first Faulkner, and perhaps Stone, was thinking of offering the completed manuscript not to Horace Liveright, Anderson's new publisher, but to Scribner's, which published four of Stark Young's books between 1923 and 1926. Young had worked with Maxwell Perkins at Charles Scribner's Sons since autumn 1922 (with Elizabeth Prall's assistance on *The Flower in Drama* [1923]). By the time Faulkner was finishing *Mayday*, Young and Max Perkins were personal as well as professional friends.[29] However, Stone, at least, was following Fitzgerald's career at Scribner's and may bear responsibility for Faulkner's consideration of that publisher and his controversial editor.

If the few surviving letters Faulkner wrote Stone are any indication of their correspondence, the Faulkner letter explaining about his "mistress" was probably little longer than his telegram. Stone heard nothing more or received only sketchy details about the New Orleans outpouring before he reported again to Four Seas on 18 April 1925: "Mr. Faulkner is still in New Orleans and has postponed for some months his departure for Europe because . . . Sherwood Anderson has been kind enough to write a novel in colaboration [sic] with him. I think this novel will be published some time in the fall. Faulkner has also just about finished a novel on his own hook. Some of his articles and verse appear in every issue of the Double Dealer. He has gotten a good deal of publicity in the New Orleans papers and suppose that you have gotten hold of this."[30]

For a few weeks Faulkner and Anderson collaborated on the Al Jackson "letters," presumably the "novel" to which Stone refers. Their first efforts on the tall tales were so successful that they may have thought half seriously of following through with the project; Anderson could even have talked in jest of placing it with Boni & Liveright. Faulkner's

April essay on Anderson, which may have temporarily chilled their relationship, may also have spelled the end of Al Jackson. By late April both men, in any case, became absorbed in work of their own, Anderson with *Tar: A Midwestern Childhood* and Faulkner with *Soldiers' Pay*. Their "novel" was never resumed.[31]

During the talks about alligators and "congress shoes" in the Al Jackson letters, Anderson, also reading the early chapters of *Soldiers' Pay,* had mentioned Boni & Liveright to Faulkner for that novel too. Hence, the Scribner's idea was abandoned, despite the allure of Max Perkins, and an Anderson letter only awaited Faulkner's completed manuscript. Neither Stone nor Faulkner, so sensitive to the feelings of children, would exhibit the same circumspection with Anderson or Young, so completely did they distinguish at that stage between a man and his work. It probably never occurred to Faulkner that the piece he wrote for the book editor of the Dallas *Morning News* might jeopardize Anderson's offer. Fortunately for him, Anderson was not vindictive. *Soldiers' Pay* was finished on 25 May 1925, and by the time Faulkner took it to Oxford in June, the awkwardness surrounding the Anderson recommendation to Liveright had given rise to the apocryphal Faulkner anecdote according to which Anderson promised the letter only if he did not have to read the manuscript. "I said, 'Done,'" Faulkner claimed, and Elizabeth Anderson took the word to her husband, who completed his part of the bargain, for Boni & Liveright took the novel in late August 1925.[32]

The "maiden lady critic" of the *Commercial Appeal* had not been so forgiving. From November 1924 Monte Cooper's promised "favorable" review had been steadily undermined by the difficult young poet, only to be annihilated by Faulkner's sexist pronouncements in "Verse Old and Nascent: A Pilgrimage," which appeared in the April 1925 *Double Dealer.* Alleging there that his poetry at first had served the art of seduction and the establishment of a bohemian persona in Oxford more than any pure aesthetic sense, Faulkner now disdained the women attracted by his method: "Ah, women, with their hungry snatching little souls!" who desired only men even while professing a literary passion. Surveying the essay and "On Criticism" in addition to *The Marble Faun* in her column "The Book of Verses," Monte Cooper attacked in the former the "sneering quality, especially in regard to women, that is half-baked and raw, and in one or two places faintly evil smelling." The poems, she wrote, issued from "an undeniably sensitive nature, so evidently now abraded." She catalogued the poet's technical lapses, found that "fifty pages of monotonous, if silvery, intoning, must prove soporific," and could praise only glimpses of "real delicacy and a pensive charm."

Phil Stone informed Four Seas that the book had been "reviewed in the Memphis Commercial Appeal on Sunday, April 6th—though the review was written by a lady who had been quite angered by Faulkner's articles in the Double Dealer." Stone was not alarmed. In fact, he thought they might turn the devastating review to their advantage: "I expect to answer her with an open letter some time soon and I shall send you a copy. This may start a controversy," he explained, sagely, "and of course, you see the value of this."[33]

Yet four months after the publication of *The Marble Faun*, it was all too clear that if Faulkner were to receive any critical attention from the New York literary center, it would have to be primed from Europe, as Robert Frost's had been. Stark Young was most influential in drama—another genre. Sherwood Anderson's talent—to Stone and Faulkner—seemed in decline. The *Double Dealer* circle appeared to be dilettantes, although on a business trip to Chicago that year, Stone used the evidence of the magazine along with the coming maturity of William Faulkner to forecast to Harriet Monroe the rise of the South as the next center of American letters. Their expectations of financial and critical success with the first book, however, were diminishing, as evidenced in the widening intervals in the Four Seas letters as well as in Stone's proposal to the *Poetry* editor, which he recounted for a Newberry curator in 1955 (who offered to buy a copy of *The Marble Faun* for seventy-five dollars): "It may interest you to know that in 1925 (I think that was the year) I was in Chicago, went around to see Miss Monroe, had lunch with her, told her that the literary star in America was passing from the Midwest to the South, and tried to get her to publish free in POETRY some parts of Bill's 'Marble Faun.' She wouldn't do this but she later wrote a little editorial about what I had told her."[34]

Four Seas could read the book trade well enough to see the fate of the volume by William Faulkner and now made few pretenses of promoting the book. Late in April, Stone requested the names of persons who had bought copies from the publisher in order to "get after the others," but by that time even his enthusiasm was dampened and the hyperbole somewhat qualified; he thought he "could sell quite a few more books." The publisher's report on May 8 shattered the last of his illusions; there were only eight names, one a duplication: Bill's Aunt Bama; Donelson Lake; Thomas Pegram and Calvin Wells, lawyer friends of General Stone; and three others.[35] If anything more were to be done, it would have to be initiated at James Stone & Sons. The correspondence with Four Seas would not be renewed until August.

Quite absorbed by his new work on the novel, Faulkner now distanced himself from the old. As Carvel Collins discovered, "When a Mississippian sent him a letter [in New Orleans] complimenting his 'true poetic lines' in *The Marble Faun*, Faulkner derided this unusable response and sent to Oxford for Phil Stone's amusement a copy of his seemingly courteous but actually ironic reply to this insufficiently analytical fan."[36]

Early that summer, Faulkner returned to Oxford with the manuscript of his novel. After greeting his family, he must soon have walked through the woods to Stone Lodge. When Stone came down, the men (followed by Phil's usual retinue of terriers) would have gone into the parlor; it was too hot to sit upstairs in the ninety-degree heat. It would be cooler below, even if the faded crimson damask and the gentlemen's chairs and sofa did smell of dust and mildew—from Miss Rosie's lifelong war against Mississippi sunlight. Phil was "ear-minded," he said, and when his mother got up from her nap and passed the darkened parlor on her way to the front porch, she could have heard the rise and fall of Bill's voice, interrupted now and then by Phil's laugh or a short interchange, then Bill's voice again. Unlike their readings of the poems or short stories, these sessions must have continued for several days.

The Bunch saw the manuscript at the office, where secretary Grace Hudson, the wife of folklorist Arthur Palmer Hudson, complained about "that tripe of Bill Faulkner's" she had to copy for several hours each day. Edith Brown, "shocked at how badly it was punctuated," volunteered to correct the manuscript, which the seemingly indifferent novelist casually permitted. Before they mailed it, Stone took the typescript to Ellaville, who read it overnight and returned it to the office full of misgivings, which Stone only laughed away. "I think it's a damn fine book," he insisted. He approved of the humor of *Mayday*—"There is a good deal in there of the broad type," he often said of the book—excusing its flaws as those of a first novel.[37] A year later, however, Stone would herald *Mosquitoes* to his friends as a much better-written book.

Bill looked thin, Phil thought, and somewhat worn. Spratling had suggested that he and Faulkner make the long-postponed voyage together in July. If Bill were to be in any shape for the walking tour he planned, Stone thought, a few weeks' rest was essential. Jack and Myrtle Stone had opened their camp house in Pascagoula as soon as their oldest child was out of school. Phil had always found it very pleasant there. Jim Stone's family were going down later. Stone would ask Myrtle to invite Bill for the interim.[38] There were a few odds and ends to see about, but those could wait. Accordingly, Bill could go down to work on a new book or on the poems for *A Green Bough*—and try to add a few pounds. With the firm in its usual summer slump, Stone could manage the preparation of the manuscript and the advance publicity he had in mind for the European trip.

Miss Rosie spent part of every spring or summer on the coast, usually at the Great Southern Hotel in Gulfport. After bar association meetings, sometimes General Stone and Phil would join her for a Pascagoula visit before returning north. With, at best, gravel roads, almost always the family made the journey by rail to Gulfport, where they caught the train to Pascagoula. Jack's chauffeur, Lonnie Townes, drove the big Lincoln to the coast for them; later in the decade Jack's whole family went down in two automobiles.[39]

Traveling by train, Faulkner, packing a typewriter "and little else," joined Jack, Myrt, and their children, "Sister," eight years old, Jack, four, and baby "Rosebud," that June for an uneventful vacation.[40] In Faulkner anecdote, however, the quieter the experience, the more romantic the tale. In reality Faulkner's most exacting labor was to keep up with young Jack Stone, who "wore him down when he was five or six," as he confessed to Phil. That and subsequent summers in Pascagoula, nonetheless, provided chapters for Faulkner's ongoing autobiography, which was transmitted in several versions to other anecdotalists, who were free to polish or embellish at will. At home, the lawyer roundly applauded the humorist as the stories filtered back, first from Canada, then New York and New Orleans, now from Pascagoula, and presently from Europe; but as he saw less of his inventive friend, it became harder even for Stone to separate the real from the fanciful. More cautious after Carvel Collins proved to Phil instances of his own gullibility, Stone took care with Robert Coughlan to qualify the Gulf-Coast stories that he knew to be "largely bunk": "I am pretty sure he was never a hand in one of the trawlers, am doubtful that he ever helped sail any big sloop in off-shore races, and know that he never did any rum-running."[41] In all likelihood Stone heard of Faulkner's brief romance with Helen Baird only from Myrtle and nothing of the boating adventures directly from their source, when the latter turned up again at the office late in June, tanned and a little heavier.

In addition to the finished typescript, which Stone and Faulkner both proofread, the newest Faulkner file had "a stack of letters about two inches thick" addressed to the British and expatriate Americans whose work filled the little magazines in Stone's walk-in closet. T. S. Eliot, Ezra Pound, James Joyce, and Arnold Bennett were among those told to watch out for the young writer whom Sherwood Anderson and Stark Young were so much impressed by. Aldous Huxley would have been included because they knew *Crome Yellow* and *Antic Hay*, but also because of Stark Young's friendship with Julian Huxley.[42]

Earlier that month, Stone had Faulkner writing inscriptions to a less illustrious company, as they took desperate measures to dispose of the copies of *The Marble Faun* in the office basement. They ransacked their lists for possible buyers and sent word to the laggards among their friends. Sometimes, apparently, they gambled and simply mailed off a volume, hoping the recipient would obligingly remit the purchase price. In the 1950s a federal judge in Yazoo City wrote Stone that he recalled "the book [of poems] you sent me to read." They inscribed another copy to a nightwatchman (an Ole Miss student found it in his trash after the book had become a collector's item and brought it to the man's attention, only to receive the slim volume as a gift). According to collector William Boozer, who in 1974 published the results of his attempts to locate extant copies, Faulkner presented another to one of Reno's Memphis friends (the copy burned with her house). On 5 June 1925 they both inscribed copies to two of their friends: "To Dorothy [Ware?] / in memory of many pleasant occasions," Faulkner wrote, with Stone adding, "Best of luck to Dot." Perhaps out of loyalty to Phil or to the friend with whom he had "spouted" Swinburne in New Haven,

Distant Company

Arthur Head either purchased a copy at the Brick Row or agreed to buy one from Phil; in any case, both men signed a volume for him that same Friday, Stone's gratitude evident in his inscription "Good old Arthur!" They probably carried Dorothy's copy with them on the last, quick Memphis trip before Bill left.[43] A few days later Phil, a few of the Bunch, and Bess Storer bid farewell to Faulkner at the office, the others still teasing Bill, Bess, and chaperone Grace Hudson about their 2 A.M. return from a swimming double date to Water Valley. Their pushing a Model T Ford through mudholes in the driving rain had endeared the author to his reluctant typist.

When the *West Ivis* left the dock in New Orleans on 7 July 1925, William Spratling and William Faulkner were aboard.[44] As in 1918, Stone little expected to see Faulkner home by Christmas. But this time his own adventures would carry him no farther away than Memphis or Clarksdale.

While Faulkner's ship steamed around the Florida coast to Savannah, Stone returned to searching titles, probating wills, and flirting with Edith Brown over fountain Cokes. The summer would not offer even a decent political brawl. Vardaman, old and tired, lived in Alabama, his career finished. Henry Whitfield, the Stones' candidate, had whipped Bilbo to succeed Lee Russell as governor.[45] Having seen "prisoner" Theodore G. Bilbo holding open house in Oxford in 1923 when he was jailed for contempt of court, Stone no doubt concluded Bilbo's perjury would hardly spell the end of his political career, and, in fact, Bilbo merely bided his time until the 1927 campaign.[46] That summer when court adjourned, checker players under the courthouse trees would see Phil and Bess drive over to pick up Abe Linker at the Bank of Oxford. Frontis L. Linker, General Stone's protégé, had in six years moved from cashier to bank president there. A dozen years older than Stone, and a widower since 1910, he would be a perennial political associate of Phil Stone. After hours it was Abe and Phil now who pulled up a chair at gambling houses such as Reno's Club Seville.[47]

There were postcards from Faulkner in Italy and Switzerland after he went ashore at Genoa on the second of August, and, more regularly, short notes after he settled into the first month in Paris, around 13 August. Because Faulkner was eager to know the fate of *Mayday* at Liveright's, Stone wrote Sherwood Anderson to inquire, adding that an introduction by the novelist might secure an audience for his friend's book. On 17 August Anderson reported Liveright's having written that "two of his readers were enthusiastic about Bill's novel, the third not so enthusiastic." The decision would come from Horace Liveright, now reading *Mayday* for himself. Anderson was optimistic. "I have a hunch he will take it." Anderson believed the introduction Stone suggested was superfluous. Instead the former advertising man, who advised Stark Young about the salability of titles and jacket blurbs, volunteered to help with the latter: "I'll be glad to do it, as I certainly admire Bill's talent."[48]

On 10 August, soon after Stone's letter to Anderson, he wrote Four Seas: "It is my understanding that under your contract with Mr. Faulkner, a statement of account with reference to 'The Marble Faun' was due the first of August. Mr. Faulkner is now in Europe and I have not heard from him as to his present address. He authorized me to make any settlement with you and I also have his power of attorney. I shall be glad to take the matter up with you as soon as possible as Mr. Faulkner needs the money."

Stone evidently forwarded the 14 August sales report to Faulkner. Only the figures from New Haven's Brick Row were still out. Hackett's manager had "bought a few copies outright," the publishers said, "and we therefore let them have a quantity for display." Stone did a bit of arithmetic on his copy of the 10 August letter. In one column he added "25, 50, 19, 11, 50, 11, 2, 12"—presumably the eight monthly sales, which totaled 180 copies. To the left he worked out Faulkner's 30-cent royalty, a dismal eighty-one dollars. After twelve months, they had learned the hard way, as Stone would write at another time, "That the world owed no man anything, that greatness was in creating great things and not in pretending them; that the only road to literary success was by sure, patient, hard intelligent work; that you reached the throne if you deserve it and not otherwise." Phil had about as much patience as quick-tempered General Stone and could easily have doubted now whether talent, work, and "unflinching honesty" would win out after all.[49] It was impossible, Stone may have thought, for two men to have tried any harder.

News of Faulkner's beard, his new novel *Elmer*, and surly American tourists must have come periodically to James Stone & Sons early that fall. In late September Faulkner began a letter he never finished on the back of a sheet from the *Elmer* typescript: "Dear Stone—I've had a look at Brittany." No other letters or cards in their personal correspondence survived the 1942 fire, which also destroyed one of the few replies Stone received from his letters to major writers in London and Paris. T. S. Eliot had taken time to answer, something to the effect "that he had met Bill in London once and would pay more attention to him than he had before," according to Emily Stone. Faulkner wrote his mother in October that he had arrived in London, had "seen a lot . . . everything, almost," but that the city was so expensive he was leaving the next day for Devon, Cornwall, and Kent. A week later he was back in Dieppe.[50] Thus, even a single Eliot encounter would have been casual indeed.

The letters had been Stone's idea after all, but his friend seems to have gone out of his way to avoid capitalizing on them. Faulkner was comfortable conversing with Breton fishermen or the habitues of the Luxembourg Gardens, but for all his talk to Spratling about Pound, Blotner writes, he apparently made no attempt to look up Pound in Italy, although Spratling thought they had seen him at a distance in Paris. They walked to Shakespeare & Company, but missed Sylvia Beach, Ernest Hemingway, and Gertrude Stein; and Faulkner staked out a café table in Paris in order to study James Joyce, but never spoke to him.[51] The nerve of the two friends evidently belonged to Phil Stone, whose shyness—although every bit as real—was not often discernible behind his barrage of words.

When Faulkner reached Paris again in mid-October, he learned that Liveright had decided to take his novel, now to be called, at the publisher's suggestion, *Soldiers' Pay*. The good news about the book, though, was soon marred by a pressing financial obligation: in October the Falkners had been presented with a bill for $21.85, which the former employee still owed the post office. The funds left with Stone were exhausted, but, rather than raise the small sum, Faulkner's attorney meant first to check out the matter with his political friends. Murry Falkner explained to the General Accounting Office only that his son was in Europe. But Faulkner could infer his mother's state of mind from her letters, and he began urging Stone to get his money from *The*

Phil Stone of Oxford

Marble Faun. Stone dictated a letter to Four Seas on 6 November requesting their "prompt attention" to "the settlement due Mr. William Faulkner on November 1st last." On 9 November, however, the Comptroller General granted a grace period until Faulkner's return.[52]

Least concerned of all, Faulkner was happily parodying Stone in his cover letter for the six stanzas of "Ode to the Louver," a work they both later swore actually to have mailed to H. L. Mencken.[53] The poem, as its typist explained, had been "conposed by Wm Faulkner," who signed it with his mark. "Typewritting and corrections & advice [were furnished] by Ernest V. Simms (American)," who also signed the papers. Faulkner poked fun both at Eliot's *Waste Land* scholarly paraphernalia and at Stone's habitual pencil work. There were eight "Orthurs notes," beginning with footnote one to "Louver" in the title: "Big house in Paris, France, Near City hall." Footnote six explained that "Herbert Hoover," used to rhyme with "Louver," was an "American church worker." Thinking not only of Stone, but perhaps also of Monte Cooper's chiding his "unforgivable localisms in pronunciation," Faulkner noted, as in footnote eight, where the verse "Dont rhyme." But the letter enclosing the poem was aimed at Phil Stone, with merely an aside at Mencken, and Faulkner mailed two copies of the letter and the poem home to Phil:

Paris, (France)
November 1st. 1925

Mr. H. Mencken, magazine orthur
Mr. H. Mencken

Gentlemen

Enclosed at your usual rate are poem by Wm Faulkner, He wants to get a start at poetry. And I advise him to try your magazine after I made the corrections because my family is long a reader of your magazine until a train reck 2 years ago. Since I have read your magazine personally since I am not 1 of those who reads only for pleasure.

I think our Americans poets will be good as any foregner with encouragments and corrections since reading your magazine feel sure you feel the same sentiment. Give young americans chances to make good with advice and corrections say I. I onely made corrections in the above poem without changing its sentiments because the poet himself quit schools before learning to write because I have a typewritter

I feel sure that you feel the same

respectfully yours & ect.
Ernest V. Simms

Ernest V. Simms
Baptist Young Peoples Union
care American Ambassador
Paris (France)
(American Citizen)

At least since 1919, Faulkner poems had gone out under the office letterhead with accompanying letters dictated by Phil Stone, no matter who signed them, a patronage that in time could rankle the humblest of men. Stone's enthusiasm could be stifling; he knew himself that sometimes the advice went on too long. Stone once admitted, after the fact, that he doubted whether "it was [Faulkner's] early ambition to be a poet as much as it was my ambition for him to be one."[54] But if Phil Stone could tell Harriet Monroe the direction of American letters, with equal aplomb he could freely revise Faulkner's phrases, while reminding their maker that in academic degrees the score was four to nothing. It was evident whose family connections earned the meager royalties for *The Marble Faun* and whose law firm furnished reams of office stationery and typewriter ribbons. Phil Stone read books "only for pleasure"; his friend's work "will be good . . . with encouragements and corrections." It was a devastating yet oblique satire; at times William Faulkner was even prophetic. It seems impossible that the parodist had not seen the—quite literally—hundreds of business letters in the Stone papers after 1931 which, like that of Simms, interlace business requests with recitals of family tragedy: Twenty years ago, when my father's bank failed. . . . One of my brothers was a prime chiseler and the other. . . . After our old house burned in 1942 and my father and brothers were dead I tried to save some of our property by. . . .

There is another way in which Ernest V. Simms anticipates Phil Stone, especially at the end, when Stone's illness exacerbated his character flaws. A letter selected at random from Stone's June 1962 Faulkner file is the usual three short paragraphs of the Stone business letter. Yet there Stone is obviously as much taken with the pronoun *I* as is Simms: "I have"; "I was introduced"; "I was still fooling with Bill";

"I took him over"; "I took Bill"; "I am the Phil Stone"; "I wish"; "I did help"; "I had him autograph"; "I got $40 or $50 . . ." Only in the last sentence of Stone's letter does he use, tellingly, the first person plural pronoun: "we actually made money."[55] The sardonic comedy of the Simms letter may be the earliest sign that the balance of their heretofore complementary relationship had shifted a degree or two as Faulkner left Woodson Ridge for Royal Street, the Gulf Coast, and the museums of Paris.

Nevertheless, Faulkner's homecoming in Phil's office at Christmas was full of good humor. The dark brown beard, as Bill responded to the secretaries' teasing, had made him look more French or Italian than American, allowing him freedom to observe the Europeans he met unobtrusively. There was a gift for Stone, one of the W. C. Odiorne portraits taken of Faulkner on the bench in the Luxembourg Gardens. And the tourist picked up where he had left off in his Breton letter describing the countryside over which the war had been fought, as he had done in letters to his mother.[56]

After the Christmas holidays, the friends settled into two months of something like Indian summer in their relationship. They played golf, joked with the Bunch, visited Dorothy Ware and their Memphis friends, and came back with some racy details about a gangster known as "Popeye" Pumphrey.[57] Faulkner briefed Stone on his work in Paris and at nights frequently came over to read. One night he brought along the inscriptions he had copied from tombstones in Savannah's Colonial Cemetery while waiting for the *West Ivis* to take on cargo for Naples.

Stone and Faulkner also shared their reading discoveries over the past months, but Faulkner there had a trump card: he had bought James Joyce's *Ulysses* (Paris: Shakespeare & Company, 1924). Within a month of Faulkner's return, Stone was writing the Brick Row for an inexpensive edition of *A Portrait of the Artist as a Young Man*. Paying for it in February, he sent DeLacey on a more difficult assignment; he wanted his own copy of *Ulysses*, though he could do without a first edition, he said.[58]

They were almost as excited about Joyce as they were about the coming publication of *Soldiers' Pay*. When Faulkner's novel appeared on 25 February, however, Oxford, like Ireland, was more shocked than pleased with its native son. Few read it, of course, but within a matter of days everyone in town knew of its scandalous contents. Miss Maud, according to Blotner, wrote her son that "leaving the country was about the best thing he could do." Faulkner, fortunately, had already returned to New Orleans. Phil Stone took a first edition over to the Ole Miss librarian, but the rumors had preceded him. The university would neither buy one nor accept a copy with the author's compliments.[59]

In returning to New Orleans, Faulkner had also escaped the unfinished post office business, which the government, however, remembered on 3 March: "Unless this matter is adjusted without further delay, it will be necessary to make the collection from your bondsmen." On the ninth Stone wrote Perrin Lowrey's uncle, Congressman B. G. Lowrey, requesting that he review Faulkner's liability. If the congressman were satisfied, Faulkner would pay the department. Lowrey soon explained that Bill had only made an error in tabulating his money orders. When Phil thanked Lowrey for his "usual courtesy," he revealed no little paranoia about Faulkner's postal entanglements: they had merely wanted satisfaction that if Faulkner paid up, the matter would end there: "It does look like the Government could manage its affairs so as not to harass a man forever." To reciprocate for the favor, Stone had collected some political gossip for the congressman; their 'mutual friend' Mooday Patton, listening out in Beat Five, reported that "Dick Denman [had] made no impression at all and that he [could] not find anybody out there who is for him." Lowrey, a long-seated incumbent, thus might rest easy during the coming election. The aging politician had heard and discounted rumors of "impending political deals against us." "To be perfectly frank," he wrote, "I cannot see why any aspiring young politician should go out of his way to incur my political opposition." Lowrey's post office report, however, presented a problem. Faulkner was short on money and to pay the bill had to borrow thirty dollars from Stone.[60]

Despite its Oxford reception, the Faulkner novel soon drew national, and favorable, reviews. On 21 April Stone began a series of letters for Faulkner to Boni & Liveright. The initial communication that Sallie Simpson typed would have been quite familiar to the *Marble Faun* stenographers: Stone inquired about sales and requested 250 stamped envelopes for his personal letters, whereby he could sell "not less than one hundred copies." He advised the publishers to hurry books to Oxford to meet the current "interest": "As you know, most people will buy a book when they can see it but will not go to the trouble to write to the publisher for it." (Stone also enclosed Bess Storer's five-dollar check made payable to him for two first-edition copies she wanted Bill to autograph.)

Three weeks later Phil endorsed Gathright-Reed's proposal to handle *Soldiers' Pay* on consignment: "These people are absolutely reliable." He also advised that Boni & Liveright send "posters or reviews" with the books. John S. Clapp, unaccustomed to Stone's promotion mania, mistook him for a bookseller. The publisher had no circulars but would gladly mimeograph a Stone letter using the reviews, which they mailed to him. Stone explained about Mack Reed's sales offer and said that he planned only to write local newspaper articles "and thus aid Mr. Faulkner in selling his book." They exchanged four letters in five days. New York also reported sales of 2,084 copies of the 2,500 printing by 19 May. Stone was "very much gratified," he wrote, at the prospect of an end to the twelve-year "drought." [61]

Soon out of money in New Orleans, however, Faulkner came home to borrow more or to find an odd job to do. Stone, it appears, had a better idea. With the good publicity from *Soldiers' Pay*, Boni & Liveright might give Faulkner a further advance on his royalties, not enough for New Orleans perhaps, but enough for several weeks in Pascagoula with the W. E. Stones. Money meant little to Jack and Myrtle; Jack was generous to a fault, and Myrtle cared very much for Bill Faulkner and enjoyed mothering him. Stone and Faulkner talked over how much he would need to finish his second novel there and how much they dared request of Horace Liveright. With the latter foremost in their minds, they agreed on fifty dollars. The letter that Faulkner signed on the fourth of June, the two surely collaborated on; indeed, the phrases, and the obvious reference to Phil's poor opinion of *Soldiers' Pay*, suggest Stone as having written or dictated most of it. After naming their business, "Faulkner" pleaded his case:

> I am about half through with "Mosquitoes", the second novel, and it is much better than "Soldier's [sic] Pay". I think it is a far better piece of work from a literary standpoint, much better articulated and is more sustained. It possesses, in my opinion, the additional merit, from a commercial viewpoint, of being quite amusing and the kind of book that any

sort of person could read and enjoy. It should easily have twice the sales of "Soldier's Pay". This is not only my opinion but the opinion of several people of intelligence and taste who have read the manuscript. I might also add that these same people did not place anything near so high an estimate on "Soldier's Pay" as you and Sherwood Anderson did. Just now I am stuck in the middle of this new novel and can't seem to go any further. I think I need a change of surroundings but have no money hence the request above.[62]

Stone's high opinion of *Mosquitoes* would not last for long. The finished product would be disappointing. Years later he wrote Glenn Carey: "I feel sorry for you if you have to read MOSQUITOES because it is a very poor book. My recollection is that it sold about 1200 copies and that was all it deserved to sell."[63]

When Faulkner went again to Pascagoula that summer to court Helen Baird and to finish *Mosquitoes*, Stone stayed in Oxford to putter in three campaigns: the congressional races, promotion of *Soldiers' Pay*, and the stage "career" of Marian Davis. In the Davis letters in July to Stark Young and Byrne Hackett, he reported, misleadingly, that Bill's first novel had already sold "into the third edition"; the second novel, to be finished in the fall, he prophesied, would sell even better because it was "much more amusing and a far better book." It was Frances Starks who wrote Stone that Young was abroad; she also reported that Scribner's was soon to publish *Heaven Trees*, the novel about Young's family, which Stone promised to buy: "We are all very proud of Mr. Stark." But Young's father had died the previous October, and although Stark Young had spent Christmas in nearby Como, where he grew up, his visits to Mississippi now would almost cease.[64]

Faulkner was "pretty near done" on another book himself, as he wrote Helen Baird in North Carolina in August on a discarded sheet from the *Mosquitoes* manuscript. The author finished the novel in Pascagoula on 1 September, having lingered on the coast after Jack and his family returned to Charleston.[65]

Although the majority of the New Orleans experiences Faulkner used for the novel were familiar to Phil only from Bill's stories, their common experience, woven through these threads, strongly colors the finished narrative, especially in incidental details. And although faithful to its Huxleyan model, *Mosquitoes'* "endless talk" seems also to suggest, as Blotner points out, Faulkner's incipient skepticism about men of words rather than deeds. The playful allusions to Yale men as well as Faulkner's hypothesis of the "sterility" of words make clear that Phil Stone, once aligned with the poet, observing in company with him the passing show, in *Mosquitoes* joined Sherwood Anderson and the rest of the world as object. Yet in the talkative Stone, the writer could also see his own reflection. In matters of money the friends for years operated as one, as Faulkner wrote Robert K. Haas in 1939: "I have a friend here, I have known him all my life, never any question of mine and thine between us when either had it."[66] The fascination with words, Faulkner perhaps suspected, might be for them a common disorder.

When Faulkner brought his typescript to Sallie Simpson, Phil had some bad news for him. Impatient to know how their first novel was selling, Stone had written Liveright late in August on the excuse that he needed the figures "to prepare some more publicity for Mr. Faulkner in this section." Clapp replied that total sales to date were 2,210: "I have told you before how much I regret that so fine a novel as this has not reached a sales figure which it so justly deserves."[67] In that letter Clapp's offer to assist Stone's publicity appears more genuine.

Faulkner evidently stayed around long enough to see the *Mosquitoes* typescript completed before he returned to New Orleans "for the winter." He was there by late September.[68] That fall Stone and the credit department at Boni & Liveright engaged in a flurry of correspondence—over Bess Storer's five-dollar check. Her bank account in Yazoo City had been closed by the time Liveright got around to cashing her April check, sometime in July. They had written Bess there that month, having "no record of Mr. Stone's address," and the letter came back; but someone finally enlightened the credit department, and Phil wrote that she was in Kosciusko, Mississippi, assuring the firm that she would pay promptly or he would cover it. But the matter dragged on.

By 8 November Liveright demanded a check by return mail. Stone replied that if the publishers were so impatient for five dollars that he had to remind them that they had his word and a gentleman's bond that they "need have no fears," perhaps another matter of money (or honor) ought to be brought to their attention. He was "much surprised," he wrote in the 10 November letter, to learn from "Mr. Faulkner the other night" that the 31 August itemized sales statement and the 31 October royalty check for *Soldiers' Pay* were both overdue: "My understanding is that you are thoroughly reliable but Mr. Faulkner has had one unfortunate experience with the Four Seas Co. and they owe him some money which he has been unable to collect. I happen to know that he needs this money very badly." Until the author was paid, Stone said, he had no intention of sending five dollars to New York. At their request he would pay that amount over to Faulkner, and they might deduct "this amount from what you owe him."

The royalty check, without a deduction, was mailed on the sixteenth; Liveright "will therefore thank you to send us your check," the publishers rejoined. On 26 November Stone informed them, as if for the first time, that he had requested Miss Storer to pay: "if she does not do so please write me and I shall," he said.[69] Thereafter in the Stone papers there is no mention of Bess Storer's five dollars.

In New Orleans that autumn Faulkner became absorbed in his first publishing venture in which Stone took no part. He and Bill Spratling collaborated on *Sherwood Anderson and Other Famous Creoles*, the collection of Spratling's caricatures of their friends in the Quarter. Faulkner contributed captions and a short parody of Anderson's style in the foreword. They sold the four hundred copies of the first printing within a week.[70]

That winter Stone had ample leisure to catch up on his correspondence, for with the collapse of cotton prices, money in the South had simply vanished. In economics as in literature Stone was an inveterate and ebullient prophet, and two years from the stock market crash the "male Cassandra" was urging his New Haven friend Al DeLacey to invest in real estate in the rural South. Phil himself had been too poor to order any new books for almost a year, but by 1928, he told DeLacey, there would be "more money in the South than there has been since the war." Not the West but the South was destined for great wealth, within twenty-five years, and because Southerners were "too urbane . . . kindly . . . humorous for money to ruin," the region would be "the most delightful country in the world to live in."[71]

In literature at least Stone's prognoses had some relationship to fact. Among the first editions General Stone and Sallie Simpson ordered as a surprise for Phil at Christmas was F. Scott Fitzgerald's *All the*

Sad Young Men (1926). He read part of it immediately, "marked it up with [his] usual hieroglyphics," and promptly revoked his scorn at Fitzgerald's "literary pretensions" in *This Side of Paradise* and *Flappers and Philosophers*. With the new stories, as Stone reported his about-face to DeLacey, inexplicably "this man Fitzgerald has become somebody and he will bear watching." The collection rivaled the best American short fiction and even approached the genius of Chekhov. He was equally effusive about Faulkner's most recent short fiction. Bill was at work on a story—"It is very good indeed"—that he hoped to sell to the *Saturday Evening Post*. "If anybody with the slightest taste for writing happens to read it they are certain to take it," Stone declared, telling DeLacey "to watch the Post for it." [72]

Although Phil had recommended the "extremely clever and beautifully written" *Mosquitoes* to the men at the Brick Row, he believed that Faulkner's stories, some then "in the hands of agents," were "much better than either one of the novels," as he wrote Carl Rollins, the Yale printer. Rollins's recent correspondence had been prompted by a Stone letter the *Yale Alumni Weekly* reprinted. Rollins seems also to have inquired whether Bill was going to publish any more poems. "He has two more books of verse," Stone replied, "but has not tried to publish any more of it and has not been writing any verse for nearly a year." [73]

For a man having "no itch for print," as Stone described himself to Rollins, the lawyer found more excuses than that of William Faulkner to sign his name to "open letters." The one Rollins had seen, Stone had sent to the *American Bar Association Journal*. Alumnus Stone was also closely following the selection of Yale's new law school dean, he told Rollins. Legal politics, like the practice of law, seemed to be holding greater interest for him as his own business expanded. However, the "growing practice" he mentioned to Rollins was more satisfying to his ego than to his pocketbook, even as his dedication to the profession still ranked behind his passion for literature. [74]

When the galley proofs of *Mosquitoes* arrived in Oxford in late January or early February of 1927, Faulkner's chief concern was for the date of the four-hundred-dollar advance for *Mosquitoes*. He may have been contemplating a travel fund, for, unlike Stone, Faulkner was "damned tired of our 99 [degree] winters of this sunny south," he wrote Horace

Liveright in February. His writing, however, was not suffering; he was at work, he also reported, both on "a novel, and a collection of short stories of my townspeople." [75]

With no money immediately forthcoming from New York, the author and his lawyer thought again of the royalties owed by Four Seas; but since August 1925 their letters to Boston, even one sent by registered mail, had been ignored, and the eighty-one dollars was still unpaid. Faulkner turned to anthologist William Stanley Braithwaite for advice. Stone owned several volumes of Braithwaite's annual poetry anthology, the earliest purchased in 1916. In 1925 the editor had included a Faulkner poem. With that introduction and knowing that Braithwaite published out of Boston, Faulkner requested information from him concerning Four Seas' credibility. "It never occurred to me that anyone would rob a poet," he wrote. "It's like robbing a whore or a child." He inquired whether he "might collect this money without resorting to legal means, which I cannot afford to do, having no income beyond that derived from more or less casual manual labor."

Faulkner certainly had grounds for suspicion, but attorney Stone, given to cynicism anyway, especially about Northerners, alarmed him even more by pointing out that legally his claim would be void after two years, a deadline half a year away—and a deadline, said Stone, Four Seas intended to exploit. Braithwaite replied, however, that Edmund R. Brown's company was in a position of "temporary financial embarrassment," but should fulfill its contractual obligations when the situation stabilized. Faulkner, though critical of Brown for not explaining himself, was characteristically generous. "I have been without money too damned often myself, to annoy anyone who is himself unable to meet an obligation," he wrote the anthologist, thanking him for the information about his "uncollectible royalties."

That contact probably was initiated as a last alternative to filing suit, a contingency more probable—because of Stone—than Faulkner admitted to Braithwaite, but, considering the expense and the amount in question, one hardly very practical. (Litigation might have greatly embarrassed the publisher, for Stone later suspected, as do collectors today, that Four Seas never printed the thousand copies their contract had stipulated.) [76] The only money Stone and Faulkner subsequently made on *The Marble Faun*, enough for both to make a profit, would come from the box stored then in General Stone's attic—and from the reputation accrued from the books about to follow. For a while, however, Faulkner must have had to interrupt his new work to paint a house or two.

9

The Major Fiction

At James Stone & Sons that rainy spring of 1927, business was slack. Between thunderstorms and rumors of tornadoes, Phil Stone and William Faulkner played golf at the university course, where the putting greens now often stood in water and the fairways were virtually washed away. One day in April, Bill dropped by the office with a letter from Boni & Liveright. The second novel would appear by the end of the month.[1] When Faulkner left, Stone began a draft announcing the approaching publication of *Mosquitoes* for the area newspapers. *Soldiers' Pay*, he wrote, had "attracted quite a bit of attention among the discerning," but, mentioning nothing more than the title of the second novel, he went on to a description of Faulkner's present work and a short paragraph about his golf game:

> Since his return from Europe Faulkner has been here at home playing golf and writing two new novels which are already under contract. Both are Southern in setting. One is something of a saga of an extensive family connection of typical "poor white trash" and is said by those who have seen that part of the manuscript completed [i.e., Phil Stone] to be the funniest book anybody ever wrote. The other is a tale of the aristocratic, chivalrous and ill-fated Sartoris family, one of whom was even too reckless for the daring Confederate cavalry leader Jeb Stuart. . . .
>
> Faulkner is quite an excellent amateur golfer and consistently makes nine holes under forty. He is planning to enter the State Golf Tournament in June and some think he has a good chance for the State championship.[2]

Since Faulkner apparently was still "not keen on photography," Stone decided to use with the publicity the Odiorne portrait then sitting on the law table in his bedroom. The bearded writer smoking a pipe on the park bench in Paris was something of an improvement over the Mississippi Byron.

By the publication date of *Mosquitoes*, over two and a half million acres in Faulkner's home state were under water. At 7:45 A.M., 21 April 1927, the levee that protected the Delta from floods broke some eighteen miles north of Greenville. Oxford and the North Mississippi hill country remained dry, but the rampaging Mississippi soon covered an area "the size of Rhode Island," wrote poet-planter William Alexander Percy, now chairman of Greenville's Flood Relief Committee. "The 1927 flood," Percy noted in his memoir *Lanterns on the Levee*, "was a torrent ten feet deep . . . ; it was thirty-six hours coming and four months going; it was deep enough to drown a man, swift enough to upset a boat, and lasting enough to cancel a crop year."[3]

Those cotton farmers who did manage to get seed in the ground would make windfall profits, but the flood ensured that banking resources, which in 1926 had finally climbed back to their 1920 levels, could grow only 11 percent through 1928, despite the river's reparation of silt, which made that year's crops so bountiful. It would be fourteen years—not until 1942—before Mississippi money again equaled even the 1928 mark.[4]

If 1927 was the year of the flood, it was also the year William Faulkner began seriously to cultivate his native soil. Taking to heart the example of Balzac and, more recently, of Sherwood Anderson, Faulkner became determined "to recreate between the covers of a book the world . . . I was already preparing to lose and regret." Fashioning characters "composed partly from what they were in actual life and partly from what they should have been and were not: thus I improved on God who, dramatic though He be, has no sense, no feeling for, theatre," Faulkner wrote. The world he conjured up of course was the mythical Yoknapatawpha County. In his thirtieth year, Faulkner watched as a character named Flem Snopes took over one short story and moved into a novel. Perhaps the manuscript, first entitled *Father Abraham*, contained the story that was to have gone to the *Saturday Evening Post.*[5]

Phil Stone, to whom literature and politics were nectar and ambrosia, would never be more enthusiastic about a Faulkner creation; for, even more than in *Sartoris* or *Sanctuary*, to which he contributed incidents and phrases, with the Snopes clan Stone could actually experience, if fleetingly, the satisfaction of incarnation. The idea was his; after William Faulkner, Stone's greatest compulsion was as self-appointed commentator on the decline of his class and, as he wrote, their displacement in "what the lingering few of the old ante-bellum ladies still refer to with calm and cultured scorn, as the 'Rise of the Redneck.'"[6] But if, to some, Phil Stone seemed to arrogate Faulkner's achievement, in justice there were darker implications of Faulkner and Stone's common storage not only of money but also of ideas.

After Phil's breakdown, for example, in one of his lucid periods at Whitfield, Stone's wife brought down a copy of John Faulkner's *My Brother Bill*. After writing his name in it, Stone turned over the title page and exclaimed, "Why, he used my poem!" and underlined the first four lines from the *Green Bough* epitaph, which John had quoted. Stone had written a little verse in his youth, some during the Faulkner period, as well as suggesting words and phrases for Bill's poetry. Perhaps Faulkner had merely expropriated "If there be grief . . ." as he expropriated General Longstreet or the Civil War games of Phil's childhood.[7] Or perhaps in using "he," Stone had meant John Faulkner, for Phil might momentarily have overlooked the acknowledgment, so that "my poem" may have been Stone's way of saying "our poem." In either case, from the first, the intimate collaboration over the Snopeses and soon on *Sartoris* would have significant effects, certainly on their immediate relationship. Without doubt it had profound later repercussions for Phil Stone; almost surely William Faulkner would not have escaped untouched.

"The Snopes Business," said Stone in 1962, "was actually generated around 1924 and 1925."[8] Having begun as anecdote, Stone's medium, the Snopes chronicles, like other sagas, would live in the spoken word for a time before being confined to print. Stone was instinctively a preserver, and until he was almost forty enjoyed the leisure of an 1890s maiden aunt to indulge his historical curiosity by listening to his father's generation and by turning over old papers at the courthouse and in the antebellum law office. Instead of entertaining other people's children with such tales—he did some of that too—he unconsciously provided a convenient storehouse for Faulkner, out of which came some of the materials for *Flags in the Dust,* which Faulkner began soon after *Father Abraham,* according to Blotner. Stone, of course, was merely one source; Faulkner, the inveterate listener, managed to assimilate virtually the collective lore of the town. But, unlike the maiden aunt, Phil Stone, who lived in the present too, found there a more engaging study than "before the wa'."

Just as Stone as a child had fought "new" Civil War battles, his imagination delighted in stories—some he himself made up—about the class represented by men like Vardaman, Bilbo, and Lee Russell. Those afternoons of play, however, would have been as ephemeral as the earlier ones had not Faulkner, fascinated himself, joined in. It is the seminal distinction between the two friends that Faulkner and not Stone gave those creatures the name Snopes. Stone could not remember at what stage that occurred, only that the "name had no connection with the Stopes [sic] trial."[9] In an area where the lower classes give their children names like Ex Senator or Fragile (frăjɔ́ lē) and the gentry nickname wives or children "Lump" (for "Lump of Sugar") or "Courthouse," it was a challenge to christen the clan. Stone subsequently supplied Faulkner with the names Admiral Dewey Snopes and Wallstreet Panic Snopes, he said.

The satisfaction in conceiving the Snopses, it seems, was to caricature—and hence in part to exorcise—the already absurd. While Stone had a youthful weakness for pranks, the antics of the characters they laughed at together for forty years were generally black farce, the portrait of a world usurped by freaks and gnomes. Below the humor lay their incredulity and horror as the South they had known and loved went terribly awry.

The "real revolution in the South was not the race situation," Stone told Faulkner, "but the rise of the redneck . . . to places of power and wealth."[10] That class had none of "the scruples of the old aristocracy," and that assured them the victory. Educated himself to assume the responsibilities of his class, Stone would have relished power, as perhaps Faulkner would not. And yet, nearly a decade after his formal education had ended, Phil Stone still played at literature and small-time politics while James Stone ran their law practice, having placed his proxy, Abe Linker, in the president's chair at the Bank of Oxford.

The Major Fiction

By the time Stone's father died, the money necessary for power had evaporated, even if he had been capable of action. As a boy, his own son Philip, too young to sense the impotence of that sardonic mirth, would be incredulous that Phil could sit laughing over Bilbo's skulduggery. Like a child, however, with Bill Faulkner's characters, Phil Stone might manipulate a world—but only so long as Faulkner tolerated such manipulation.

During 1927 Stone was clearly casting about for a vocation. According to the autobiography, he was seriously considering becoming a professional gambler. Characteristically, with money or without, having decided on the experiment, he kept the road hot to Memphis. Sometimes Faulkner went with him. On one trip, in July, while Stone was closeted with Berryman and his fellows, Bill played the wheel. By the time Stone redeemed his chips, Faulkner had lost over three hundred dollars, or so he wrote Horace Liveright. Stone, it seems, was in no position to help him. At any rate, without authorization Faulkner had "drawn a draft on" his publisher for two hundred dollars, "against my next advance, the mss for which I shall send in to you by Sept. 1," he explained. Somewhat less than pleased, Liveright honored the draft. In his letter of thanks, Faulkner elaborated on the other streak of bad luck responsible for his "case of dire necessity," obviously a tall tale, about the authorities' having confiscated his cache of twenty-five gallons of whiskey through the perfidy of "one of our niggers," who "had smelled the whisky out, dug it up, sold a little . . . been caught and told where the rest of it was." [11]

As early as the winter of 1926–27, Blotner thinks, Faulkner had been pulled away from *Father Abraham* and the other stories by his work on *Flags in the Dust*. "At last and certainly, as El Orens' sheik said, I have written THE book, of which those other things were but foals. I believe it is the damdest best book you'll look at this year," he wrote Liveright in mid-October 1927, just before mailing the manuscript. Though enamored of the Snopes idea, Stone had shifted with him, embracing enthusiastically the new game of populating Yoknapatawpha County with people from Woodson Ridge, the square, the Big Place, North Lamar, Stone Lodge, the university, as well as Ripley, Clarksdale, and Memphis. *Sartoris*, Phil Stone said later, "is really factual." [12]

Had their countrymen been readers, Stone could easily have found himself defending Bill Faulkner for libel. But just as the Sartoris house is an amalgam of four or five houses in Oxford, so Miss Jenny, for example, is in part a Falkner, a Carter, a Stone, an Alston, and probably others. No libel suit would ever have stood up in court.

By August the book was "half done." Meanwhile, there was the constant irritation about money. Stone and Faulkner sent a revised article on Sherwood Anderson to the *New Republic* in August, hoping that a small check would accompany the publication of an article clearly superior to the one they had read there earlier. Faulkner had asked Horace Liveright late in July whether he might "be prevailed [upon] to look at a book of poetry?" but Liveright was not inclined to publish Faulkner poetry.[13] Sallie Simpson had patiently retyped the ragged copies of short stories as they returned from the *Post* or *Scribner's* or *Collier's*, and on their trips to and from the post office Stone and Faulkner recorded the dates of submission and rejection on the suitbox lid. A drawer in Stone's desk filled up with printed rejection slips.

Stone's conversations with the older lawyers drinking cider in his backyard or with his colleagues during recess at the courthouses around the circuit were now occasions for research, or a filching of anecdotes. In Ripley one afternoon attorney Orbrey Street disclosed an intriguing addition to the Falkner family history. Even though Faulkner had already finished the *Flags* typescript, in September 1927, perhaps during the preparation of the final copy, Stone wrote asking Street for a complete version of his story, which Street mailed two days later, on 7 October. The tombstone story he had told Phil, Street observed with a lawyer's penchant for facts, was "hearsay," but he would shortly check it himself and report later. The story Street recalled was this:

> Col. W. C. Falkner killed a man named Bob Hindman, brother of General Thos. B. Hindman of the Confederate army. It seems that Hindman was going on the Colonel with a knife, and he shot him. The family out of a spirit of revenge . . . had inscribed on his tomb this sentence: "Murdered by W. C. Falkner." Col. Falkner who seems to have been promptly acquitted of all charges that may have been preferred against him, didn't like the idea of that sentence standing as it was inscribed. He applied for a Writ of Injunction, which was granted and sustained compelling the family to take the word "Murdered" out of the inscription. They complied with the order of the Court by striking out the word "Murdered" leaving

The Major Fiction

the word itself plainly visible and inserted over it the word "Killed" leaving the balance of the sentence as it was inscribed before.

Less than a week later there came another letter from Street, who in the interval had visited the Hindman family plot: "Clearly there has never been any inscription on the tomb except what now appears there. It is this: 'Robert Hindman . . . Born 1823. Killed by William C. Falkner in Ripley, Miss., May 8th, 1849.'" The chancery clerk's office had most of the county's old files, he wrote, but those were not in chronological order, so he had given up the attempt to trace the injunction. In the penultimate episode of *Flags in the Dust*, Miss Jenny and Isom tour another graveyard where a man with a chisel had effaced an earlier inscription on Colonel Sartoris's monument and "added beneath it: 'Fell at the hand of ____ Redlaw. Aug. 4, 1876.'"[14]

When Sallie Simpson had typed too far into the text for any more of those last-minute revisions, Stone and Faulkner talked excitedly of the book's prospects. Bill was certain that not "even the bird who named 'Soldiers' Pay' can improve on my title." Not only would it sell, as Stone believed, but *Flags in the Dust* would be the novel to establish Faulkner's reputation as a writer, according to the novelist himself. Sherwood Anderson could no longer regret having introduced William Faulkner to the world of letters.[15]

While they waited to hear from New York, Faulkner was again "working spasmodically on a book" which, he thought, "will take three or four years to do." It may be, as Blotner thinks, that he was working again on the Snopeses, the "rural tribe" whose progeny were becoming so numerous that it would take years to exhaust the vein.[16] That would be welcome news to Stone, who was steadily enriching and expanding the saga.

But Stone and Faulkner were to be sorely mistaken about *Flags in the Dust*, the novel Phil said he had more to do with than any other. Liveright saw it as a book with "a thousand loose ends," lacking "plot, dimension and projection." The publisher would not even recommend extensive revisions; the book simply had no "story to tell."[17] On the contrary, it may be that the novelist had too many stories to tell, stories pressed upon him by Phil Stone virtually until the last sheet came out of the typewriter. It was a recognizable pattern to those who had been force-fed books from Stone's lending library. Overflowing with energy and ideas, Stone had not the patience himself to whittle those down to fit the printed page; he needed Bill for that. Phil's critical tenet, moreover, was that genius disseminates an abundance. Later he would protest Faulkner's exhaustion of every creative detail.[18] Liveright might have said that after *Flags in the Dust* Faulkner learned to weave together his thousand strands. But they were both right in a way. The first Yoknapatawpha novel was to be a nursery for much of the Faulkner canon.

That winter for Stone and Faulkner, 1927–28, marked the nadir of their hopes for Bill's career. The November rejection had come as a shock to Faulkner, as he was to write two years later: "My first emotion was blind protest, then I became objective for an instant, like a parent who is told that its child is a thief or an idiot or a leper; for a dreadful moment I contemplated it with consternation and despair, then like a parent I hid my eyes in the fury of denial." Immediately he requested that Liveright return the book, unless they were "holding the mss against that super-advance." But it was apparently three months before Faulkner could bring himself seriously to consider resubmitting the novel—or starting another. If anyone else took the Sartoris book, he wrote his publisher in February, "at least I'll have incentive to light in and bang you out a book to suit you.—though it'll never be one as youngly glamorous as 'Soldiers' Pay' nor as trashily smart as 'Mosquitoes.'" He had "a belly full of writing, now, since you folks in the publishing business claim that a book like that last one I sent you is blah. I think now that I'll sell my typewriter and go to work— though God knows, it's sacrilege to waste that talent for idleness which I possess."[19] Stone, who had had such hopes for a popular success, was equally disenchanted when *Sartoris* initially "fell flat":

> That was the time in desperation, that I suggested to him to write anything he wanted to, any way he pleased, and perhaps he would get prestige and later could make some money. That was the day when he said he didn't know why he kept on writing—he supposed he did it just to stay out of work, that he was sure he would never make any money writing and was quite sure he would never receive any recognition. I felt the same way at that particular time (I can pick the spot on the university campus where we stood and talked about it) and I didn't dare tell Bill because I was the only one who believed he could do anything, and I was afraid if

I told him he would lose heart. I should have known better. You can no more stop a professional from writing than you can stop a dope fiend from taking dope.[20]

After the rejection, Faulkner had set aside his Snopes novel to crank out short stories written deliberately to sell. Late in February 1928 the first of these were being peddled in New York by his friend Ben Wasson, who had left Greenville for New York and now worked for Leland Hayward at the American Play Company, a major literary agency. When Liveright returned the *Sartoris* typescript in December, Faulkner, still in shock, decided to ask "several of his friends" to read it, according to Douglas Day, who edited the uncut version of the novel published finally in 1973. But the consensus was that Horace Liveright was correct. Even though later it was a standard Stone criticism that Bill's work lacked "dynamic design," presumably Phil Stone did not vote with the jury.

That winter the godfather of *Flags in the Dust* could have been no more objective about it than Faulkner himself. After their university conference, Stone continued to keep quiet about his own despair, and in only a short while Faulkner was working over the typescript, consigning some of it to the stove or fireplace, rewriting and rearranging the rest, getting sick of it and shelving it for a while, but finally in resignation typing a coherent version and sending that manuscript as well to Ben Wasson: "Will you please try to sell this for me? I can't afford all the postage it's costing me." But as Wasson carried Faulkner's third novel in and out of eleven more publishing houses, the question of Faulkner's professionalism was being resolved back in Oxford. Any self-doubt too seems to have dissipated by early March. "I have got going on a novel," Faulkner wrote Horace Liveright, "which, if I continue as I am going now, I will finish within eight weeks." Seven months later (October 1928), in New York City, Faulkner completed *The Sound and the Fury.*[21]

Whether he felt in part responsible for the failure of Faulkner's third novel or whether after fourteen years even Phil Stone could hope no longer, he seems at that point to have pulled back, perhaps to hide from Bill his hopelessness, as he said, but in some measure also in reaction to the writer who emerged from the creation and seeming destruction of *Flags in the Dust* to write for himself alone. In the period after

Mosquitoes was written and *Flags* rejected, definitely through most of 1927, both Stone and Faulkner had virtually lived in Faulkner's fiction, in quarters as close as Phil's sitting room on York Street. And if at times Bill Faulkner was one of the damnedest human beings God put upon this earth, Phil Stone—swearing, threatening, pleading—was one more. Although as open-handed as General Stone, Phil was his mother's child too, and in the long financial drought before the *Sartoris* advance (in the fall of 1928), William Faulkner, Maud Falkner's child, had to rely for money upon Phil Stone, a dependency perilous in the simplest of relationships.

On one occasion, in Pascagoula, according to Tom Kell, his friend Bill Faulkner, so often flourishing in poverty, had felt "crowded" by his lack of funds. It seems that the writer owed over seven hundred dollars. "Phil Stone lent me that money," Faulkner told Kell, "but I'm not gonna be obligated to him. I'm gonna pay that money back." There was more, as Kell reconstructed the conversation for Blotner: "Nobody dictates to me what I can write and what I can't write," Faulkner had added. But Phil often did not confine his advice to literary matters—and in January 1927 Estelle Franklin had returned with her children to Major Oldham's, with divorce proceedings already under way.[22] Phil Stone and William Faulkner would go on as before, but psychologically they began to live apart.

Much of the late spring, while Faulkner was working on *The Sound and the Fury*, Stone determined to get himself elected a delegate to the 1928 Democratic National Convention. Vardaman and Bilbo had come to power in state politics as the planter-dominated caucus system for nominating political candidates gave way to primary elections, though it remained an essentially one-party system: most of the votes in presidential elections went to the Democratic nominee, no matter who he was. Although Theodore G. Bilbo now sat again in the governor's chair, in the Democratic machinery Senator Pat Harrison held together a coalition still usually able to outvote the governor's men. Having established his party credentials by working tirelessly for the lackluster 1924 ticket, and his loyalty to "our cause" by daring to oppose Lee M. Russell, a hometown man, Phil Stone at thirty-five was well known to the congressional delegation, who occasionally looked to him for help in local matters. With General Stone's connections and his own contacts in court and in the bar association, Stone easily made his way from county convention to district caucus to the state nominating convention in Jackson. When the train left the state capital for Houston in June 1928, Phil Stone was a member of the Mississippi delegation.[23]

Despite the party's suicidal dogfight over the nomination in 1924, the Democrats ducked the most controversial issues of the day in their platform, and prohibition, farm relief, and the tariff were expected to provide the fuel for the 1928 convention. Two classes went to Houston, said *Time*, the "lean, hungry" congressmen from the South and West, conventional Democratic strongholds, and the "jovial, well-fed city bosses from the North and East." The issues split between them: "South versus Cities, Dry versus Wet, Protestant versus Catholic, the Field versus Candidate Smith." The Texas hosts had made the "suggestion to all delegates that Houston fashions will demand linen suits"; they had built Sam Houston Hall with enough fans and water coolers so that in the "torrid June weather" the Democrats would enjoy an "igloo in the desert." Although the Coast Guard in May had seized liquor cargoes near Houston presumably designated for convention visitors, when delegate Stone got sick soon after his arrival, the doctor on call prescribed that he have a cocktail. Having more or less adhered to his pledge of abstinence for twelve years, until 1926, it became his custom for three consecutive quadrennial sessions to weather the political storms with alcohol.[24]

Thanks largely to the floorwork engineered by Franklin Delano Roosevelt, the convention proceedings that opened on 26 June were remarkably amicable—except for a fistfight among Mississippi's delegates. On the first ballot, the Mississippians were committed to cast their twenty votes for native son Senator Harrison, but on the second day of the convention, as it became apparent that the odds on the nomination of Roosevelt's "Happy Warrior" were nine to one, the state delegation retired to discuss a "swing to Smith." An Associated Press reporter eavesdropped:

> Sounds that rang out over the transom told of the fury of the debate that was being waged within. Voices grew excited and appeals at times verged upon the hysterical as a woman delegate proclaimed that she had spent her "life working to put liquor out," and found her state desperately near "a vote for a wet candidate."

Another delegate declared in a voice that could be heard far down the corridor that "Al Smith will be nominated and we will be in a more favorable position if we vote for him."

There were shouts, cheers and cries of "No, No." Another man implored the delegates, the crowd outside the closed door, and the business district of Houston, "For God's cake [sic], don't let Mississippi vote for Al Smith."

Three hours later they emerged "coatless and hatless and perspiring," and, having refused "to recognize the proxy of Gov. Bilbo," with the vote deadlocked: 9½ for Smith and 9½ against.[25]

On the convention floor, a slightly intoxicated Phil Stone watched the Dry forces' prohibition film *Deliverance*, soon to be distributed to the nation's YMCA's; but Stone voted with the majority on a platform again aimed at "conciliation through vagueness." Explained "Boss Brennan" of Illinois: "No sensible Democrat ought to worry. . . . Only one person in 25,000 thinks, and only one in 50,000 reads the party platform. Do you?" Hardly twenty-four hours after Roosevelt introduced New York's governor, the roll call began. Smith listened by radio as on the first ballot Ohio gave him the nomination. The fistfight among Stone's colleagues apparently occurred sometime within that interval. When the secretary reported the vote that put the name of Alfred Emanuel Smith in the almanacs, Pat Harrison had received 8½ votes and Bilbo, 2½; only nine members of the Mississippi delegation, including Phil Stone, it seems, had voted with the convention majority. With such malcontents, the Democrats were unable to nominate Al Smith by acclamation.[26]

Although historians now contend that no Democrat could have beaten Herbert Hoover in 1928 and that Smith's Catholicism and his notorious bungling of the prohibition issue had little or no effect at the ballot box, in Mississippi, as in the Deep South generally, there was bitter anti-Catholicism in evidence during Smith's candidacy. Phil, Abe Linker, Bill Anderson, and Jack Stone actively campaigned for the Democratic nominee, in matters of substance clearly the more conservative of the two candidates. Politics in Mississippi, especially since the introduction of the Vardaman and Bilbo constituency, was frequently a matter of knives and fists. During the 1928 Neshoba County Fair, still an annual political forum, the four North Mississippians sensed trouble as soon as they arrived. They abandoned the speech-making shortly thereafter, for one of their group "had to take out a pistol" to the threatening crowd in order for his friend to finish. They walked to the car, "with this man with the pistol walking backward shielding them," as William H. Anderson recalled. It was his last political rally.[27]

In a more peaceful setting, "three or four nights a week over a period of three or four months," as Stone told Carvel Collins in 1954 and repeated to James B. Meriwether in 1960, "I had an experience that no other human being has ever had or ever will have: this was that I sat night after night in Bill's little room in the little tower of the old Delta Psi chapter house and had him read THE SOUND AND THE FURY to me page by page."[28] Stone may in fact have been "ear-minded," as he called it, but although he recognized immediately the "idiot of the Chandler family" in the opening narrator, he understood very little else the first night. "I could not make head nor tail of it," he told his wife, "and asked Bill and he kept telling me—'Wait, just wait.' " "God knows he's the world's worst reader," Stone often complained of Faulkner.[29] But "as soon as we got into the part about Quentin, the whole thing began to unfold like a flower." Stone was very much impressed, and quite satisfied to discover that Faulkner had returned from the apprenticeship with Joyce with new pencils and brushes and yet with the ability to paint portraits other than those of Stephen Dedalus or Leopold and Molly Bloom.

From the time *Ulysses* had been serialized in the *Little Review*, they had talked "endless hours" about Joyce, Stone "drilling into Bill that Joyce was a pioneer and that fiction would never again be the same after *Ulysses*." But the debt to Joyce in *The Sound and the Fury*, as Stone later argued with Carvel Collins, "is the debt an empirical writer would owe, a matter of method purely." Stone contended that Faulkner "has no theory of aesthetics at all," a notion he recognized as "atheism to the Faulkner idolators," directing a barb at Collins. Collins had discussed his theories of the novel at length with the Stones before publishing "The Interior Monologues of *The Sound and the Fury*," but had returned to Massachusetts with neither party having changed his mind one jot. When Collins sent them his "pamphlet" in 1954, although Phil admired its craftsmanship and admitted the plausibility of Collins's argument, he continued the argument with a five-page letter of dissent "for the record," a practice of correction and elaboration he often employed with Faulkner critics. "The trouble about it," he wrote Collins, "is the same trouble that besets so many beautiful theories. . . . it happens to be contrary to fact."

Stone belied Collins's assertion, for example, that Faulkner ever began a novel with any "conscious well-organized structure of plot," explaining that consequently the short stories were "so much better" and the novels, "from the standpoint of overall design," nothing but "a series of episodes." Collins's ideas of the indebtedness of Faulkner in the fourth novel, not just to *Ulysses* but also to *The Divine Comedy*, *Macbeth*, and the theories of Sigmund Freud, Stone also would have no part of. "Bill is not ill-read but he certainly is not widely read and never has been," he countered. It was an opinion he had enunciated before to Louis Cochran; to Stone's mind, it was a corollary to Faulkner's distaste for "literary talk": ". . . the reason is a natural weariness after writing about 5,000 words every day. Lawyers don't like to talk law business while they are playing golf," he had reminded Cochran, nor did "a professional writer . . . care to spend his leisure time reading books," he told Collins. Stone doubted whether Faulkner had read Dante at all. He also claimed that the completed manuscript had no title until they both "thought about it and finally I suggested, since it was a tale told by an idiot, that we call it THE SOUND AND THE FURY," to which Bill agreed, "since he could not think of a better title." Until that time there had been no mention of *Macbeth:*

> I realize that you have to shift gears to fully understand how impossible it was in those days for me not to know what Bill was doing and why. . . . Remember at that time he was entirely dependent on me not only for faith in his ultimate success, but for ideas and advice concerning the actual writing because he had no one else to whom he could turn. You know me and know that I have to know why. So I always made Bill tell me why. This does not mean that he always agreed with me. He frequently disagreed with me and more often than not he was right because of his insistence as a writer.

Had there been any "hint of Macbeth carrying such an important part" as Collins speculated, Stone insisted, "I certainly would have known of it." [30]

A number of details in the novel in which the critic traced Freudian

The Major Fiction

lines, Stone believed, came rather from Faulkner's lifelong observation of persons such as the Chandler man, Stone's brother Jim, and the Falkner servant Caroline Barr. Stone declared that Jason Compson, for example, had been modeled on James Stone, Jr.: ". . . between him and my mother, as I told you, there was a typical harmless but complete Oedipus and Jocasta complex. Anybody who knew Jim Stone could recognize him from the way Jason talks . . . and many have actually done so." Later, Stone returned to the parallel: "Jason does act with more decision than Jim Stone would have acted but he does act entirely for the benefit of Jason as Jim Stone always did and he was tied to his mother as was Jason. You are wrong about Mrs. Compson not loving anyone. She loved Jason beyond a doubt." Stone did admit that Collins's theories were reasonable, but attributed those patterns in *The Sound and the Fury* at best to "purely . . . subconscious result." From before the time of the *Marble Faun* preface, Stone's preference, his ideal in writers, was for one lacking in self-consciousness. In his exhaustive attempt to refute Carvel Collins, curiously there are no references at all to Caddie Compson, and only one reference—the one above—to Quentin.

In the autumn of 1928 Faulkner took the book with him to New York where Ben Wasson, through Harrison Smith, had finally placed *Flags in the Dust* with Harcourt, Brace. Faulkner's three-hundred-dollar advance came, however, with strings attached: the 20 September 1928 contract for *Sartoris* stipulated that the 600-page manuscript be cut to approximately 110,000 words by the 7 October delivery date. Faulkner quickly let his agent know that he planned to take no part in the surgery.[31]

While Faulkner was in New York, an occasional letter went to Phil Stone in Oxford, one postmarked 11 November 1928, the tenth anniversary of the Armistice; but many of Stone's former services for Faulkner were now being performed by others. Wasson, as official agent and temporary editor, was actually being paid fifty dollars for the pencil work Stone had done gratis for fourteen years. It was Bill Spratling who suggested the strategy to be implemented over the now bothersome Liveright contract. Faulkner manuscripts were no longer typed by legal secretaries, just as James Stone & Sons had been replaced as central rendezvous. The novelist, revising more than before, typed his own manuscripts—or Wasson's secretaries handled final copies. Lyle Saxon's flat in Greenwich Village served as social center, but, as at home, not the place to write. Miss Maud had even taken over from Phil the chiding of Horace Liveright: she had written accusing Boni & Liveright of "cheating Bill on his royalties," Wasson remembered.

Evidently Faulkner had hoped that he might place a few short stories as well as *The Sound and the Fury* during his New York stay. "What he wanted," Blotner concludes, "was to go home with money to live on until *Sartoris* brought financial success." But when he caught the train for Oxford in December, he was again living off his friends. If on another trip he had appealed to Stone—"Can you send $10.00 or maybe $15.00, or perhaps $8.00 or $4.50? A circumspect [?] man can buy it for $4.50. If you can't do more, send love and best regards."— there were now others to rescue the impoverished writer.

In Oxford that fall Stone had handled incidental local Faulkner publicity, passing along to the *Mississippian*, as Blotner hypothesizes, the news of the *Sartoris* acceptance, and bringing Bess Storer Condon up to date on their mutual friend, probably in an exchange of notes at Christmas. Stone still believed in the third novel, but his opinion about its salability had been revised somewhat. *Sartoris* had "none of that flip and youthful smartness of *Soldiers' Pay* and *Mosquitoes*," he wrote Condon, "but is a sad and lonely simple book," although superior, frankly, to any he had expected Faulkner capable of at that stage. The author was convinced of a financial success, but Stone now believed it "too good to sell." He did predict that it would "make Bill's literary reputation and sell his future books." Still committed to the idea that humor would be Bill's forte, Stone described Faulkner's evolving mastery of the comic: "There's a good deal of humor in it, and it is the humor of people in action, not mere cleverness or wit." [32]

The returning novelist was scarcely home before family duties called him away from his typewriter. Almost at once Faulkner was bullied into joining a political campaign. Phil Stone may not have succeeded in moving Al Smith to Pennsylvania Avenue in 1928, but he did have a hand in sending his college friend and fellow gambler Wall Doxey to Capitol Hill. Consequently a special election had been called in February to fill the post Doxey had vacated, and J. W. T. Falkner, Jr.,

Rosamond Alston Stone, Phil's mother, September 28, 1895.

Phil's oldest brother, "Jack,"
W. E. Stone IV, born in 1879,
February 1903.

Phil's older brother, Jim,
James Stone, Jr., born in 1881,
about age eighteen.

"Preacher," Green Liggin, with Philip Stone.

A bearded William Faulkner was photographed in Paris by William C.
Odiorne, 1925. The Cofield Collection.

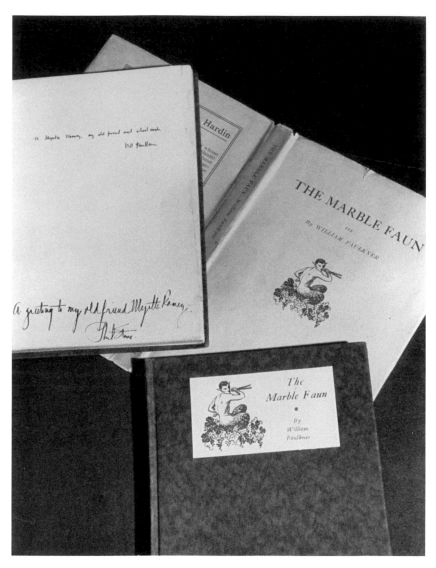

Presentation copy of *The Marble Faun* signed by Faulkner and Stone, 1924.
Copies signed by both are exceedingly rare. Louis Daniel Brodsky Collection,
Southeast Missouri State University, Cape Girardeau.

VII.

Mississippi Hills : MY EPITAPH.

Far blue hills, where I have pleasured me,
Where on silver feet in dogwood cover
Spring follows, singing close the bluebird's "Lover!"
When to the road I trod an end I see,

Let this soft mouth, shaped to the rain,
Be but golden grief for grieving's sake,
And these green woods be dreaming here to wake
Within my heart when I return again.

Return I will! Where is there the death
While in these blue hills slumbrous overhead
I'm rooted like a tree? Though I be dead,
This soil that holds me fast will find me breath.

The stricken tree has no young green to weep
The golden years we spend to buy regret.
So let this be my doom, if I forget
That there's still spring to shake and break my sleep.

William Faulkner.

William Faulkner

Typescript of one of William Faulkner's "Mississippi Poems" that Faulkner
gave his friend Myrtle Ramey in 1924. Louis Daniel Brodsky Collection,
Southeast Missouri State University, Cape Girardeau.

The Stones' antebellum
Oxford residence
(1892–1942),
College Hill Street.
This is the house as
William Faulkner
likely knew it.

Phil and Emily during the Stones' financial crisis in the Depression; Phil's
mother, Rosamond, in the background, January 3, 1938.

Emily and Phil posing for writer Harry H. Kroll during the Southern Literary Festival, April 1940, three months before Philip was born.

Emily, Philip, and Phil at the "little house" shortly after the 1942 fire.

Phil visiting with Philip at the tuberculosis Preventorium in south Mississippi, summer 1949.

Phil with his daughter, Araminta, at the "little house" in the early 1950s.

Thirteen-year-old Philip in residence at the library at Ole Miss, 1953, where he read *Finnegans Wake*.

Phil Stone and William Faulkner
in Stone's law office during
the 1952 filming of the Faulkner
documentary for *Omnibus*.
Louis Daniel Brodsky Collection,
Southeast Missouri State
University, Cape Girardeau.

Phil Stone in his rooms at James Stone & Sons in the early 1960s. Martin J. Dain,

Phil Stone and Mack Reed walk at the head of Faulkner's casket as it is
carried to the grave in St. Peter's Cemetery. The Cofield Collection.

Phil and Emily Stone in Jackson, Mississippi, spring 1966, the year before his death. Taken by Emily's colleague Rod Smith at All Saints' Episcopal School, Vicksburg.

Bill's uncle, was among those filing to run in the Third District U.S. attorney's race. Although Stone had little respect for Judge Falkner, it was expedient to return the office to Oxford. But it was apparent that Falkner's supporters had a fight on their hands. His Bilbo connection, surprisingly, worked against the candidate in the northeastern district, hence the foray into Chickasaw County with Mack Reed. It was still necessary to run a full-page ad in the *Eagle* just prior to the election. General Stone, Phil, Major Oldham, and Bob Farley all came out publicly for J. W. T. Falkner. Nonetheless, Falkner carried only three of the district's seven counties and lost by seven hundred votes.[33]

In the same month Hal Smith and his new partner Jonathan Cape mailed William Faulkner a contract for *The Sound and the Fury*. The transfer to Cape & Smith, his fourth publisher in five years, was amicable, as is evident from a letter that Faulkner wrote Alfred Harcourt: "About the Sound & Fury ms. That is all right. I did not believe that anyone would publish it; I had no definite plan to submit it to anyone. I told Hal about it once and he dared me to bring it to him. And so it really was to him that I submitted it, more as a curiosity than aught else. I am sorry it did not go over with you all, but I will not say I did not expect that result. Thank you for delivering it to him." He was writing also to thank Harcourt for his copies of *Sartoris*, a courtesy postponed, with other correspondence, because he was a month into a new novel (*Sanctuary*).[34]

Like *The Hamlet* later, as Phil told Carvel Collins in 1954, the book that spring "grew out of a series of sketches [Faulkner] had been experimenting with over a number of years." One, Faulkner himself believed "the most beautiful short story in the world." It was a story with the subtlest of plot lines, a story "about the Luxembourg gardens and death" that Faulkner had written to his great satisfaction during his September in Paris. When he had completed it, he wrote his Aunt Bama from Europe, he walked over to a nearby mirror: "Did that ugly ratty-looking face, that mixture of childishness and unreliability and sublime vanity, imagine that? But I did. And the hand doesn't hold blood to improve on it."[35]

Later Stone would remember that in 1929 Faulkner "had run out of something to write about and I happened to know the background of all of that [i.e., the prostitutes, gamblers, and bootleggers of *Sanctuary*] and he was just writing something to be writing."[36] But this is a very late, and hence a more suspect claim.

At the time, Stone had little faith that a book based on their "research" in Clarksdale and Memphis could be anything more than a potboiler. The "bad" book they would not let Sallie Simpson type had always been something of a joke on the girls of the Bunch. Stone believed, as he often repeated, that "the day of the shocker was over!" (He was wrong, as he later confessed, "on both counts.") But the reviews of *Sartoris* that Harcourt sent to Oxford might easily have undermined a man "just writing something to be writing." In any case, by 25 May 1929 William Faulkner had finished typing the potboiler that Stone had seen in manuscript. Stone routinely read through Faulkner contracts, and probably had checked the one for *Sanctuary* that arrived earlier in May. At least someone wanted to publish the work, but, again, Faulkner's terms with Cape & Smith could hardly be grounds for celebration. Nor, to Stone, was the news reaching him through gossip around the square: late in April, Estelle Franklin's divorce had come through.[37] Phil Stone knew very well what would follow.

Stone also knew that it was impossible to swerve any Falkner once he was in motion. "Pope said that fools rush in where angels fear to tread," he remarked, but thinking perhaps of Judge Falkner's arrogance at the wheel of his automobile during the recent campaign, he continued, "Falkners rush in where fools fear to tread and usually get away with it." Although the lawyer would have been privy to the size of Bill's bank account, as well as to his literary prospects, even Phil Stone knew when to say no more. Over twenty years later, correcting Robert Coughlan's *Life* manuscript, Stone dictated a short note about 20 June 1929: "Bill and Estelle were married in the old Presbyterian Church at College Hill by the revered late Dr. W. D. Heddleston [sic]. . . . They ran off to get married like two children."[38]

With a loan from a Falkner relative, the William Faulkners left on their honeymoon, spending most of the remainder of the summer on the coast in Pascagoula, where Estelle's children sometimes played with Rosebud Stone. The Faulkners evidently felt more comfortable around Jack and Myrtle than with Phil. Nevertheless, Faulkner would see to it that Phil received the promotional pamphlet his publishers made from the enthusiastic response of poet-novelist Evelyn Scott to *The Sound and the Fury* manuscript. And when Bill and Estelle moved into Elma Meek's apartment on University Avenue that fall,[39] the chats between Stone and Faulkner at the post office and at the Gathright-Reed Drugstore apparently were resumed. When *The Sound and the Fury* was published on 7 October, Faulkner inscribed one of the usual author's copies to Phil Stone and brought it by the office.

That fall William Faulkner wrote *As I Lay Dying* to the rhythm of the dynamo at the university power plant where he found a job. A month later he mailed the typescript to Hal Smith. It was the last of the Faulkner novels with which Stone said he had "anything to do," and for it he seems only to have served as a first reader.[40] Ironically, by that time in Oxford, it was a well-established secret that the "truth" of the matter was that Phil Stone was writing those books: Faulkner "didn't have sense enough to do it." He had never written a line of Bill's books, Stone swore when someone put the question to him. If he had, Stone joked, the novels would have been better punctuated. But Phil had no specific criticism to make about the Bundren novel. In retrospect he believed *As I Lay Dying* "the best thing [Faulkner] ever wrote," even though as with the others he could often identify myriad details from which it sprang. As he read that manuscript, for example, Stone recalled vaguely "some funeral of . . . Bill's people [in which] there [had been] water in the grave and they had to bore holes in the coffin" to make it sink.[41]

The reviews of *The Sound and the Fury* in the autumn of 1929 were gratifying to Stone as well as to Faulkner. At last someone else appreciated the talent Phil Stone had seen for fifteen years. Although there began to be fan mail, there was still no money. Thus, after the sixth novel left Oxford, Faulkner initiated another assault on the national magazines. Sometime that winter he submitted a story called "Smoke" to the *Saturday Evening Post*. It marked the first appearance of Harvard-educated, "loose-jointed" county attorney Gavin Stevens, "with a mop of untidy iron-gray hair." A bald, double-jointed, Yale-educated Phil Stone would be greatly amused.[42]

The legal hackwork Faulkner asked of Stone in January 1930 would hardly have interested Gavin Stevens. Phil drew up a preliminary five-year lease between Faulkner and a man named Mayfield for a house and acreage east of Oxford on which Faulkner would begin annual payments of $500 in November, with an option to purchase the property later at $4,500. Stone may have opposed the idea in light of what followed. The agreement, at any rate, was never consummated.

Later that spring Ike Stone, from Coffeeville, came over to handle the final details of a sale for Maggia Lea Stone's parents, Mr. and Mrs. Will Bryant. He stopped at the office on Jackson Avenue to speak to Cousin Jim. Garrulous and folksy, Ike Stone was a walking caricature of a country lawyer. Yeah, he told Phil, he remembered getting the letter in 1924 about that boy's poetry book. So this was the same fella'. During a time when credit was drying up—after the summer, the Bank of Oxford and other banks in the area would have no money to lend— Faulkner purchased a house and four acres of land, agreeing to pay Ike Stone's client six thousand dollars at 6 percent interest, or seventy-five dollars a month. Fortunately, by the time the Faulkners began unpacking at the old Bailey home in the summer of 1930, *Forum* had taken "A Rose for Emily," the *Post* had accepted "Thrift," *Scribner's* at last had bought a Faulkner story, "Dry September," and another was to appear in the *American Mercury*. Two more had been sold to the *Southwest Review* and *American Caravan IV*. Not only that, but in June came the first British edition of *Soldiers' Pay*, and Arnold Bennett's observation in London's *Evening Standard* that Faulkner "writes . . . like an angel." [43]

Phil Stone in the interim had become enthralled by the news coming out of the state capital. Bilbo had convened two special sessions in 1928 and 1929, to force the legislature to commit the state to a system of permanent highways and a reorganization of the shockingly corrupt and inept Highway Commission, a political football since 1927. "Roads," said the demagogue, "rule the world. . . . Permanent highways are the only royal lines in democracy, the only legislature that never changes, the only court that never sleeps, the only army that never quits . . . the exodus from stagnation in any society, the call from savagery in the tribe, the high priest of prosperity." Bilbo was perfectly serious about paving highways with "state-produced vitrified brick." Some of his constituents even missed his joke in suggesting that "when the topside of the bricks was worn out, they could be turned over and used on the other side."

The 1929 special session, however, got sidetracked into investigating

Bilbo's attorney general and the State Tax Commission. In fact, hardly a day passed during his second term when the weakened but feisty opposition was not on Bilbo's trail. The counterattack was devastating. In only one arena, the governor replaced the presidents of the four major educational institutions and fired hundreds of faculty members known to be anti-Bilbo. (One ousted librarian left Mississippi State College for Athens, Georgia, where she befriended a college junior named Emily Whitehurst. After a year's exile, Alice James returned to Mississippi and helped her young friend get her first teaching job there.) Finally, early in 1930, the Highway Commission was reorganized once again, removing political appointees and providing for the popular election of three state commissioners. Stone's friend Abe Linker would have to run for the job he had held since January 1929. Phil Stone volunteered to manage Linker's campaign.[44] It would be a vicious one, but Abe won and for three consecutive terms, as long as Phil Stone ran his campaigns—the popular Linker would be highway commissioner for the Northern District.

When Emily Whitehurst taught her first class at University High School in Oxford in the fall of 1930 and talked to students like Hugh Miller Surratt about literature, it was some months before she realized that to them the word "literature" connoted only campaign literature or political broadsides. Apparently the man of letters at James Stone & Sons had himself temporarily abandoned the pursuit of literature to compose reading matter for Abe Linker's constituents. Phil's Yale friend Herb Starr in Los Angeles had written him in the spring, with a customary paragraph or two of literary talk. Stone wrote the lawyer back at the end of June:

> I would have answered your letter sooner but a local man and a friend of mine has been a candidate for Highway Commissioner for this District and I have been managing his campaign. In spite of this he got elected finally. I am sending you a few of the circulars, which, although I wrote, I think are pretty good political flap-doddle.
>
> If I ever get a chance to read another book I will read the book to which you refer. I am going to work like the devil . . . in order to be a lawyer one of these days.
>
> Bill is married and, surprisingly, still married. Wish you would come to see us sometime.[45]

Later that year a busy Phil Stone passed two young women on the street, only part of his mind registering that one had "cut her eyes around at him." The women had been discussing the "dearth of men" in Oxford when Emily Whitehurst looked in Stone's direction. "Now, *there's* a man I'd like to know," she said. But her friend Sallie Cummins only laughed, "Hon, better women than you or I have been after Phil Stone and nobody's ever got him yet." That year Emily and another friend were assigned to a school survey in the northwest section of town, where the Stones lived. The woman told Emily that they were wasting their time to stop at General Stone's, but Emily Whitehurst, who had written one novel herself, would not pass up an opportunity to meet the man she had been told had "educated" William Faulkner. She had read *The Sound and the Fury* in college, walking the floor in her excitement. Besides, as she recalled, "there was the interesting-looking house." So they went in and talked to Rosamond Stone.

"I led Miss Rosie on about the books and things so that she sent me upstairs," Emily Stone recalls, "and I saw that hall full of books and peeked in the door of Phil's bedroom and saw books all over the tables and all over the floor. He had a law table such as they have in their office there and it was piled up with books. . . . So I was 'interested.' "

But unless Mack Reed stocked a few copies of the new Cape & Smith book, Emily Whitehurst would have had to approach Stone or Faulkner himself to read *As I Lay Dying*, which had appeared in New York on 6 October. And even this early in his career, Faulkner was not easily approached. That fall Myrtle Ramey, married and living in New Jersey, appealed to Phil Stone to have Bill sign two books for her. In his letter to Myrtle Demarest, Stone unconsciously made his debut as go-between, the role he would play in the second phase of his relationship with William Faulkner:

> . . . I think Bill will autograph "Sartoris" and "As I Lay Dying" for you but I will have to catch him in the right mood. He is continually being worried about autographs since he has gotten well-known and is sick of it. Still, if you will be patient and let me use my judgment I think I can get him to autograph the two books . . . since you and he were children together and he likes you very much. . . .
>
> Bill has sold four stories to the Saturday Evening Post. . . . He got five hundred dollars for one of them and seven hundred and fifty a piece for the other three. So you can see that he is made as far as money goes.

The Major Fiction

Let me know whether or not you have an autograph copy of "The Marble Faun". If you haven't I have one that I will give you. If you hear of anybody else who wants one I have five or six more that I wish to sell. The price for the present will be five dollars apiece. It is a good buy from a collector's standpoint. There were only one thousand copies . . . printed and with the exception of a few presentation copies, nobody has an autograph copy and nobody has the slightest chance to get an autograph copy. Of course, since you and I are friends I shall be glad to give you one.[46]

With the worsening financial situation, legal fees were beginning to disappear, and some of his father's creditors had begun worrying. Phil Stone, who delighted in calculation, evidently determined that the hour had come to capitalize on his poetry investment.

Unexpectedly another Faulkner work surfaced that same autumn. Hal Smith had decided that he was willing to risk the publication of *Sanctuary* after all. But when Faulkner received the galley proofs for the book, he would agree to its publication only if he were allowed to revise it. So in November and early December, Faulkner paid "for the privilege of rewriting [*Sanctuary*], trying to make out of it something which would not shame *The Sound and the Fury* and *As I Lay Dying* too much." Stone may not even have seen that version. It would be, however, the one book he later reread in print. (Generally he saw Faulkner's work only in manuscript, he claimed.) During a bout of flu sometime in the 1950s, he returned to *Sanctuary*, and that time pronounced it "a damn good book, one of the best from [a] writer's standpoint."[47]

With *Sanctuary* the deluge came at last, according to Stone, after seventeen long years of "drought." Bill's fortune, he surmised, was now "made." When the magazines began clamoring for Faulkner stories, Phil Stone asked a single favor of his successful pupil: "Bill, there's one thing I want you to do for me. I hope you'll go look at that suitbox we nailed up on the wall . . . and send the same stories to the very first magazine that turned them down. Don't even retype them, will you? . . . Send them what they wouldn't take before." The vindication, however, was bittersweet. By *Sanctuary*'s notoriety, neither Phil Stone nor William Faulkner could derive much satisfaction from "the vice of spoiling good white paper with little black marks."[48]

If Stone's request carried a valedictory tone, it may have been because, like Faulkner, he had been dealt a devastating personal blow in the winter of 1930–31. Estelle and William Faulkner's first child,

Alabama, had been born on 11 January 1931—to live only nine days. Faulkner in time could in part assuage his grief at the death of his first daughter with his delight in the second, for he would dote on Jill, according to Stone. By contrast, Phil Stone hardly realized the longevity or the depth of the curse leveled at him on the morning of 27 December when General Stone telephoned the office to ask him to come over to the bank. On 29 December 1930 the Bank of Oxford would not open for business.[49]

10

For Honor and For Love

THE STONES' PREDICAMENT was a familiar one that year. Fifty-six state banks and three national banks had failed in Mississippi earlier in 1930; another fifty-six would close in 1931. Among other factors, the reduction in the number of banking institutions, evident as early as 1925, had increased real estate loans with the survivors, so that investments soon accounted for a disproportion of their assets. In May of 1931, when state official James S. Love supervised the Bank of Oxford's reopening as a corporation owned by depositors, the new manager intimated in his public promises the nature of the errors contributing to the bank's failure. There would be no more borrowing money to lend, or protecting frozen or undesirable loans; no longer would the institution carry accounts free of service charges or add interest to the face of notes. Second mortgages were henceforth abolished.[1]

Lafayette County had first learned of the examiners' closing General Stone's bank on Monday, 29 December 1930. Despite initial disclaimers of executive misconduct, knavery as well as folly had contributed to the collapse. Some time before, James Stone had naively employed an officer of good family fired from the smaller Guaranty Bank and Trust Company—only to discover that the man was indeed a thief. After their apparently acrimonious confrontation, the dismissed employee spread rumors precipitating a run on General Stone's bank. The embezzler was subsequently convicted for his part in the failure of the former institution and died in the state penitentiary. But restitution for the Stones from that quarter, of course, was impossible.[2]

Phil Stone's father assuredly felt each of his seventy-six years on 24 January 1931 when he convened a stockholders' meeting at the courthouse at 9 A.M. As he had announced in an open letter in the *Eagle* two days before, he was to meet with the depositors at the same forum at one o'clock. Those in debt to the bank of which he was president were to assemble the following Monday morning. "I believe our deliberations may result in better understanding and the working out of some plan by which the stockholders, the depositors, and the general public may be benefited." He relinquished the chair early in that meeting in order to present a full report. The *Eagle* was clearly in sympathy with the old man: "He sat while he spoke and at times his voice did not carry throughout the room but he was given close attention and unquestionably the faith of the men and women who had done business with the Bank of Oxford during the many years he has served it as its guiding spirit was not in the least shaken by the closing of the bank." Others in town were not so gentle.[3]

Under the plan negotiated that spring, one proposed by Superintendent Love, shareholders of the bank were personally liable to the depositors. They agreed to pay into the new bank 100 percent of their liability; moreover, a stockholders' committee would assume and liquidate "an equivalent amount of the slow and bad paper which originally caused the trouble." As major stockholders, the Stones were financially ruined, although depositors, one of them Emily Whitehurst, eventually were repaid with interest. The Wohlleben sisters and numbers of the family's other friends also suffered during the liquidation. (Phil Stone, according to Blotner, later sold the collateral for the Oldhams' defaulted beverage company loan.)

The situation for General Stone, owing additionally thousands of dollars for his farming and timber speculation, was hopeless. Friends in neighboring towns rallied to his defense, but his creditors were at his heels. Although the family owned land once worth $300,000 to $500,000 (including 3,000 acres of virgin timber in the Delta), General Stone's debts stood at well over $50,000. His unofficial committee of advisers—Judge Julian Wilson of Memphis, his first Oxford partner; J. T. Thomas, president of the Grenada Bank system; and M. P. Stur-

For Honor and For Love

divant, a Glendora planter—recommended that James Stone declare bankruptcy. Such a move was unthinkable, but the Stones' prospects of meeting the notes were dim indeed.

Significant revenues at James Stone & Sons depended upon corporate accounts already suspect because of the debacle on Wall Street. Jack, like Phil and his father, lived on his capital; little could be expected from Jim. "Land-poor," their only recourse was to bid for time, to hold out until land values improved, even slightly. Meanwhile, Jack's Charleston house was heavily mortgaged, Phil borrowed as much as his $18,000 life insurance policies allowed, and the Stone attorneys pledged their law practice—and their honor—to make good the rest.[4] In reality powerless to protect the old man's serenity, nevertheless Phil Stone was prepared to sacrifice his most vital self to that endeavor. "Bill," he told Faulkner without irony that spring, "you don't need me any more, and I have to make a living for my old folks."

With the energy that before had been devoted to the promotion of *The Marble Faun*, Phil Stone threw himself into the defense of his father's name, with results equal to those of the campaign of 1924–25, but, ironically, with small operating costs covered by sales of that very book. A week after the bank reopened, Phil wrote a family friend in Sivley's old position with the Illinois Central for a list of Chicago's rare book dealers. Bill Faulkner had just learned from his publishers that an unsigned copy of *The Marble Faun* had recently brought twenty-five dollars. Suddenly the box marked "Four Seas" in the attic seemed a small gold mine. Evidently there was little interest from the Midwest, for in July Stone placed an ad in the *New Republic* offering "a few autographed presentation copies," and sent letters specifying four such copies to Byrne Hackett in New York and Al DeLacey in Cambridge, who, like Carl Rollins that October, renewed their lapsed New Haven ties with accolades for Stone and Faulkner for the latter's recent success. DeLacey enclosed a letter to Faulkner, noting how much he relished "pushing" Bill's notorious books with the local "Watch and Ward Society." Only DeLacey bid on the collector's items, but Stone was asking a steep fifty dollars each—one-third off the price he quoted, however, to the collectors answering his advertisement (by autumn his hoard grew to "six" copies). To each inquiry Stone summarized his history with the book and with Faulkner, the restrictions on future

Faulkner autographs, and thus his "corner" on a very small and active market.[5] One condescending New York dealer rebuked him for exploiting Faulkner, unaware (only a short while) that Faulkner had suggested the scheme to his friend, in part to repay loans drawn on Stone over seven or eight years during his apprenticeship.[6]

Faulkner autographed the rest of Stone's copies in return for ten dollars on each sale and continued to hand over to Stone requests for the volume of poetry and to relay news from New York about its current market value. Over the next thirty years, the "five or six" *Marble Faun*s that Phil Stone owned in 1930, like the loaves and the fishes, would multiply as he sold individual copies to collectors and critics. Although his prices never soared to those of the 1990s, not even V. K. Ratliff could have done better.

The link between Stone and the author of his collector's item was supposedly restricted then to Stone's return on his investment in Faulkner. Had there been an actual break, or a drastic redefinition of their relationship, however, Stone might have sold Faulkner manuscripts when rumors that he owned them swept rare book dealers in New York in the fall of 1931. Other evidence too gives the lie to Stone's professed emancipation from Faulkner business. He made no such declaration to Carl Rollins in October, speculating that his disappointments in Faulkner's evolution as a writer might stem from his too close engagement in the novels' genesis, marring his objectivity about the completed texts. Clearly his intimacy with Faulkner continued, for he wrote Rollins too of their periodic "fooling with" the Snopeses in a "fragment of a book" over the last "two or three years."

Faulkner's Oxford literary agency had not closed down either. After a busy season in fall court, a somewhat harried Stone agreed, as a favor, to research the town archives for Faulkner juvenilia at the request of Cape & Smith, whose office was preparing a bibliography to meet the new academic (and collector) interest in their author. But the topic of money continually interrupted Stone's literary avocation. Conventional notes executed to cover the Stones' bank liability would have expired in December 1931. In November Phil begged Faulkner in New York to stimulate the now sluggish *Marble Faun* market, his desperation apparent in his last lines: "If there is anything in the world I can do to make some money for God's sake send it to me. If I can't get hold of four or five thousand dollars between now and January 1st, we may lose everything we have."[7]

Mary Stone, Jim's oldest daughter, a stenographer in the firm, apparently typed that appeal. Over the same summer and fall, however, her father in public exhibited few signs of his brothers' anxieties. The *Eagle* reported that Jim Stone, Jr., had helped the Scouts prepare dinner for the Rotary Club, and that he had entertained the Tri Delta sorority in his daughter Evelyn's pledge year with Brunswick stew and a 'possum hunt at Hillcrest. "One of my brothers had all the load he could carry," Phil Stone wrote in 1960, "and another brother, a likeable sort, never succeeded in carrying his own load."

In the 1940s, in a memorandum to his son Philip bordering on frenzy, Stone characterized the latter's response to the financial crisis of that winter, or to a similar one later: "Your Uncle Jim was not a bad man but he was completely irresponsible, was dishonest in small ways and was a prime chiseler. . . . When our troubles came on and our property was about to be sold for taxes I raised all the money I could to save the property but finally lacked a few dollars. Your Uncle Jim had that money in his pockets but would not contribute that much to keep the home of our own father and mother from being sold for taxes."[8]

If Jim Stone would not help, perhaps that year, as later, it was Bill Faulkner who rescued Phil, and with more than moral support. In December Faulkner tried to locate the Gavin Stevens manuscript "Smoke" to resubmit it to the magazines. Unspecified circumstances compelled his request for an advance from his publisher sooner than he planned too. Either Faulkner was also in financial straits or he was sharing his limited resources with Phil; in April attorney Stone argued to the State Tax Commission that William Faulkner owed the treasury no money for the past year.[9] Whatever stopgap measure was adopted for Stone's relief, in the interim he had had another Faulkner assignment as a temporary diversion.

Jackson lawyer Louis Cochran, Ole Miss class of 1920, revisited Oxford in late 1931, requested an interview with Stone about Faulkner, and apparently unleashed in Phil a torrent of facts, opinions, and anecdotes. In a pattern established for the next thirty years, Stone asked to see the manuscript of "William Faulkner: A Personal Sketch" and mailed almost two dozen corrections and amplifications in detail to

Cochran, not the last critic to suffer such discomfiture. Their correspondence continued into the next spring, as Cochran placed the piece finally with a Dallas woman's magazine; by fall 1932 the *Commercial Appeal* reprinted it. Stone's remuneration, also setting a pattern for the future, was "thanks for everything." [10] Faulkner spent a more lucrative spring and summer in California learning the motion picture industry, returning to Oxford only after his father's death in August.[11]

Except for Jim's university salary, lost when the state treasury failed in 1932, the Stones' financial situation stabilized somewhat by summer, and Phil went as delegate to the Democratic National Convention in Chicago—the convention that nominated Franklin Delano Roosevelt. Some of his expenses apparently were covered by a *Marble Faun* sale in April; the residue he hoped to meet by selling two rare books from his personal library, a secondary money source initiated the year before when he invited DeLacey's bid on a numbered, autographed first edition of Masefield's *Sonnets.* That contingency was comforting in light of the campaign instigated in May by Bruce Humphries, Inc., to reprint a limited edition of the Four Seas volume. The Stones' continuing sense of disgrace, however, is evident, for none of Phil's Eastern friends knew of the bank catastrophe, Byrne Hackett having ended his 1932 letter, "I hope this economic depression leaves you unscathed." [12]

Roosevelt's nomination and vigorous campaign that summer and fall gave General Stone and his sons reason for hope. Jack Stone began to talk to his children about the family's attending the Century of Progress Exposition in Chicago the next May. But responsibilities weighing upon the eldest son had taken their toll. Jack suffered a heart attack in October. It was a mild one and he was ordered to bed. Three days later, in defiance of his doctors, he got up to try a lawsuit, when massive heart attacks killed him on 23 October 1932.[13] Following his father's death that summer, Faulkner, again at MGM, could afford to renovate the old Bailey place—by now called Rowan Oak—and provide for his mother after she quickly exhausted Murry Falkner's estate. After Jack's funeral, bachelor Stone could look only to a seventy-eight-year-old father and to farmer Jim of Hillcrest—and break the news to Jack's widow of the realities of their predicament. Two weeks before Christmas, Faulkner and Stone met again in common grief when Bill brought Stone's copy of *Light in August* around to the office.[14]

For Honor and For Love

Understandably, there appear few Faulkner references among the scant Stone remains from 1933; Phil was too busy in the law firm. He knew of Bill's publishers' plan to gather manuscript poems for a new (and final) volume, but he later noted sarcastically only the title change from "Greening" to *A Green Bough:* "I guess he's arrived now." Stone no doubt was as relieved as the others of Faulkner's friends when the second Faulkner child, Jill, was born healthy in June, and if he deemed Faulkner's obsession with flying inappropriate for a new father he kept it to himself, probably joining the family at the christening festivities in October, where he might have met publisher Harrison Smith.[15] Making money was foremost in Stone's mind in 1933, but his resolve to turn his back on literature was perhaps undermined from another quarter that year.

Stone and Faulkner now were continually besieged with manuscripts from aspiring young writers. They had assisted Mississippi poet Hubert Creekmore's assault on New York in 1930. At Rowan Oak one afternoon in the early thirties, Faulkner had graciously entertained questions from future poet George Marion O'Donnell and others in his group attending a university journalism clinic. The famous writer had easily awed a silent Emily Whitehurst and mesmerized the young O'Donnell with a deadpan recital of the time he "died"—one of Faulkner's apocryphal plane crash yarns.[16] But Miss Whitehurst's infatuation with the man behind the writer appeared doomed to failure. The eligible lawyer up town considered himself "crippled" because of his baldness and rarely attended social functions in Oxford. Finally, librarian Alice James, whose influence had brought Emily to Oxford, intervened again, through her friend Percy Rainwater on the university faculty, asking Rainwater's help in getting Stone to read a Whitehurst manuscript. "Phil Stone is as slow as tar in the wintertime about doing anything," Rainwater told Alice, "but if he says he'll do it, he will, and I'll ask him."

When Percy approached Phil, the lawyer claimed to have "sworn off talking to people about writing—and about politics." If anyone asked his advice about either, he would say, "Don't!" If the writer or politician "takes your advice," Stone explained, "he hasn't got the stuff anyway, and if he has got the stuff, you couldn't stop him for all hell." Nevertheless, Stone accepted the manuscript from Rainwater that summer. A month passed, then three. By October, Emily's patience was exhausted. With Alice's advice, she typed a formal letter: "My dear Mr. Stone, I suppose, since I have not heard anything from you, you consider the work Mr. Rainwater left with you as of no value, so suppose I come by your office to pick it up at your convenience."

Stone's reply came by return mail: "Dear Miss Whitehurst, Indeed I do not consider the novel of no consequence. It was my understanding that you had left and gone to New York [she had talked of enrolling at Columbia]. Will you please come by the office tomorrow afternoon and we will discuss the matter." Miss Whitehurst was ecstatic. She dressed with great care for the occasion, but Stone, later admitting to extreme self-consciousness and embarrassment himself, launched into a frenetic monologue on aesthetics that so captivated the young woman she spoke hardly a word. They met at the law office a few more times, Stone read and criticized her work, and once, in January 1935, Stone tried in vain to reach her by phone when publisher Hal Smith was in Oxford to see Faulkner.[17]

Emily Whitehurst shared vague, uninformed literary aspirations with several young Oxonians in high school or at the university. Among those was Dale Mullen, brother of the new editor of the *Eagle*, who in the spring of 1934 proposed a community literary venture which Phil Stone was persuaded to join.[18] Emily contributed a woodcut entitled "Nicodemus' Mystery"; Phil's friend Ella Somerville gave Mullen an essay on Stark Young. Stone himself had promised a series of articles on Faulkner. Six days before the first issue of the *Oxford Magazine* was to appear (1 April 1934), Phil finally sat down to his task. In the short, last-minute foreword he complained first of having broken his vows to "abjure both politics and literature," in the present case "sinning for nothing" (i.e., for free); his chief excuse in agreeing to chronicle the career he had served as "midwife" and "wet nurse" was that "If I do not make a permanent record of it, . . . William Faulkner will never bother to do it." He would attempt later (after Bill's vehement protests) to keep silent about Faulkner's biography; the prospect of his ever becoming a Boswell, he had told Louis Cochran, was dim indeed.[19] Stone's plans, nevertheless, were to provide the requisite life history of William Faulkner: both "the sanest and most wholesome person I have ever known . . . [and] the most aggravating damned human being the

Lord ever put on this earth." Stone reserved greater space not for adulation but for a discussion of the techniques of Faulkner's craft through *Light in August.* He apologized if the series inevitably recorded "too much of Bill and me," confessing the likelihood of there being "too much of ME and bill," but ended with a caveat: "Carp who will. You don't have to read it."

Although Stone again procrastinated in writing his essay for the 1 June issue, completing it on 27 May, he was deliberate in his research, writing Smith on 10 April for permission to quote from the published works[20] and interviewing the Falkners about the family history. But consulting Bill Faulkner was another matter. Stone's facts, he said, came "not from Bill, God knows! It's too hard to get Bill to talk." In his essay the anecdotes of Falkner genealogy were organically structured, Stone beginning with a capsule history of his inanimate origins: "It is impossible to understand a tree without knowing its source, the soil in which it grows and the nature of the country which surrounds it. So it is with man." In the paragraphs covering the "Rise of the Redneck" in the South, Stone prophesied again that the Snopes saga was to be "Faulkner's greatest book and possibly the grandest book of humor America yet has seen." The background chapter ended abruptly in the June issue, perhaps for lack of space. The 1 November sequel picked up with the Young Colonel's generation and Faulkner's immediate family, whom Stone had known since boyhood. Instead of moving then to the author's own biography, however, Stone turned again to Oxford, though far more specifically than in the overview of "the land" the issue before. Such information was in part sentimental—"I know that in all my memory there has never been a time when I have left [Oxford] without sadness or returned to it without joy"—but the implicit audience to whom Stone recited familiar details were not natives, but Faulkner's Northern readership. It was not the last time that the "male Cassandra" intuited correctly his responsibilities as historian of a man and an era.

Nevertheless, the final pages sounded a strident note as Stone remembered Oxford's scorn or indifference to his earlier prophecies, and his sometimes despairing, more often arrogant associate in response to that rejection: "There was no one but me with whom William Faulkner could discuss his literary plans and hopes and his technical trials and aspirations and you may be sure I kept his feet upon the ground. Nay, I stood upon his feet to keep them on the ground." As he voiced repeatedly, he was skeptical whether Faulkner had the humility of the truly great. The essay's concluding paragraphs, however, were Stone pastoral:

> Here, out of the contemporary mad rush, we have time and quiet to think and savor the taste of things without having to gulp them down. Here we can see the stars. Here on frosty nights of fall we have only to listen to hear, faint and afar, the bay of the hunting hound, as in "Sartoris"— "mournful and valiant and a little sad." Here, as I sit writing this ["in the room next to the room where I was born more than forty-one years ago"] it is quiet enough to hear the cool rustle of the leaves of the ancient oaks and the mellow liquid call of the whippoorwill from the front yard.

The series, projected to run for six issues, died with the magazine in that third issue. Faulkner's own contribution, though promised, also never materialized.[21]

Phil Stone was not the only one marking the passing of time. Before Faulkner left again for Hollywood, he had Stone draft a new will naming Phil and Faulkner's brother Jack (Murry C. Falkner, Jr.) as executors and testamentary guardians of his infant daughter. The will stipulated that in the event of his death his wife was to use his property until her death or remarriage, holding it intact for Jill; the Franklin children should consider Rowan Oak their home; and revenues from *Soldiers' Pay* and, ironically, *Sanctuary* were to secure his mother's income. Stenographer Mary Stone, Faulkner's hunting companion R. L. Sullivan, and R. L. Holley, a businessman and Stone's friend, witnessed the will in Stone's office.[22]

For several years in the 1930s Faulkner's attorney agreed to a more personal favor as well. James Stone & Sons would serve as "mail drop" for Bill's letters from Meta Carpenter, whom he had met in Hollywood. Phil Stone was commiserative over how painfully unhappy Faulkner's marriage had become for him, and, though saddened by the turn of events, Phil believed Bill justified in the affair. Moreover, Stone was gratified that Faulkner would call upon him for that service too.

During Faulkner's intervals in California, he and Stone maintained a "fragmentary correspondence," as Phil wrote later. On Faulkner's first trip west Stone had given Bill the current address of his Yale law classmate Hubert Starr, and Faulkner and Starr had revived the New Haven literary and drinking sessions when Faulkner finished for the night at the studios. In the summer of 1934 the prosperous Hollywood attorney lived "on the beach, in a canyon," as Bill wrote his wife on the day he moved in with Starr.[23] When Faulkner and Starr got together on one of Faulkner's later sojourns in California at the end of 1935 and the beginning of 1936, there was startling news of their friend: Phil Stone had married Emily Whitehurst.

Emily had finished work on her master's degree at the university the summer before. When she learned that her art classes were among the school budget cuts scheduled for fall 1935, she talked with Phil Stone again of further graduate work at Columbia. Stone had promised to write an odd—and probably useless—assortment of people on her behalf, including Jim Farley, Roosevelt's postmaster general, who as FDR's campaign manager would have made it a point to meet delegates to the 1932 convention. However, New York was prohibitively expensive, and it seemed more practical to both that she adjust her career aspirations to the economic and political climate. Thus she applied instead to Tulane University's School of Social Work. Phil sent for her the day of her Ole Miss commencement to give her the names of New Orleans contacts and to say good-bye. She was leaving Oxford the next morning for a few weeks at her mother's in Georgia. Once again he did all the talking, and, too soon for the young woman, she had to meet friends at a farewell picnic, and Stone walked her to the door. But as they passed out of the middle room together, the two brushed against one another and, with that, Stone turned and kissed her. Astonished at himself, he immediately apologized, "Oh! I ought not to have done that." "I've been wishing for a long time that you would" came the weak but more candid reply. But the nineteenth-century gentleman had misbehaved: "Here I am, a middle-aged old man taking advantage of a young woman . . ." Their dialogue of apology and mild protest continued to the door. A dazed Phil Stone later found himself sitting up in his room at home, oblivious to the intervening hours, saying aloud, "My God, I want to marry the woman."

In romance as in business Stone was never catapulted into action until the eleventh hour; even then he appeared more often to hesitate than to act. Emily's departure was set for the next morning. It took him an hour and a half of telephoning to reach her early that Saturday, but at noon, after a revision of her travel schedule, Emily joined the flustered Stone household for dinner. When his parents excused themselves for afternoon naps and the servants retired to the kitchen, the younger couple at last had no need to talk aesthetics. But still Stone did not propose. He could not see her that night, oddly, because he had to stay with his "old folks," but he asked to call on her Sunday afternoon. Emily rearranged her travel plans once more. Arriving in a somewhat rumpled white linen suit, her caller spent the first quarter hour apologizing; his last fresh suit had split when Stone dressed that afternoon. But he did explain the mystery about Saturday night, clarifying his intentions as well. Full of misgivings, Stone had told his parents about Emily. His mother and father were not only immeasurably pleased, he said, but relieved. Their chief worry about dying had been the thought of leaving their youngest son alone.

By Monday, Stone had assumed command of Emily's trip to Georgia, seeing the young woman—but not her luggage—safely aboard her bus to Tupelo and wiring her brother to meet her in Macon, Georgia, where she was to stop overnight. Phil had also asked a political friend to drive Emily across Tupelo to her train, but after the man dropped her off at the station she found that she had missed the train, and had to hail a taxi herself to return to the bus station. Romance suffered further when her bus finally pulled into the Macon terminal. Unaware of her change in plans, her worried brother was meeting every train at the Macon depot. Meanwhile the young woman found herself paying in advance at the desk of the Dempsey Hotel because she had no luggage. Her brother rescued her after midnight that night, but she was tearful for hours, after the emotional upheaval of the last few days. Phil Stone must have spent the day and night cursing himself for his ineptness.

When Emily's luggage finally did arrive in Gray, Georgia, Mrs. Whitehurst began to question the character of the man her daughter revered. For her vacation reading, Stone had given his protégé volumes of Krafft-Ebing's excursions into abnormal psychology. Mrs. Whitehurst could not quarrel with Stone's attentiveness, however. There were long letters and two long-distance telephone calls from Oxford; because of the poor connection Emily had taken his second call at the small exchange in Gray, and they ran up a twelve-dollar bill. Stone was also to meet her in New Orleans before her classes began. He would propose only in person, he wrote her, because of Miss Rosie's longstanding resentment at James Stone's proposing to her by letter.

Phil Stone had good reason for his fortnight delay. There was no money; he had other, major responsibilities; he was Emily's senior by sixteen years. Yet after their lunch at the Court of Two Sisters in the Quarter, Stone asked the question his letter had promised, and Emily accepted him. Both were chastened, however, at the financial impediments to their marriage and agreed that it would be foolish for her to forfeit her Tulane investment. They would wait until she got her degree before being married. Their resolve, however, was tested as soon as Stone's train pulled out of the station, Phil waving good-bye from the rear platform. At one signal from her, he said later, he would have jumped off the departing train and married her on his first trip to New Orleans.

Out of sight of one another, it was difficult to remember why he had not so romantically risked his neck that September afternoon. They soon determined to marry even if Emily continued her studies at Tulane. Stone was in New Orleans again on 18 October. Although his fiancee affected a youthful "atheism" then, she wished still to be married in a church. So Phil telephoned the dean of the cathedral on St. Charles, explained their not being able to afford a traditional wedding, and asked him to marry them. No, the minister lectured, the Episcopal church did not approve of hasty marriages. Stone grew irate at the man's tone. "After all," he argued, trying to control his temper, "she's twenty-six and I'm forty-two, and I wouldn't call that hasty!" When Phil replaced the receiver, he was fuming: "I thought I was talking to a rector, not Jesus Christ, Jr."

The couple were nervous but more politic at their appointment with the Reverend Charles Monroe at St. Paul's the next morning. And when Monroe leaned back in his chair, Stone later declared, "I *knew* we had him." The rector would marry them at noon the same day. The bride's attendants—her roommate Katherine Davis and Sallie Cummins from Oxford and Mary Alice Boyett from Tulane—were soon assembled at the altar in the chapel. The groom, teasing Emily for having cried throughout the ceremony, told the wedding party that it was difficult for a woman even to read the marriage vows without tears.

After a brief honeymoon at the Monteleone Hotel, Stone, as they had agreed, rode somberly north to Oxford. One month later, however, Emily Stone abandoned her Tulane studies and Phil met her train in Sardis on a cold November morning and drove her home.

Despite her happiness, when the bride entered the Stone house only for the third time, she was disheartened by the Victorian clutter of the interior, as by the country food they ate downstairs with Stone's parents. It would be a year before she assumed supervision of their meals, but she found Miss Rosie quite amenable to her desire to redecorate the upstairs for the new couple's living quarters. The first (and only) time William Faulkner came over to read after their marriage, he looked with approval at the new arrangements: "I can see another hand than Miss Rosie's here." "You surprise me," Emily replied. "Phil says you never see anything." "I see everything," Faulkner declared, as both found themselves abruptly on serious ground. The challenge to Phil's authority was a novel experience for her, but she dismissed it, embracing her husband's versions of reality, especially with regard to one William Faulkner.

That winter the Faulkners invited Alice James and her friend Kenneth Gatchell to a dinner party in honor of the Stones. The author with dramatic flourishes made the salad dressing from an array of bottles brought to the table by a servant; Estelle announced over dessert that the white bowl centerpiece on the table was the Faulkners' wedding present to the Stones. Throughout the evening the two husbands looked on in amusement as their wives appraised one another behind facades of polite female chatter. On 20 February 1936 Stone wrote Faulkner's agent in New York: "We had dinner with Bill Faulkner and his wife Saturday night and I am now proof-reading the manuscript of Bill's next novel [*Absalom, Absalom!*]. It goes very well but I think it could be made to go better if I could persuade him to abandon some writing peculiarities which he has but this I seem to be unable to do. However, I think the book will make a grand movie. It is supposed to be in the hands of Smith and Haas [actually Haas at Random House] by March 1."[24]

Even proofreading was more stimulating than Stone's law practice during the Depression years. Clients had become so rare that he finally accepted the government's offer to join seven Mississippi attorneys searching titles for the U. S. Corps of Engineers' Sardis Reservoir project northwest of Oxford. Abstracts were legal hackwork of the dullest sort, but apparently Phil's standards never fluctuated with the task, or with the size of the fee. He worked out a system, "accurate and very neat," according to his colleague D. R. Johnson, greatly impressing their Pentagon coordinator.[25]

Although the Stones were still in financial straits at the time of Phil's marriage, General Stone not only shared his domestic animals and flocks with the new couple, but gave Emily a two-year-old bay mare for her riding pleasure.[26] The milieu into which she had married was not always a quaint anachronism, however, for the Stones' was a violent world too, as she soon discovered. At Christmas, because they could not afford a turkey, Emily bought a box of cartridges and asked her husband to shoot one of the guinea fowl for Christmas dinner. But she had failed to notice the manner of his assent. There was a heaven tree in front of the garage at Stone Lodge, and, farther down, a pecan tree, and at their approach with the gun the guineas flew up into the top of the latter. Stone shot at them two or three times before hitting one, and the pecan tree became alive with squawking as the bird fluttered forty feet to the ground. Emily started when Phil threw down the .22 and turned abruptly back to the house, "I'll never eat another one if I have to kill it!" It had never occurred to her that he would react in such a fashion; Stone was a hunter, or so she thought.

The incident almost ruined their first Christmas, although eventually he tried to explain. In the firm's liquidation of the bank's bad paper, Stone had incensed a farmer in the Yocona bottom, a brutal man, who threatened to kill him. Before walking to the office in that period, Phil confessed, "I got a one-ounce medicine bottle and filled it full of water; I knew that if he attacked me, I would tell him I was going to throw acid in his face." Emily was horrified; a county school superintendent's daughter, one whose grandfather had run plantations and the genteel Whitehurst Academy, had never known such men before. Phil went on then to tell her of his aversion to guns after his experience as a boy with the deer.

Some months later, when Stone came in for lunch and Emily greeted him with an embrace, she felt something under his coat: "What is this?" There was a pistol in a shoulder holster under his arm. "I've got it for ____ [an unscrupulous lawyer]; I hope I don't have to kill him, but if he says any more about me, I'm going to have to kill him," Phil said. Emily had trouble getting her breath, "Darling, you couldn't kill the guinea. How *could* you kill a man?" "The guinea was helpless," Stone replied. "He hadn't done anything to me, and ____'s like a rattlesnake; the world would be better off without him." Those emotions found outlet instead in courtroom litigation over General Stone's debts.

Against such a background in 1936 Phil Stone again tried to lose himself in the nurturing of literary talent in another. He had begun the Emily Whitehurst file at his office on 22 January 1936 with a letter to Faulkner's story agent Morton Goldman enclosing Emily's stories "Hail, Caesar!" and "The Fur Coat." Goldman had already submitted her novel, *Sublimest Word*, to Viking. (Her novel's title alluded to a remark by Robert E. Lee: that duty is "the sublimest word" in the language, a principle she was observing her quixotic husband apply literally, with disastrous result, in assuming his father's debts.) After Viking's rejection of the novel, Goldman and Phil Stone discussed the problem with Emily's work, Goldman thinking it too abstract, Stone, curiously, believing her too much concerned with psychology.[27]

Phil evidently reassumed direct control over their correspondence with the magazines in March, for they kept a calendar of submissions and rejections similar to the Faulkner suit-box lid, at least until early 1937. In a cover letter to *American Mercury* Stone included a paragraph that, with variations, became a standard feature: "I have seen the manuscript of no one since Faulkner that impressed me as do those of my wife." After five months of rejection slips, his point was stronger: Emily Whitehurst (she wrote under her maiden name) had "more potential ability than Bill Faulkner had. She certainly has a better sense of design." Stone's belief in her inevitable success was as complete as his faith in Bill all those years: Phil carefully dated her manuscripts and typescripts; he marked her poem on L. Q. C. Lamar's house and books "May 9, 1936" and "First Manuscript Copy." Stone assisted her research too, as with Faulkner; one letter to Wesson Oil, Wesson, Mississippi, requested background for her current novel.[28]

For Honor and For Love

That spring and summer Stone shared with his wife another interest that he had supposedly abjured. She attended her first precinct, county, and state Democratic caucuses, seeing in Jackson also her first gambling establishment. There Stone won enough on her turn at the dice to cover their expenses to Philadelphia, for the teasing the new couple endured from Phil's friends in Jackson had culminated in a surprise honeymoon trip. Soon after Phil's election as delegate to the national convention, a man had risen to his feet, assembled his rhetoric, and nominated Emily Stone as an alternate delegate. "They haven't been married long. You know they don't want to be separated," he argued, evidently persuasively. In June the Stones voted with the majority in Philadelphia to continue Roosevelt's New Deal. When the convention adjourned, they returned home by way of New York and Washington. In Manhattan, Byrne Hackett took them to lunch and presented Phil and Emily with a belated wedding present, a bas-relief profile of Napoleon from his office wall at the Brick Row bookstore. And in Washington, Senator Pat Harrison had made an appointment for them with the president. During their fifteen-minute conversation, Stone reviewed Mississippi politics for Roosevelt, and the president inquired whether they had seen a new TVA dam. But as Roosevelt smiled and talked, an intimidated Phil Stone turned white in the face. FDR, like General Longstreet, apparently numbered among Stone's demigods.

The Stones had made another stop in New York, at the Viking Press, where they talked with Harold Guinzburg about *The Conquerors*, Emily's novel-in-progress. The publisher asked to see a chapter of it, which they rushed to New York that summer. But while they awaited Guinzburg's return from Europe, there were catastrophic changes in the Stones' lives. Letters to the Viking Press would not resume until January 1937.[29]

Throughout the decade the law firm had defended its senior partner in the suits brought by his creditors, and Phil had sold large tracts of land at a loss to cover their liabilities in crisis after crisis. The Stones' income in that period was so negligible that Phil and Leon Holley, the Oxford Ford dealer, often borrowed fifty cents from one another for household groceries. Under the strain of those daily humiliations, Stone believed he could discern a sinister pattern. One afternoon in Memphis, his wife, after finishing her shopping, waited hour after hour in the lobby of the Peabody Hotel while Stone played poker upstairs with Bob Berryman. They had already missed one bus, Emily was frightened for him in such company, and her agitation had even attracted the curiosity of the hotel's house detective. When at last Stone came down, although he was apologetic and moved by his wife's distress, he could not stop exclaiming over how he had missed such great pots by "incredible odds," a dozen times by drawing a queen, for example, instead of a king. "It had gone on and on and on." He was visibly shaken, as if incredulous that since the bank fiasco his luck had so viciously turned. In nightly blackjack games with his father, though playing as they did for matches, against all odds again, as General Stone dozed over his cards, Phil lost hand after hand. Although thereafter he eschewed games of chance, Stone's lucklessness at cards was, he concluded, an "objective correlative" for his life, over which he often returned to brood in the dark years ahead. Contrary to the laws of probability, the brilliant, well-educated Phil Stone was capable only of failure.

Phil's father, a man of quite different temperament, was no less sensitive to public disgrace. The family had lost fifteen hundred acres in 1935 because they could not raise the dollar-an-acre drainage tax (one of Governor Bilbo's ideas for refilling the state coffers). General Stone had retained title to the land at the hunting camp, however, and the old hunters, as was their custom, went to Stone Stop at Thanksgiving in 1936.[30] Jim Stone thought his father to be more than usually depressed that autumn and rode down to the camp to "comfort" him, deciding somehow to shield General Stone from his mood by bringing his father back with him to Oxford. When the old man learned of his plans, he cursed Jim roundly, in full view of his companions, and kicked him out of the shack.[31]

When his temper subsided, General Stone's black mood returned: "If it were not for Miss Rosie," he said, "I wish I never had to go back to Oxford." The next morning, after the other hunters left at dawn, James Stone got up out of his chair, walked across the room to fill his pipe, and fell dead on a cot.

In Oxford the telephone rang in the Stone hall that Monday morning by chance just as Phil walked in the front door for lunch. Usually his mother compulsively dashed for the telephone. ("She thought that

when God called her," Phil said, "He was going to call by telephone.")
On the other end of the line one of the hunters, a Midwesterner, gave
Phil the message: "General Stone's dead down here at the camp. You'd
better send somebody down to get his body." On the day of the funeral
Oxford's merchants closed up the square for the onetime banker, an
honor paid to L. Q. C. Lamar, as, thirty years later, to novelist William
Faulkner.

After Jack's death in 1932, Myrtle Stone's black handyman Will
Kelly had quite literally sustained the widow and her four children
in Charleston for almost two years. To provide the family's "fireplace
and stove wood" during the Stones' most destitute winter, Kelly had
bartered his week's labor felling trees for a neighbor in exchange for
half the wood and the use of the man's wagon and mule team. However, Myrtle finally exhausted her limited resources and moved her
children to General Stone's. After his death, Allie Jean, Rosebud, and
their mother slept in his bedroom, the front one downstairs, and Jack
and "Sister," young Myrtle, in upstairs bedrooms across the hall from
Phil and Emily. It was a difficult solution for all concerned, but three
survivors of the experience mention only pleasant memories.[32]

Their routine, however, was hardly established before the Stones
received a second shock. Jim Stone's friends and family had worried about his emotional state after General Stone's death. There was
a physical reason for concern too. Rotund like his father and older
brother, Jim had taken no heed of his short-windedness as his girth
increased. After a quiet Christmas morning at home, Jim had been
persuaded by his hunting friends to accompany them to Stone Stop,
perhaps in an attempt to get him away from his family before he tried
to numb his grief via a bottle. Christmas night, after Jim's family had
retired, Phil and Emily were knocking at the front door at Hillcrest.
"Mat," Stone told his sister-in-law, "Jimmie is dead. And, Mat . . . he
drowned!"

There was an artesian well at the camp, and under the pipe installed
there a steady stream of water formed a shallow pool before flowing
off into the woods. Jim had left the cabin, either to relieve himself or
to get a drink of water, but he may have been drinking and slipped
and fallen, knocking himself unconscious. He drowned, according to
the first report, in three inches of water. Later his daughter Evelyn

closely questioned the coroner, fearing that in anguish over his disastrous relationship with his father Jim Stone might have committed suicide. Although there was no autopsy, the family concluded that, like Jack and his father, he had had a heart attack.[33]

Matsy's grown daughters would work to support her, with Rosamond Stone's assistance, if not Phil's, although in the years ahead Phil and Emily tried to see that his brothers' children did not miss the necessities of childhood and early adolescence: a bicycle or a birthday dance, a graduation suit or a trip to Memphis. With the children under his roof Phil could be especially attentive. Santa Claus might be a myth, but the Easter bunny was not, for Allie Jean and her uncle had seen him among the spring bulbs of the front lawn. Stone's nephew, Jack, resented the loss of his tenth-grade friends in Charleston, but Phil eased the transition for the boy by engaging him with readings from his Latin and Greek books. Phil's dependents ate salmon croquettes and canned English peas for weeks when the garden vegetables were gone, but Stone invited Jean to a seven-course meal with the dignitaries at ribbon-cutting ceremonies for the Sardis Dam. Having observed the Stones' financial prospects at first hand for over a year, however, Myrtle Stone realized that her children's security depended solely upon herself. The widow found a better job, and moved her family into a small house.[34]

In the month following Jim's funeral, Phil and Emily Stone were both sick with influenza, but she finished the first draft of *The Conquerors*, retrieved the chapter at Viking, and promised Guinzburg a revised manuscript by 1 March. Two weeks after mailing it, however, Stone read in the *Jackson Daily News* that Harper editor Edward C. Aswell was coming south to scout for manuscripts. He wrote Aswell about Emily's novel, baiting the North Carolina native with the names of Stark Young and William Faulkner. And he continued to write to Guinzburg, only now he began to play one editor against the other. Aswell telegraphed the Stones to hold the manuscript for him until early April. Not without scruples, Stone explained in full about Guinzburg's prior claim—but he promised also to show Aswell his Faulkner manuscripts.

Stone had business in Washington in early April—federal court opened on the nineteenth—but the editor and his wife evidently ad-

justed their itinerary to include a night at the Stones' on their way to
New Orleans. In the meantime, the manuscript was rejected by Guinzburg. Having demanded that Viking return it by 15 April, Stone could
not have been surprised, and Guinzburg had written a personal letter. But the risk seemed slight; Phil no doubt hoped for a more serious
reading from the fellow Southerner.[35]

After Aswell returned to New York, he wrote to thank Stone for his
hospitality and for letting him see "that priceless letter written by the
postal inspector to Faulkner." He tactfully overlooked Phil's ace-in-
the-hole: his promise to give his book on "the life and work of William
Faulkner" to whoever accepted Emily's novel. Even after Harper's rejected the Stone novel—the manuscript was mailed to Simon & Schuster in June—the correspondence with Aswell continued; the editor said
he wanted to give a dinner party for them whenever the Stones came
to New York.[36]

It was small consolation to either Phil or Emily Stone that the third
issue of Oxonian Dale Mullen's *River: A Magazine of the Deep South*
(June 1937) published her story "Hail, Caesar!" Nevertheless, they
would persevere, sending out, with "Unto the Third Generation," two
new biographical stories that June: "Great Man's Son" and "For Honor
and For Love." Stone advised *Scribner's* with those submissions, "In
the year and a half we have been married, she has already improved
more than William Faulkner did in his first ten years." By November
1937, *The Conquerors* had gone on to Macmillan, the fifth publisher
to see it. Stone called the editors' attention there to paragraph two of
Stark Young's "New Year's Craw" in the *New Republic* to substantiate
the Faulkner reference he had cited in his November letter.[37]

The publishing fervor dwindled in 1938, although five more publishing houses and a Hollywood agency read the novel. The Whitehurst file
lapses entirely by August, not to resume, except for a half dozen letters,
until October 1939.

In public nothing seemed amiss for the family. Emily Stone made her
entry into Oxford society in March of 1938, giving her first large party
when Jack's oldest daughter, Myrtle Stone, married. Estelle Faulkner's daughter Victoria Franklin, "Cho-Cho," received at the door that
afternoon. As the guests began to arrive, Rosamond Stone, not without

complaint, took her seat in a chair in the receiving line; she had been persuaded to relinquish her invalid's role for an afternoon. Nina Culley, Phil's college friend, greeting the bride's family there, stopped to exclaim over Mrs. Stone: "Oh, *Miss Rosie,* I'm so glad to see you; I haven't seen you in such a *long* time." "Well, Nina," the matriarch rejoined, "you're younger than I am, you've got a car, and you know where I live, and if you had wanted to see me very much, you could come." Another guest complimented Emily on the decorum of the Stones' servant Green Liggin; she felt that she needed a coach-and-four to be worthy of him. Liggin, dressed in a white coat, had been stationed out front to direct traffic.

In the spring of 1938 a more private Emily Stone labored eight hours a day to illustrate a friend's children's book for an Alabama publisher. Stone objected strongly, especially in light of her recurring fever. One physician suspected she was contracting tuberculosis, but Dr. Ashford Little had dismissed that diagnosis the previous fall. Yet Phil wanted a third opinion to be sure, for the Stones desired confirmation about the safety of Emily's having children. Phil requested Dr. Henry Boswell of the state sanitorium to examine her in April, when Stone had business in Jackson. The report was favorable: she did not have TB. In June Phil wrote for a pamphlet on expectant mothers, and in August they took out a medical insurance policy for Emily; after a year, the insurance would cover maternity expenses. Money was tight for them. The sanitorium fee of twenty-five dollars had been prorated to fifteen dollars, on the basis of their negligible income, and Phil had even written about the loan value of Emily's small investment account. Embarrassed by such nickel-and-dime efforts, they may have viewed with envy Faulkner's "stroke of good fortune" in selling *The Unvanquished* (1938) to MGM for $25,000 and his purchase of Greenfield Farm in the same spring.[38]

Although unsuccessful thus far, the Stones still dreamed of financial relief from Emily's novel. In July Faulkner, after reading the manuscript, told them that he would "be glad to write a foreword" to the book, but they were unable to find a publisher. In the meantime Emily turned to Susan Myrick, a Whitehurst relative on the Macon (Georgia) *Telegraph* who, at the recommendation of Margaret Mitchell, would spend eight months in California perfecting the Georgia accents of the cast of *Gone With the Wind*. Myrick tried to interest her boss George Cukor and the movie's producers in the manuscript by her Mississippi cousin. By late August, Faulkner gave the Stones the address of Hawks-Volcke, Inc., and signed a letter to Bill Hawks that Phil wrote for him endorsing *The Conquerors* as a Hollywood production. All their efforts, however, came to nothing. Faulkner tried to comfort Emily, saying that three hundred rejection slips were required just to get up to zero.[39]

One explanation for the break in their letters to publishers that year is that Emily was again writing; in February 1939 they mailed her new children's book and drawing to Edward Aswell. Queries went out to the Pan American Union and to the Argentine consul general, whom they had met in New Orleans. The Stones were pursuing background for a story Emily had encountered in her social work among the exotic but destitute gentility in the Quarter, persons like Miss Jennie Fortier and her invalid sister, a former nun.[40] Yet it was not literature that preoccupied the Stones that autumn, winter, and spring, for as the Whitehurst file diminished, the Land file for 1938–39 had grown.

The nightmare so often narrowly averted in the decade seemed upon Phil Stone at last. His creditors demanded he settle his father's estate. That his wife tried to interest rare book dealers in the nineteenth-century Mayes library is one indication of how few options were open to them. When Judge Wilson, "Tol" Thomas, and Mike Sturdivant were summoned again for their advice, they could recommend to Phil as before to his father only one rational strategy: Stone should declare bankruptcy. Their resignation, however, spurred Stone into further schemes to preserve the family name. The moment of disaster, it seemed, was the only time he could act. When the Stone property was put up at public auction for their debts, it was Phil's friends who ensured that there were no other bidders and who loaned Emily the cash necessary to redeem the property. Stone's family could breathe, temporarily.

In January, Emily opened a stock account of $1,800 with a Memphis broker; on the thirty-first Phil wrote that she was "interested in selling land she bought the other day."[41] Although the Stones speculated in a small way in the stock market throughout the year (some were Republic Steel shares), Phil apparently had badly miscalculated the patience of his creditors. Another man sued him that spring. Phil raised a thousand dollars and turned, in yet another desperate time, to William Faulkner, who wrote Robert K. Haas in March 1939:

> I have a friend here, I have known him all my life, never any question of mine and thine between us when either had it. His father died few years ago, estate badly involved, is being sued on $7000.00 note, which will cause whole business to be sold up. He must have money in 3 weeks. How much can Random House let me have? Of course I will sign any thing, contracts, etc. I should be able to realise something when I cancel insurance policy, can use sum you mentioned in your letter. I have all my original manuscript, most of them in handwriting. I will sell or mortgage. Can you suggest anyone I might approach? $6000.00 is what we have to raise. He has $1000.00. I don't have to tell you matter can not be compromised. I would not have mentioned this sum if any less would do. If you will name what sum you can allow, I will know then just what difference to try to raise. It will probably be hard to find anyone to buy mss. but that is best chance I see now. I would not want to sell any of it unless I was sure of getting what he must have.

Haas by return mail sent a check for $1,200; with Faulkner's insurance money, Phil had the amount he needed—for two months.[42] By May, Stone was in danger of losing the law office. He reluctantly borrowed another thousand from Emily's widowed mother, Mrs. M. E. Whitehurst. "I am going to have this office property clear as Bill does not want any security. . . . Bill understands that you are to get all of your money back before he gets any of his,"[43] he wrote her.

By autumn, all their land titles were clear, except for the plots on which the house stood, and all were then in Emily's name. In an effort to increase their monthly income, they moved a four-room servant's house at the "back door" of the Stone residence across the street as rental property. That fall too Emily wrote William Faulkner a check for twenty-five dollars to begin to repay their loan (one of two installments made in Phil's lifetime).[44] The tension evident in both contemporary files noticeably lifts by November 1939 as the beleaguered son seems at last to have contained the effects of the bank failure. That winter the household tried to adjust itself to singular good news: there would be a baby at Stone Lodge in the summer of 1940. The Stones had leisure now to write, and think, of trivial concerns: Emily's mare's performance with the Como trainer to whom they soon sold her, or the eight cherry trees Miss Daisy Rogers of New Albany had given them. They might return to literature too.

When the Stones read Harry Harrison Kroll's review of a Hamilton Basso novel in the *Commercial Appeal* in August, they had initiated a friendly correspondence with the Tennessee writer. Kroll, then an instructor at the Martin branch of the University of Tennessee, was something of a literary curiosity, having taught himself to read and write after his twenty-first birthday. In April 1940, when the author of *I Was a Sharecropper* (1937) addressed the Southern Literary Festival at Ole Miss, he was the guest of the Stones. As a memento of his visit, Harry Kroll posed the expectant parents in front of their house for the photograph later reproduced in *William Faulkner of Oxford*.[45]

In the same period the Stones seemed uncertain how to proceed with the Whitehurst career, for the manuscripts were as usual numerous, but more various. While continuing research on her novel set in antebellum New Orleans, Emily reviewed a book for the *Commercial Appeal* and submitted "Ballad of the Burned-Up Son" to the *Atlantic Monthly*. Phil, and Bill also, believed Hawks-Volcke might wish to reconsider her unpublished novel *The Conquerors*, "since studios will want to make their own versions of Gone With the Wind."[46] As before, however, Hollywood was indifferent to Stone's advice.

The direction of another career was also in doubt in the late 1930s, according to Phil Stone. When he saw William Faulkner one morning on the square, the writer was depressed. "I've written out," Faulkner announced. Stone responded in the derisive manner he had once employed with a novice in his twenties: "All right, so you haven't got the stuff."

"A man has in him just so much," Bill returned. "When he's written that, he's through. He can't do any more."

"That's the second-rater," Stone said. "Look at Leonardo da Vinci. Look at Sophocles. He was in his nineties . . . when he wrote *Oedipus Tyrannus*. . . . Why don't you go back to the Snopeses," Phil suggested. "You never have written all those books we planned and talked about."[47]

Stone believed too that he had contributed fresh material to the Snopes chronicles during Faulkner's composition of *The Hamlet*. Canvassing Lafayette County for Phil's gubernatorial candidate in the summer of 1939, Emily Stone had heard from her companion "about the only son of the WIDOW SOMEBODY who had . . . 'taken up with a cow,' " and lost his senses. " 'That,' said Phil, 'is made to order for Bill,' " and he passed the story along to Bill Faulkner. Faulkner never enlightened the Stones about his apparently much earlier acquisition of the story, maintaining a customary reticence when the Stones remarked with satisfaction on the appearance of Sir Isaac Snopes and his bovine lover in the manuscript Faulkner brought for Phil to read. Stone wrote Harry Kroll in mid-November that the first volume of the Snopes trilogy was to be published in February 1940.[48] It is apparent how much Stone welcomed even a semblance of the former intimacy.

That Faulkner kept at least Emily Stone at a distance did not escape either Stone, however. Her attempts to discuss Freud or Jung or Thomas Mann with him were always fruitless. Not infrequently, Faulkner "did not just fail to reply; his silence was like a mallet on my head," she observed. She thought his reserve formidable, except with "children or old ladies," but at a cocktail party in 1939 or 1940 she assayed that reserve, in full knowledge of the risk she ran, because she suspected that her husband's old friend might in part redeem the self Stone had sacrificed to family honor. She asked Faulkner whether he had decided to whom he would dedicate the first Snopes book. The author "looked away above that lifted neck of his as though to get me out of his world and said in that high-pitched, tentative voice of his, 'No.' " But she had gone too far to retreat. " 'I wish . . . you'd think about dedicating it to Phil,' " she continued, to which Faulkner "did not answer at all."

The matter was not mentioned in the conferences the two men had over revisions of Faulkner's will, which Stone finished on 27 March 1940.[49] But on 1 April *The Hamlet* was published with the dedication "To Phil Stone." Emily, silent about her conversation with Faulkner, asked Phil whether he would thank him. "Hell, no," Stone replied, "Bill wouldn't thank me!" The gesture from the past had probably raised more specters for Stone than it had laid to rest.

The birth of Philip Alston Stone on 7 July was a safe one, although it was an eighteen-hour delivery and he arrived early, weighing five pounds, seven ounces. "Aunt" Mary Smith moved in with the Stones to help with the baby. Their friends telephoned or sent letters, telegrams, flowers, and presents in numbers that astounded, and gratified, the servant Green Liggin; when one acquaintance addressed a card to Philip from Berkeley, California, Preacher was awestruck. "Yo' name's gonna be known farther than yo' face!" he told the baby.

Jill Faulkner had been christened by the local rector, Dr. McCrady,[50] but Phil asked the Episcopal bishop in Jackson to perform the sacrament for Philip in November. Godmother Jennie Fortier was too feeble for the train ride from New Orleans—Evelyn Way, classics professor at the university, served as her substitute—but Congressman Wall Doxey left his duties on the House Judiciary Committee in Washington to stand with Miss Kate Skipwith and William Faulkner as godparents at the christening of Philip Alston Stone at St. Peter's Episcopal Church on Armistice Day, 1940.

11

Compensations But
No Reprieve

IN THE EARLY 1940s neither the war nor his customary pursuit of literature most engaged Phil Stone. He was meeting the legal liabilities of
his father's debts as they came due, but honor demanded that he fulfill
his moral obligations to the creditors as well. And as a new father at
the age of forty-seven, Stone had to move quickly to secure his own
son's future. The South's economy, however, still languished in the
Depression.

Late in 1939 Phil had displayed a curious interest in a WPA sewage
project in Oxford. The ineptness he observed in public work near his
residence provoked not only his private curses but also a characteristic
volley of letters to national Democratic leaders.[1] Within a year, ironically, he too had determined to profit from a local application of New
Deal dollars, for it was not T. Edison Avent who developed Oxford's first
subdivision; it was "aristocrat" Phil Stone. Over more than a decade he
would carve one hundred acres west of his home into tiny lots for inexpensive, middle-class homes financed through the Federal Housing
Authority. He drew up the first deed in September 1940.

Stone worked diligently on the project, attacking such tedious and
dull matters as the paving of an adjacent road with his usual flurry and
enthusiasm. He was sure enough of success early in 1941 that he could

afford to be generous, executing deeds to two lots in Stone Subdivision as gifts to Myrtle Lewis Stone and Matsy Greene Stone. His veneer of prosperity, however, raised the suspicions of his brothers' families, who believed the youngest son somehow to have swindled the rest of the family out of a Stone fortune. Jim's family had been displaced from Hillcrest in the late thirties when General Stone's land there had to be sold; Jack's widow, after a period of meager charity, had built a small house for her family near the Faulkners. Stone's tactic of putting the property he salvaged in his wife's name no doubt fueled their mistrust, for when he offered the lots, Myrtle apparently refused to be "bought off" with a pittance, as she saw it, and returned the deed to Phil.

The family quarrel over the Stones' fortune in notes was already moot, as any financial analyst could have foreseen as early as 1941. Stone could admit later that he had always been too frightened to borrow sufficient investment capital, and multitudes of short-term loans in the next two decades were renewed and renewed again. A more serious flaw in the real estate scheme was Stone's unfortunate timing. After the Allied victory, land would appreciate 300 percent over its 1941 valuation. Avent's Acres would flourish in the booming postwar economy.[2] Almost a dozen lots in Stone Subdivision had already been sold when the United States entered the war. The trickle of real estate income did relieve Stone's daily expenses, but neither that venture nor an improving law practice would ever generate enough money to make significant headway against the old notes. The Land files among Stone's papers too soon become fatefully predictable: three hundred, five hundred, or, later, a thousand dollars from the sale of a lot went immediately to pay an overdue note.

During his son's first two weeks, Phil Stone had stayed home in Oxford when the Democrats assembled in Chicago to renominate Franklin Roosevelt. Stone had missed his fourth consecutive session not because of the new baby, but because of principle: he "wouldn't vote for Jesus Christ for a third term." From Philip's third week until he was over a year old, according to a diary Emily kept, the baby cried continually with the colic, exhausting his mother and fraying his father's temper. They tried a score of remedies, "everything except catnip tea the old blind negro brought." One doctor's suggestion in early October had alleviated his most dangerous digestive problems, but Philip's crying continued through the spring and into the summer of 1941 (the baby had also contracted the family's usual winter influenza).

In the rare intervals when he was not ill, Philip was "a friendly, merry, intensely alive baby." But fatherhood was proving traumatic for Phil Stone. Fearful that he might not live to see the boy grown, Phil began collecting letters, newspapers, programs, photographs— and then Philip's own drawings and stories—and to write accompanying memoranda to his son in a series of Philip Alston Stone files. Yet he was somewhat jealous of the boy too; for over the past five years he had enjoyed his wife's complete attention. At dawn one morning, after the child had cried for several consecutive days and nights, Stone fell back on chauvinistic privilege, although neither parent had slept well in weeks. *His* work that day was ruined, he snapped when Emily suggested that he go to the crib. Stone's distraught wife turned away to the baby: "Well, *I'll* look after him." Philip grew healthier after they took him to a Memphis pediatrician at thirteen months, but the incident had marked a subtle turning point in the family's relationships.

After Myrtle and her children moved from the house, the Stones engaged a series of Ole Miss coeds to live downstairs with Miss Rosie. In her eighty-third year, during the winter of Philip's colic, she almost died from a severe heart attack, compounding the responsibilities of her son and his wife. The Stones sold some timber to meet their growing doctors' bills, and to pay for a bleak Christmas.[5]

Phil Stone's surrogate writer persevered through that year too. House of Field's glowing response to Emily's much-traveled historical novel had tempted her to make a dedication in 1940: "THE CONQUERORS is for Phil who is one." But the publisher's deep interest had been a trap. Stone wrote them in great bitterness at the discovery: "Many years ago I learned better than to pay a publisher to publish a book."[4] The next spring they discussed a new series of articles with Mrs. Sewell Haggard of the magazine department at Curtis Brown Company. Mrs. Haggard was a friend of Hal Smith, and an acquaintance of William Faulkner. Stone had in mind repossession, for Emily's subject, once again, was to be "the decline of the true old aristocracy in the South and the rise to power and affluence of the poor white." Further along in the consultations, the topic shifted, at the agent's suggestion, to "Mr. Faulkner's personality and his inside literary history"; Edith Haggard advised against the Stones turning literary critics. But responses elsewhere to the idea were not promising: "As I feared," Mrs. Haggard wrote Phil, "Mr. Stout has reported that the chances of their buying an article on William Faulkner are so slim he does not believe they should encourage you to write it for them." That initiative too was primarily financial; Phil pulled what strings he could through influential Jackson friends, but he was turned down at least twice that spring for large subdivision loans. In May 1941 more short stories went off to Edith Haggard; they promised a new novel "as soon as the baby allows Emily to work again."[5]

The Stones were not so preoccupied with literary markets that they were heedless of the war in Europe. Emily packaged Stone's binoculars to mail to the American Committee for the Defense of British Homes, designating the gift for Oxford, England. During the Blitz, she recalls, the couple and William Faulkner had talked seriously of "stocking up some place way out in the woods" with guns and supplies. If Oxford were occupied, they were "just the sort to be liquidated." In reality the roles the war assigned them were patently inglorious. Phil Stone was appointed in February 1941 to the district appeal board of the Selective Service. In 1940 Oxford's mayor had recommended William Faulkner for the post of "aircraft warning chief." By the summer of 1941 Faulkner distributed the booklet "Meet Your Air Warden" and guides to Oxford's air raid procedures from his new office over the square.[6]

Stone had not been surprised when *Life* magazine failed to interest Faulkner in "a biographical picture story" the year before, but when the magazine's photographer came to Oxford in August 1941 on an assignment about John Faulkner's WPA novel *Men Working*, Phil talked with Johncy and Phil Mullen of the *Eagle* downtown one Sunday morning while Philip posed from his stroller. Later that month Emily Stone wrote William Faulkner a second twenty-five-dollar check, which the air warden used to pay his city taxes.[7] (The balance of Stone's debt was to remain in arrears for the next quarter century.)

That autumn, as Phil Stone's onetime protégé completed *Go Down, Moses*, Harry Kroll asked to come down around Thanksgiving to consult

Phil, "the literary leaning post," about his book with Bobbs-Merrill. On 4 December 1941, not long after Kroll's return to Tennessee, a homesick serviceman mailed the Stones a Christmas card from the Pacific. A. W. Sturgis was stationed at Pearl Harbor.[8]

Mobilization would scarcely alter civilian life in the small mercantile and farming community; in fact, in Oxford the phenomenon most remarked of the first winter of the war was the weather. Temperatures fell below freezing and stayed there, in a region where Faulkner once complained of 99-degree winters. Young Jack Stone and his Deke brothers skated on the iced-over pond behind the Stone house. The weather was hardest on the elderly, and Miss Rosie's cold began her monthlong confinement in bed; soon she required private nurses around the clock. Overlooking the family quarrel, Myrtle and her daughter Jean relieved Emily one night before Christmas by taking the housebound toddler with them to see the Christmas lights in town. Philip was more interested in the neon signs on the square, where he could point out and name the letters. When his aunt turned down South Lamar, the eighteen-month-old was indignant: "Round the square; round the square!" On New Year's Day Miss Rosie had to be admitted to the hospital, with pneumonia. She responded to treatment, however, and was discharged on Friday, 9 January.[9]

The next morning the thermometer read three above zero; by early afternoon it had climbed only seven degrees. Allie Jean Stone and her friends were out riding bicycles when they heard sirens in the cold, still air, and followed them in great excitement—out to Uncle Phil's. The Stones had discovered an upstairs fire at 2:30 that Saturday afternoon and already had carried Philip and Miss Rosie out of the house when the small crew of fire fighters arrived. A hearth fire upstairs had apparently spread into the walls through a defective chimney. While futile attempts were made to keep the water in the firehoses from freezing, other men were soon passing the downstairs furniture out the front door. Two of them lifted a breakfront full of crystal and china and set it outside on the grass without cracking a goblet. Jean and her friends were allowed to take smaller things to safety from the men on the veranda, until the heat drove them all back. The fire was still burning ten hours later at midnight, the firemen able to bring it under control then only because the top floor's collapse almost smothered the flames beneath. The family spent the rest of the night with the Lewises, their neighbors down the road. Five days later, Phil wrote Mayor Branham Hume thanking the city for the firemen's efforts.[10] But Phil Stone would groan in his sleep for the next six months.

In an insurance claim of $3,548.50 for the house's contents, the Stones listed, with the lost antiques, an autographed photograph of FDR, three family coats of arms, a 1655 map of Europe, a gold cigarette case, a Smith-Wesson .32 pistol, a gold-headed ebony cane, a silver-mounted one, and Miss Rosie's hospital bed and ultraviolet lamp. There was also a grossly understated tally of the books, twelve hundred volumes valued at only two dollars each: autographed first editions of Faulkner, Pound, Robinson, and others, and complete volumes of *Poetry*, the *New Republic*, the *Double Dealer*, and "others now quite rare." The two policies paid a total of four thousand dollars. The family later salvaged a furnace, the grillwork from around the porches, radiators, pipes, and other plumbing; but there were a score of assorted bills for wrecking the rest of the structure as well as for repairing the rental house across the street into which they moved in the spring.

Stone's greatest anguish was over the books and the ten-by-fifteen closet off his bedroom that had been stuffed with the bound stacks of magazines and shelf after shelf of Faulkner's apprentice poetry and related correspondence—as well as manuscripts by Emily Whitehurst. Ten days after the fire, it occurred to his wife that perhaps some of the papers "might be under the cinders where they had fallen through from the second story." Without upsetting Phil, she called to Preacher to get a shovel and croker sacks, and they dug through the cinders about a foot or two deep, and there indeed were "a lot of manuscripts." The two were dirty and cold, and they put most of the charred papers and books in the sacks, stored them in one of the farm buildings—and forgot them, for Philip had to be hospitalized the next day with influenza, Miss Rosie was still weak, and there were bills to pay and a stack of sympathy letters to answer.

For Phil's forty-ninth birthday, on 23 February, Emily gave him the first book for the new library, volume one of Douglas Southall Freeman's biography of Robert E. Lee. Stone's burned copy of the book had been a 1934 present from General Stone. Faulkner promised to replace his presentation volumes as soon as his publishers could locate them.[11] Phil lost a collection of pipes in the house too, and Bill Faulkner gave Stone one of his Dunhills. All but two chapters of Emily's current novel survived the fire because the finished manuscript was being typed at the office. By March she was rewriting the missing sections.

That May, Stone sent his wife and son to her mother's in Savannah, but Emily could not forget the situation at home. "I don't know, sweetheart, whether I can stay out the week or not away from my love,"[12] she wrote her husband. Phil dreamed of rebuilding, she knew, but for the present they would watch the ruins from the small frame house in the former calf's lot across the street.

When Stone read his advance copy of Faulkner's new book, *Go Down, Moses,* he may have taken note of a sardonic (and perhaps only coincidental) passage about the Beauchamp house fire: "a peaceful conflagration, a tranquil instantaneous sourceless unanimity of combustion, walls floors and roof: at sunup it stood where [Isaac's] uncle's father had built it sixty years ago, at sundown the four blackened and smokeless chimneys rose from a light white powder of ashes and a few charred ends of planks which did not even appear to have been very hot."[13] After the Stone house burned, the author was reluctant to accept Phil's invitations for cocktails at the little house. "I don't think I could bear to come there," he demurred.

At the requests of mutual friends, Stone agreed to several Faulkner assignments in 1942, though sometimes indulging parenthetically in acrid criticisms. Arthur Head apparently mentioned Stone's papers and his influence with the writer to librarian Robert Daniel, who was organizing a Faulkner exhibition at Yale. Explaining that the manuscripts and "about twenty" presentation copies of *The Marble Faun* had been lost in the fire, Phil scouted around Oxford for the materials Daniel wanted, but added that he was skeptical whether he could persuade Faulkner to help, though he promised to try. Meanwhile, Daniel should be wary of the "fairy tales" Faulkner spread among the gullible in Oxford and appreciate that the writer once so ignored was currently much "overrated":

> The truth is that none of the contemporary novelists have the stuff that the old ones seem to have had although in the last book which Hemmingway [sic] wrote, he seems to have been better than ever before. The present day boys seem to make a virtue of being half undressed. I am not talking about their literary morals but about their performances. They,

especially Faulkner, seem to make virtues of all their literary faults and seem to think that it is a cardinal sin to be coherent. They usually copy all the faults of James Joyce (who had something of genius) and very few of Joyce's virtues. I am reminded of what Oscar Wilde said about Zola when he said that Zola had said genius was never clever and that Zola had proved that if he could not be a genius, he could at least be dull. Our contemporary novelists seem to prove that if they cannot be geniuses they can at least be obscure and incoherent. Several weeks ago, Faulkner gave me a copy of his last book of short stories "Go Down Moses". I think the best prose in it is in the dedication to Aunt Caroline. What Faulkner should do is to strike out on a new vein like "The Hamlet". If he ever completes the Snopes saga, it will be the best thing that he has done yet. For several years, he has mainly been rewriting Faulkner at Faulkner's worst and I think he is all washed up unless he breaks the mold and starts over again. This disappoints me a great deal.[14]

Fulminations would become Stone's metier, especially later; but whatever inspired his acrimony in the spring of 1942, its effects seem to have dissipated somewhat by summer, when, as Faulkner prepared to sign away seven years of his life to Warner Brothers, guest editor David Cohn, a friend of Stone and Faulkner, commissioned a short essay by Phil for the Deep South issue of *Saturday Review*. Cohn was interested in "what the proletariat, the loafers around the courthouse, now think of William Faulkner." "David, of all people," Stone explained to his readers, "should know that 'proletariat' is not the word to describe these highly individualistic Southern white people." Stone went on to explain the rise to fame of "Count No Count," concluding, "If [Faulkner] should completely lose out as a writer and should cease to be a commercial success and should begin to write in a new vein—and a greater one? Well, until the New York critics should say that his new writing was greater than his old and until he made a lot of money thereby any claims for him [like those of Phil Stone] would again be met by polite, derisive smiles."[15] Cohn mailed Stone his fifteen dollars, and the essay appeared in the 19 September issue of the magazine, along with others by Roark Bradford, Harry Kroll, Eudora Welty, Cleanth Brooks, Robert Penn Warren, and Mrs. John McClure.

The editor, David Cohn, a native of Greenville, Mississippi, had made a fortune with Sears, Roebuck in New Orleans before turning to his second successful career as a writer. He was best known for his 1935 book on the Mississippi Delta, *God Shakes Creation*. Faulkner, who introduced him to the Stones, probably met Cohn either at William Alexander Percy's or through Roark Bradford. One morning before Philip was born, Faulkner, who had just returned to Oxford from Roark Bradford's place outside New Orleans, saw Phil and Emily at Avent's Drugstore and related a funny anecdote about the deluge of tourists showing up at Bradford's gate. When Cohn visited the Stones a few days later, he claimed credit for Bradford's troubles, for, as a practical joke, he had printed his friend's address in his column for a Boston newspaper, telling readers that Bradford loved to see his admirers, particularly those from the Boston area. But Roark Bradford devised a sweet revenge, Cohn later admitted. Will Percy, knowing how dependent both writers were on black materials, took his houseguests Cohn and Bradford one night to a black church in Greenville, where Bradford was courteously invited to the pulpit to "exhort." In condescending mimicry of a black evangelist, Roark extemporized an elaborate tale of the Lord's having inscribed, "in letters of fire," a personal message to sinner David Cohn. As he wallowed in drunkenness, venery—and wealth—in a New Orleans hotel, Cohn had been directed to return to his native place to give away his fortune to the town's churches. The "philanthropist" had been compelled to escape Greenville that night, as Cohn told the Stones, " 'cause already Percy's yard was full of Negro preachers there asking for money."

Phil Stone probably revived the anecdote for Faulkner collector William Wisdom, a friend of Cohn in New Orleans, with whom the Stones spent a memorable afternoon in the autumn of 1942. "Wisdom," Stone wrote later, "has the finest and most interesting mind with which we have ever come in contact except, possibly, that of Mr. Justice [Felix] Frankfurter [a guest lecturer at the law school in the 1950s]." The *Commercial Appeal* provided another note on Stone's activities that fall. On 22 October "a forum led by two of this section's literary lights was held at Ole Miss. Harry Harrison Kroll and John Faulkner spoke with Phil Stone acting as emcee. Under the latter's gracious influence largely, Oxford comes as near to being a literary center as any community in the Mid-South."[16]

Compensations But No Reprieve

In 1943, as before, the Stones in public masked their financial straits, even from their closest friends. David Cohn liked to tease Emily about mindless women's magazines and club work. After joining the Marines as a war correspondent, Cohn had Simon & Schuster mail the couple an excerpt from his book *Love in America* on Emily's birthday, which renewed the topic.[17] David Cohn seems never to have suspected the seriousness, or the ulterior motives, of the Stones' continued pursuit of literature. Emily sent another novel to Edward Aswell in June. At a time when even small fees were precious, attorney Stone also steadfastly refused Maud Falkner's money for some legal work he had done for her. (Several weeks later, however, Bill's mother sent around a portrait she had painted of Philip.)

Although Phil Stone had paid off half of his father's $50,000 debt, and might be released from the rest for $5,000 more,[18] the Stones failed to secure adequate loans in the early years of the war and scrambled again for petty cash. Emily worked part-time at the university teaching drafting to servicemen, reviewed books for the *Commercial Appeal*, and tried to sell five or more anecdotes to *Readers' Digest* for the feature "Life in These United States."[19] She and her husband lost some stock when a Chicago railroad went bankrupt, and in the summer there was another capital loss. Preacher forgot to turn the hay in the barn behind the old house; it was wet and fermented, and the barn exploded in flames.

That autumn Phil Stone was allowed publicly to acknowledge a bereavement he had actually felt all his fifty years. On 27 September his mother fell and broke her hip. Miss Rosie lingered for almost a month, dying at dawn on 21 October, at the age of eighty-five. She was buried beside General Stone in the Batesville Cemetery.[20] At the hospital Phil had momentarily acquitted himself, the forsaken son: "I'm the only one who stayed with her completely to the end." Indeed, he had never left his mother's house, not when he married, not even after the place burned. She had removed with his wife and son across the street to the "little" house. In the familiar psychological pattern, however, the self-doubts, the compulsions to duty and honor that Stone attributed to his mother, would only intensify *after* her death.

If Phil and Emily saw William Faulkner between the summer of 1942 and the summer of 1943, it was only during his month's leave of absence from Warner Brothers at Christmas, but after August 1943 Faulkner was home for six months, working on his farm and beginning a new novel, "a fable, an indictment of war perhaps," as he wrote Harold Ober.[21]

The rudimentary correspondence that Stone had had with Faulkner in California in the 1930s apparently all but ceased in the 1940s, though Faulkner may still have used Stone's office address for private letters when he was in Oxford. In the war years, perhaps to atone for lack of a military record as well as out of a genuine sense of family and civic responsibility, Phil initiated an extensive correspondence with those who had left to serve their country: Cousin Polly with the Red Cross in Washington, his nephew Jack Stone with the Army Air Corps in New Mexico, hometown men like Dale Mullen and George Fenger, Staff Sergeant Sykes Kennon, Lieutenant Colonel Louis M. Jiggits, and numerous others. In weekly letters to Lieutenant Jack Stone, Phil wrote of Philip and his paid companion, a ten-year-old black boy nicknamed "Hambone"; of the case he was working on, and whom he had seen on a Jackson trip; of Emily's book, and her election as district club president. Philip, who had been reading with ease since his third birthday, typed a letter to his cousin in May 1944, and Jack Stone kindly asked about "Philip's man Friday" in his report of seeing the Pope while on leave in Rome. (Most of the soldiers, like Jack, rendered compliments to the proud father, but one tactlessly admonished Phil not to put Philip on a pedestal.) After Jack was assigned as bombardier to a Liberator in Italy that autumn, his uncle continued to supply family and Oxford notes, including news of county war bond drives. But Phil's November letter was returned unopened. W. E. Stone V had been shot down over Hungary on 17 November. Not until Christmas Eve would the family receive word that Jack was "well and all right." Although the first of their letters to the American POW were returned—one of Phil's cautioning Jack, "do not be foolish enough to try to escape"—soon Phil Stone was regularly corresponding with #9056 Stalag Luft 3, Germany.

In the spring of 1945 Stone's correspondence with servicemen increased both in volume and intensity as the men anticipated the war's end. Major David Cohn, on his way to China, wrote that he had "heard and thought" about Phil at General D. I. Sultan's headquarters: "This is no place for a country man to be but here I am trying to scare up some Democratic votes in Burma against the next election." Cohn wrote, more seriously, of having "seen a lot of war and a lot of Americans. They are a greater people than they know," but his letter ended on a light note: "I trust, sir, that you and Miss Emily are flourishing; are fighting the sinners and backsliders; and are generally setting an example of austerity for the community."[22]

Roosevelt's death on 12 April was a shock to Phil Stone. Although often admitting "distress at FDR's perpetuating himself in office," Stone cried at his desk when he heard the news. The world looked even bleaker when Corporal James E. Gooch, with the Third Army in Germany, mailed a V-letter to Stone with an appalling account of "Bucheniwell," a camp where fifty-one thousand lives had been exterminated.[23]

On Wednesday, 15 August 1945, the day after the Japanese surrender, Oxford's mayor proclaimed a holiday at "the return of peace" and encouraged attendance at a memorial thanksgiving service in the First Baptist Church that morning, which the Stones attended. As he filed the mayor's proclamation, Phil wrote a memo about the war for Philip: "Before you were born . . . Hitler and his like were overrunning Europe and practising all sorts of cruelty and beastality [sic] on innocent conquered people. We talked about it and wondered if we were going to be sorry that you would be born and if you would live out your childhood beaten and cowed by some Jap or German. I told Emily that all we could do was to trust in God and God did work it out all right."

By the last year of World War II, as Joseph Blotner records, "almost all of Faulkner's seventeen books were . . . out of print." In 1944 Malcolm Cowley, an editor on the *New Republic*, had received a rare Faulkner letter giving his blessings to the article Cowley had proposed to write to correct that situation. Stone probably missed the first Cowley essay in the *New York Times Book Review*, but he read Cowley's article in *Saturday Review* and congratulated the author in a letter of 30 April 1945: "It is the best article on [Faulkner's] work that I have yet read. In fact it is the only one that I have read that has any great degree of accuracy and that is at all well based. However, you are all wet about a number of things."

What followed was a familiar Stone recital: praising *Sartoris*, fault-

ing *The Wild Palms* and *Absalom, Absalom!* as the work of "a literary extrovert" (i.e., without comprehensive design or aesthetic theory),
denigrating Faulkner's style as "merely a personal mannerism." Faulkner, Stone told Cowley, "keeps on rewriting *Sanctuary*"; unlike those
of Shakespeare and Balzac, with few exceptions, his "characters all
talk like William Faulkner writes." Explaining the place of *The Hamlet* in the Snopes saga, he observed, oddly, that the "incident about the
calf . . . ruined" the novel, one indication of Faulkner's characteristic
"complete lack of aesthetic taste." Stone invited Cowley to Oxford to
continue the discussion; "It would take several days," he added. Cowley
need not answer his letter, Stone concluded, and he mailed a blind copy
to his university friend Dr. James C. Rice.[24] Phil had often accused
Faulkner of those transgressions to his face, but over the last few years
the two friends had seldom found the time or the occasion for serious
discussion.

For his part, William Faulkner's desperation to escape Jack Warner
with soul and pocketbook intact seems to have inspired his nostalgia
for all things at home, including even a critical Phil Stone. Faulkner
had heard, of course, that five-year-old Philip Stone shared his godfather's penchant for drawings and stories; but the child was merely an
excuse for a commemorative gesture William Faulkner made in 1945.
When he visited Stone at his office at Christmas, he brought for Philip
not his usual silver dollar, but the first carbon typescript of *The Hamlet*.
Inside he had inscribed: "To My Godson, Philip Alston Stone / May he
be faithful / fortunate and brave. . . ."

Two months later, Faulkner autographed Phil's replacement first
edition of *The Hamlet*. Stone was too watchful for a decline in Faulkner talent not to have observed the retrospective nature of the other
books Faulkner gave him that year: Cowley's *Portable Faulkner* and
the Modern Library edition of *The Sound and the Fury and As I Lay
Dying* (with the Compson appendix).[25] Their rapprochement was further hindered by reticence and jealousy. Stone was never disabused of
the notion that, as he warded off insolvency, Bill was earning fabulous
sums in Hollywood.

In the war years, as the Stones' income did at times meet their expenses, Phil's legal expertise had begun to draw state and even national
attention. The *American Bar Association Journal* asked that he review

Charles E. Merriam's *Systematic Politics*, an essay which he meticulously prepared in 1945. He had been an occasional contributor to legal publications since he argued for stricter training for state lawyers in the 1930 *Mississippi Law Journal*, and Stone now chaired the advisory board for the state's law review. He also presided in Mississippi over the ABA's Committee for the Improvement of the Administration of Justice. From 1944, too, he would be elected each year to the State Bar Commission.[26] Despite his growing reputation, however, significant fees continued to elude him.

A decade after his father's death Phil Stone was compelled to examine a pragmatic proposition, at which his instincts revolted. The last Stone attorney was under pressure to desert the family firm. Other men less gifted than he had thriving practices; in a large, money-making firm, Stone would not have to search titles; clerks could leave him free for the appellate work at which he excelled. The argument his wife constructed was irrefutable. On 22 May 1946 Phil answered a job advertisement in the *ABA Journal*, but without enthusiasm: "I might be interested in your proposition," he began, and he recited his education, background, and accomplishments. He wished not "office work alone," but "principally trial work and appeal court work, especially trial work before juries." Yet he had not enclosed references, and concluded the resume in a tone of resignation: "If you are not interested you need not bother to reply to this letter."[27] Stone talked also with Thompson and Thompson, a Mississippi firm, but either position would have necessitated his leaving Oxford, and although the summer before Philip began school was an obvious time to move, Stone let the matter drop—unable to quit his native soil.

At any rate, by temperament Phil Stone was hardly suited to the pace or the competition of a busy corporate law firm. His languid practice afforded him if not money then a gentleman's leisure, in which he might still cultivate his public image (certified by his Faulkner associations) as a man of taste, intelligence, and social charm. In May 1946 Stone tried to convince William Faulkner to lure the visiting Russian Ilya Ehrenburg into the Stones' backyard for a Tom Collins and an afternoon's cross-examination about the Soviet system. The State Department's advance man had telephoned Phil to intervene to arrange a meeting for Ehrenburg with Faulkner. The reclusive Faulkner, claiming to be engrossed by his work on *A Fable*, told Stone he was not interested in talking "ideas." Further negotiations finally effected a grudging invitation. The visitor's party, however, responded with hauteur to the writer's munificent offer of an audience for fifteen minutes, and bypassed Oxford, Mississippi, on their American tour.[28]

Stone, while appreciating a working author's natural aversion to literary talk, himself relished social debate on politics or art. The Stones liked to entertain and, despite their limited budget, were perceived as congenial hosts. David Cohn, who had threatened to spend three or four years at their home eating "frying chickens and mustard greens" upon his return from Burma, was twice their houseguest in 1946. The couple marveled at the conversational skills of Cohn, "one of our best friends," as Phil wrote Philip. English professor A. Wigfall Green and his sister shared Christmas dinner with the Stones that year, according to another memo, and later that evening another university friend, Mrs. Anita Hutcherson, joined them, with two members of her family.[29]

In April 1947 the Tenth Anniversary Southern Literary Festival was scheduled at the Lowreys' Blue Mountain College, a short drive north from Oxford, and the Stones, with their Ole Miss friends, made plans to attend the day's lectures. Perrin Lowrey was to introduce one speaker, and Harry Kroll was to talk that afternoon on "Resources in the South for Historical Writing." Kroll also introduced writer Jesse Stuart, who gave a morning address. The Stones had become friends with the Baptist educator Charles D. Johnson of the Baylor faculty, who had originated the Mississippi conferences, and they attended a number of those sessions in the late forties and early fifties. While increasingly dominating the conversations at those gatherings, the state's most famous author, an absent William Faulkner, steadfastly refused all Festival Association invitations.

The author had been more gracious about a recent Stone request. When Emily completed another novel in 1946, Phil asked Faulkner whether his agent might be willing to look at it. Bill had given him Harold Ober's address and had mentioned the book in his own letter to Ober in late June: "I haven't seen it. I have known her husband many years, have confidence in his judgement, I mean literary. . . . It may not be salable but I don't believe it will be trash."[30]

The homage paid to Art in the Stone house did not escape the intel-

ligent, sensitive child growing up there. At ages five and six Philip's
Christmas requests, with one exception, were for literary equipment:
story records, books, a desk and chair, a blackboard and chalk, crayons
and tablets, pencils and a pencil case, a roll of newsprint and sten-
cils, a "movie projector and some films." The Stones as yet had been
unable to have other children (Emily had two miscarriages between
1940 and 1948), and Philip's prodigious feats, which his father meticulously documented, must sometimes have wearied the couple's social
acquaintances. The boy read forty-two books in first grade; his first
poem went into the files in 1947; his radio scripts were mentioned in
the Memphis paper. When book editor Paul Flowers enclosed a children's story for him among his mother's review assignments, Philip,
relieved that it was "not another Jesus book," responded with a review of *The Adventures of Winnie and Bly* for the *Commercial Appeal*.
Like his parents, the child also corresponded with authors whose books
he approved; he suggested to Howard R. Garis that he set his next
Uncle Wiggley story in New England. Phil Stone filed every scrap, even
when in temper Philip's fantasies turned macabre: "Cemetery Ticket /
Killing / Oxford Graveyard / Today / 10:30."

Collecting memorabilia for Philip had evolved also into casual autobiographical exercises for Phil Stone (a mirror in which he later fashioned less accurate self-portraits). He had reason to be proud in 1947
and 1948. The May 1947 issue of the *American Bar Association Journal* had carried a signed editorial by Phil Stone, "What Is the Matter
With Our Law Schools?" Phil thought it time the professors taught
the *A* students "lawyering" as well as law. In the same issue Stone's
name appeared with his friend Wesley A. Sturges of New Haven as
a member of the advisory board of the national publication. "This is
really an honor," Stone wrote Philip; he was the single board member
from the Mid-South and one of only three from the "entire South."
Furthermore, the editor-in-chief had been "kind enough to say" that
Stone's unsolicited article was "so good" that the month's layout had
been redone "to include my editorial therein." [31]

Stone's colleagues in Mississippi awarded him another professional
honor when the state bar convened on the campus of the University of
Mississippi in 1948. Stone, a four-year veteran on the Bar Commission,
was elected without opposition as president of the State Bar Associa-

tion for the coming year. But Phil Stone was almost the only topic the lawyers could discuss in Oxford without raising their blood pressures. Even though a full century had elapsed before a white majority had returned to Mississippi with the 1940 census, the war's blurring of social class, the Democrats' wooing of black support, and President Truman's integrated armed forces and Civil Rights Commission had quickly unsettled that conservative majority. A states' rights address by Stone's friend "Major" W. Calvin Wells was taken up by an angrier Resolutions Committee, and in a heated debate of the final session, the convention voiced "emphatic opposition to President Truman's 'so-called, misnamed civil rights recommendation,' to Mr. Truman's renomination . . . and to the nomination of 'anyone else who makes similar recommendations to Congress or harbors similar ideologies.'"

The Memphis *Commercial Appeal* reported that the Dixiecrat measures were adopted unanimously; according to Stone's summary for the *ABA Journal*, however, "The actions voted were vigorously debated and were by no means unanimous." Stone's article had begun by noting the lack of precedent for the greatly politicized debate by the bar. But whether the state bar discussed rules for civil procedure or the qualifications for state justices at Jackson and Biloxi in Stone's last fourteen years of active participation, the issue was raised and raised again. "Is the South . . . to be called upon to ENDURE A SECOND TRAGIC ERA?" one speaker at the 1948 convention wanted to know.[32]

In his largely ceremonial post Phil Stone could enact a few reforms— he set up a new standing committee to explore "the legal implications of the age of air travel"—but his most pressing responsibility was the association's shoestring budget, historically and incessantly in the red because of the great numbers of attorneys who refused to pay their dues. Finances had been strained further during the war when attorneys in uniform were exempted from dues payments. The new president's campaign to collect delinquent dues fared as poorly as those of his predecessors, but most of his friends in the state knew enough of his personal indebtedness to resent the pointed irony or supreme cruelty of Jack Hancock's column "Under the Ding-Dong Domes" in the Jackson paper for 24 August 1948:

> Phil Stone of Oxford, the current president of the State Bar, has sent word down the line that he expects every lawyer in the state to pay his dues—

and points out that legally no lawyer is supposed to practice unless his dues are paid up. As a rule nobody but the secretary of the State Bar worries about this little item. But Phil, who has definite ideas about the way an organization ought to be run, says that lawyers certainly should pay their debts before they write letters to people threatening suit for nonpayment. He threatens to make certain committees of the State Bar go to work on some slow-pay members if they don't change their habits. Me, I hope he does it. I still remember that some of these letters I used to get were kind of mean—especially along about the 3rd round. And I bet I never got 16 years behind, either.[33]

Phil Stone, bracketing the item for Philip, incredibly took the piece at face value. He never made Hancock's malicious if inevitable connection, for there was no question that Phil Stone meant to repay his 1930s debts. Shyster or even just lazy lawyers needed to be shamed into remitting their delinquent, legally imposed dues. Good fortune may have blinded him, for he was enjoying his new position; his income had stabilized; and by August six months of excited apprehension were safely behind the Stone couple: they hoped for another child in the fall.

One afternoon in mid-summer Phil telephoned Emily that a Mr. Collins and his wife from Cambridge were at the office and that he would like to invite them out to the house for a drink. Carvel Collins, then an assistant professor at Harvard, was preparing to devote a graduate seminar to novelist William Faulkner. The scholar, although listening politely to Phil's yarns, upset Emily that afternoon, for he seemed rather skeptical of Stone's less than modest claims about his role in the Faulkner career. When Phil mentioned the fire, however, she remembered the papers that she and Preacher had salvaged from the ashes in the bitter cold of 1942. Six years later, in blazing July heat, Carvel Collins and Emily Stone rummaged in storage areas of the old stable, the bull house, the smokehouse, turning at last to a small tin structure glaring in the oppressive heat. After their eyes adjusted to the dark interior, they could see the grillwork from the old house and other junk; but behind that in the back there was a large toolbox.

"Carvel, let's see if we can get over there; it may be there," Emily said. Collins climbed over the junk and raised the toolbox lid, and there they were. Many of the papers were Whitehurst manuscripts, but among the remains were over a hundred sheets of Faulkner poetry. When the Collinses returned north after their proof of "the written word," the professor mailed them a copy of *Forms of Modern Fiction*, which included Robert Penn Warren's essay on Faulkner. Emily Stone signed their names in the book with a note, "From Mr. Collins, of / Harvard, who made / us a little visit." [34]

Rather than resent Collins's scrupulous accuracy, Phil Stone was a great admirer of his new friend's exactitude. After filing the program for Philip's stage debut as a page in a campus production of *Antigone* later that month, Stone wrote, "They spelled your name with two 'ls' which offended you very much. I don't blame you but I feel sorry for you because, as you grow older, you will find out, as I have found out, that very few people are very accurate about anything. . . . so many people do not seem to know or care that if a thing is not done exactly right it is entirely wrong."

To whatever degree Philip imbibed those standards, his fledgling literature continued to reflect the world of his father. After the summer's elections, the young librettist wrote "Vote Early and Often: A Political Operetta in Two Acts"; after Phil's September trip to the American Bar Association convention, Philip printed the script "The Lawyer's Trip to Seattle," its cast to include "The Lawyer's Friends, Pat Murphy and Virginia Parker."

The fifty-five-year-old president of the Mississippi State Bar had suffered not a little teasing when his colleagues heard that he was again an expectant father. Many of his contemporaries had grandchildren older than Philip. Herbert Fant, Jr., a Sardis attorney, threatened a recall of the May election: "We've made a mistake, Phil; we should have elected you president of the Junior Bar." When the Stones' seven-and-one-half-pound girl was born two days before Thanksgiving, Phil Stone assumed a grandfather's prerogative, to spoil her. He had always bemoaned not having a sister, Miss Rosie's two daughters having died as infants before his birth, and the special gentleness he exhibited with his nieces now found expression with a daughter of his own. Dr. James C. Rice, head of the pharmacology unit at the university medical school, and his wife Bernice accepted responsibility as godparents to the second Stone child, as did Katherine Lawless Compton, Stone's friend in Charleston in 1920. The baby was christened Araminta Whitehurst Stone, for her mother's sister and her maternal great-grandmother.

Shortly thereafter, Philip's godfather gave him another distinctive

Christmas gift in 1948. Faulkner typed and bound one of two new copies of his 1920s children's story *The Wishing-Tree* for "Philip Stone II."[35] The baby very much interested the boy, who sketched her first portrait in pencil at five weeks as she was being patted to sleep in her crib by an adult hand. After the holidays, their father collected the drawing, newspaper notices of Araminta's birth, and, a new compulsion, stamps on envelopes that Stone said "may have some value someday," for the initial volume of the Araminta Whitehurst Stone file.

The Stone household was diminished by one the next spring when their servant Green Liggin died. The obituary Stone wrote for his son's file, though trite, was sincere: "He used to tell you stories up at the smokehouse and around the barn and was very kind to you and loved you dearly. You are probably the last little white boy who will ever have stories told him by an old colored man Uncle Remus style."

On the front page of the issue of the *Eagle* with Araminta's birth announcement there had been a story about the university's offer of assistance to MGM, which was considering filming Faulkner's *Intruder in the Dust* in the author's hometown in the spring. Stone had not yet read the book Faulkner had inscribed to him on publication day, 27 September 1948, and was too busy to do so before the shooting began. In the first quarter of 1949, he was preoccupied with the subdivision, a proposed office addition, and his first stirrings of oil lease fever. Philip's movie madness, however, ensured that the Stones would not escape the town's hysteria that March. Perhaps to distract his son from Preacher's funeral the day before, Stone accompanied Philip up to the jail where the Hollywood crew was filming on the seventeenth, and the boy got the autograph of Claude Jarman, Jr., the young actor who retraced an incident from Phil's boyhood for the picture's opening scene.[36]

Stone's duties as state bar president also continued to make demands on his time. Dean Robert J. Farley of the Ole Miss Law School invited him to address a luncheon at the Southern Law Review Conference later that month.[37]

Although he hardly relished the speaker's podium, Stone was a more willing lecturer than his aging mentor Stark Young. The Stones' friend Dean Dudley R. Hutcherson of the graduate school inherited the task of inviting literary figures to the campus when the university hosted the 1949 Southern Literary Festival. John Crowe Ransom agreed to participate, as did younger writers like Harry Kroll and one of the university's junior faculty members, Mrs. John Rusher, who had just published a first novel, *Fire in the Morning*, under her maiden name Elizabeth Spencer. But the invitation was declined by alumnus Stark Young. However, late in the night, days after his rejection, the phone rang in the Hutchersons' home. It was "Mr. Stark, well into his cups, and he'd decided to come," Dudley told Phil and Emily the next morning. "The next time we ask Mr. Stark to come down here, we're going to send a quart of bourbon with the invitation."

At 7:30 on the evening of Friday, 22 April, the Phil Stones with other festival participants gathered for Stark Young's address "Lights from Strange Lamps." There seems nothing singular in his topic, the luminosity a knowledge of languages afforded the student of English poetry. But by all accounts (not excluding his own), Young's eloquence that night commanded attention. The audience listened enthralled.[38] Phil Stone glimpsed again the man who had opened his mind.

The homecoming otherwise was most unfortunate, for, to an omniscient observer, a recurring absence of circumspection had soon soured the reunion of three old "friends." In the past Faulkner and Young had clashed more than once over their fluctuating evaluations of Sherwood Anderson, whom both had known well in the twenties. Relations between Stone and Young had fared no better. That Stark Young's was a minor, effete talent had become the transparent theme of Phil Stone's letters and comments to Young himself in the intervening years. Young's revenge upon Stone's excessive candor was often petty—laughing with Ella Somerville over Stone's idiosyncrasies—but Stone's words obviously rankled. Stark Young was inebriated one night months after Phil's scathing letter about *So Red the Rose* (1934), Young's most popular work. "Stark tonight has been drinking Bourbon, tone rather fresh, chirography vague," he wrote Somerville. He had another confession too: he was "stealing a sentence" from one of Ella's letters, "about doing nice things—not, as Phil would say, as great as Medici, Congreve and Aristophanes, but very trim and lovely."[39]

Somerville, in whose house Young was a guest during the Southern Literary Festival, gave a dinner party for him to which Faulkner and the Stones were invited. (Afterwards, Young worried whether Elizabeth Spencer had thought him "a fresh old man," excusing his behavior to his hostess because Spencer's "eyes [were] so full of wild flights and the glass so full of your bourbon.") However, Mr. Stark had not seemed to notice Bill Faulkner's cold and resentful glare—and abrupt exit— after Young began to satirize Sherwood Anderson. In a letter to his sister, Young mentioned the Somerville dinner and other social events before concluding, "Then Phil Stone would have us there, with a writer from Tennessee, whose name hit me wrong from the start and I can't remember it."

Young had left the Stones and Harry Harrison Kroll that night with one of Emily's stories, which he promised to recommend to a publisher. However, the manuscript was not in his luggage as he "rushed from" Oxford after the weekend, according to his apology. Subsequently, Phil mailed "For Honor and For Love" to him in New York. When it arrived, Young, drinking again, began a letter to Somerville promising to read and return the manuscript that day. Emily Stone, he wrote, "has good qualities and is alive, and so may they rest in peace. What is peace? . . ." And Stark Young went off on a comparison of Italian and Yankee tombstones.

His report to the Stones was apparently more guarded. Phil Stone saved the return envelope from "the celebrated dramatic critic," who had "liked" the story, according to a note that he directed to his daughter; Araminta should know that Mr. Young was "quite a friend" of her father.

Several months later Young expressed outrage at being asked to read a manuscript by the Somerville boarder, a university professor. "There are not six people in the world I would ask to read a manuscript of mine," he wrote, "any more than I would ask Doctor Culley [Ella's brother-in-law] to take home some of my blood and let me have an analysis."[40] Phil Stone again should have expected no help from Stark Young.

Six weeks after the conference, Stone delivered an impassioned lecture of his own, the president's annual address before the state bar. His title was "Let Us Turn to Liberalism," and while a different audience might hear the perfidy of "states' rights" beneath his rhetorical repetitions and his sometimes Latinate, sometimes pungent Anglo-Saxon prose, Stone's argument for the liberty of the individual at the encroachment of a centralized, "faceless, nameless" bureaucracy was neither racism nor Agrarian elegy. He sounded at times more like a Henry David Thoreau converted to New Testament Christianity. Americans by their inactivity—and indefensible prejudices—had permitted the federal government its incipient socialism; "we have indolently sprawled supine while money was wasted by our own people, and education languished, and roads were quagmires, and individual rights denied." "The admonition to do unto others as you would have them do unto you," Stone argued, "is stern economic necessity apart from being good ethics." Once they had set their own house in moral order, advocates of true liberalism, historical Adam Smith capitalism, should "match the passion of those who cry for security." They must not appeal "to the emotions of greed, of intolerance, of cruelty, of hate, but to the spark which ever lifts the face of man toward the stars, to that tiny essence of God that is resident in every human being."

Nettled in his own quest for solvency by the IRS, FHA, Social Security, even Washington's expropriation of offshore mineral rights, at which he loudly complained in the speech,[41] Stone was not yet embittered, his anger still under control. The nightmare decade ahead, however, was to crack the reasoned conservatism.

Before the convention closed, the retiring president was elected Mississippi's representative to the American Bar Association's House of Delegates, but the year's rumors of Stone's being considered for a federal judgeship came to nothing.[42]

That summer, as Phil tried to double subdivision profits by investments in oil rights in Tennessee, their son's "night terrors," marked pallor, and weight loss gave the Stones grave concern. The doctors agreed that a few months at the "Preventorium," an adjunct of the tuberculosis sanitorium in South Mississippi, would not be unwarranted. Philip accepted the verdict with a show of adult sensibility.

On 13 June the Stones received his first letter: "Please don't think for one minute I haven't written you because I didn't want to. I've been dying to write you. It's just that they only let us write home once a week and that's the *only* reason, believe me," the eight-year-old began his dozen pages, feeling "a little guilty" at his mother's more frequent correspondence and apologizing because his pen was out of ink. Philip was working hard to gain his requisite eight pounds by eating and sleeping, but admitted less success in playing outdoors, with the depressing rainy spell, which contributed to his being "sort of homesick once in a while." But there was a movie theater, and, though Mrs. Jones confirmed that "the children down here are pretty destructive on comics," Philip asked his parents to send "that crate of comics, right away." After two weeks, visitors were allowed "anytime," although a journey would involve "too much trainfare," he knew, and the possibility of his increased homesickness at their departure. "That doesn't mean I don't want you to come. . . . Absolutely not!" He had a "proposition" about the ten pounds of his parents' goal; he would gain eight pounds in four weeks and come home for his birthday to gain the last two: "Will you take me up on it? Please do it, Mother." Trying another tack, Philip wrote that no doubt they were "glad to get rid of me for the summer." There might now be "some peace and quiet around there." His bravado crumbled further at his final request, for a "good-bye kiss."

It was torture for all three of them, but at their visit on his birthday, Philip's weight was up only four pounds. After six weeks he wrote: "I think it would be better if you came only once every *three* weeks and as I said, a surprise would be nice." After three months Philip returned to Oxford stronger, but with a child's security, perhaps, never again complete.

That autumn Phil Stone finally began to read *Intruder in the Dust*, finishing it on Sunday night, 2 October. "A skillful job, Bill, but it seems too trickey [sic] in places and there is too damned much talk in it," he first wrote. Then he recorded a note for his children: "This tale grew out of a suggestion I made to Bill and he wrote it in six weeks to sell to the slicks because he needed money and the slicks rejected it. Then MGM bought it for fifty thousand dollars and made a movie of it. The premiere will be here Tuesday week, Oct 11, and Mother and Philip and I are going." (Phil asked Stark Young in 1951 whether he remembered that Faulkner's agent "could not get the Post to take it because [as Bill told ME] the story did not glorify the negro?")

Stone was vexed at having to buy his own movie tickets; nevertheless, the Stones did attend the Oxford premiere, leaving Araminta "at home asleep with Mrs. Hattie Morgan." For her benefit, Stone made another note: "It was a pretty good picture but not the best I have ever seen." He collected all the accompanying publicity for his children's files, even the program for the PTA's "Intruder at Its Wu'st, An Operatic Travesty in a Dozen Scenes," which might be "of some interest."[43] But Faulkner's movie sale seemed a fantasy to a man who still owed the IRS four hundred dollars for 1948. The expiration of another note in December was overlooked with the baby sick, the cook sick, and the Stones' having to milk the cow themselves, as he wrote one creditor.[44]

On the first day of the new decade, Phil completed a more recent Faulkner book with his highest praise for the title story "Knight's Gambit": "A damned good job." The baby was asleep, Philip "singing in the bath-tub," his wife "reading a brief of mine."[45] Even with outside irritations, the husband and father was more than content. But during the 1950s General Stone's son and William Faulkner's character model was to be hounded from that sanctuary inch by inch. The harvest of talent and honor and friendship would rot with the diseases of failure and self-justification.

12

The Embittered Friend

THE MAIL that attorney Stone retrieved each morning from the post office more often than not included a letter with questions about William Faulkner. Those student requests and others came so often now that Stone sometimes declined help to the less tactful or sincere inquirer, but rarely failed to answer at all. More typically, he relished setting the facts straight, as with Glenn O. Carey's research on Faulkner humor in 1949 and 1950.[1] To the brightest and most industrious of the rising Faulkner scholars on junior faculties, particularly in the East, Stone was often willing to offer friendship along with anecdote and artifact. Most of the serious correspondence he filed in three Faulkner files, apparently comprehensively between 1949 and 1962.

Carvel Collins, one of Stone's three major correspondents, typically mailed to Oxford publications garnered in his research, shared news from his academic and publishing contacts, and carried Stone's regards to old friends like Stark Young. Stone in turn answered questions and reported on the current Faulkner: "I saw Bill at the post office a few minutes ago and he says he is not feeling well again. He has not been feeling well for almost a year, off and on, and I am gently needling him now to get him to go through the Clinic but he probably won't do it. As I told you, the Faulkners think they can even defy the laws of Nature."[2]

Early in 1950 a persistent *Life* magazine had offered Collins fifteen hundred dollars for a Faulkner essay, finally even agreeing to one less personal than Malcolm Cowley's on Hemingway. But Collins was still hesitant. In April he discussed its possibilities with Stone, for whose assistance he offered a third of the commission. Phil was more uncertain, "If there is anything in the world I do not want to do it is to commercialize on my friendship with Bill, one of the finest things in my whole life." Faulkner's approval was necessary before Stone could accept any money, but his "tentative opinion" was that the critic should enjoy the entire fee for his labors. Stone would help, of course, preferably as a silent partner, although his support would be there in the event of a challenge.

Neither man had pursued the matter very far by May. Collins, unwilling to write about a "celebrity," was mulling over the ethical issues involved; Stone, busy in court, had not yet seen Faulkner, but worried whether Collins was deferring too much to him. Phil's offhand advice about the biographical chapter was not "gospel": "You know more about it than I do." On 7 May Phil Stone finally put Collins's project before Faulkner, who at once opposed the idea, vehemently; "quite disturbed," Faulkner even saw Phil later at home to try to "prevent it[s] being done."

In a letter to Collins written the following day (a copy of which went to Faulkner), Stone at Bill's request explained the latter's objections on the grounds of privacy (which Stone accepted but did not share) and because of Cowley's prior claim of having "graciously complied" with Faulkner's veto during an earlier *Life* initiative, a scruple with which Stone concurred. Furthermore, after his family, Stone continued, "I am fonder of Bill than . . . of anybody in the world." If Faulkner's "profound faith in my integrity and in my personal loyalty to him" were destroyed, "it would be a very saddening shock to Bill, even more than he realizes," Stone wrote, adding, "although maybe I am now being vain." Collins's research was sure to profit later from Faulkner's goodwill and generosity. Phil asked that word of the matter's being closed be mailed immediately. Stone's dilemma, a dilemma he had not foreseen, was resolved with Collins's wire on 15 May. According to Mr. Faulkner's wishes, there was to be no *Life* essay by Carvel Collins.[3]

A five-hundred-dollar commission was not an insignificant amount to Stone, but his business affairs were somewhat more orderly in the early fifties, after he consolidated his smaller loans in a large note with J. C. Jourdan, a legal friend in Iuka. Because the Stones' first automobile, Mrs. Whitehurst's ancient green Chevrolet, was more and more unreliable, Stone also borrowed from the creditor for a 1948 Ford sedan. His friendships with Faulkner and Collins too had survived the *Life* matter. After Faulkner dropped by the Stones' house one night in August, Phil passed along to Collins Bill's admission that he had not read Carl Jung. The writer was more interested then in his corn crop: "Bill told me . . . that he stood in one spot on his farm and reached out and touched 27 ears of corn." In another letter written the same month, Stone told the scholar that although Faulkner's *Collected Stories* was out, he was tardy in remembering to bring Stone's copy: "I shall probably have to go after it, as usual." Faulkner autographed the book forty-eight hours later, but it was a week before the Stones drove the new car "down to Bill's / house and got this book on Sunday morning."[4]

From that August weekend until after he left for the ABA's annual meeting in Washington in mid-September, Phil Stone engaged in an embarrassing, frantic correspondence with the Most Reverend R. O. Gerow, Bishop of Natchez. At issue was the rumor of a black parochial school. Stone feared that the school would lower the value of adjacent property—specifically, his remaining subdivision land, on which his financial house of cards rested. Father Edgar Smigiel called on Stone in Oxford to explain that the Franciscans' interest was only in a residence, but not before Stone's wife drew Bishop Gerow a map of the racial distribution in town, while Stone protested overlong that he harbored neither racial nor religious prejudice. If a quarter of Oxford's black population would not validate his helpfulness to the race, he would "sell out and leave the county." He had close Northern Catholic friends, he wrote Gerow: the late Jim Hoey of New York and Postmaster General Jim Farley; ABA president Harold Gallagher of New York, a "prominent Catholic layman," had appointed him to the reception committee for the September convention. Moreover, he saw the church as the "best nucleus against Communism."

After Gerow ordered Smigiel to abandon his pursuit, Stone polled his homeowners, who had no objections to a Franciscan home; but Gerow and Smigiel had agreed to give up. By the time the bishop reported to Stone on the order's having bought a Greenwood "place," Phil was not the only one relieved: "for now this will occupy their attention," Gerow concluded.[5]

There was little rationale for Stone's panic; but the single move, from his perspective, appeared to belong in a series pointing toward checkmate. Its context is not without interest, for the incident too laid the ground for what followed. Stone's debilitating paranoia, according to his wife, manifested itself initially in what he called the conspiracy of "Yankees and niggers." In 1950 Phil wrote of Faulkner, self-revealingly, "It is a civilization that is gone for which he mourns." The death of his cousin Lemuel Augustus Smith, Sr. (a fellow Alston devotee) left a Supreme Court vacancy in October, and Phil Stone headed the list of possible candidates in the *Commercial Appeal* pages. His comment was that of a man in whom hope too seems to be dying: "It will amount to nothing as I am not an applicant for the job." The first of the later numerous secretive letters also appears in the 1950 file. Phil asked that classmate Paul Bowdre meet with him before a trustees' meeting on campus for a talk about some business that Stone would not mention in print. The conference was postponed, but Bowdre made a point of praising Stone in the month of the news from Stockholm: Faulkner "deserved [the Nobel Prize] and you deserve a *great* deal of the credit too, because you steered him in the proper course before he knew how to handle the oars." Then Bowdre added, "Hope you are feeling all right again."[6]

When Phil Stone learned sometime on Friday, 10 November, that the 1949 Nobel Prize for Literature had been awarded to William Faulkner, the word would not have come from the recipient; even Faulkner's daughter heard the news at second hand. Rumors culminating in the days before the announcement no doubt had prepared Stone in advance, but whatever he felt in private, his public reaction was understated. There is no record that he beat a path to Faulkner's door with the reporters, but neither did he offer at once a private handshake of silent congratulations as did their mutual friend Mack Reed.[7] Phil had to be coerced into writing a reminiscence for Phil Mullen's paper, but then professions of reluctance for print were a long-established *modus operandi* for attorney Stone, as unstudied for him as Faulkner's flights from publicity.

It was Tuesday before Stone completed his portion of "I Know William Faulkner" for Thursday's *Eagle*. He rehearsed their years together from the summer of 1914 to the attention that followed the publication of *Sanctuary*. The story, told so often, would have written itself. Its leitmotif, more distinctly than before, articulated that of the *Oxford Magazine* and *Saturday Review* essays: Stone's quarrel was not with Faulkner, but with the town. They had laughed; they had sneered; they had begrudged Stone a dollar and a half for *The Marble Faun*; most often, the community had been simply oblivious to what he and Faulkner were about. Only Mack Reed, Maud Falkner, and Stone had cared; and Oxford might dismiss the others, but not to believe Phil Stone? As Stone's tale of rejection ended in present time, he turned from the town to Faulkner:

> . . . Bill and I are getting to be old men now and perhaps someone who knows should say it, someone who knows that he is even greater as a man than he is as a writer. A lot of us talk about decency, about honor, about loyalty, about gratitude. Bill doesn't talk about these things; he lives them. People may persecute and revile you but this would only bring Bill quickly to your side if you are his friend. If you are his friend and if the mob should choose to crucify you, Bill would be there without summons. He would carry your cross up the hill for you.[8]

Perhaps the sanctuary of his family would never have been enough for Phil Stone.

But Faulkner had his own demons, and, like Phil's father, he escaped to the woods to exorcise them, though not before informing the Swedish Academy that he could not be present at the awards ceremony. The dean of his hunting party, Ike Roberts, recognized Faulkner's warning signs, but had small success in getting him to take a little soup for nourishment as alcohol destroyed his appetite. Meanwhile, embassy officials were concocting elaborate and awkward schemes of persuasion designed to deliver one American novelist to Stockholm by 10 December. Lucy Somerville Howorth, a onetime subscriber to Stone's lending library, now a colleague in the state bar, was contacted by Washington's envoy Muna Lee, who had family ties in North Mississippi. Howorth advised Miss Lee to telephone Phil Stone or her cousin Ella Somerville. According to Joseph Blotner, Ella steered Lee away from Stone—the two men were "on the outs"—and suggested Hugh Evans, another hunting companion. Evans's influence, however, proved indecisive when the hunters brought Faulkner back to Oxford, put him to bed, and took turns with the family sitting up with their friend, who continued to drink.

It was Estelle Faulkner who finally telephoned Phil Stone: "Won't you please try to help us with Billy? He's drinking and he swears he's not going to Sweden." "Stelle," Phil replied, "I'm sorry, but, no, I won't." Having quit drinking himself after the long struggle in college, he explained, he had little patience with those who refused to stop. "Bill doesn't want to quit," he said, "or he would. There's nothing to do until he decides himself to stop." But when she told him of Faulkner's having promised his daughter the trip abroad, Stone relented: "Well, that puts a different face on it. I'll come over and talk to him."

He had to argue with Faulkner at some length—"Bill, Jill's counting on this trip; you promised her; you can't break a promise to a child"— but Estelle's suggestion had proved the turning point. The family still resorted to moving the calendar up to accelerate Faulkner's drying-out, a plot exposed when the patient heard stadium cheers from the campus: "They don't play football games on Monday," Faulkner declared. "I'm going to drink for two more days." Yet when Stone went over the morning of his departure, Faulkner was sober, and more than a little irritable. Not for the first time, Stone made the mistake of advising too often: "Now, Bill, you do right." "Faulkner glared and retorted, 'I'm so damn sick an' tired of hearin' that. Everybody from the Swedish ambassador to my nigrah houseboy has been tellin' me to do right.'" Three months later, Stone wrote Stark Young, "I believe you have forgotten that if you live with a Faulkner you have to wear spurs constantly and have to use them often. Otherwise, Faulkners seem to become unbearable." In the interval before Faulkner left for Stockholm, the men had managed a brief conference too on the acceptance speech: "For God's sake, make it short," Phil suggested. "I never heard a bad short speech in my life." Later, Emily recalls, Stone would be effusive in his praise for Faulkner's Nobel address: "The best damn thing Bill ever wrote." At Christmas the author perhaps made his version of an apology, leaving a five-dollar-bill and the note "Merry Xmas to Philip II" with Stone at the office.[9]

Late in January the two men were in the office together reworking Faulkner's will. Phil and Bill's brother Jack Falkner were again named

The Embittered Friend

Jill's guardians in the event of her father's death, and if Miss Maud also were deceased, the two executors were to use half of his Penn Mutual policy to educate his niece Dean Faulkner. Stone and Faulkner's brothers were to choose one complete holograph manuscript and notes each, and after the brothers completed their sets from Faulkner's first editions, Stone might complete his, with the remainder kept for Jill. There were other family legacies, and Item Fourteen bequeathed Faulkner's Bulova watch to his godson Philip Stone.

Item Fifteen touched Stone even more directly: "If my friend, Phil Stone, shall, at the time of my death, owe me any amount, including any note payable to my mother . . . said indebtedness shall be canceled. However, if the said Stone shall insist on paying such indebtedness . . . (and he probably will), he is to pay the same either to my mother, my daughter, or to the Trust Fund." The endowment to which Faulkner referred was the $25,000 Nobel Prize account he also instituted in the document. Stone witnessed the "Trust Instrument" portion of the will, but he was not included with Mack Reed and two of the Falkners among the three trustees.[10]

Faulkner was to leave for California two days later, Phil wrote on 29 January in his new copy of Faulkner's *Notes on a Horsethief,* "for the / purpose—he says—of doing / a job for Howard Hawks."[11] It was the winter of the "Ice Age" in Oxford. For a fortnight, temperatures hovered at zero; snow was inches deep on the ground; and most households were without water, the pipes frozen far into the ground. After Emily's family called from Savannah to tell her of Mrs. Whitehurst's death, Malcolm Franklin drove his stepfather and Emily Stone to the Memphis airport in Faulkner's jeep.

In a letter to Faulkner in Beverly Hills in mid-February, Phil explained having postponed the will revisions because of his wife's exhaustion after her return from the funeral. Promising the new paragraphs soon, he advised Faulkner to have a tax expert forward Stone data about the tax implications of the new will and trust fund. Heretofore Phil had not spoken of the trust, "because I did not consider that any of my business." After Faulkner's departure, Stone had had an idea. The principal might draw interest of 5 percent from "entirely safe" real estate loans, for which Stone could prepare all legal papers and "make a little money." He had handled thirty-thousand dollars in similar loans for Abe Linker; he asked whether Faulkner might be interested.[12]

Apparently, Faulkner required no further legal—or business—assistance from Stone in that period, but there were two literary matters to which the lawyer turned in March 1952. James T. Babb, of the Yale University Library, asked Stone's help in persuading William Wisdom of New Orleans to donate his "very fine" Faulkner collection to Stone's alma mater. Inviting Wisdom again to North Mississippi, Stone promised only to tell him in person the farcical tale of "getting Faulkner off to Sweden."[13] In the same month Phil sought Stark Young's counsel about theater producers and agents in New York. In 1950, after the continued rejections of her novels, his wife had written a play depicting the ironic consequences of white juries' leniency with black defendants, who then merely victimized other black citizens. Margo Jones, a Texas producer, had liked *Here Come God's Chillun*, but could not stage an integrated cast in Dallas. Phil argued that the drama's controversy would gain it valuable publicity. But Young, suggesting that they consult agency ads in New York publications, offered no encouragement. If Emily converted the script into fiction, he would offer it to Scribner's: "the leading publisher in the world," Young preened, "and they think I am something, may I say?"

Stone felt that Emily might actually be a better dramatist than novelist; at any rate, by May he tried to interest a Natchez segregationist acquaintance in privately financing production of her play "as a great public service." At the time the man was advocating Harry Truman's impeachment and Douglas MacArthur's appointment as "Defense Minister" or "Dictator."[14]

Again context is important, for in the same season Stone began what became a long-term, monomaniacal letter assault on his (white) renter about excessive water bills; the February bill was thirteen dollars, he opened: "I just can't stand this." (It would be a decade before he realized that the ancient pipes were riddled with holes.) After Stone's tiny cotton crop was harvested in early fall, he informed a black community leader that he was "breaking with" his lazy sharecropper; the federal government could "support him if they wish."[15] The catalyst for Stone behavior was money; his new racism was a toxic effect, not a cause, and a symptom without precedent in his papers before 1950.

Anxiety had been rampant in the Stone household that spring. Emily was becoming alarmed at the prevailingly dark mood of their son's drawings. Their local doctor saw nothing physically wrong with the ten-year-old, but psychiatrists in Memphis were sufficiently concerned to order a cephalograph. His father meanwhile exchanged deliberately veiled letters on some legal or public matter with a Jackson attorney, the Honorable Ross Barnett. Although the nature of this business—now indescipherable—may have been innocuous, both attorneys avoid specificity, as if wary of leaving a paper trail.[16]

During the play correspondence Stone had complained to Stark Young of Faulkner's recent behavior:

> He came back from California several weeks ago but he hasn't been anywhere near me since. . . . After all the time I have spent running down to his house and worrying with him trying to sober him up and get him off to Sweden, he is going to have to look me up if and when he wants to see me. [Stone commiserated with Young about Faulkner's never answering his letter.] Also I am afraid that he is taking himself and his greatness too seriously and that sort of thing always makes me tired. I suppose you have heard that he got the Legion of Honor.[17]

Later that spring, after Jill Faulkner invited the Stones to her high school graduation, Phil saved the newspaper covering the event and Jill's thank-you note. "Mr. Phil said that perhaps you would be out of town and unable to attend the graduation exercises," she had written Emily Stone. "I hope you were there for Pappy's talk was most impressive and we all were so very proud of him." Delegate Stone, however, had returned from his New Orleans judicial conference by the night of 28 May. Before filing those items, he gave Philip another explanation for their absence: "Your Godfather made a talk . . . but we did not go out there because I knew it would be so crowded that it would be almost impossible to get a seat."[18]

Stone now filed other complete newspapers too, most of which required memoranda. One mentioned his trip to the annual bar convention: "Your mother went with me and she was very much pleased that when the question came up of re-electing me as the State Delegate to the House of Delegates . . . no one knew exactly whether my term expired this year or next year and the members just decided to elect me unanimously this year and then, if necessary, just to re-elect me again next year." Another *Eagle* headlined recent atomic tests; Phil filed it with the comment, "This is probably history." [19] (An apple crate discovered in the office in 1976 contained virtually a complete file of local papers for the 1950s, a few with attached Stone memos.)

In the late summer of 1951 another *Life* reporter came to Oxford and held fast to a bridgehead at Rowan Oak until his publicity-shy subject relaxed and offered him a beer and a short interview. Later Robert Coughlan made his way from Phil Stone's office to the couple's backyard.[20] The Stones were prejudiced against the Luce publications for what they saw as deliberately biased and arrogant reporting, but they came to admire Coughlan's professionalism. In an interview he revealed nothing while eliciting his subject's confidences. Bob Coughlan was to become a second major correspondent in the 1950s files. Exasperated by Faulkner's behavior of late, Stone grew candid with the reporter as he reviewed the writer's life and career, but he asked, as usual, to read the completed manuscript, to which Coughlan agreed.

In autumn Stone bet against long odds on two chances for instant financial and personal vindication. When state geologists released news of "Potential Oil Structures" in Lafayette County, his ventures in oil and gas rights were redoubled. The young attorney Robert Nichols, Jr., who had clerked for the Stone firm as a law student, kept an ear to the ground for Phil in Jackson legal circles. Their business association in the early fifties produced promising but never satisfactory results for Phil Stone. The Stones' literary hopes, likewise, had been revived enough for an infusion of capital in 1951. With Coughlan's encouragement, they invested in a trip to New York for Emily to confer with literary agents. While Stone went ahead to the ABA convention, she stopped overnight en route in Chicago at the home of Madeleine Kilpatrick, an editor at Reilly & Lee. "Pat" Kilpatrick had embraced the Stone family after Philip's letter to her about her firm's Oz books. The reception for Emily Stone in New York was much cooler, her talks with Mrs. Sewall Haggard and others less than encouraging, as she reported to her husband when they rendezvoused as planned in Manhattan after

Stone's meeting. But before boarding a train for home, they telephoned Stark Young, just back in town from his summer place, who invited them over for lunch.

At Young's apartment, however, the door was ajar, and at Stone's knock there came a wavering voice from inside, "Phil?" Young, semiconscious, lay crumpled on the floor where he had fallen from a stepladder while hanging draperies. He would not let them call a doctor, and for three hours they argued with him, Emily kneeling beside Young cradling his injured shoulder while Phil rummaged in the kitchen cabinets for liquor. Fearing that he was in shock, Emily had first waved ammonia under his nose, but he had thrust that away. After Stone located a bottle, Young refused Phil's offer of a tablespoon of whiskey too: "Pour me a drink such as you serve at your house." After three or four highballs, he finally agreed to their calling an ambulance. (When the hospital receptionist asked whether the Stones were friends or family, Young interjected, "Kinfolks!") He confessed to Phil later by Special Delivery letter that he remembered nothing from the time they walked in until the moment he regained consciousness in the hospital with a shattered shoulder and broken arm. A grateful Stark Young, aware that without their timely arrival he might have lain for hours unconscious, showered the Stones with presents in the months ahead: manuscript pages of *The Pavilion*, a presentation copy of the memoir itself, and later a Chinese cigarette box.[21]

That October in Oxford Phil Stone finished two books by old friends, but his compliments were reserved for Stark Young. Faulkner's prose in *Requiem for a Nun* might rival the "damned good writing" of *The Pavilion*, but Young's excursion into autobiography was much happier than Faulkner's into drama. "After all, in a play," Stone scribbled at the end, "I would think your audience would have to have some inkling of what the actors are talking about." *Requiem*, he repeated for Young, was a "shoddy job."

In November Stone echoed his own commentary also to Carvel Collins, to whom he had sent a bothersome State Department man on some Faulkner mission: "I told [the official] that any Faulkner is likely to assure you that he knew God when God was just a poor boy working for a salary." Stone said he had refrained from mentioning *Requiem* to Faulkner at the office for, if asked for his opinion, he would have had to answer candidly. Yet arguing for proper perspective on the unfavorable reviews that were confirming Collins's own disappointment about the book, Stone advised the critic to remember that Faulkner was "a very good writer and a very fine person."[22]

Dividends for the Stones from their September literary investment, however, came not from Emily's New York trip but from her stopover in Chicago, and in a form quite unexpected. Philip's precocity at age eleven, perhaps more than before, made heavy emotional demands upon the boy; the normal traumas of puberty certainly seemed more serious because the boy was so articulate. In February 1952 Philip staged the typical runaway from home complete with note: "Goodbye forever—I am sorry you do not love me anymore, and from now I will not trouble you any more. I am taking my pen, my tablets, my money, my raincoat and my overcoat. I will send you my future address in a few days, and please have all mail forwarded to it. Please keep up the good work and read Uncle Wiggley to Araminta every night." The prodigal was welcomed home warmly, but Pat Kilpatrick's invitation for Emily to return to Chicago with Philip must have done more to satisfy his demand for attention. The editorial staff at Reilly & Lee were "astounded" at the brilliant child, and Pat asked to read his book "Sonny in Oz." Phil proudly relayed word of Philip's conquest to Young and the Faulkner critics; Emily's comment, he repeated, was that they "should have disregarded the old maxim and . . . sent a boy to the mill long ago."[23] A number of Philip's manuscripts are extant, but another not mentioned to Kilpatrick, in all likelihood, bore the title "Hitler and Oz: A Fantasy of Bloodshed, Murder and Oz."

Emily Stone had been unable to sell a copy of *The Marble Faun* for $150 in Chicago, but even though their major creditor was replaced by a man much stricter about note deadlines, the Stones were not yet confined to Oxford by lack of funds. Phil and Emily heard the results of Hudson Strode's horoscope of Faulkner over drinks in their hotel room at the 1952 Southern Literary Festival held in Jackson (Phil, at Strode's request, had secured details of Faulkner's nativity from Miss Maud). And Stone's wife had driven the whole family, including Fanny, Araminta's nurse, to Biloxi for the bar convention, where Stone again was returned to the House of Delegates without opposition. Their only sadness of the first half of 1952 came when Anna Liggin, the cook, died in May.[24] The Stones gave a eulogy at her funeral.

"Old families" in Oxford were not invariably provincial, but the Stones found more compatible friends among the numerous new faculty Ole Miss began to hire after the war. That autumn the "second Yankee invasion" brought Arthur and Zoe Kreutz to the university. Arthur, who joined the music department in the fall semester, had impressive credentials; once a chemical engineer, the violinist had won two Guggenheim Fellowships and a *Prix de Rome* in composition. In 1945 he had served a month as guest conductor for the New York Philharmonic. Zoe Kreutz, soon supporting Emily Stone's transfusions of serious literature into the Woman's Book Club, had published a novel with Macmillan, written plays and librettos, and done a stint of gagwriting for Edgar Bergen. She had also at one time studied law.[25] The couple inevitably interested the Stones, although Phil was more reserved in the friendship than was his wife.

The year also brought more Faulkner books and letters to James Stone & Sons. Ward L. Miner's *The World of William Faulkner* and William Van O'Connor's *Two Decades of Criticism* were added to the Stones' Faulkner library. O'Connor had been in Oxford the previous Christmas; Miner had written Stone from France. Stone confessed to the latter how much the growing tide of Faulkner literary criticism saddened him, for it smacked of "literary obituaries." After all, Phil continued, "the Nobel Prize was for work he did between 1928 and 1940 and he has done very little since then of the same stature." [26]

Robert Coughlan's *Life* manuscript also arrived in Oxford in late September 1952. Stone read it twice with care, pronounced it "extremely good"—and dictated eight pages of corrections and amplifications about details that he or his wife had noticed. There were three general points, he said, requiring greater tact or a different emphasis. In his "Freudian" analysis of Faulkner's allegedly complex personality, Coughlan had overemphasized "that Bill occasionally, very occasionally, throws a drunk. . . . On the whole he drinks very little." Although Coughlan's portrait of Faulkner's father was accurate, Stone hoped that Bob would "tone this down" rather than "offend needlessly . . . Miss Maud, a grand old lady." Moreover, Stone praised Murry Falkner's financial support of "Count No 'Count" from the perspective of the years before the Nobel acclaim. The article had omitted too William Faulkner's particular rapport with "young children and old people, . . . one entire side of the man and one of his few attractive sides as an individual."

Except for perpetuating the myth of a Four Seas typesetter's having inserted the Faulkner "u," Stone's recollection seems accurate. Stone had first concluded, on pages five and six, with family news: Emily's books "still not selling," and Philip's "Miss Minerva" book for Reilly & Lee. He reserved more space for Araminta, "a darling [who would be] four in November. She is sweet most of the time, is the only member of the family who is not absent-minded . . . is most amenable as contrasted with Philip, and is a very satisfactory child. She does not have the brilliance that Philip has but has a head full of sound practical sense." Stone ended by thanking Coughlan for his treatment in the article: "You certainly did me justice, if not more."[27]

But after the postscript on Bill's father, there were three long impassioned paragraphs cautioning Bob Coughlan about relying on the *Oxford Eagle*'s editor, transplanted Southerner Phil Mullen, a personal Stone friend, but one whose Faulkner lore came at second and third hand. Mullen's comprehension of Faulkner was necessarily shallow: "It takes a second generation [for] Yankees to really become authentic Southerners." The crux of Stone's chauvinism glared out in his final diatribe. Mullen, it seems, opposed segregation. Stone's counterargument was that equality was not the issue; Southern opposition to black voting rights "is a natural attempt to prevent happening what has happened once before and what we have reason to think will happen again, complete negro domination." Then his attack swung to Coughlan: "When you Yankees get your negro population up to 50% and we get ours down to 10%, we shall be glad to join you in helping the negroes get equality." Stone's 10 October letter to Coughlan, with another page of corrections, was more restrained.[28]

The following November Stone appraised Coughlan's piece for Carvel Collins and reviewed the most recent Faulkner business into which he had himself been drawn. For the record, he said, he was not Bob's source on Bill's drinking and Bill's father, about which he had registered a protest. Stone claimed to have confined his remarks to "the production of the books," guessing that Coughlan's primary biographical sources had been Faulkner's brother John and their uncle. The other project, to which Collins had alerted him in the spring, had afforded Phil Stone a television role: "The Ford Foundation has been here making a TV movie for their History of America series and they took shots of me and Bill all day long one day in the office. Bill was just as gracious and patient about this as possible, and I am quite alarmed about him. I want to get him to a doctor soon to be sure that he is not developing a split personality."

Although the Stones were "dreaming" of a new car and a journey together to next year's bar association meeting in Boston (where they might see the Collinses' new house), Stone's law practice promised "no chance of daylight" before January. Twice Phil spoke of both the Stones' being "just driven" that year.[29] Indeed, financial records for the period, as for the decade, suggest that it was Phil Stone, not William Faulkner, who was maintaining a double identity in 1952. The dignified aristocrat in the *Omnibus* film is a remarkable facade, behind which a frenzied man now fought off symptoms of mental illness.

Stone had made many friends among the television crew, despite his complaints, and Howard Magwood, the director, had left a bottle for him at their departure. It was "quite welcome," Phil wrote, for he had risen at 5 A.M., driven eighty miles to Carroll County for a full day in court, and returned home only at seven-thirty that evening. He did not "patronize the bootleggers," Phil told Magwood, and getting to Memphis was virtually impossible with his current work pace. "It was a pleasure to both of us to know you," he remarked. "There are so many phonies these days that it is very nice to meet a genuine person."

But Howard Magwood was soon to witness another Phil Stone. Letters from Oxford poured in over the next three months. The town had no CBS affiliate, and Phil labored to obtain a print of the program so that an increasingly feeble Ike Roberts might see the film before it was too late. Faulkner also was said to be "anxious" about the print, but he was off to Princeton early in 1953, and would not return until he brought Jill home from junior college at Easter. Stone finally passed over Magwood and wrote directly to producer Boris Kaplan. His participation in the film had been freely given, Stone said, but he had done so at no little inconvenience. He wished the print first for Faulkner's godson Philip Stone; more essentially, Ike Roberts's recent shock at the death of his youngest son made it imperative that Stone have the movie for a private showing without delay. A copy of Transfilm's "Bill Faulkner and the Nobel Prize" was thus filed with Stone's pages of the shooting script in the family's archives. In thanking Kaplan, Phil wrote that he "was glad to help with the film on account of Bill, but I told him I certainly would be glad when he got through being famous. It takes up too much of my time."[30]

Before Faulkner's departure, Stone had prepared at his instruction a codicil to the 1951 will naming Saxe Commins, his editor at Random House, as Faulkner's literary executor. Nevertheless, other provisions affecting Stone remained as before.[31]

Someone at the Ford Foundation may have complained of Stone to Faulkner, but Phil's letter to the author at Random House in April would have done little to ameliorate any strain in their relationship. Wes Sturges, dean of the Yale Law School, and his wife were in Oxford, and their New Haven friend Carl Rollins, now virtually blind and close to death, had asked the Sturgeses to convey his regards to the young men with whom he had discussed Swinburne on York Street in 1918. It was impossible for Stone to see Rollins, or New Haven, again, but Phil would not or could not explain that aspect of his insistence on Bill's going. "I feel sure that you wont [sic] do it," he wrote, "but it would be a very kindly deed if you would get off your caboose just one day and run up to New Haven and go to see Mr. Rollins. It would not be much trouble to you and he would appreciate it deeply." (As Stone learned only later, Faulkner's drinking on that trip had put him in the hospital in New York.)

A few days later Stone wrote Collins, defending Faulkner's making television money with his story "The Brooch": "Surely it is not as bad as being a slave to the movies." On the basis of his look at part of *A Fable* in manuscript some years before, Stone predicted that the much-heralded novel would exhibit "some marvelous Faulkner prose," but would be "a flop as a whole." To Collins, as to Coughlan a fortnight later, Stone likewise commented on Estelle Faulkner's hospitalization that spring, revealing not only his disgust at the couple's habitual drinking, but also how little Faulkner had confided to Stone of their recently serious medical problems.[32]

While Stone himself pored over outlandish get-rich schemes in *Reader's Digest,* his anticipation of the oil companies in Tennessee and South Mississippi converging on his area gave him a comfortable hoard of oil rights when more than three hundred new wells were drilled in the state in 1953 and lease fever struck the local chancery clerk's office. Stone's public plans to put a small grocery and service station near the subdivision also suggested a different, shrewder business sense. And his reputation in legal circles was being sustained. Stone co-directed state fund-raising for the new ABA Center in Chicago and delivered an address on "Ethics" before the junior state bar. At the opening of the autumn Supreme Court session, Phil was invited to deliver the eulogy for attorneys who had died in the past year. Their memory might best be served, he said, by a vigorous opposition to " 'tyranny and oppression' of the individual citizen through a determined effort to see that 'no one—young or old, white or black, richer or poorer—fails to attain justice.' " [33]

Stone's wife too was yet to be counted out. At Zoe Kreutz's instigation, Harold Latham at Macmillan, the editor who had discovered Margaret Mitchell, came to Oxford and asked that Emily Stone submit her novel *Hark, Hark, The Dogs Do Bark* to him personally in early summer. When Stone informed Coughlan of this development, he added, "Considering our usual luck we are very much afraid that he will drop dead before we can get it to him." In July, making no promises, the publisher requested detailed revisions in her story of the "rise of the redneck." One character in the novel had assumed the burden of his father's debts, but Macmillan editors worried rather over its resemblances to Faulkner and to Robert Penn Warren's *All the King's Men.* Stone explained the common source for his wife and Faulkner at that time, but when the associate editor suggested a foreword by Faulkner for the book, Stone wrote that he and his wife would prefer "not to trade on" Bill's friendship.

By mid-August the manuscript was back on Latham's desk. For a month the Stones allowed themselves to hope. Notice of rejection came that time by telephone, not by printed slip, but neither Macmillan's courtesy nor the sympathy of friends such as Robert Coughlan and Carvel Collins tempered their bitter disappointment. Coughlan had heard Emily's editor remark that "there were 'brilliant' books in [her] future." And Latham himself explained soon afterwards that the editors had been "all very enthusiastic"; it was the sales department that had vetoed the book. Stone wrote Collins in September that Emily would "quit if I'd let her but I won't." Salvaging what they could, the Stones wrote for permission to use Latham's letters in her attempts to sell her short stories.[34]

When Coughlan's "The Private World of William Faulkner" appeared in the *Life* issue of 28 September 1953, Phil Stone, as he had promised Bob, listened out for the explosion. It was not long in coming. "Miss Maud is as mad as a wet hen," he wrote Coughlan two days later, and, the next day, the article "has the town stewing." Stone's own reaction to the advance copy Coughlan had sent was that the article had actually improved in print. Dismissing Faulkner habitually now because of his drinking—"any man over 30 . . . who gets drunk the second day is just a damn fool"—Stone had told his son Philip that, yes, Faulkner would read the articles, and then pretend not to have done so.

Although Faulkner was incensed at the invasion of his privacy, he accepted Phil Mullen's disclaimer of responsibility at face value, according to Blotner, and in New York in October when Coughlan met Faulkner at lunch, according to Malcolm Cowley, "There had been no drama." Table talk had ranged from crops to *A Fable*, Coughlan wrote Stone about the meeting, but there had been not one word about *Life*. Faulkner's mother canceled her subscription to the magazine, but that either she or her son took the matter up with Phil Stone is quite doubtful. The Falkners themselves had not exactly been uncooperative with Coughlan. "They surely can't blame those family photographs on me," Stone wrote Bob. Before the second installment, "The Man Behind the Faulkner Myth" (5 October 1953), arrived in Oxford, Stone caught a spelling error and corrected Major Alston's name in a note published in *Life* on 26 October. Atypically, he refrained from commenting further, on essay, author, or subject.[35]

Coughlan's account of Stone's role in Faulkner's career evoked a half dozen letters from Phil's lawyer friends. Whitney North Seymour, an associate in the American Bar, like the others, had been surprised at what he read: "You have been exceedingly modest with us all these years in never telling us about what a large part you had in getting your fellow townsman up in lights." The title "The Man Behind the Faulkner Myth" tempted Phil's modesty, however, and he told one of those who wrote him that friends in town had likewise believed "the man behind the man" to be an allusion to him, so that he had (vainly) put the question to Robert Coughlan for a definitive answer.[36]

The Stones exchanged a number of letters with Coughlan in October, one in which Phil expressed relief at Bob's reporting Faulkner's improved appearance: "I am glad to know he is looking better because he certainly looked like hell before he left here." But Coughlan had become involved also in the campaign to get Emily published and was instrumental in persuading Houghton Mifflin to consider *Hark, Hark, The Dogs Do Bark* after the Macmillan rejection. Not content to leave their luck at that, the Stones opened a second front with Houghton Mifflin through the publisher's best-selling author Mildred Spurrier Topp, the resident creative writer at Ole Miss that fall. Mississippi author Elizabeth Spencer joined in too before the second rejection, offering her New York agent and subsequently recommending the novel to Edward Dodd of Dodd, Mead and to William Raney of Henry Holt, both of whom wrote to see the manuscript, which they too, however, did not take.[37]

That autumn Phil Stone could vent his frustration only at work, threatening to sue the city about unauthorized dumping on his land, engaging in another "secret" oil deal, and, most obviously, howling at the Illinois Central for setting afire his twenty-five-acre pasture and fence. Fearful too of losing the office, like the house, to fire, it became his habit to have the gas cut off at Jackson Avenue from April to October. Stone must have huddled there some nights in his overcoat, for that year also, he said, he was working "five nights a week on my law business."

His relationship with the Faulkners appeared unchanged, however. After Estelle Faulkner left on a trip to Mexico City, Stone handled the papers for her recent minor automobile accident. Then Coughlan wrote from New York after Thanksgiving that when Faulkner heard his articles were to be reprinted in book form, he had offered to help with the revision, citing merely two errors: Maud Falkner's corrections that she had not bought her son any dress suit and that he had never even once had "plasma injections" during a drinking spree (Coughlan noted that he had written only "injections"). Faulkner was to read the essays—for the first time, he claimed—and discuss them further with Coughlan in the new year. Estelle mentioned to Stone her husband's upcoming flight to France in November, but Phil, as he wrote Collins, had to discover from the newspaper that the trip concerned a film script set in Egypt. Bill's knowing nothing about Egypt should prove no hindrance to a Faulkner, Stone said. But Phil was now devoid of jokes, for he added, "Strictly between us and completely off the record, I am *just about* fed up with Bill and as far as I am concerned I don't care *much* if he never comes back [italics mine]."[38] Qualifications were as inevitable for Stone in his denunciations of Faulkner as in his former praise.

A "quite dissatisfied" Philip Stone was also undergoing "a hard period" in late 1953, but with some relief offered by a journey the newspaper featured in December: "Young Phillip [sic] Stone will be missed in the *Eagle* book department and the University Library for the next few days. He's going to Chicago to visit . . . publishers of the Oz books." The Stones had sent him for the first time alone, Phil wrote Carvel Collins, the trip had given him confidence, and "at last Philip, himself," was listening to their idea of his going East to school, a move Collins seconded. A man from Exeter would be down in February to interview the boy. Philip would be fourteen the next summer, but he had already ransacked the town's meager library resources. He was not reading children's books at the university library, however; among his fictional exercises in 1953 was a "parody of *Finnegan's Wake*," according to his father.[39]

Until Faulkner's months of foreign travel drew to a close in April 1954, the Stones' professional and social activities rarely allowed time for comments on William Faulkner. Stone, hoping to accumulate sufficient operating capital for his business, negotiated another refinancing of his debts with a Batesville federal savings and loan association, where his classmate D. R. Johnson was a director. Coincidentally, in February the Stones gave a dinner party for Finland's finance minister, an Ole Miss lecturer, who had been instrumental, Phil wrote Philip, in his country's paying its World War I debt "a few weeks ago." In a letter to the *Commercial Appeal* and at the American Bar convention, Stone continued at that period too his active endorsement of the proposed Bricker Amendment, to restrict presidential powers. Stone had tried to interest one ABA colleague that year in oil investments in Mississippi, but the venture appeared too risky to the Wall Street attorney.[40]

Money and politics, however, were not Stone's only concerns. As chairman of the vestry at St. Peter's Episcopal Church he conferred with the bishop about a new rector for the parish in 1954. In March the family attended the campus premiere of the Arthur Kreutzes' third opera, *The University Greys.* They had met other talented university friends too that school year: the sculptor Leo Steppat, who opened a show in New York in February, and his wife Annaliese, whose hand-wrought silver jewelry was carried by galleries in New York, Philadel-phia, and Washington. As with Arthur and Zoe Kreutz, however, Stone left to his wife the pleasures of cultivating the friendship.[41]

Although Stone was considering sending Emily to the University of Alabama to study with Hudson Strode, Zoe Kreutz was now a full part-ner in the promotion of Emily, reviewing her work for the Woman's Book Club, encouraging her to apply for the Eugene F. Saxton Award (a fellowship Zoe had won), and keeping publisher Harold Latham at Macmillan interested in the new novel. Emily was also auditing Mildred Topp's creative writing classes at the university. But it was Phil's move that gave his wife's career new life. Scanning advertise-ments for New York agents, an old suggestion of Stark Young, when his eyes fell upon the firm of Annie Laurie Williams, Inc., Stone looked no further. Any woman named Annie Laurie, he declared, *had* to be a Southerner. Williams, whose grandfather had been born in Oxford, Mississippi, specialized in selling published novels to the theater or to motion pictures; however, her affiliate, McIntosh & Otis, was interested in reading the new Whitehurst play. Shirley Fisher, a young assistant at McIntosh & Otis, was more impressed by the Whitehurst novels, but her first report on 6 April was liberal in its praise. Robert Coughlan rec-ognized the promise of such a letter from a firm that was "among the very best agents" in New York and urged Stone to invest in another trip north. The Stones could ill afford such extravagance in their current financial bind, and Emily began explaining her "literature of affirma-tion" to the agent through the mails.[42]

In mid-April, at the appearance of Faulkner's "Mississippi" article in *Holiday,* Robert Coughlan solicited Stone's help again, for final re-visions of his Harper's book. Grateful for Bob's continuing assistance,

Stone readily complied, offering full answers about what he knew, asking around town for what he did not. Coughlan had added that Faulkner's publisher believed the writer would never again live in Mississippi, for Faulkner feared he could no longer work there. *A Fable*, Coughlan reminded Stone, had been finished in New York. Stone admitted that he too had suspected such a move by Faulkner, in part because the Nobel Prize had "ruined" his writing anywhere and because he sensed that the Faulkner marriage was at an end. To Stone's surprise, nonetheless, Faulkner returned home not in July, as his wife had told a reporter he would, but on 25 April. But two days later Stone still had not seen him.[43]

The Stones were soon too much upset to worry over Bill Faulkner's comings and goings. It was not, as one might expect, "the Supreme Court decision regarding segregation" (Stone's dispassionate note as he filed the *Commercial Appeal* announcement for Philip). It was a minor personnel change at McIntosh & Otis. The agency, to season their promising junior colleague, had determined to assign Shirley Fisher to their office in England. Elizabeth Otis, Nelson Algren's and John Steinbeck's agent, henceforth would handle client Emily Whitehurst. The long, intimate relationship of the two women, however, began with misunderstandings. Otis was somewhat taken aback at Phil's role in her client's correspondence and asked whether she should address her remarks to husband or wife. And Fisher's gentle, complimentary critiques were abruptly exchanged for more perspicacious criticism from Elizabeth Otis, at which Emily seemed like "a felled ox," Stone complained to Otis.

The Stones distrusted the new agent and wished for some way to return to Mrs. Fisher, as they wrote Coughlan. At the end of May, Emily submitted a story she thought at last tailored to Otis's requirements: "I can see that learning to be commercial is going to be a bitter lesson. I shall try, however, to learn." Phil snarled that in his opinion the story was trash. Otis, to their surprise, agreed; she and Emily were having major difficulties communicating through the mails. Emily's talents were those of the classic storyteller as well as artist, and "she must never again write about a flimsy little bride raising chickens."[44] Phil Stone set about to find the money to arrange a meeting between the writer and her agent.

The Embittered Friend

A few days before Emily left alone for New York, William Faulkner brought over his long-promised novel *A Fable*. Like *Requiem for a Nun* in 1951 and *The Town* in 1957, it was inscribed to "Phil, with love / Bill," ironically, the only extant autographs so affectionately inscribed. Faulkner and Stone may have chosen to avoid discussing civil rights that afternoon, but it is not unlikely that Phil kept quiet too about Emily's trip. The Stones were pointedly restrained to that date in trading upon Faulkner's name with the New York agency.[45]

Although it was Emily Stone who drove their car on trips of any distance, she, like Myrtle Stone before Jack's death, had grown dependent upon her husband's instinctive chivalry. In the train diner on her way to New York she folded her napkin, nodded thanks to her waiter, and walked out of the car before realizing that she was to pay for the meal. Phil had asked the agency to arrange comfortable but inexpensive accommodations in the city, and when Emily tried to check into the Algonquin Hotel at three in the afternoon, it took a phone call from Elizabeth Otis before the clerk was set in motion. But as Emily was walking up to 18 East 41st Street for her appointment at McIntosh & Otis, the awkwardness of her journey was forgotten. For the first—and last—time, the dream seemed tantalizingly near. Elizabeth begged them to be patient; in time Emily's books would sell. But Phil Stone could only remind the agent that they had already been patient for twenty years.[46]

On his son's fourteenth birthday that summer, Stone exhibited a rare candor with Philip about their finances: "For a long time you have wanted a typewriter badly and I wanted to get you one, but we just could not spare the money." The Faulkners' invitation to the marriage of Jill and Paul D. Summers, Jr., in late August likewise proved a financial embarrassment. The Stones could not afford a wedding present, and Emily finally sent the bride an antique decanter that she had bought for a few dollars in New Orleans during the Depression. On the eve of the wedding Faulkner had Stone again redraw his will, naming Jill as executrix, but the provisions affecting Stone's loan and his son's bequest continued as before. Earlier Phil had told Carvel Collins how much he liked Faulkner's fine daughter, but he was adamant in refusing to join the Collinses, Ben Wasson, and old friends like Arthur Halle and Jim Kyle and Katrina Hudson at Rowan Oak on 21 August.[47]

Carvel Collins's monograph "The Interior Monologues of *The Sound and the Fury*" had preceded him to Oxford by a week. Collins and the Stones had argued his points before, and although Phil knew "it is not going to do any good," he dictated five pages of rebuttal, "for the record," and, without thinking, mailed a copy to Collins's department head at M.I.T. before Collins left Cambridge. Later that night, Stone was shocked at his stupidity, fearing his page-by-page disagreement with the article might harm the critic's career. By air mail the next morning he offered to explain to the department head that he had been "largely kidding" and that Collins was, in his opinion, the preeminent Faulkner critic. Phil had spent a sleepless night worrying about it, and sought reassurances that his blunder was not a serious one.

While the scholar and his wife were in Oxford for the wedding, they paid a brief visit to the Stones and the debate about the "conscious" design of *The Sound and the Fury* resumed with vigor on both sides. But Collins's points had "licked" him, Stone admitted in late August, and he temporarily retreated. That the critic might be right had Stone "in a perfect stew," as he put it. But Phil requested one concession while admitting the truth of Collins's proving Faulkner a " 'secretive writer' "; he deemed it "a result and not a cause." "The real thing is that Bill is a taciturn writer," Stone countered. "I base this opinion on my close association with him for so many years. . . . If I had asked Bill what was the significance of the dates to the different parts of the *Sound and the Fury* he would have told me right off." But Phil Stone had not thought to ask, and though Stone claimed always "to know himself," the reticent William Faulkner had set him up for a rude awakening. In writing Carvel Collins's department head, Stone referred to Collins as "THE authority on Faulkner," primarily, it seems, because of the critic's discovery of "certain facts about Faulkner's life that occurred during the fifteen years that Faulkner and I were almost daily associated . . . which I did not know myself." [48]

Stone acknowledged aftershocks from the Collins theory even two weeks later, when he answered attorney Whit Seymour's letter from New York; but Phil's reiterations there about his treadmill progress at work continue as the major theme in his correspondence through 1954 and beyond. Seymour and Bob Leavell, a mutual friend, were growing concerned at Phil's enslavement to his law practice, and Whit's calculated threat to send an ABA delegation to Oxford to picket the twice-absent association member elicited a lengthy but less than candid account of Phil's financial morass. Stone knew that his oil speculation was largely folly, that the quarter interest in oil rights he usually gleaned from hours of paperwork for the landowner and investment partners was so much paper, while his energies for the burgeoning law practice, his "meat and bread," were steadily eroded—unless the companies drilling just over the county line struck oil, a climax from which Stone could not turn away his eyes. His twenty-five-year-old debts and "all that Uncle Sam takes away from us for the more abundant life" forestalled the reasonable option of his taking a law partner; there was no way "to guarantee some young lawyers that they can eat." Stone could only make excuses for sadly missing his friends at conventions, confine his reading to a hurried glance at the *Commercial Appeal* over his six o'clock breakfast, and return to the office every night after supper. Meanwhile, his wife listened when her friends the Steppats remarked that her drafting talents would earn a high salary for the Stones in a city.[49]

In growing desperation Phil Stone tried to play the stoic that fall and winter, abdicating his interest both in Faulkner and in his wife's writing rather than lament any longer past or future failures. Estelle Faulkner, in the office about a passport, talked of hurrying off to her daughter in the Philippines before her husband's return from New York. "What this means I don't know, but it probably means nothing, as most of what Estelle says means," he wrote Robert Coughlan. Stone's not seeing Faulkner himself for more than a month, he claimed, "suits me exactly. I feel rather relieved at the prospect of being free from Bill forever." Two days later, though, he had found time after all to read and to praise Coughlan's *The Private World of William Faulkner*. And Stone's brief correspondence with a man in São Paulo, Brazil, in the same season, is noticeably free from rancor at Faulkner; there he is only mildly ironic about latter-day idolators; but then Osmar Pimentel's remarks about the "creative spiritual comradeship" of Faulkner and Stone had been very gracious: "I know he was the fire, and you, the hearth."[50]

Although a publisher had asked to see her book, Emily spent the autumn of 1954 revising *Trampled Steel* under Elizabeth Otis's instruction, but in his letter to Coughlan renouncing Faulkner, Stone declared himself also to have "finally given that up." The New York publishers would never "buy" her work: "If Emily wants to go on and write for fun that is fine but I have enough troubles without having to go through the situation of her being taken up on the mountain top and then cast down repeatedly." She had wanted to stop writing ten years before, Stone admitted, but he had "kept on after her and made her keep on writing." Her revised novel was at Knopf in November, but before as after its rejection there, Emily's letters to her agent sound the contagion of Stone's despair: "I have been at this so long, so long. And Phil, who kept me writing when I would have quit long ago, now has given up and wants me to quit, for, he says, when you say it is well-written and readable and still can't sell it, I might as well kiss it goodbye."[51]

Stone was sixty-one in 1954, but, like Jay Gatsby, he had an extraordinary and naive capacity for hope, and an elemental perseverance of steel, not clay. Indifference to the two writers upon whom his vindication depended had been long ago impossible. But he must have been shocked when his older contemporary Abe Linker met a sudden death in an automobile accident in December.[52] There would no longer be easy small loans or business from a friend. Now he had always politely to beg, to the IRS or office stationer for extensions of time, or to creditor D. R. Johnson to replace the four old tires on his aging sedan. Linker's estate did pay Stone a one-thousand-dollar fee, surely one of the largest to date in his practice.

Whatever pleasure Phil enjoyed emanated from his family, though within that circle there were sometimes symptoms of his inner trauma, as when Stone, listening to the 1955 Sugar Bowl game over the radio, spent the afternoon "raging" at the Rebels' broken tackles and missed blocks. Ole Miss, he said, looked like "a consolidated high school team" in its 21–0 loss to Navy.[53] But, more generally, Stone could hide his anxieties and the real nature of his finances from the children, sometimes even from his wife. In the spring Philip kept house with his father when Emily and Araminta made a "sentimental journey" to visit her Georgia relatives. In Atlanta Emily discussed Faulkner's work for "a mink coat crowd" at the invitation of Phil's friend the attorney Frances C. Dwyer. Phil wrote Mrs. Dwyer that his wife "thinks more of Bill as a writer than I do."[54]

But Phil Stone was also at odds with Faulkner the man that year.

Faulkner's letter to the *Commercial Appeal* of 20 March 1955, in which he seemed to be speaking out for an integrated school system, had prompted a caustic reply from one Mississippi legislator. Dave Womack was confronting the political time-bomb of financing a dual school system in segregationist Mississippi in the year after the Supreme Court decision on *Brown vs. The Board of Education*. What alternate solutions had the Nobel winner to offer to "mortal men"? Dave Womack wanted to know. Did not William Faulkner hold degrees from those "inferior Mississippi schools"? Stone's sympathies lay with Womack rather than with his friend Bill Faulkner, as he wrote the former, elaborating upon Faulkner's vulnerability to Womack's charges because of his "Mr. Greta Garbo" hubris, and, ironically, eighth-grade education.

Writing Emily's cousin Susan Myrick on the Macon *Telegraph* a few days later, Stone threatened to answer Bill in print if he succeeded in his, to Stone, ulterior design of getting a subsequent "smart-aleck Faulkner letter" reprinted in the national press. That the writer pontificated on matters in which he was ignorant infuriated Phil: "My idea is that he is not getting as much attention now as he did when he first won the Nobel Prize." However Stone reacted in person to Faulkner during that year's press notoriety—Phil handled minor legal transactions for him in March and again in June—the unusually brief Faulkner references in the 1955 files are all negative ones: Stone telling William Van O'Connor of Faulkner's being ill-read, for example, or the *Chicago Review* that "Bill would not be interested in anything except a good-sized check."[55]

Stone, however, had outfoxed the editor of the *Chicago Review*, who had naively hoped to get something of Faulkner's through Stone. Phil would not waste the opportunity to find a critical audience for a much-revised story his wife could not sell because, according to McIntosh & Otis, the female protagonist was a masochist. He offered Samuel Blazer the original version of Emily's once "beautiful," now "butchered" story. Later that year the Stones were miffed when the magazine demanded further revisions and postponed its publication. The spring 1956 issue of the *Chicago Review*, however, published among others an essay coauthored by Marshall McLuhan, translations of two poems by Ranier Maria Rilke, and "Feet of Clay," a story by Emily Whitehurst Stone of Oxford, Mississippi, "her first appearance in print."[56]

The victory was a pyrrhic one for Phil; Stone too would have preferred "a good-sized check."

By the time of his mother's publishing debut, fifteen-year-old Philip Stone was finishing his first year at Hotchkiss, having won a scholarship there (and one to Phillips Academy in Andover), despite his limited high school background. William Faulkner had driven Philip and Estelle's granddaughter to meet their Memphis train after the Christmas holidays, a trip that for Philip was exceedingly uncomfortable, for, taking his cue from Stone, he no longer approved of his godfather. At the end of the school year Stone would crow about Philip to Carvel Collins. His son, then six feet three inches tall, had won the Latin, Greek, and French prizes at the prep school and was to manage the literary magazine and perhaps to have his play produced in the next term. After reading Cicero on his own for two weeks (he had never read him in class), Philip missed taking first place in the state Latin contest by one percentage point.

Increasingly, Stone's moods were swinging to inexplicable extremes. A month later, for no good reason, he wrote Philip's Hotchkiss tutor in great disgust. "Friendly talks" with his son, as he knew from ten years' trial, accomplished nothing. He urged the man not to spare their feelings; Philip was worse than the tutor admitted. Throw him out, or threaten him with the loss of his scholarship; then he would come around, for Philip cared about the scholarship.[57] Only a half hour with the father's business files in 1956, however, would have provided an epiphany for the no doubt puzzled Hotchkiss tutor. The financial pressure and attendant shame and panic he tried to suppress were destroying Phil Stone. Trifles now evoked his daunting rage. Not even a precocious teenager could have understood when Stone's fulminations struck Philip himself.

13

Cataclysm

By 1956 Phil Stone's paranoia was rampant. In his scrounging around for money over the past quarter-century, not infrequently he had embarrassed his friends by asking for loans and then by not meeting the personal notes on time. Credit for Stone in Oxford was becoming no longer available. That spring he called in his political capital. Attorney General Joe T. Patterson, with Governor J. P. Coleman's approval, was searching for a small sinecure in state government meeting Stone's requirements, four or five hundred dollars a month to cover his office overhead. Stone told Patterson that someone at the First National Bank had refused him a loan because "they" were "after his land cheap." It was a charge he made elsewhere: "Now don't breathe this to a soul because I can't prove anything, but I do know that there are a lot of people around Oxford who have never known how to make any money except by getting some man in a pinch, squeezing him and getting his property cheap. That is what scared me," he confided, repeating the need for secrecy. Oil fever had subsided once more, even while Stone maintained a more than weekly correspondence with his former clerk and fellow speculator Bob Nichols. Someone in the state bar, Stone wrote Nichols, was also out to replace Phil Stone as the state's representative in the House of Delegates.[1]

Stone dallied with his remaining property throughout the year. Only a few of the subdivision lots were left; by his estimate they were worth seventy-five thousand dollars, and he owed only twelve thousand, he kept telling himself. Southern Bell might wish to buy the property adjacent to his office; another piece of property was fifteen hundred feet short of the site for the new airport, Phil told D. R. Johnson. But every day, it seemed, another note came due. "Can you think of anything to do? I don't seem to have any brains left myself," he begged of Johnson. A Kosciusko banker was at first helpful with a personal loan for a thousand dollars, and in June, Stone expressed his appreciation for such "encouragement" in the face of "so many licks . . . and so many dirty ones from people that I thought I could trust." But when the man tried to collect the overdue note in August, the governor himself had to rescue Stone by cosigning a renewal.[2]

Phil's working four to five nights a week "for four years," with the concomitant financial anxiety, necessitated immediate relief, Stone wrote Coleman's attorney general, returning to his theme of a conspiracy: "You do not seem to take seriously the fact that I am suspicious that someone is lying to the Governor about me." He asked to be given the opportunity to answer those enemies out to get his property "at sacrifice prices." "Neither one of you has realized what this is doing to my nerves," Stone said. "I just can't stand it forever." When Patterson immediately replied, explaining that there was no part-time state job that would allow Stone to continue his law practice as he wished, he offered instead a full-time Jackson post for $8,000 a year, which Phil might take for as long as he needed the money.[3] But once again the prescience that Stone claimed to have inherited from his grandfather—his reiterations there and later about his going mad—evoked at best an embarrassed skepticism, at worst, indifference.

It was not chance that gave Stone his principal contacts with younger men in 1956. Many of his older friends could not meet his eye; men in their twenties were too much self-absorbed to notice the thin facade of Phil Stone's pain. Two young graduate students, for example, wrote for Stone's help with their Faulkner dissertations in that year. Donald P. Duclos of Michigan received only a brief and strident note about "Old Colonel" Falkner, but the charm and breeding of South Carolinian James B. Meriwether, Jr., at Princeton, subsequently the third major correspondent in Stone's Faulkner files, evoked a warm response from the Stones. "Knowing you, even slightly, is one good thing we can credit to Bill," Emily Stone wrote that autumn.[4]

Cataclysm

As early as April 1956, Stone had asked Robert Nichols's advice about offering his present law clerk, William Waller, a position in the firm after graduation.[5] Phil was finally acting upon his friends' suggestion to share his practice with a partner. Waller probably had better offers— he would be elected governor of Mississippi later in his career (1970– 74)—but his replacement that fall as student clerk at James Stone & Sons would move permanently into the antebellum office on Jackson Avenue, and into a close association with Phil Stone. Thomas H. Free- land III, from Port Gibson, had family ties with the owners of Windsor, now in ruins, but once one of Mississippi's most elegant mansions. Hal Freeland was "a money-maker," the Stones invariably commented, and Phil's onetime worry about providing a young man enough to live on soon evaporated, for as Freeland finished law school Stone's practice multiplied, despite his lack of timely cash.

At some point during that same year, Philip's junior year at Hotch- kiss, Stone made a startlingly pathological move. He simply ceded the management of his finances to D. R. Johnson, the Batesville attorney and creditor. The transfer appears not to have been made gradually, although Johnson's power over Stone's business did increase in the months ahead. Johnson's substantial loans to Phil Stone were there- after more secure, but the creditor had not sought, he said later, such dependency. The law firm was actually generating profitable revenues, Johnson agreed, but Stone's problem was in cash flow. Sixty percent of his practice came from the difficult and slow appellate work at which Stone excelled, but fees paid through his associates' firms were often delayed, or so Stone wrote the now incensed Kosciusko creditor. In a recent case, as Johnson verified to the banker, a Grenada man had "beat him out of his fee in full."

Johnson's orderliness and calm to a degree forestalled those habitual crises, and he soothed other lenders who threatened suit while estab- lishing Stone's monthly payments to Batesville low enough so that Stone made most of them on time. Probably it was Johnson to whom Phil listened about taking a partner, for the one man whom he trusted in his paranoia inspired in Phil a reverence as absolute as his suspi- cions of others. Stone tried to throw oil business Johnson's way that year, and in September 1957 he named as his executor the man "who has helped me world without end."[6] It became Stone's monthly habit to carry his passbook in person to Panola County—to save postage, he said, but also as an excuse to consult the onetime Ole Miss "plodder."

As before, Stone's relationship with Faulkner and even Faulkner business remained colored by the state of his finances—and the widening gulf between his failures and the world renown of his friend. Of late, Faulkner had become "insufferable," he wrote Carvel Collins in December (and repeated to Meriwether early in 1957):

> Recently an incident occurred which is typical. Several weeks ago there was visiting here a Jewish woman from Long Island who formerly lived here and who went to all our parties with us when we were young people and of whom we are quite fond. Estelle had a supper for her and invited us down with other friends of Florrie [Friedman]. Bill is such a knot on a log on social occasions and so completely devoid of making any effort to entertain his guests except to mix them drinks that I would not have gone at all if it had not been for Florrie. During the reminiscences of old times Florrie asked Bill if a certain character in a certain story had been taken from a lady who used to teach music here. Bill reared back in the usual Olympian, Faulkner manner and announced: "No. I can invent much more interesting people than God ever made." Emily said that if she had not been in Bill's own house she would have murmured, "Poor God!" I told Emily I would have added, "He done the best He knowed how."[7]

Necessarily Stone's response to Faulkner's success contaminated other relationships as well. Like his father, Philip was of several minds with regard to his famous godfather, but for complex reasons he was instrumental in the request Stone received from Hotchkiss in January 1957 to deliver a lecture on Faulkner the following May. Phil wanted to accept the invitation, even making suggestions about the format he had discussed with Philip, but only if "next week early" he could borrow enough money to prevent the school from canceling Philip's scholarship because of their overdue account. Another invitation to go north in the spring arrived less than a month later. James Meriwether had interrupted his thesis research to assemble a Faulkner exhibit opening at Princeton on the first of May, the publication date of *The Town*; Meriwether wanted the Stones to come up for the opening festivities. The previous autumn, reading galley proofs with Saxe Commins at Random House, the young scholar had tried to correct discrepancies between *The Town* and the first volume of the Snopes trilogy.[8]

It was news to him, Stone responded, that the second Snopes book would also bear a dedication to Phil Stone; when Faulkner had offered the manuscript for his customary perusal the year before, Phil had explained that time permitted his reading only law books and the morning news. Out of politeness, Stone continued, he had suffered in silence his host's absence of modesty at the dinner party at Rowan Oak for Florrie Friedman; but the blatant "arrogance and egotism" with which Faulkner had recently refused to address an English class on campus had shocked even Phil Stone. Faulkner had first informed the woman who invited him that "he never did that sort of thing." Then, reminded of his imminent departure for Charlottesville to become writer-in-residence at the University of Virginia for the spring semester, he had "replied that when he made a public appearance he always wanted to do that in a time of crisis when he could do some good." Hearing of the exchange, Phil said, he determined to urge Faulkner at their next meeting "to appoint a deputy" and leave his name and address with Stone, so that upon those occasions of Faulkner's "two-weeks' drunks the whole world would not fall to pieces for lack of management."[9]

Stone's wife packaged and mailed the typescripts of *The Hamlet* and *The Wishing-Tree* for Meriwether's exhibit, but, although Stone's letters to Meriwether and to older correspondents frequently cover several pages, most often in his Faulkner file that spring Phil pleaded haste or lack of time. The Hotchkiss lecture was subsequently abandoned; Philip represented the family at the Princeton dinner and seminars; Stone could not spare the energy to correct mistakes in the exhibition catalog Meriwether sent; he had time only to read the *Post* excerpt from *The Town* (though commenting, "Bill can hold his head up with anybody who ever wrote a short story in English"); neither Phil nor his wife could accept their friend Robert Holland's invitation to review the book that summer for the *Mississippi Quarterly*.[10]

In 1957, despite Stone's vociferous protests, Emily had become an English instructor at Ole Miss—in order to cover their household expense. Moreover, she continued to mail out short story manuscripts, exchange letters with her agent, to complete a historical novel based on her Georgia family, and to work with Zoe Kreutz on a second play, this one having to do with a Lincoln assassination conspiracy. (Zoe had at least William Faulkner's compliance with her own idea for a

Faulkner opera at Ole Miss; the university administration, however, preferred to keep its distance from a man some perceived as a rabid integrationist.) [11] Emily Stone, meanwhile, began to plan a different writing project. Looking through the 1920s office files that spring, she had discovered there Faulkner manuscript poems, "a good deal of correspondence" between Stone and Faulkner, and a few canceled checks that Stone had written to the once penniless author. Collins (and presumably Meriwether) was invited to see those remnants, but Stone intended them for her use in "a reminiscent account of my association with Bill." "She insists that it should be written down," Stone told Collins, "and I shall never do it myself." [12]

When Meriwether visited the Stones that summer before beginning his search for a teaching job, he took notes on the new discoveries, no doubt nodding politely when Stone made him a forecast of Faulkner's behavior in the coming months. Phil repeated the prophecy to Carvel Collins on his new dictaphone in mid-July: "For some time now Bill has not been getting publicity. My prediction is that between now and October 1 he will do or say something that will again attract public attention. Watch for it. I have no idea what it is because I have not talked with Bill since he got back from Virginia." Sixteen days short of Stone's deadline, the *Commercial Appeal* printed a letter from Oxford, Mississippi, under the headline "Faulkner Predicts Graver Dangers / South's Resistance to Integration Invites Them." Phil mailed Collins and Meriwether copies of the clipping in exulting letters on 16 September: "Nobody knows Bill as I do." [13]

Philip Stone was leaving that day for his senior year at Hotchkiss, where he would be editor-in-chief of *The Lit*. Philip had amused himself during his summer vacation by, in part, fabricating copy for the ninetieth anniversary issue of the *Oxford Eagle*. In October Stone reported to Collins that his son had written a novel as well in six weeks that summer. In the family's eyes, "A Long Way from Home," the original version of *No Place to Run*, was a high-spirited, outlandish satire of Mississippi politics—though Phil had not yet found time to read it. McIntosh & Otis submitted the manuscript to Knopf in November. Stone, quite cautious after his wife's "two last-minute disappointments," shared with most of his correspondents the "secret" of the publisher's request for "certain revisions," while postponing his own celebration until "the ink is on the contract." His son was "very smart, perhaps too smart," Stone wrote a Yale classmate after Christmas when the book was again at Knopf; Philip could "dash this stuff off just like a professional." [14]

Philip continued to accumulate academic honors as he began to compete for scholarships to the Ivy League for the fall—while still indulging his precocious child's wit. In his January school campaign to preserve traditional class privileges, Philip spearheaded the defense against "mixed tables" at Hotchkiss with propaganda sheets parodying the conflict then in its fourth month in Arkansas. "Both of the Negroes in school," Philip declared proudly, had signed his petition.

Philip's father was also following the initial major confrontation over civil rights as if it were a prep school game: "[Governor Orval] Faubus has the National Administration in a box over at Little Rock. They want to turn loose and they don't know how to do it without being completely ridiculous," Stone reported to the Yale friend in January 1958. The integration issue also prompted Stone's exchange of notes with Maud Falkner in February: ". . . I thoroughly agree with you. It sounds like Alice in Wonderland when you consider that the taxpayers have had to pay out over $800,000 apiece to keep nine negro children in a school when they, the negro children, have a brand-new million-dollar school just a few blocks away. . . . How crazy can we get?" According to a note reprinted in the *Eagle* in March, William Faulkner, when asked to comment on Little Rock at a Princeton seminar, responded that the Supreme Court decision had ignored that the races "simply don't like one another" and that it was the white man's responsibility to "change the Negro from acting and thinking like a Negro. How? The answer is just one word—education." [15]

Even though shortly thereafter, at Harold Ober's request, Stone drew up a codicil to Faulkner's will concerning film rights to *The Hamlet*, the papers were still unsigned in mid-May. Faulkner had been back from Virginia for some time, but he had not come by Stone's office. "I am glad to do this and I do things like this for Bill free, but I have too much to do to run Bill down," Stone wrote Ober's secretary, suggesting that Ober prod Faulkner from New York to attend to his business at James Stone & Sons. Stone was frequently out of town in court, and preferred to be in the office "if and when Bill executes the codicil, to be sure that it is done correctly." But it was not until mid-October that Faulkner and his attorney managed the simple ten-minute signing at Stone's desk. Faulkner warned the lawyer that he would "probably misplace" his copy of the paper, asking him to file it in Stone's safety-deposit box, Phil informed the agent.[16]

Stone's participation in any other Faulkner matters was quite infrequent during 1958, but his practice seems to have been active that year. Hal Freeland, having graduated from law school in January, joined the firm upon Stone's offer of a guaranteed income "substantially greater" than that usually afforded novices in the state bar. Despite his having practiced alone since 1936, Stone was by no means " 'sot in his ways,' " Freeland observed; Phil welcomed Hal's immediate implementation of a new bookkeeping system. However, Stone instructed D. R. Johnson subsequently to mark his mail "personal." The Stones also embarked on some necessary improvements; Phil borrowed funds to rewire and air-condition the office; Emily determined to repaint the house herself with supplies purchased in Memphis sales. They began payments for a new car that August. By September, however, when Philip left for Harvard, Stone was again devastated by debts. His son's triumphs that year were to offer Phil Stone both a measure of compensation and new worries. Was there "anything honest" he could do? he asked D. R. "Perhaps the whole trouble is that I am crazy and don't know it." [17]

After Knopf turned down Philip's novel, Elizabeth Otis submitted it to Viking, and the Hotchkiss student—the first to have a book accepted while still in school—sold "A Long Way from Home" to the second publisher, for a thousand-dollar advance. The word went out to the Faulkner critics and family friends in late April, although Stone somewhat dampened his son's glee with fatherly advice. "I think from the talk I have given him he doesn't expect to get rich and famous in just a year or two," he wrote Otis. Phil asked Philip's tutor for suggestions for a graduation present "sparing no expense," and when the family arrived in Lakeville for commencement, Stone gave Philip an eighty-dollar record player he had bought in New York the day before. Philip graduated cum laude, with prizes in Greek and French. Both Yale and Harvard had offered him $1,100 scholarships and Princeton, one only $100 less.[18] Although Hotchkiss had traditional ties with New Haven,

Philip, disappointing his father, chose Harvard, perhaps as a gesture of independence.

Yet Phil Stone's gifted son was still very much a child. When the new author stopped off at Viking on his way home, his editor presented him with twenty-five pages of suggested revisions. That summer, as his work proceeded fitfully, his parents nursed his wounded ego as well as his infected foot and wrenched knee. Because of his "invalidism," when Philip moved to Cambridge in September, Phil lobbied through a local Southern Bell attorney for the prompt installation of Philip's telephone. While Philip, enamored of "the Winslow Boy" (a television hero), established a Rex Thompson Fan Club at Harvard, it was Philip's father to whom Robert Ballou turned to check his revised satire for probable libel. But Philip himself felt quite old; in November he wrote a reflective letter to Araminta for her tenth birthday, praising her study of French and the violin, and observing that her "outgoing," "warm-hearted" personality would make her happier than he had been. After recounting his search all over Boston for her birthday gifts (an Eloise book and a Girl Scout compass), he advised his sister to avoid his mistakes in loving books too much: "remember you can always read when you have nothing else to do, and I hope you will play more with the other girls, and be less bossy, and so on—because I do love you." [19]

In October 1958, during the time when Philip was unhappily completing his revisions for Ballou, his agent Elizabeth Otis finally accepted the family's long-standing invitation to visit Oxford. She could not stay a week, Elizabeth protested, and she had rather spend her time in a rocking chair than at football games and ladies' luncheons, but she was interested in the prospect of a trip into the Delta and in their offer to take her "to a church session of the Sanctified." ("They are a sect of colored people who think they cannot sin," Phil had explained.) Elizabeth returned to McIntosh & Otis after her brief vacation with bolls of Delta cotton and jars of homemade jellies,[20] her souvenirs, like her itinerary, Phil Stone's standard program for touring Yankees.

But Elizabeth Otis was no longer a casual friend. In their correspondence she had introduced Emily Stone to the ideas of George Ivanovich Gurdjieff, the mysterious Caucasian Greek who had attracted a coterie of English and American disciples in Paris in the early twenties. In

1923 Gurdjieff had won a minor literary notoriety for allegedly imposing character-building "exercises" upon a dying Katherine Mansfield. (The American author of *Cane*, Jean Toomer, was another of Gurdjieff's followers.) Philip Stone later would share his mother's intensive study of "The Work" in books such as *In Search of the Miraculous* (1949) by Gurdjieff's apostle-biographer P. D. Ouspensky. Phil Stone, however, remained decidedly uninterested in his family's excursions outside traditional Christianity.

Another Stone friend, Jim Meriwether, had met with a similar resistance from Phil for over a year whenever he supplied names of possible buyers for the Faulkner material in Stone's possession. The burned papers especially required immediate professional care, Meriwether pointed out. "If it is possible I never want to sell it because I want to save it for our children," Stone responded at first. "Frankly, if I were going to give it to anyone I would give it to Yale Library." Meriwether, however, continued to press the matter, and after his first semester in Austin made an Oxford appointment at Christmas to present the University of Texas's offer to buy Stone's Faulkner papers. They looked forward to his visit, Phil replied, but he still wanted to keep the manuscripts for Philip and Araminta. Although he did sell the scholar a *Marble Faun* during his visit, Stone stalled Meriwether about the institution's offer of two thousand dollars for the manuscripts. Meanwhile, Stone consulted Elizabeth Otis, who assured him that the papers were Stone's "to dispose of as you wish," and that, in light of the depressed manuscript market, Meriwether's price was a good one. The manuscript of Steinbeck's *The Grapes of Wrath*, she said, had been sold to a California university for the same amount.[21]

Phil Stone worried, procrastinated, and equivocated virtually until the purchase voucher was typed on 19 January, but Meriwether maneuvered to assuage each of his doubts. He would not be in dire need of the money after 1 February, Stone parried, and might not wish to sell at all—or another purchaser might make him a better offer. Ostensibly it was Philip's condition that secured the deal. After Viking's "hoopla" over Philip's successfully completed revision, the boy had returned home at Christmas in "a very bad fix," his father said. Stone feared that unless something were done, Philip would suffer a breakdown. The doctor ordered him to forget about school and go to bed. There were unpaid Harvard bills from the fall (as well as old Hotchkiss notes) and also no money to meet Philip's expenses for the spring semester. After Philip got some rest, Stone called a family conference to discuss the Texas offer and the decision whether to relinquish portions of his literary inheritance for his Harvard education was left to Philip (now deeply resentful of his godfather), who said yes. Even then, Stone hesitated, but eventually Meriwether came to Oxford to carry the "Burned Papers" to the University of Texas.[22]

On 4 February 1959 William Faulkner, writing about his shock at the Calvin Browns' intent to publish their late daughter's copy of *The Wishing-Tree*, mentioned another friend to Harold Ober: "By now I should certainly have got used to the fact that most of my erstwhile friends and acquaintances here believe I am rich from sheer blind chance, and are determined to have a little of it. I learned last week (he didn't tell me himself) that another one gathered up all the odds and ends of mine he had in his possession, and sold it to a Texas university; he needed money too evidently. So do I—the $6000.00 of my cancelled life insurance which paid a mortgage on his property 20 years ago which I'll never see again."[23]

Stone and Faulkner had enjoyed an autumnal, and final, flowering of their friendship when Araminta was a little girl, before the repercussions from the Nobel Prize. Without their former bond of literature, however, there was little opportunity then for both proud, vulnerable men to disclose even obliquely their deepest pain. For a long while neither friend had been privy to the extenuating circumstances prompting the other's apparent coldness; consequently, their misunderstanding, and hurt, only intensified, though neither spoke of it. Stone never knew of Faulkner's shock at the Texas sale. The apprenticeship papers Stone had "kept for Jill" because long ago her father "would not fool with them" would be safely preserved at a major university for the use of scholars; they could not be reproduced without permission. Stone's own child might be temporarily shielded from the stigma of public debts if the compulsive hoarder relinquished possession of the proof of his central role in the Faulkner career, compromising too at no small cost his view of himself as an honorable man, for Stone's silence to Faulkner was no oversight. And Phil Stone would manifest his unceasing loyalty to Bill Faulkner in other, even more disastrous ways.

Phil Stone of Oxford

On the Sunday morning after Faulkner's letter to Ober (of which Stone of course was unaware), Phil dictated a note to D. R. Johnson: "It certainly did me a lot of good to see you, as it always does, and I don't know what I would do without your faith and comfort. I am inclined to be a little bit depressed this morning so I just decided I would come up here and go to work and not give way to it."[24]

A major worry for Stone at the time was his son, whose temperament sometimes reminded Phil of his own father. Philip had used some of the money from the sale of his book to buy his father a pedometer for his sixty-sixth birthday, but had paid less than a third of his freshman expenses. His father had underwritten Philip's vacation visits with Northern friends too, as well as the sizeable phone bills originating from Cambridge. The $825 payment remaining from Philip's Viking advance, his part of the almost $2,000 from his British publisher Frederick Muller, and his half of the $6,500 advance from Dell for paperback rights simply evaporated in Philip's hands; but to Stone, the money was Philip's, and, unlike other parents perhaps more sensible but also less respectful of their child's independence, Stone never appropriated or even asked for any of that money, although in the summer of 1959, for example, he certainly could have used it. Apparently it never occurred to him that infringing upon his son's financial liberty might actually draw them closer together, for in fact the child was beginning to feel himself unloved—and perhaps unneeded—in the family. Philip complained later that the talk at home had always been of aesthetics and of the law—never, in other words, sufficiently about himself. (It is no small wonder that art and the law were the Stones' conversational bulwarks.) But Phil Stone more and more rarely would allow the boy to glimpse the depths of his financial, and mental, distress.

And Stone's son was too finely attuned to his father's opinion of him not to sense that one Stone novel and a few thousand dollars had not satisfied Phil Stone's great need after all. After his feverish composition of a play called *Till Morning Is Nigh* in December and January, the usually prolific writer found himself in the throes of a first writer's block. The school psychiatrist whom Philip consulted early in 1959 diagnosed his condition as "narcissism" and prescribed sleeping pills for the insomnia as evident in his play's title as in the gaunt Viking photographs made of him before Christmas. He begged his parents to fly him home at spring vacation and talked of quitting Harvard after June exams. His novel was to be published on 16 April, however, and, presumably, Philip had already given the confident interview announcing an eventual ten to twenty novels in his own emerging Mississippi saga, the interview in which he spoke too of having purposely avoided reading Faulkner, not wishing " 'to write in Faulkner's shadow.' " [25] But any hopes Philip had for a triumphant homecoming as he packed his advance copies of *No Place to Run* at spring break were to be grievously thwarted.

Although Phil Stone, with some difficulty, canceled important legal business to spend as much time as possible with his son in his week at home, in Oxford as the parents were leaving for the Memphis airport, Phil had said, "That plane is sure to be late; I think I'll take along one of Bill's books to read." His wife stared at him in disbelief; but Stone was strangely adamant about taking the Faulkner book to greet the homecoming author. That night the boy, heartbroken, cried on the sofa after his father had gone to bed: "*Why* did Daddy do it? *Why?* " The impossible grace that Philip's father required could be bestowed only by one who was Phil Stone's "personal property," a category, paradoxically, to which Philip Alston Stone did not belong.[26]

During his week's vacation Philip left an autographed copy of his novel at Rowan Oak for "Mr. Bill and Mrs. Bill," inscribed 27 March 1959. John Faulkner's letter welcoming Philip into "the circle of Oxford's writers" had been posted four days before. But other friends, or even relatives, who offered congratulations or attempted to flatter the boy by requesting his autograph were sometimes stupified at the response they got from either father or son. Jack Stone and the Walter Armstrongs of Memphis received indignant replies to their requests for autographs; Philip, like William Faulkner, they were told, would give autographs rarely, to keep their monetary value high. And to comments such as Coughlan's—"no doubt that you have a genius on your hands"—Phil might answer that though Philip did "write like a professional," his subject matter was not to Stone's taste; or, that while his wife wrote of the actual South, Philip, like Faulkner, had adopted the

"Yankees' point of view," the reason they were published and she was not. Stone wrote Meriwether of his suspicions that his son had expected "to win the Nobel Prize with his first novel."[27]

The generally deflating reviews could not have caused Philip more anguish than such comments by his father, though, mercifully, he probably read none of the latter. Fortunately too, Philip claimed that he would follow Faulkner's example and not read his reviews either. The *New Yorker*, the *Herald Tribune Book Review*, *Saturday Review*, *Time*, and the *New York Times Book Review*, with the local media, all gave space to *No Place to Run*. A few reviews noted the fad of publishing precocious children after Françoise Sagan's recent best-sellers, although Viking's advertisements maintained that their seventeen-year-old author was "the *least* remarkable aspect of this bold, deeply knowing, and often shocking novel." The *New Yorker* thought that Philip wrote "uncommonly well for one of his age," but predicted that the "bookish boy . . . of almost unbearable innocence" would live to regret the publication. Frank H. Lyell in the *New York Times Book Review* complimented the "*Wunderkind* with keen eyes and ear" on the clarity of his style, only to sneer at the turgid prose of his famous godfather.

Shirley Ann Grau in *Saturday Review* struck the most typical note, objecting to the melodrama, stereotypes, and naivete of the young Faulkner and Erskine Caldwell imitator.[28] Although Philip's editor warned the Stones that it was futile to answer reviewers, the all but explicit charge of plagiarism infuriated Philip's parents, who were reading every word in the Yankee press. Phil could not refrain from denying Faulkner's influence to the *New York Times Book Review* editor: "If someone in Mississippi should write a novel in Sanskrit, the Northern and Eastern critics would say it was modeled after Bill Faulkner." Stone advised that Lyell reread *Pylon*, *Wild Palms*, *Light in August*, and *Absalom, Absalom!* to note the absence there of the kind of "incident and humor" that Philip's source Phil Stone had contributed to *Sartoris*, *Sanctuary*, and the Snopes saga.

While his parents, reeling with each blow, longed to protect their older child, Philip's youth and periods of self-confidence allowed him an easier time of it. Philip made no defensive sounds when he told *Cosmopolitan* that summer of his "several pages of a book for children" at age three and his (first) seven-page tragedy in verse at age six. Since learning his alphabet at eighteen months, Philip said, he had "been putting letters and eventually words together, and when they began to make sentences, I knew I was in business." In August, when the interview appeared, Stone wrote Meriwether, however, of his regret at Philip's decision not to pursue the interest of a Broadway producer who wanted a stage version of his novel. During his "rough" summer, Philip had worked instead on a new play, reached an impasse with it, though still believing in its promise, and struck out "at everyone else who doesn't think so," his father complained.[29]

Earlier that season Oxford learned of the William Faulkners' having bought a house in Virginia, although their plans were also to keep Rowan Oak. Except for the autumn news of Stark Young's stroke, others of Stone's friends likewise were prospering in 1959. The Hubert Starrs of Hollywood had left for another European tour in April, and Whit Seymour was serving as president of the American Bar.[30] Phil Stone, by contrast, could not afford to buy his ten-year-old daughter the horse she wanted so badly. His law firm hired three Ole Miss student clerks that summer to help with his pressing caseload, but "ill luck" was delaying the arrival of one especially anticipated "fat fee," Phil wrote D. R. Johnson. Less than a week later Stone again wrote to Batesville, "I can't get either you or Hal to realize and face that the trouble with me is this hoodoo that has been pursuing me for five years about getting money when I run out of money. That is just a fact that has to be faced. The thing that has postponed this hearing would not happen once in 20 times. . . . I confess I feel mighty low." One month later, the "hoodoo" had struck a third time, leaving Stone sleepless after 2 A.M. Another month passed; it was August, and Phil wrote of " 'cold sweat' nights" over a delinquent note. In September there was more about the "hoodoo." Writing, ominously, about a life insurance loan, he told Johnson, "Sometimes I think I am a nuisance to everybody around me."[31]

Still Stone carried on an increasingly nostalgic Faulkner correspondence, in June relating the funny 1919 "Kubla Khan" story for Hal Smith, then editor of the *Saturday Review*, who published it. In another letter Stone included "two items" he believed might amuse Bill Faulkner when he wrote the writer in December apologizing for his belated thanks for *The Mansion*. Two months before, Elizabeth Otis had asked Phil whether he was not "surprised and pleased" at the third Snopes book dedication. Phil admitted only that he had not been surprised. When Faulkner had brought by the usual autographed copy, he had been "in another county," for court.[32] Gerry Gafford, subsequently a Stone partner, was one of the three student clerks busy in the office in 1959. Gafford remarked that, when he knew them, Faulkner would come into the office "hungry to see Mr. Phil" but that Stone would slip out the back door, afraid that Faulkner too had come for his money.

The world Phil Stone now most frequently inhabited was one of relentless anxiety. Once, hurrying back to Oxford before dark from a business trip, he literally awakened to find his car in a roadside ditch; he could give no account of how he had gotten there, just that two passing country boys had pulled him out. Stone's wife, because of her mother's strokes, knew something of the symptoms, but could not convince Stone to see a doctor, even though it was apparent that he was quite frightened himself. Phil had never driven well enough to exceed forty-five miles an hour on the highway (for that reason and out of frugality usually catching rides to court—too often—with fellow lawyers),[33] but in his last years he frequently drove very fast, especially on his way home. He also began gradually to drink again, after forty years of moderation. The rare daylight hours when he would leave his work at the office, the beleaguered man spent clearing the rampant undergrowth from the vacant lot at the old house site, mumbling to himself as he furiously attacked, for the most part vainly, the fecund honeysuckle vines there, the roots of which, through long neglect, grew often as thick and as gnarled as an old man's wrist.

Only Philip Stone, a sophomore at Harvard in 1959–60, now seemed reasonably happy, diverted by his first serious if short-lived romance and relieved temporarily from his writing, by order of his doctor, editor, and agent. But in 1960 Elizabeth Otis was still trying to interest New York publishers in her first Stone client, who was moonlighting then as a census taker as well as teaching at the university. The strain of the Stones' desperate pace, however, was telling on Emily too; she was hospitalized in January with acute nephritis and choleceptitis. In March Phil Stone wrote to Elizabeth Otis, begging, Let's quit. He needed peace at home at least. "It was no time to give up . . . God forbid," Otis replied,[34] assuredly less than pleased again at his perennial, and often harmful, interventions in her clients' careers. But she, like others who saw Phil Stone daily, did not decipher then how very sick he was.

Robert Farley had been so often the lucky recipient of political forecasts from Stone's crystal ball that on election nights at the courthouse he began to take a grim (but silent) satisfaction in noting how continually Stone's prophecies were wrong. Phil was especially partisan in the 1960 presidential and congressional races, convinced from May 1959 that Lyndon Johnson would win the Democratic nomination, John Stennis would be appointed to the Supreme Court, and Governor Coleman would fill Stennis's Senate seat.[35] After John Kennedy's election, he was just as certain that the senator from Massachusetts had promised to name Coleman of Mississippi as his attorney general.

Another late personality trait concomitant with Stone's egoism and paranoia was a tender nostalgia, one, however, by no means unusual in a man of retirement age (Phil was sixty-seven in 1960). His friends were dying on him: Araminta's godfather Jim Rice, who had retired two years before, and J. C. Jourdan of Iuka, by far his most cordial creditor, whose death the next summer touched Stone deeply. In other ways too he was conscious of time's passage. His daughter graduated from the sixth grade in June (winning a silver dollar from her father for her honor report card): "Of course next year you will be going to High School and I won't have any girl coming by to see me in the afternoon after school before we go home. Of course I shall miss it very much as I did when Mr. Philip went off to High School."

On 7 July 1960, writing Jim Meriwether puzzling "corrections" to his *Princeton University Library Chronicle* exhibition catalogue, Phil reminded Meriwether that it was Philip's birthday, his twentieth, and that Meriwether had once shared Philip's birthday dinner with them "several years ago." Stone felt so much older than another Faulkner correspondent, Professor Richard P. Adams of Tulane, that, although "not given to 'first-naming,' " he took the liberty of calling him "Dick" in his first letter after Adams, another colleague, and a student writer, Kraig Klosson, spent a pleasant weekend in Oxford in October, just before the Stones' twenty-fifth wedding anniversary.

Perhaps the most disturbing symbol of mutability came for Stone when eighty-eight-year-old Maud Falkner died in a coma a few days later. Phil Stone was a pallbearer at the family services at her home and at St. Peter's that Saturday afternoon (which few Oxonians attended, Stone wrote Klosson, "because they knew the Faulkners didn't want a big crowd"). Klosson had raised the question of whether Faulkner would now move permanently to Virginia. Stone answered that he did not know but neither would he ask—"if Bill has anything he wants to say to me he will say it." Stone suspected that Charlottesville had had sufficient time to tire of the fallible man behind the celebrity,[36] implying, perhaps hoping that Faulkner might soon seek sanctuary again with his own kind.

With the Tulane men and other serious writers or scholars that year, Stone's graciousness continued, but during the winter of 1960–61, a particularly frenzied time in his practice, he lost his temper on the phone with an impertinent Pennsylvania Faulkner fan who bedeviled him one night. Although his business tax return in 1960 listed receipts of over twenty thousand dollars (and an IRS lien on the Stones' incomes was canceled early in 1961), the dearth of ready cash in mid-December incited yet another attack of Stone's paranoia, this time directed mainly at his partner Hal Freeland, whom to others Phil accused of "impudence" and gross incompetence. As he began one letter to D. R. Johnson, "I think there is no doubt that I simply have to get rid of Hal." But at the end of January Stone took Freeland into his confidence about his proof, finally, of the corruption of a legal colleague who had also, Stone believed, unethically opposed him for the ABA's House of Delegates.[37] However, Stone's resumed trust of Freeland thereafter returned only intermittently.

Phil's suspicions rarely lighted upon his Faulkner correspondents. Indeed his affection for them almost rivaled that for D. R. Johnson in the period.[38] By the time of Richard P. Adams's return to Oxford with his wife in the summer of 1961, the Stones had virtually adopted the Tulane scholar, as they had elected Collins, Coughlan, and Meriwether before. Before the Adamses came again in August, Jean Adams affirmed to Emily the sincerity of their feelings too. "The reason we want to visit with you is to visit with YOU!"—however futile it was to promise that Faulkner would not dominate their husbands' conversation. Phil sent Jean word later that talking Bill Faulkner with Adams was something he quite enjoyed, though it was not his practice to converse so freely with "everybody." The Adamses, like Jim Meriwether, were by then receiving family reports too, Philip's return by plane from his six weeks' New Jersey "job," and Emily's flight home after a week in New York going over a manuscript at McIntosh & Otis.[39]

It was Meriwether, however, who had noticed Philip Stone's "gestures on behalf of the classics" reported by the Associated Press the previous spring.[40] Donning a toga, the junior classics major had delivered "an impassioned speech in Latin" protesting Harvard's adopting the vernacular for the school's diplomas. The role Philip had assumed after exams that summer may also have owed something to his flair for histrionics. Philip's "job" in reality was that he had joined a New Jersey farm community, where after a day's haying, sheep-shearing, or garden work, the assorted American, British, and Estonian members convened for evening readings "of unpublished material by Gurdjieff." Philip's goals remained primarily scholastic and aesthetic ones—he worked on a new novel there—and in the second six weeks of the summer of 1961 he mingled at home with a far more conservative group, the Mid-South's Rotarians, from whom he solicited scholarship money for study abroad after his senior year.

There is little doubt that Phil Stone would have taken great satisfaction in successfully engineering for his own son the last campaign of his career. In their pursuit of a scholarship Philip's advocate was as zealous as the man who had tried to get another young writer to Europe in 1924–25. No law office in the region missed an opportunity to recommend the multilingual Harvard novelist for a 1962 Rotary Foundation Fellowship. How much the experience meant to Stone is apparent in his memo to Philip dated 31 August 1961, after they went together to a Holly Springs Rotary luncheon: "I had such a good time because I have had so little time in your whole life to go with my boy and I was so proud of you in every way. You made a very shrewd statement that is likely to get you the scholarship. You looked so fine and so manly that I was very, very proud and very, very happy." [41] But it was not to be. Although Philip was among the ten finalists, his Harvard advisors told Philip later that his grades were too inconsistent for the fiercely competitive Rotary as for the Rhodes Scholarship for which he also applied in vain.

When the district governor informed Philip on 18 September 1961 of the scholarship committee's decision, the senior was disappointed, but too hopeful of other prospects to react strongly. Neither was his father lacerated by the familiar failure, but not because of the resilience of his hope. On Wednesday, 13 September, Stone had had a terrifying experience, so that he had taken "a day off," actually "more than a day off," as he wrote D. R. Johnson. He had been "right on the edge." By the next week Phil could explain, somewhat; upon reflection he considered what had happened a "serious, though not dangerous situation." In his words, that Wednesday afternoon he "had gone to jerking in the daytime when I quit and went home to bed." Apparently Stone had had another mild stroke. He must have mentioned something of the episode to Dick Adams, for in closing a long letter of questions about Faulkner's apprenticeship Adams wished for another trip to Oxford soon, and "better health for you." [42] Still he refused to see a doctor.

After such a scare, Phil Stone may have had unconscious motives for providing Freeland with a young, full-time associate in the week of his exchange of letters with Adams. G. A. Gafford, the former Stone clerk, who had known Phil since 1956, was invited to practice law in the busy firm in July 1961. With their work load, Stone noted, "Gerry" was a "godsend." In October 1961 the young Gafford, like Freeland in 1958, was taken in as a full partner at James Stone & Sons on the strength of his superior work, not, as was more customary, via a large financial settlement. [43]

One of the longest hiatuses of the now sporadic Faulkner correspondence began less than two months later, after Stone's apathetic response to Jim Meriwether's 22 November 1961 letter. Meriwether had seen Robert Holland of Mississippi State at an Atlanta convention— the Stones had known and respected Holland as an Ole Miss graduate student—and the two wanted permission to reprint Stone's *Oxford Magazine* essay and critique of Louis Cochran's Faulkner memoir in an article designed for, and eventually printed in, the *Mississippi Quarterly*. "I just don't remember what I said about all of this stuff," Stone replied, but he agreed to the scheme if he might read what they planned to publish. Six months later he told a man who wrote him from New Orleans that to get his work done he had "had to swear off answering letters about Bill Faulkner." [44]

The case that was devouring the last of his energies was the $400,000 contested estate of Philip's wealthy godmother Kate Skipwith, a suit that Stone had been handling since 15 May 1961. During those months of detailed preparation Stone, nevertheless, wasted hours in D. R. Johnson's Batesville office or by dropping in to interrupt other out-of-town attorneys he knew, even while his nemesis the IRS garnished his wife's university check and Philip's accounts continued deeply in arrears. The son's embarrassment was now freezing into a bitterness that his Ole Miss friend Evans Harrington observed; after Christmas 1961 Philip would refuse to come home. Stone confided to some of those lawyers not about Philip but of the assorted intrigues against him; other matters he trusted to the office files alone, scribbling at the bottom of one "Monthly Summary of Business," presumably the work of a Stone partner, "This is as phony as it can be." On 16 January 1962 Stone executed a secret, grossly paranoid codicil to his will.[45]

"Philip did throw away some money for a while," Stone confessed to the Harvard Linen Service, to whom he remitted a small sum in May 1962, "but really he has had a very hard time of it lately" in the wake of the family's "indebtedness." It was becoming Stone's habit to reflect his own condition in his sympathetic allusions not just to Philip but also to Emily—and to Faulkner. Yet after six years' experience, Philip was as adept as his father in postponing all but "the most immediate bills." And, had the thirty-year-struggle not benumbed Stone's other memories, Philip's collect telegram on 31 May 1962 might have stirred a nightmarish déjà vu: "FOUND TODAY THAT UNLESS YOU SEND ME $250 WITHIN WEEK TO PAY DEBT I CANNOT GET MY DIPLOMA. CAN YOU? PLEASE REPLY RETURN WIRE. AFTER THIS YEAR'S BLOWS THIS IS ONE MORE THAN I CAN STAND."[46] Philip Alston Stone did leave the campus that June with his Ivy League degree. But the family were not in attendance at his graduation—and Philip would not return to Mississippi for more than two years.

Phil Stone's correspondence with Faulkner scholars increased after they too were freed from classes in late spring 1962, and his answers were coherent but lackluster, and apologetic for his inability to rekindle the past on paper for their benefit. Stone still believed that he could do so in anecdote, if they would only come to see him in Oxford. Adams, working on Faulkner's apprenticeship, and Meriwether, requesting Philip's *Hamlet* typescript for a collation before a new Random House edition, almost besieged their Faulkner source through the mails. Stone's personal notes with his answers were gentle, even paternal, as he encouraged Adams in his long task and praised Meriwether's careful textual work or relented and risked sending the valuable manuscript to Meriwether despite his fears. But too often came the phrases "I confess I simply can't take time . . ." or "I confess I do not remember . . ."

Even more chilling, however, was his postscript to Adams on 8 June 1962: "Don't repeat this to anyone, but Bill has been home for a few days and I saw him on the street the other day. I have never seen him look so old before. It is not his eyes, but the skin around his eyes; looks like that of an old man, and he looks to me like he has aged about five years since I saw him a few months ago."[47] Stone too had visibly aged in recent months.

On Thursday, 12 June, William Faulkner inscribed an author's copy of *The Reivers* "To Emily and Phil / from Bill" and left it at the office with the secretary. What possessed Faulkner to include Emily's name for the first time after a quarter-century is problematic. The widow now believes, from the Stone portraits among Faulkner's characters, that the writer at least unconsciously had foreseen the logical development of her husband's personality under the pressures Stone confronted. Faulkner had made other conciliatory gestures, most notably his 1957 dedication in *The Town:* "To Phil Stone / He did half the laughing for thirty years." Especially after that "grace note" to the Snopes dedications, Emily had determined finally to thank Faulkner herself for having so transcended "the second mile"—despite her conviction, borrowed from Phil, that Faulkner would be indifferent to the gesture. But with the Faulkners so often in Virginia she "never had a chance, not even that Sunday afternoon two or three weeks before [Faulkner] died," when she persuaded her husband for the sake of his long friendship not to reject the Faulkners' invitation to Rowan Oak.[48] She knew, though, with Mack Reed, that those intense eyes missed very little. So perhaps in some way Faulkner had sensed the nearing climax of the tragedy of Phil Stone and grieved for the fiercely loyal survivor.

A different level of communication, however, was in evidence the day after Faulkner brought Stone *The Reivers.* "I know you don't like talk over the telephone, and hate it much more than I do," Phil dictated in apology for his letter, "and I don't know when I might see you personally." Phil appreciated the gift "a whole lot" but added, automatically, that he did not know when he could read it. The letter closed in the traditional manner, "Best of luck. / Your friend, Phil Stone." But Phil did see or talk to William Faulkner again, perhaps at the party his wife mentions, for he wrote Meriwether on the fifteenth of Faulkner's having been "thrown by another horse" and "having trouble with his back again" (Faulkner had suffered a serious fall in Virginia in January). "I told him he was going to break his neck one of these days," Stone said, too accustomed to the stamina of the foolhardy, seemingly indestructible Falkners to be seriously alarmed.[49]

On 6 July 1962 Phil's friend the Hollywood attorney Hubert Starr heard on the radio that William Faulkner had died of a heart attack about one-thirty that morning. He sat down at once to write Phil Stone, "It's sad. Everything's sad. Life's sad. . . . If he were like me, he had lived too long anyway." John Faulkner had telephoned Phil from the funeral home early that Friday morning. Stone was not aware that in the last weeks Faulkner had attempted to assuage his excruciating back pain with drugs and finally alcohol too, or that on Thursday Estelle and his nephew Jimmy Faulkner had admitted Faulkner to Wright's Sanitarium in nearby Byhalia, where he had died. Consequently Johncy's information simply astounded Phil Stone. But as minutes passed the words reached him, and Stone reeled at the void distending in him at Bill's departure.[50]

John Faulkner asked that Phil and Mack Reed be honorary pallbearers at the family services the following afternoon, but in the hurried arrangements did not specifically invite Emily Stone. Even after her phone calls to Faulkner relatives failed to clarify the family's intent, she surprised herself at her audacity in accompanying her husband anyway. Only later did she realize her compulsion: Stone's shock was so extreme that he might not be able to comport himself. But after the ritual, as Reed and Stone stood near the coffin in front of the fireplace and the literary celebrities and critics clustered around the widow just before the mourners left for the cemetery, Stone's grief took a gentle turn, reconciling for him in a way an old discord. No, he said later, Estelle Faulkner's emotional upheaval as she left the house was not Oldham dramatics; "Stelle and Bill loved one another in spite of their difficulties their whole lives."

That Saturday morning when Stone had made his habitual trip to the post office, he asked the *Eagle* delivery boy for two copies of the flier announcing the town's closing between 2:00 and 2:15 P.M. in memorial to William Faulkner. He wanted them for Philip and Araminta. That afternoon as Phil rode through the square in the cortege with the Reverend Duncan Gray and University of Virginia professor Joseph Blotner, impressions and memories assailed him: the few open businesses of the town's renegade Snopeses, who refused to lose a nickel honoring one of their betters; the courthouse, the Bank of Oxford, scenes of glory and humiliation for another gentleman farmer to whom the square had paid its respect, a man now safe within the pages of Yoknapatawpha. But Stone was able to verbalize little of what he felt, instead irritating Faulkner's biographer with his incessant, seemingly irreverent chatter. At St. Peter's, again Stone and Reed stood aside, waiting to follow the six younger men bearing Faulkner to the grave under the white oak, at the site below the hill where Stone himself would rest after almost five years more. After the short graveside service, Gray and Blotner drove back in another car.[51]

Stone's world accelerated to dizzying speeds in the following days and weeks. In the middle of his Skipwith case preparation, almost thirty letters were added to the Faulkner file. Faulkner's death was "much more of a shock to me than I had anticipated," Phil replied to Adams's sympathy letter on 9 July, "and I still don't have much brains (if I ever had any)." Their early August appointment, however, need not be canceled; Stone's important case was scheduled four weeks later, and it would be "long enough after Bill's death." After seeing Adams's book into print, however, Phil vowed "to quit," to devote himself to advising Jill Faulkner about the most lucrative, tasteful, and accurate recording of the famous life so intertwined with his own, for which Stone would himself refuse all money, rather than share the company of those "picking Bill's corpse." He had warned Faulkner's daughter of such predators when she was in Oxford.[52] That time Phil's insight was prophetic.

Stone was cultivated most assiduously by senior editor John Starr of McGraw-Hill, would-be publisher of the authorized biography, for intervention on his behalf with the Faulkners and information about the probating of Faulkner's will, news which, out of politeness, Stone supplied. He told Starr that Dick Adams was "not interested" in biography, but that at the proper time he intended to pursue his own ideas of recommending James Meriwether to the family as biographer-editor of Stone's repository of anecdote and artifact, for which Meriwether was already planning by 13 July. In cordial correspondence with Jill's husband, Paul D. Summers, Stone that month twice renewed his offer to assist the family in selecting a biographer. Faulkner's widow and daughter were sure to contact Stone in Oxford in August, Summers informed "Mr. Phil." To other entreaties by letter or in person, like that of H. E. Richardson, Stone answered that it was his desire "to help any Southerner and anybody interested in William Faulkner," but the sheer volume of such requests, and his grief, made that now impossible.[53]

Despite the clarity of his Faulkner letters, Stone's darker self reemerged in his financial affairs. Although no mention of it appears in print, his attention to the probating of Faulkner's will must have derived from more than courtesy, or even curiosity. He wrote John Starr with some satisfaction on 20 August of the Virginia lawyers' becoming ensnarled in Mississippi procedure when they "attempted to file Bill's will." Earlier Stone had written Starr of having told Faulkner "some years ago" that he "didn't want to have anything to do with [the will]. . . . It would be too sad a job."[54] In fact, the last record among Stone's papers of his work on Faulkner wills was the greatly protracted signing of the 1958 film rights codicil. But, at best, the Faulkners' move to Charlottesville, or, at worst, Faulkner's belief that he had been betrayed in Stone's Texas sale, might have had more to do with Faulkner's change of attorneys. The family soon engaged the Oxford firm of Roberts & Craig to assist in probating Faulkner's will, and that must for Stone have raised a graver possibility: Had the provision for the forgiveness of his debt been retained in the document revised in Virginia? The answer was no. But by the time Stone could have confronted that knowledge, his mind was gone.

The penultimate crisis came in August. Philip Stone, from the spring under the care of another Harvard psychiatrist for a "depression neurosis," mailed his parents a letter on 5 August. He considered his father and mother failures as persons and as parents, Philip said in a detailed attack, and he never wanted to see them again. Phil Stone had already hired a man to carry the Skipwith court papers in the trunk of his car to prevent Stone's partners from seeing them; one memo to Hal on 24 July had told Freeland that he knew him to be too busy to work effectively in that suit, so Stone would not burden him with it. Phil Stone's disintegration in the face of Philip's letter, however, undermined the wall for Emily Stone that neither love nor loyalty could breach before: her husband was indeed quite ill. Accepting her subterfuge that it was she who needed professional help, Stone was persuaded that month to accompany her to a Memphis psychiatrist, who verified Emily's fears that Stone was dangerous, but told her that until the "climax" it was impossible to commit her husband for psychiatric care without his consent. On 14 August, Stone wrote Meriwether that after his major lawsuit in September he was "going to take off and get some rest, provided I am still here on this earth,"[55] so at times Stone too sensed the seriousness of his condition, though he continued to resist the idea of professional treatment.

On the eighth of September the Skipwith case opened in the Oxford courthouse with James Stone & Sons representing the defendants. Although not inherently talented as a trial attorney, Phil Stone, who argued the initial defense, had sometimes realized his ambition to master his father's courtroom facility. On another occasion Freeland had watched the adroit appellate strategist reduce twelve lower-court jurymen to tears. Although his firm won the Skipwith case too, earning Stone one of the largest fees of his career, he was noticeably clumsy in those first two weeks in court, and was distracted enough about his health at its adjournment to agree to another appointment with the Memphis psychiatrist. On 21 September, however, Stone scribbled a hurried telegram to the doctor: "DISREGARD LAST LETTER. EVERYTHING BEAUTIFUL. LETTER WILL FOLLOW."[56]

In the same month, of course, rationality and madness contended for other minds than that of Phil Stone, during the "constitutional crisis" entangling the Lyceum on campus, the executive offices at the state capitol, and John F. Kennedy's White House. In January 1961 Air Force veteran James Howard Meredith of Kosciusko, Mississippi, had applied to study political science at the segregated University of Mississippi. The conflict had begun with some dignity in the initial court battle; by September 1962 it had descended into farce. Those affirming civil liberties would blame the equivocation of Mississippi

Governor Ross Barnett. The sane of both camps would observe with re-pugnance the "sometime U.S. Army general Edwin A. Walker, a Texan who had commanded Eisenhower's troops in Little Rock. In September Walker's inflammatory rantings summoned to Oxford a bigoted rabble to resist federal power. But even federal officials from John Kennedy to Chief U.S. Marshal James McShane would not be excused from a role in the slapstick playing through the afternoon of Sunday, 30 Septem-ber. With nightfall the farce exploded into the climactic chaos of the ugliest tragedy.[57]

Emily Stone, returning to an empty campus for a book that Sunday morning in late September, had noticed there with relief the absence of the recently omnipresent patrolmen. Beginning in mid-afternoon, however, military transports were flying low over the Stone house, to land federal marshals at the nearby municipal airport. After James Meredith and a special escort were secretly locked in a campus dor-mitory, the Stones and two university couples, their dinner guests for the evening, had driven to campus to observe at first hand the situa-tion at the Lyceum. Because of the masses of people already there, the Stone party saw only the white columns of the administration building, the "ring of white helmets" at its base, and then the orange bullet-proof vests and "short, white-muzzled" tear-gas guns of the encircling squads of U.S. marshals. Facing the marshals was a student crowd, which seemed idle, innocuous, and silly to the six adults who were themselves indignant at the show of force, but not yet alarmed.

Throughout the evening Phil Stone's response to the event seemed abstracted, disengaged, his theories of states' rights, Southern history, and race relations delivered over dinner almost by rote, with a modi-cum of passion. Phil indicated no interest in testing his theories at the scene, to which his wife was compulsively drawn twice more that night. She even drove Araminta and a friend near the center of the steadily disintegrating confrontation, because she believed the girls ought to see the brute force of a vexed federal power. They would have seen and heard a demon-possessed mob had they remained an hour longer, for the stalemate there was soon jeopardized by reinforcements to both sides. Early that evening those answering General Walker's summons had relieved the fraternity boys in sufficient numbers so that at the ar-rival of the newly activated local National Guard, the first government reinforcements, the crowd facing the Lyceum began to hurl concrete and lead pipes instead of pep rally insults.

Around nine-thirty, agitated by the muffled sounds of pandemonium from the campus, Emily Stone reached again for her car keys. Stone sat reading, offering no objections. As she walked through the tear gas, flying bricks, and overturned garbage cans of the nightmarish landscape, a student reproached her: "Lady, you got no business out here by yourself." "What good are you doing? Let it alone," she naively shouted to three or four other young men. "You ought to be ashamed of yourselves." Those "students" ignored the English professor. Genteel order could not be imposed upon anarchy. What if the mob turned away from the soldiers to the town's unarmed blacks? Filled with horror, her nerve gone, Emily Stone quickly drove home.

"I knew you had no business," Stone remarked at his wife's return, "but I wouldn't tell you," he said quietly. Phil slept through that noisy night of tear-gas bombs and screams, the night also in which two men were murdered. His wife lay in bed awake, going over their attempts on Saturday to educate a New Jersey reporter about the history of Southern race relations, Emily trying too to believe her husband's version of that history even while admitting the evils of bigotry. Phil Stone had committed more than one unconscious non sequitur in that newspaper interview, and Emily winced, worrying how foolishly Stone quotations might appear in print, in full sympathy then with William Faulkner's reticence or evasiveness with the press over the years.

At four-thirty, sounds from the street drew her outside in housecoat and slippers. A convoy of Army jeeps was transporting guardsmen with fixed bayonets to the university campus. "There in the half dark, gas-masked monsters, most of them looking steadily, unrelentingly ahead . . . were ripping past our house to make us do what . . . our very government . . . was set up to ensure that none of us should have to do," Emily Stone recorded later that morning in her diary of the "Oxford Riots." "I knew that I was trying to tell every one of them that I scorned, hated, vituperated, blasted their use of physical weight, piston, gun, unseen hatred against our soil, alien to them but familiar to me, over which they rode." But among the defenders of the embattled Lyceum that night was Captain Murry C. Falkner, one of William Faulkner's nephews; he, like more than two hundred others, had received broken bones and gashes from the racist mob.

Men like Phil Stone did not riot and murder; but beneath his public demeanor during the autumn weeks of civil tension, Stone too was riddled with inarticulate fears. His adversaries, like the mob's, were no longer faceless, and they were now entrenched not only at the office but in his very home. For his wife in those weeks, the terror was of what action Stone might take in his delusions. One day she had seen his distorted features pressed against the door of her university classroom; Stone had rushed back to Oxford at 75 m.p.h. to catch his wife in imagined marital infidelities. Measures were underway to evict Freeland and Gafford from the office. At another time a gun had appeared, then disappeared in the kitchen at home. Each night after his family went to bed, Phil sat alone drinking.

The morning after Sunday's racial violence, 1 October, some of the weary National Guard units pitched their tents in the Stone pasture behind the old house. The monsters upon whom Emily Stone had vented her private terrors had become human beings again. Sixteen hundred soldiers had been ordered to Oxford, Mississippi, overnight more than doubling the population of the university town. After initial arrests were made and eyewitnesses interviewed and reinterviewed, both the military and the press who had preceded them to North Mississippi followed student James Meredith from class to class or watched in boredom as maintenance crews cleared away the wreckage. A fire alarm sent the press corps racing out to the Stones' that week, but the media would find nothing of interest in an ancient smokehouse accidentally burning to the ground. Phil Stone would have a new anecdote about Yankees.

Carvel Collins had been in Oxford just before the weekend riot and inquired of Stone later about the "army encampment" he was reading about in the newspapers. Phil replied on 11 October. The community under martial law "was not bad at all." "Most of the soldiers have gone, but they were awfully nice when they were here and we were glad to have them," he added, serenely. Stone's court schedule was full again in November, so that Collins should inform him far in advance of his winter visit. Stone's wife was "still not feeling quite well," Phil mentioned casually. In the last letter of the Faulkner file, also to Collins, on 29 October, Stone, after thanking the editor for his copy of *William Faulkner: Early Prose and Poetry*, returned to the subject of his wife's health. Attributing Emily's "illness" to overwork, Stone predicted her recovery "after a while." [58]

Just before Thanksgiving, Emily Stone was startled one morning to find her husband's law partners waiting for her in the hall after her class. Stone had made wild accusations against all three of them, as before, but that morning he had threatened as well to kill Hal Freeland—and Emily. She went home only to pick up their thirteen-year-old daughter and to collect their things. While she packed, her husband plaintively beseeched Araminta "not to go away and leave her poor old Daddy."

On the Monday after the holiday, after consultation with the Memphis psychiatrist, Hal Freeland admitted Stone to the psychiatric division of the University Medical Center in Jackson for observation and treatment. Phil was transferred to Whitfield, the state mental institution east of the capital, in January, one month to the day before his seventieth birthday. Ironically, because Stone was overage, Emily was forced to accept the intervention of Governor Ross Barnett to get him into the state asylum, the only place their finances would have permitted. The final diagnosis, "Chronic Brain Syndrome associated with Cerebral Arteriosclerosis with Psychotic Reaction." Even the cacophonous medical jargon does no justice to Stone's thirty-three years of anguish. The miracle—and the horror—is that Phil Stone could have endured so long.

Afterword

On 30 September 1964 lawyers for the Faulkner estate filed a claim against Phil Stone's guardian Emily Stone for $10,000 in debts. Stone's affairs were hopelessly entangled, Freeland writing Emily at that time of discovering another $45,000 in notes for which neither he nor D. R. Johnson could account.

In the fall of 1964 Emily Stone had left Oxford to teach at All Saints Episcopal School for Girls in Vicksburg, where she enrolled her daughter and where she could be closer to her husband, less than ninety minutes away by automobile. Stone's mind at intervals was lucid, though generally he suffered an acute "expressive aphasia," as evident in his correspondence as in his halting speech. At the institution he penciled innumerable letters to his wife and children and to other family and friends, some ranting about Emily's having "railroaded him to Whitfield," others full of love and gentleness, accurately contributing to Emily's renewed Stone-Faulkner research. One Christmas she took to Whitfield a recent recording of Handel's *Messiah*, to which Phil listened intently: "It almost makes you believe in God again, doesn't it?"

Philip Stone learned of his father's commitment by accident from Carvel Collins in Cambridge, but the sole reunion possible was with his mother and sister, whom he saw in 1964. During his father's confinement, Philip was himself hospitalized for psychiatric treatment in Massachusetts and later at the medical center in Jackson. But by the school term of 1965–66, when he taught classics at the Indian Springs prep school outside Birmingham, Philip was writing very well again, making close friends, and apparently recuperating at long last from old traumas and guilt.

On 30 May 1966, however, after three days of intestinal discomfort, Philip Alston Stone died in his sleep of natural causes. His school's infirmary had prescribed paregoric to soothe him the Friday night before. His body was discovered in his rooms on Monday morning. Philip's autobiographical stories such as "The Dead," which the *Southern Review* published posthumously, as well as his medical history of near-suicidal depression, were sufficient for his mother to request an autopsy. Indeed a frequent misconception among those who know of Philip Stone's sudden death at age twenty-five is that he died by his own hand. The 10 June 1966 report by pathologists C. Elliott and Albert E. Casey attributed Philip's death "to septic shock secondary to superior mesenteric vein thrombosis." A blood clot had caused an abdominal vein to explode; shock and death followed in rapid succession, according to another physician.

His agent Elizabeth Otis, writing out of their common Gurdjieff experience, consoled his mother with the words "this planet did not suit him very well." Lines from Book 12 of *The Iliad* that Philip had translated in college might be a more fitting obituary: "Now, however, the spirits of death are standing in hosts, and / Never a mortal man can turn them aside and escape them . . ." (lines 326–27). Philip had always said that he would die young and die in his sleep.

That autumn, after enrolling Araminta for her freshman year at Duke University, Emily Stone joined the English faculty at Huntingdon College in Montgomery. There was a substitute lecturer one morning early in the second semester of my sophomore British literature survey course. Mrs. Stone would miss one or two classes, we were told, because of a personal problem.

After recovering from multiple seizures in recent weeks, Phil Stone had been transferred from the general hospital back to the infirmary at Whitfield. But there, about five o'clock on the morning of 20 February 1967, Stone's temperature rose sharply and he went into "respiratory distress," declining "rapidly . . . thereafter." He died at 5:30 A.M. The immediate cause of death was another cerebral thrombosis. The Stone women, his law partners and legal associates, Mack Reed, Jack Stone, Evans Harrington and James W. Webb of the university faculty, with others, assembled once again on the hilltop overlooking William Faulkner's grave.

Many of the Stones' university friends had fled the campus following the 1962 racial violence, older Oxonians who knew of Stone and

Afterword

Faulkner remembered most vividly the jealous, failed man of the fifties and sixties, but after four-and-a-half years of bitter exile from Oxford, the man buried beside Philip at St. Peter's Cemetery that afternoon had at last come home.

When Phil Stone's will was probated on 28 December 1967, the Faulkners, with the other creditors, were paid twenty-eight cents on the dollar.

A Note About Sources

IN 1973, when I approached Emily Stone with a proposal to write a biography of her husband, she had long been convinced that the relationship of Phil Stone and William Faulkner was an important though minor tributary of Faulkner scholarship. In the spring of 1957, at her discovery of Faulkner artifacts in Stone's office files, she had tried to persuade Stone to record "a reminiscent account of [his] association with Bill." But Phil had transferred the responsibility to his surrogate writer Emily Whitehurst Stone: "She insists that it should be written down," he wrote Carvel Collins, "and I shall never do it myself" (May 17, 1957).

Although in the early 1960s Charles East at Louisiana State University Press restated the need for a Stone memoir, the nightmarish decade would spell the end of Emily Stone's project. In the autumn after Faulkner's death (the autumn too of the "Ole Miss Riots") Phil Stone suffered his mental collapse. That winter came the commitment to the state mental institution. Early in his confinement his mind cleared at intervals and he strained to articulate his Faulkner history for posterity. In 1963, as part of his therapy, Stone penciled a sixteen-page, third-person "Autobiography," a halting, disjointed narrative. (The staccato recital is virtually devoid of references to William Faulkner the writer, although Faulkner figures prominently in the New Haven tales.)

After the shock of Stone's breakdown in 1962, Emily was compelled to re-valuate the man whom she had loved and revered as "Mr. God" for thirty years. Unaware of the onset of Stone's arteriosclerosis, and his resulting paranoia, she had believed him when he told her that he "knew" himself. Moreover, she had accepted without question the anecdotes chronicling the seventeen years he had spent "fooling with Bill." After 1962 all that she believed about her husband demanded reanalysis. In May 1966 their son, twenty-five-year-old Philip Alston Stone, died suddenly at a private school in Alabama where he had been a classics instructor. Nine months later Phil died at Whitfield. After those deaths, Emily Stone had no heart to pursue such a study in print. Faulkner critics knew the outlines of the Stone-Faulkner relationship; Carvel Collins, the scholar whom the Stones believed to be the most reliable, had the details. Perhaps the needs of scholarship were served.

A Note About Sources

What I proposed was somewhat different, a close look at Stone in his own right, with the hope that by understanding his character in its temporal and geographic context scholars might be in a better position to evaluate the fictional effects of the Stone-Faulkner alliance. The Faulkner biographies that soon began to appear, however, seemed more than reluctant to acknowledge Phil Stone's elemental place in Faulkner's work. Indeed, the generally perjorative line on Phil is now assumed definitive: His support of and belief in the writer were probably indispensable to Faulkner early, during the long years of neglect; but Stone, primarily out of rank envy, if not blatant self-aggrandisement, greatly exaggerated his small part in Faulkner's achievement.

Perhaps the earliest recorders of a great man's life are inevitably predisposed to idolatry. Awestruck by genius, we forget that as Virginia Woolf, among others, reminds us, art is also mundanely explicable, dependent necessarily on sufficient living expenses, the requisite solitude, and supportive lovers and confidants. One *must* take Phil Stone into account before hoping to understand how one of the major literary figures of the century emerged from such unpromising beginnings.

Yet the failed, jealous man whom the now-published scholars met in Oxford at the writer's death invited skepticism, even disdain, rather than an objective evaluation. Stone's garrulous, boastful discourse then certainly betrayed little of the deep insecurities that within weeks were manifest in psychosis. The impression Joseph Blotner came away with, moreover, was apparently underscored by the testimony of Faulkner's widow, Phil Stone's chief and eternal "rival"—whose fallibilities only recently, with Frederick R. Karl's biography, have been publicly acknowledged. Without book-length rebuttals from those scholars who knew Stone earlier and more intimately, significant periods of the Stone-Faulkner alliance were at first overlooked (the Charleston and other 1920s episodes, for example), and the received bias has been passed down largely unchallenged.

Perhaps the greatest injury to Phil Stone's literary reputation has resulted, ironically, from a humane gesture. Joseph Blotner's 1965 interview with Emily Stone coincided with Phil's illness, Philip's emotional crises, and the Stones' financial distress. Although candid with the scholar, as is her character, she sought one concession from him. In an attempt to shield her now sick husband from societal disgrace and ridicule as a "lunatic," she requested that the biographer refrain from mentioning Stone's commitment to as, later, his death in the mental asylum. Although Blotner had at first asked permission to question Phil Stone in the hospital, the gentleman-scholar readily agreed, unintentionally excising from his narrations the key that explains much of Stone's character and behavior. Paradoxically, the fateful omission from Faulkner studies of

A Note About Sources

Stone's long descent into madness presents Phil Stone to the world as a fool— rather than the tragic figure he more accurately appears. By the late seventies a complete Stone biography, then, seemed an essential corrective.

Because the majority of the family's written records burned with the Stone house in 1942 and because so few intimates of Stone and Faulkner before 1930 now survive, this version of a life rests in part upon hearsay, for a primary source is Emily Stone, a woman who first met Stone and Faulkner in the early thirties, when their literary colloquy seemed at an end. That it is perspicacious hearsay derives from Emily Stone's commitment to a continuing analysis of the lives she had observed—observation sharpened by forty years of writing novels and poems herself. For the sake of recording the truth, she was willing to look again at the particulars in the kaleidescope. She would not restrict my research or attempt to censor its results at any stage. Since my initial taped interviews with Mrs. Stone in Montgomery during six weeks in June and July 1973, we have periodically talked at length about the details and anecdotes she remembered, but neither of us could be content to trust to memory alone. Mrs. Stone encouraged her husband's acquaintances to contribute "whatever they may feel free to offer is the truth concerning [Stone and his family]," but I also interviewed or corresponded with other persons whom she does not know.

At the outset Mrs. Stone turned over to me the family papers, in the main, legal-sized file folders measuring more than ten-feet high. Among the family archives I began to appreciate the formulaic quality—and amazing longevity— of the Stone anecdote. Phrases or whole stories I heard from Emily Stone in 1973 recur almost verbatim in Phil Stone's correspondence: the 1900 General Longstreet story, in a 1950 letter to Glenn O. Carey and in 1954 to Robert Coughlan; a 1918 Yale anecdote, in a 1953 letter to William Faulkner and in 1959 to Carl P. Rollins; Faulkner's reading Stone *The Sound and the Fury* "page by page," in letters to Carvel Collins (1954), James Meriwether (1960), and Elizabeth Y. Grosch (1962).

"Twelve large folders" of Faulkner correspondence and manuscripts had been lost when the Stone house burned (Stone to Fred D. Wieck, September 19, 1952). Nevertheless, the extant papers are remarkably complete—because of Stone's pack-rat tendencies in evidence from the forties and because of his concern to preserve the past for his two children (born to Stone's middle age). There are six major files: land and bank account folders, on the one hand, but also series of files for Emily Whitehurst, Philip Alston Stone, Araminta Stone (his daughter), and for William Faulkner. The earliest surviving Faulkner files, with most of the extant Faulkner poems in Stone's possession, are the "Burned Papers" now in the Humanities Research Center at the University of Texas at Austin. Letters there begin in 1922 and continue into the early thirties.

A Note About Sources

The files still belonging to the family begin in the thirties and continue until Stone's forced retirement. Louis Daniel Brodsky has since purchased the three remaining Faulkner files, dating from 1945, which contain Stone's extensive correspondence concerning the novelist with critics, graduate students, journalists, old friends, and celebrity seekers. Periodically, into the fifties, Stone would also file there the wills he drew up for his most famous law client.

Not surprisingly, there are few letters from Faulkner to Stone in the entire collection, in part as a result of their almost daily contact. References to Faulkner, however, are ubiquitous, not only in that file but in the other five series as well. Although Stone began Philip's file in 1940 and Araminta's in 1948, those folders are especially rich in anecdotes and memorabilia about persons and events prior to 1940, many from the early 1900s and before. Stone made hundreds of memoranda to accompany the programs, ticket stubs, photographs, letters, news clippings, and the like that he kept for his children. The extensive Whitehurst file, charting his wife's finally unsuccessful writing career, offers intriguing explicit and implicit parallels to Stone's early promotion of William Faulkner. Consequently, it is rare that the anecdotes Stone transmitted to his wife are without some confirmation among the papers.

Fortunately, by the time I began to write, Joseph Blotner's monumental *Faulkner: A Biography* (2 vols.; New York, 1974) was in print. The exhaustive work provided copious details and contexts against which I could easily align and measure the materials I had gathered in interviews and in the Stone Papers. Likewise, Blotner's *William Faulkner's Library—A Catalogue* (Charlottesville, 1964) and *Selected Letters of William Faulkner* (New York, 1977) became invaluable to my pursuit, as to anyone at work in the field. With regard to Phil Stone, however, the late Carvel Collins and James B. Meriwether had the advantage of Blotner (and me). Their so astutely recognizing the worth of seeming trifles has rescued from near oblivion documents I, for one, have found indispensable: the Texas papers, in which both scholars had a hand, but also Collins's *William Faulkner: Early Prose and Poetry* (Boston, 1962), *William Faulkner: New Orleans Sketches* (Rev. ed.; New York, 1968), and numerous other research, not to mention the illuminating responses his questions elicited from Phil Stone. Meriwether's "Early Notices of Faulkner by Phil Stone and Louis Cochran," *Mississippi Quarterly* 17 (Winter 1964) makes readily accessible to us all Phil Stone the biographer-critic. Their correspondence as well gives shape to Stone's last years.

Although the lives of Stone, Faulkner, and Stark Young only occasionally intersect, I found in John Pilkington's *Stark Young, A Life in the Arts: Letters, 1900–1962* (2 vols.; Baton Rouge, 1975) a captivating and useful reconstruction of their era. Outside the Faulkner novels, the first intimations I had of

A Note About Sources

Phil Stone's world came from the evocative and perennially readable *William Faulkner of Oxford*, edited by James W. Webb and A. Wigfall Green (Baton Rouge, 1965). I am pleased, and no longer surprised, that as with my project, Charles East had no small part in that volume too.

For a complete record of the sources I have employed, please consult the Notes below.

Notes

CHAPTER 1. Family

1. Chapters 1–9 of this biography appeared in an earlier form as "Phil Stone of Yoknapatawpha" (Ph.D. dissertation, University of North Carolina, 1978). To avoid excessive text intrusion, I omit here references to my taped interviews with Emily Whitehurst Stone in Montgomery, Ala., June–July 1973, and to periodic conversations with Mrs. Stone from 1966 to the present. I cite rather the written confirmations of oral history, taking care, however, to note any discrepancies either in the text or in documentation. Unless otherwise indicated, miscellaneous brochures, clippings, photographs, and the like are among the myriad minor documents of the Phil Stone Family Papers, Charlotte, N.C. The three Faulkner files (Stone's Faulkner correspondence, 1945–62), his presentation Faulkner volumes, and a number of other items that were among the Stone Papers when I began have been subsequently purchased by Louis Daniel Brodsky. Cf. catalogues of his collection, principally Louis Daniel Brodsky and Robert W. Hamblin (eds.), *Faulkner: A Comprehensive Guide to the Brodsky Collection* (5 vols.; Jackson, Miss., 1982–1989). Other early Stone books have since been sold to William Boozer.

2. Portions of Stone's conversations and stories as recalled by his widow appear in the text as direct quotations, a practice justified, I believe, by the formulaic quality of the Stone anecdote and by the veracity of Emily Stone.

3. J. A. Groves, *Alstons and Allstons of North and South Carolina* (Atlanta, 1901); PS to Morris E. White, 13 May 1959; interview with W. E. Stone V, 10 August 1975; W. E. Stone V to Susan Snell, 31 July 1982; program, 1959 dedication of Ravenscroft Chapel, Tenn.; Arney R. Childs (ed.), *Rice Planter and Sportsman: The Recollections of J. Motte Alston, 1821–1909* (Columbia, S.C., 1953).

4. C. John Sobotka, Jr., *A History of Lafayette County, Mississippi* (Oxford, 1976), 20–21; PS letter reprinted in *Life*, 26 October 1953, 19–20; Mrs. Marilou Alston Rudulph to PS, c. November 1953.

5. Interview with Pauline Alston Clark and Philip Alston Clark, 31 August 1975. Pauline Clark also allowed me to examine the Alston Bible and other family records.

6. Dunbar Rowland, *History of Mississippi: The Heart of the South* (4 vols.; Chicago, 1925), 2:760; Sobotka, *Lafayette County*, 30–31; A. Wigfall Green, "William Faulkner at Home," *Sewanee Review* 40 (1932): 297.

7. See Emily Whitehurst Stone, "How a Writer Finds His Material," *Harper's*, November 1965, 159.

8. "Mrs. Alston's Death Grieves Host in Delta," *Clarksdale Daily Register*, 5 December 1932.

9. W. E. Stone V to Susan Snell, 31 July 1982. Dunbar Rowland, *Military History of Mississippi, 1803–1898* (1908; rpr. Spartanburg, S.C., 1978), 547, identifies P. S. Alston as a major in the Fourth Regiment–Cavalry, organized 6 September 1864.

10. Lunceford Cooper was later a criminal court justice in Memphis. See William D. Miller, *Memphis During the Progressive Era, 1900–1917* (Memphis, 1957), 99; Memphis *Commercial Appeal*, 18 April 1902.

11. Interview with Pauline A. Clark and Philip A. Clark.

12. PS to Hotchkiss School, 9 December 1955.

13. "Mrs. Alston's Death," *Clarksdale Daily Register; Commercial Appeal*, 22 October 1943 (Rosamond Stone's obituary).

14. "Mrs. Alston's Death"; *Commercial Appeal*, 22 October 1943.

15. Interview with Pauline A. Clark and Philip A. Clark; "Mrs. Alston's Death," *Clarksdale Daily Register;* Elizabeth Pauline Alston Clark (Mrs. Walter Clark) Diary, from 20 February 1897 into the early 1900s, in possession of Pauline A. Clark, Clarksdale, Miss.; mayoral appointment certificate in Clark Diary.

16. Belle Kearney was the first woman to serve as state senator (1924–28), according to Charles S. Sydnor and Claude Bennett, *Mississippi History* (Richmond, 1939), 323, and the first woman to run for the U.S. Senate from Mississippi, according to John K. Bettersworth, *Mississippi: A History* (Austin, 1959), 412.

17. *Biographical and Historical Memoirs of Mississippi* (2 vols.; Chicago, 1891), 2:847.

18. According to the Stones, Wilkes County, Ga., had been established by the House of Burgesses for younger sons of Virginia gentlemen otherwise landless because of primogeniture. Washington is the county seat. "They called it 'Washington-Wilkes,' as they do in Virginia." Interview with W. E. Stone V.

19. PS summarized the Stone genealogy in a memo to his son in the late 1940s.

20. W. E. Stone V, who otherwise corroborated Emily Stone's anecdote, says, however, that the mine was in Nevada.

21. Interview with Philip Thornton, Jr., 16 March 1976; PS memo to his

son, c. 1948; Lt. Col. James Darwin Stephens (KMI historian) to Susan Snell, 10 October 1983.

22. Telephone interview, Office of Admission and Records, University of Mississippi, 20 June 1977. "Preparatory classes" there were not discontinued until 1892, according to *Bulletin of the University of Mississippi*, March 1909, p. 24.

23. According to Col. Stephens's research, the Philimathean Literary Society awarded Lt. James Stone, Bachelor of English, a Gold Medal for the best Commencement Day oration, a manuscript still extant in 1937 (PS to Col. C. B. Richmond, 17 June 1937, KMI records).

24. Bettersworth, *Mississippi*, 385; interview with Philip Thornton, Jr. A newspaper [*Commercial Appeal?*] clipping dated 29 August 1929, in KMI files, says Williams and Stone were KMI classmates. Extant records list Williams's school residence only for 1867–68, 1868–69, according to Col. Stephens, though the two were exact contemporaries. Stephens cannot corroborate Thornton's dates either, though Thornton's son showed me the elder's KMI scrapbook.

25. *Biographical and Historical Memoirs*, 2:847.

26. *Oxford Eagle*, 28 November 1936 (James Stone's obituary).

27. Telephone interview, Office of Admissions and Records, University of Mississippi, 20 June 1977; *Biographical and Historical Memoirs*, 2:847. There is no record of his degree, but pre-1900 university records are in disarray.

28. Emily W. Stone, "How a Writer," 160. See Joseph Blotner (ed.), *Uncollected Stories of William Faulkner* (New York, 1979), 296–310.

29. *Biographical and Historical Memoirs*, 2:847; PS memo to his daughter with a poem Perrin had sent her; Perrin Lowrey to PS, March 1950. General M. P. Lowrey founded Blue Mountain Female College in 1869. Oxford *Globe*, 19 June 1892: "Mr. Lowrey of the firm of Stone and Lowrey of Batesville has been in the city for court." The Stones would have already moved to Oxford by that date. Perhaps Stone in Oxford and Lowrey in Batesville continued as partners "for years," as PS claims.

30. Joseph Blotner, *Faulkner: A Biography* (2 vols.; New York, 1974), 99; *Eagle*, 15 March 1905.

31. See also William Faulkner, "Mississippi," *Holiday*, April 1954, 35.

32. "The Avent-Stone Home," *Eagle*, 10 December 1936; Oxford *Globe*, 24 December 1891. Chancellor Mayes was also Lamar's biographer (*Lucius Q. C. Lamar: His Life, Times, and Speeches* [1896]). See James B. Murphy, *L. Q. C. Lamar: Pragmatic Patriot* (Baton Rouge, 1973), 5.

33. "Avent-Stone Home."

34. [Philip Alston Stone], "Built By a Man Who Wanted to be a Southern Aristocrat: The Stones Lived There for 50 Years," *Eagle*, 22 August 1957;

"Avent-Stone Home." The source of Philip's unsigned account of the Avant legend was probably Phil Stone. In 1957 seventeen-year-old Philip and a friend found summer jobs on the *Eagle*, primarily for this ninetieth anniversary issue. Philip, who also wrote his novel that summer, often freely mixed fact and fiction. His article on James Stone in the same issue, however, is almost a verbatim recital of anecdotes corroborated elsewhere. His Avant article elaborates on but does not deviate from the shorter 1936 *Eagle* article except in the spelling of Tomlin's surname. There he follows his mother's spelling, *Avant*. How much of Philip's article is historical remains problematic; the details have not been corroborated by sources outside the family. By 1957 Philip had adopted his father's critical attitude toward Faulkner, so it is unlikely that the tale began as a conscious imitation of the Sutpen story. More probably, Philip and Faulkner heard from PS versions of the same story that they in turn embellished at will.

35. Property abstract for the Stone homesite.

36. "Avent-Stone Home," *Eagle*, 10 December 1936, mentions only Memphis, which Philip Stone omits.

37. Ibid. and Emily Stone. In his 1934 *Oxford Magazine* Faulkner essay, PS recalled only one pane, however, inscribed "U. S. Grant 1862." See Phil Stone, "The Man and the Land," excerpt reprinted in James W. Webb and A. Wigfall Green (eds.), *William Faulkner of Oxford* (Baton Rouge, 1965), 6. But the engraving detail Faulkner employs in "Ambuscade" in *The Unvanquished* derives from another Oxford home, Stone says there.

38. William Faulkner, *Sartoris* (London, 1932), 8. Although the Sartoris house has features of the Stone mansion, the former seems a composite of several Oxford homes.

39. PS to Robert Nichols, 24 April 1953.

40. *Eagle*, 31 March 1926.

41. Oxford *Globe*, 15 September and 28 July 1892; *Eagle*, 4 June 1904; interview with Pauline A. Clark, 20 July 1976. *Eagle*; 9 and 30 July 1903; Pauline A. Clark.

42. William Faulkner, *As I Lay Dying* (New York, 1930), 76.

CHAPTER 2. Childhood

1. James Stone's sentiments are reflected in *As I Lay Dying*, although in Addie Bundren's defense of her beloved Jewel, not of the rejected Darl: "He is my cross and he will be my salvation. He will save me from the water and from the fire. Even though I have laid down my life, he will save me."

2. "Phil Stone: An Autobiography," a sixteen-page, third-person narrative

penciled at Whitfield, the state mental institution in Jackson, in autumn 1963 (later typed by Mrs. Arthur Kreutz, a family friend).

3. Phil Stone Papers.

4. Interview with Allie Jean Stone (Mrs. A. S. Scott, Jr.), 9 August 1975.

5. Joseph Blotner, *Faulkner: A Biography* (2 vols.; New York, 1974), 63.

6. [Philip Alston Stone], "Folks Fearless in Fever's Face," *Oxford Eagle*, 22 August 1957.

7. *Eagle*, 9 October and 5 June 1902 (the office was above what later became Parks' Barber Shop), and 22 January 1903; C. P. J. Mooney (ed.), *The Mid-South and Its Builders* (Memphis, 1920), 121; Julian C. Wilson to Mrs. James Stone and PS, 20 January 1942; *Eagle*, 2 July 1903.

8. Memphis [*Commercial Appeal?*] clipping dated 29 August 1929; *Eagle*, 28 November 1936 (James Stone's obituary).

9. *Eagle*, 17 and 24 September 1903.

10. William Boozer, *William Faulkner's First Book: "The Marble Faun," Fifty Years Later* (Memphis, 1974), 19; Mooney, *Mid-South*, 241; *Eagle*, 5 June 1902.

11. Boozer, "*Marble Faun*," 19; Blotner, *Faulkner*, 63; *Eagle*, 24 February 1898 and 22 October 1903 (death notice).

12. [Philip Alston Stone], "County Landmark for 44 Years," *Eagle*, 22 August 1957.

13. Ed Meek, *Birmingham News*, 7 February 1961 (interview with PS).

14. PS to Memphis paint firm, 23 February 1959; Ed Meek, *Birmingham News*, 7 February 1961.

15. "County Landmark for 44 Years."

16. Edith Brown Douds, "Recollections of William Faulkner and the Bunch," in James W. Webb and A. Wigfall Green (eds.), *William Faulkner of Oxford* (Baton Rouge, 1965), 50–51.

17. "County Landmark for 44 Years."

18. Interview with Robert J. Farley, February 1976.

19. *Eagle*, 16 October 1902; Blotner, *Faulkner*, 52; John K. Bettersworth, *Mississippi: A History* (Austin, 1959), 364.

20. *Eagle*, 24 June 1904 and 28 May 1903.

21. Ibid., 1 January and 5 November 1903, 3 July and 9 October 1902, 9 and 30 July 1903, and 10 September 1903; PS to Glenn O. Carey, 5 April 1950; Blotner, *Faulkner*, 90; *Eagle*, 31 March 1926.

22. The Longstreet anecdote appears in two typescripts: PS to Carey, 5 April 1950, and one dated 27 January 1955, submitted to *Reader's Digest*'s "Footnote to History," accompanied by PS's offer of an affidavit swearing to its truth. The latter version, probably written by Emily Stone (and tailored for the *Digest*),

differs from PS's version only in its greater length and in setting the Holland meeting on the beach.

23. Rowland, *History of Mississippi*, 3:170–73; *Eagle*, 5 June 1902, 24 December 1903, and 4 and 11 December 1902; interview with W. E. Stone V, 10 August 1975; Rowland, *History of Mississippi*, 3:173; *Eagle*, 26 June 1902. Telephone interview with Mrs. Singer, Office of Admissions and Records, University of Mississippi, 20 June 1977, provided only partial verification, for their records are incomplete.

24. Interview with W. E. Stone V.

25. Rowland, *History of Mississippi*, 3:170.

26. *Eagle*, 10 and 24 September 1903, apparently confuse Will and Jim. *Eagle*, 3 December 1903 and 24 June 1904, document Jim's year in Okolona.

27. Telephone interview with Office of Admissions and Records, University of Mississippi, 10 and 20 June 1977; interview with Mrs. A. S. Scott, Jr., 9 August 1975.

28. James Stone, Jr., to James Stone, Sr., 29 April 1910; Mrs. James Stone, Jr., to James Stone, Sr., 16 December 1911.

29. Mrs. James Stone, Jr., to James Stone, Sr., 16 December 1911; James Stone, Jr., to James Stone, Sr., 29 April 1910.

30. Photograph that Rosamond dated February 1903, with PS's note, c. 1953.

31. PS to Carvel Collins, 16 August 1954. The 1940s memo from PS to Philip with the James Stone, Jr., correspondence mentioned above is a frenzied, almost manic warning to his son about financial dealings with the Jim Stones.

32. PS to Whitney North Seymour, Sr., 5 October 1953; "Autobiography"; Emily Whitehurst Stone, "How a Writer Finds His Material," *Harper's*, November 1965, 159; *Eagle*, 30 July and 10 September 1903.

33. P. M. Carmen to James Stone, 23 March 1904; W. M. Stebbins to James Stone, 17 March 1904, with PS memo to Philip, n.d. (after 1942).

34. "Autobiography"; Emily W. Stone, "How a Writer," 159.

35. PS to Alston Clark, 29 November 1905, in possession of Pauline A. Clark, Clarksdale, Miss.

36. Interview with Evelyn Walton Stone (Mrs. Herbert Ray), 5 March 1980.

37. *Eagle*, 14 January 1904.

38. "County Landmark for 44 Years."

39. *University Training School Announcements*, 1905–1906, 1907–1908, 1908–1909, and 1909–1910, Cooke Papers, Mississippi Collection, University of Mississippi. Unless otherwise indicated, UTS details are from these sources. PS's University of Mississippi transcript lists as his high school credits (Carnegie units): English 3, History 3+, Algebra 1½, Geometry 1, Greek 2, and

Latin 3+. Although he may have enrolled at UTS only in 1906, his finishing grades 4 and 5 in public schools and then 6 through 9 at UTS to complete the then conventional nine grades (*Eagle*, 9 June 1955), is not inconsistent with his transcript either.

40. *UTS Commencement Announcement*, 30 May 1907, Cooke Papers, Mississippi Collection, University of Mississippi.

41. "Autobiography."

42. Blotner, *Faulkner*, 379.

43. Robert W. Hamblin and Louis Daniel Brodsky, *Selections from the William Faulkner Collection of Louis Daniel Brodsky: A Descriptive Catalogue* (Charlottesville, 1979), 21. The poem, which Brodsky and I discovered together, appears in pencil on p. 260.

44. Charles R. Pettis to PS, 9 April 1959; interview with Mrs. A. S. Scott, Jr.

45. "Autobiography."

46. Memphis [*Commercial Appeal?*] clipping dated 29 August 1929, KMI records.

47. *Eagle* clipping, n.d., 1904.

48. *Eagle*, 3 August 1907. Stone's detailed summary of the 1907 campaigns is correct. See also William F. Holmes, *The White Chief: James Kimble Vardaman* (Baton Rouge, 1970), 177–95. On Vardaman's more famous second Senate race, see William Alexander Percy, *Lanterns on the Levee: Recollections of a Planter's Son* (1941; rpr. Baton Rouge, 1973), 140–55.

49. Blotner, *Faulkner*, 130–31.

50. *Bench and Bar of Mississippi: A Pictorial and Biographical Directory* (Jackson, 1938), 7. In "Autobiography" PS apparently mistakes L. A. Smith, Sr., for McGowen.

51. 1908 DuVal-Stone contract; H. R. DuVal to James Stone, Sr., 23 July 1908.

52. In an 8 April 1959 memo to Philip, PS dated a postcard print of the house as 1917, when his mother was away for the summer and his father had had the yard graded over, for the trees were in leaf in the photograph and the crepe myrtle bush on the east of the veranda was in full bloom, yet there was "no grass much" on the lawn. Perhaps the anecdotes telescope two different projects.

CHAPTER 3. The Hunt and College

1. *Oxford Eagle*, 14 January 1904 (Stone as vice-president); *UTS Announcement, 1909–1910*, Cooke Papers, Mississippi Collection, University of Mississippi.

2. Joseph Blotner, *Faulkner: A Biography* (2 vols.; New York, 1974), 133.

3. [Philip Alston Stone], "County Landmark for 44 Years," *Eagle*, 22 August 1957.

4. PS memo to Philip attached to 29 August 1951 issues of the *Eagle* and the *Commercial Appeal*.

5. Oxford *Globe*, 1 December 1892.

6. *Eagle*, 27 November 1902.

7. Evelyn Walton Stone (Mrs. Herbert Ray) to Susan Snell, 9 August 1976.

8. Emily Whitehurst Stone, "How a Writer Finds His Material," *Harper's*, November 1965, 157–61, the primary written source for the hunt details, is based in part upon an extant tape and notes she made with PS at Whitfield, 2 November 1963, material recapitulated in a tape she made with her daughter, 8 and 9 September 1969.

9. PS to Alston Clark, 29 November 1905, in possession of Pauline A. Clark, Clarksdale, Miss.

10. The first nickname denotes a black servant who was of normal stature except from his knees down. The black man Ad (or Add) Jones appears under the pseudonym Ad Bush in John B. Cullen, with Floyd C. Watkins, *Old Times in the Faulkner Country* (Chapel Hill, 1961), 29, 43, 111.

11. All of these men, and others too, no doubt, hunted with the Stones, but they may have done so over a 35-year period. I know very little else about them. In the *Eagle*, 22 August 1957, Philip mentions Van Tankersley, W. V. Archibald, and Walton "Bud" Waller. In *Old Times in the Faulkner Country* (p. 13) Cullen says that his hunting pal and contemporary R. Walton "Uncle Bud" Miller also hunted with the Stones. Miller's photo appears in the *Eagle*, 12 July 1962. Philip's "Walton Waller" may mistake "Walton Miller." Emily Stone named Mathis (Arthur, Harmon, or Harvard?) as another 1930s hunter, when she too mentioned Tankersley. She also identified C. W. Callicott, in Blotner (*Faulkner*, 177) mistaken for Buster Callicoat, the Faulkner's hired hand. Phil Thornton, Jr., said that his father hunted with James Stone and that he himself had killed two bears at Stone Stop, as had a Dr. Walker of Charleston. Interview with Thornton, 16 March 1976.

12. Emily W. Stone, "How a Writer," 159.

13. Cullen, *Old Times*, 27–28.

14. Emily W. Stone, "How a Writer," 160.

15. "Phil Stone: An Autobiography," a sixteen-page, third-person narrative penciled at Whitfield, the state mental institution in Jackson, in autumn 1963.

16. Emily W. Stone, "How a Writer," 160.

17. "Autobiography."

18. Ibid.

19. Emily W. Stone, "How a Writer," 160.

20. Ibid.

21. Perhaps this land lay north of Oxford on the river; according to Emily Stone, the hunters referred to it only as "Section 14."

22. PS to Robert Coughlan, 30 September 1952; PS memo to Philip: "Attached are some deposit slips of Stone and Sivley for the year 1917 and they are for the land at Stone Stop and not for law business. Your Grandfather and Mr. Sivley had ceased to be law partners long before that." Stone Stop seems to have remained in the family until after James Stone's death in November 1936; Sivley died in February 1936.

23. Interview with W. E. Stone V, 10 August 1975.

24. "As I Knew William Faulkner" (interview with John Cullen), *Eagle*, 12 July 1962.

25. PS to Robert Coughlan, 30 September 1952.

26. PS memo to Philip. The principal source for Rainey details is the typescript "The Raving Rainey," by Vickie Therease Berryhill, a student of George Boswell, University of Mississippi folklorist, in 1973. Chancellor W. H. Anderson, whom I interviewed on 14 July 1976, had been her principal source of anecdotes and news clippings. He gave me the Berryhill paper, which has no documentation, and showed me his clippings, most undated, including Jackson *Clarion-Ledger*, 14 November 1965, and Memphis *Commercial Appeal*, 22 August 1965. Cullen (*Old Times*, 27) cites a Rainey article in *True*, October 1957.

27. Sales list, Tippah Kennels, Cotton Plant, Miss., c. late 1910; pamphlet for field trial champion Llewellyn setter, listing "E. Shelley," manager, with beagle pedigree and PS memo to Philip.

28. PS memo to Philip with a small snapshot "of the Lodge at Stone's Stop" taken by Mary Stone, James Stone, Jr.'s oldest daughter, dated July 1926. PS marked through the inscription "Tallahatchie Co. Miss." and wrote "Panola." The camphouse was on the eastern side of the river because in winter the Tallahatchie was too swollen to cross.

29. PS memo to Philip; Cullen, *Old Times*, 27. Philip Thornton, Jr., remembered Rainey's twice coming down to Stone Stop. Thornton interview.

30. Sales list, Tippah Kennels, Cotton Plant, Miss.

31. PS memo to Philip.

32. Philip Thornton, Jr., said that his father had sent him off to college up north (c. 1917) over his protests because the bears were almost gone from the Tallahatchie and he did not want to miss the last hunts. Cullen (*Old Times*, 28) recalls that the beginning of the end of the Mississippi bear hunts occurred after fires swept Delta canebrakes in autumn 1914; the bears surviving the fire apparently migrated.

33. Emily W. Stone, "How a Writer," 161. Another account of the formulaic deer story, on which I chiefly rely here, survives in Emily Stone's tape with her daughter, 8 and 9 September 1969.

34. Emily W. Stone, "How a Writer," 161.

35. "Autobiography."

36. Principal sources for PS's Mississippi undergraduate work, in addition to his transcript, are *Bulletin of the University of Mississippi*, March 1909, and *Ole Miss* yearbooks, principally 1910, 1913, 1916, Mississippi Collection, University of Mississippi.

37. *Eagle*, 13 May 1954.

38. "Autobiography."

39. Interview with W. H. Anderson, 14 July 1976.

40. John Pilkington (ed.), *Stark Young, A Life in the Arts: Letters, 1900–1962* (2 vols.; Baton Rouge, 1975), xxiv, xxiii.

41. William Faulkner, *Flags in the Dust*, ed. Douglas Day (New York, 1973), 12.

42. Interview with William McNeil Reed, 15 August 1975. Reed's nickname is variously "Mac" or "Mack" among Faulkner acquaintances and scholars. Although PS (or his secretaries) is also inconsistent, I follow here his more usual Mack Reed.

43. Interview with D. R. Johnson, 16 March 1976.

44. PS once brought Emily Stone several poems written in an office ledger. She remembers only one about "that square cotton house." With the Stone Papers replete with unsigned manuscripts by Emily and Philip Stone, it is difficult to determine whether any of Phil Stone's poems survive.

45. Bettersworth, *Mississippi: A History* (Austin, 1959), 402.

46. Blotner, *Faulkner*, 145.

47. Emily Stone to Elizabeth Otis, 28 September 1954.

48. Interview with Robert J. Farley, February 1976; Blotner, *Faulkner*, 132.

49. Blotner, *Faulkner*, 149.

50. Dunbar Rowland, *History of Mississippi: The Heart of the South* (4 vols.; Chicago, 1925), 3:173.

51. Blotner, *Faulkner*, 149.

52. *The Mississippian*, 22 March 1913. Lee M. Russell managed the Opera House for a number of years. See Blotner, *Faulkner*, 115–17, 125–26.

53. PS's 1913 experiences with poker and alcohol are recounted in detail in "Autobiography."

54. Mrs. Herbert Ray to Susan Snell, 9 August 1976.

55. *Eagle*, 2 July 1903; Walter P. Armstrong, Jr., to Susan Snell, 26 July 1976.

56. William Faulkner, *Mosquitoes* (1927; rpr. New York, 1955), 115.

57. Dating Stone's anecdote, most probably 1913 and not 1917, is complicated by feminine vanity. It seems unlikely that in 1913 Carter (born 30 July 1895?) began her second year at Fairmont, as her son believes (Interview with Jim Kyle Hudson, Jr., 16 May 1978), for Blotner (*Faulkner*, 152), citing two issues of the *Eagle* for 1912, places her in Oxford in autumn 1912, whence she and Estelle Oldham attended Vardaman houseparties in Jackson. A Woodrow Wilson inaugural postcard note (n.d.) among Carter's papers mentions "Fair Mount," but Carter and her mother were back in Washington in 1917 too, during Carter's YMCA work, although the canteen job would have postdated Wilson's second inauguration, with the April 1917 declaration of war. Furthermore, to qualify for canteen work, according to Hudson, Carter forged records of a false birth date, thereafter obscuring family records: Carter, allegedly born in 1895 (twenty-one and twenty-two during World War I), would probably not have been underage for the YMCA. Perhaps she was more nearly Stone's contemporary.

58. Interview with Peyton W. Williams, Jr., 5 June 1978.

59. Unless otherwise indicated, basic scholastic information here derives from Stone's transcript, *The Course of Study in Yale College and in particular The Prospectus of Courses Offered to the Sophomore, Junior, and Senior Classes for the Year, 1913–1914*, 12 March 1913, and Yale *Banner and Pot Pourri*, 1913–14, Yale University Library. PS studied French either with medievalist Raymond T. Hill or Horatio E. Smith, later general editor of Scribner's French series and editor-in-chief of the *Romantic Review*. The course, on nineteenth-century authors, probably resembled the pedagogy of the Holt textbook *Advanced French Composition* on which Hill and Smith collaborated in 1916.

60. John Donald Robb, "A Memoir of Yale, 1911 to 1915," *Yale Alumni Monthly* 39 (November 1975): 7.

61. Ibid., 4–7.

62. George Wilson Pierson, *Yale College: An Educational History, 1871–1921* (New Haven, 1952), 281.

63. Minott A. Osborn (ed.), *Life at Yale* (3d ed.; New Haven, 1920), 45; PS to E. Melville Price, 8 January 1953.

64. "Autobiography."

65. Osborn, *Life at Yale*, 42.

66. Henry Tetlow to PS, 9 January 1958.

67. PS memo, 1952: "Several years ago I gave a few things to the Yale Library." The Beinecke Rare Book and Manuscript Library, Yale University, dates the gift February 1947. PS later reiterated that he had given Yale a copy of *The Marble Faun* (e.g., PS to James Meriwether, 19 February 1957). But

in January 1977, Beinecke librarians told Michelle Lamphiere, my research assistant, that the two typescripts were PS's only gifts. William Boozer, *William Faulkner's First Book: "The Marble Faun," Fifty Years Later* (Memphis, 1974), 23–24, says there are two Yale *Marble Fauns*, one "purchased in 1943 . . . [with] no marks of provenance," another the gift of Cole Porter, class of 1913.

68. Osborn, *Life at Yale*, 86.

69. See William Faulkner, *The Sound and the Fury*, new, corrected edition (New York, 1984), 86–88.

70. Emily W. Stone, taped speech, "The Writings of William Faulkner," probably delivered at All Saints Episcopal School, Vicksburg, Miss., where she taught after leaving Oxford in 1964.

71. Yale *Daily News*, 14 April 1918.

72. The clearest written confirmation of PS's prejudices occurs in a sarcastic short correspondence now in the Humanities Research Center at the University of Texas at Austin: Benjamin Hauser: New and Rare Books, New York City, to PS, 5 and 10 November 1931, and PS to Hauser, 13 November 1931. Hauser asked Stone to name his price on his "nice things by William Faulkner"; he had heard about the *Marble Fauns* and "various manuscripts" in Stone's possession; his rich customers were eager for Faulkner material, having "already acquired everything that Faulkner ever did." Stone was selling only the former at $75 each (in that first year of financial crisis). Hauser took umbrage at PS's "huge letter" (7 November), called his price "ridiculous" and "absurd," accused him of encouraging price gouging, and wondered whether Faulkner was aware of the price, "as it seems to me that our conscience would trouble us forever if we asked someone to pay" such a sum. "You must bear in mind not to make ridiculous prices," he concluded. Stone told Hauser that his letter "amused me a great deal. It is so typically Yankee in its ignorance, patronizing arrogance, and discourtesy." Then Phil explained about Faulkner's having suggested the idea, reminding Hauser that the price was still $75, but that there was "no law requiring" him to buy them.

73. Osborn, *Life at Yale*, 15, 87, 43–44.

74. Blotner, *Faulkner*, 161.

75. Brick Row advertisement, Yale *Daily News*, 18 June 1918: "Here it is possible to see the great books in English Literature, in folio and quarto, First Editions, Association Items, Original MS, Autograph Letters, etc. etc. No one is ever asked to purchase. There are quiet nooks at the service of the reader and the Book Shop plays no inconsiderable part in the lives of the thoughtful and bookish undergraduate. The shop will be open during the long vacation and visitors are cordially invited to stop in at this literary retreat to inspect

our shelves." PS's extant Brick Row correspondence (chiefly for 1922 and 1927) is now in the HRC.

76. Stark Young to Howard Phelps Putnam [16 August and 10 November 1915], in Pilkington, *Stark Young*, 60, 72–73; *The Elizabethan Club of Yale University* (New Haven, 1924). Carl P. Rollins was also a member.

77. Pilkington, *Stark Young*, xxiv, note to 169. Hackett (1883–1962) had been a charter member of the *New Republic* editorial board, in 1914; he was also editor of the Chicago *Evening Post*'s *Friday Literary Review*. From 1918 to 1943 he published nine novels, biographies, and studies of his native Ireland.

78. Volume Index, Yale *Daily News*, 1917–18. Club records for that year are missing.

79. Osborn, *Life at Yale*, 30, 43–44.

80. Yale *Daily News*, 8 April 1918.

81. Ibid., 17 March 1914.

82. John Unterecker, "A Yeats Chronology," *A Reader's Guide to William Butler Yeats* (New York, 1959), 298–99. It is clear that PS did attend Yeats's 1914 lecture. One can speculate that Stone and Faulkner's comic encounter with a famous poet occurred instead in 1918, but with Alfred L. Noyes, whose metronomic beat and facile rhyme could easily have provoked their mirth.

83. "Away" is a favorite Yeats word, but PS may be remembering "The Hosting of the Sidhe" from *The Wind Among the Reeds* (1899): "The host is riding from Knocknarea / And over the grave of Clooth-na-Bare; / Caoilte tossing his burning hair, / And Niamh calling *Away, come away* . . ." (lines 1–4), *The Collected Poems of W. B. Yeats* (New York, 1956), 53.

84. If Stone and Faulkner's encounter was with Yeats, and not, as I suspect, with Alfred L. Noyes, or, less likely, John Masefield, then the poem alluded to might be *The Wanderings of Oisin* (1889). See *Collected Poems*, 380, "We will tear out the flaming stones and batter the gateway of brass / and enter, and none sayeth 'No' when there enters the strongly armed guest; / Make clean as a broom cleans, and march on as oxen move over young grass."

85. "Autobiography"; diploma at Freeland & Gafford, Attorneys at Law, Oxford, Miss.

CHAPTER 4. Phil and Bill

1. Phil Stone to Richard P. Adams, 4 October 1961. Excerpts from the letter appear in Susan Snell, "Phil Stone of Yoknapatawpha" (Ph.D. dissertation, University of North Carolina, 1978), 181–82.

2. Interview with Jim Kyle Hudson, Jr., 16 May 1978. Unless otherwise in-

dicated, the Carter-Wohlleben material is from this source or Emily Stone.

3. John B. Cullen, with Floyd C. Watkins, *Old Times in the Faulkner Country* (Chapel Hill, 1961), 74–75. Joseph Blotner, *Faulkner: A Biography* (2 vols.; New York, 1974), 479, note to line 10, also cites Faulkner's variation on "Wohlleben" for a character's name in *Elmer.*

4. *Oxford Eagle,* 22 August 1957, 2 April 1903, and 28 August 1952 (business history for Neilson's department store); advertisement, *Ole Miss,* 1898.

5. Interview with Allie Jean Stone (Mrs. A. S. Scott, Jr.), 9 August 1975.

6. O. B. Emerson to PS, 23 October 1956. The sole extant Balzac volume of PS's library, apparently not from his brother's set, is George Saintsbury's edition of *The Rise and Fall of César Birotteau,* trans. Ellen Marriage (London, 1916), with many underlinings and marginal notes in pencil by PS, now in the William Boozer Collection, Nashville, Tenn. Among the Balzac at Rowan Oak is an 1897–99 set of *La Comédie humaine,* according to Joseph Blotner (comp.), *William Faulkner's Library—A Catalogue* (Charlottesville, 1964), 90–92.

7. Blotner, *Faulkner,* 160.

8. Interview with Jim Kyle Hudson, Jr.

9. Ibid.

10. Interview with Robert J. Farley, February 1976.

11. Interview with Jim Kyle Hudson, Jr.

12. Ibid.

13. Horace Benbow echoes Stone in the remark " 'You see,' he said, 'I lack courage: that was left out of me. The machinery is all here, but it wont RUN.' " William Faulkner, *Sanctuary* (New York, 1931), 11.

14. William Faulkner, "Verse Old and Nascent: A Pilgrimage" (1925), reprinted in Carvel Collins (ed.), *William Faulkner: Early Prose and Poetry* (Boston, 1962), 114.

15. "Phil Stone: An Autobiography," a sixteen-page, third-person narrative penciled at Whitfield, the state mental institution in Jackson, in autumn 1963.

16. Phil Stone, " 'I Know William Faulkner,' " *Eagle,* 16 November 1950. See Malcolm Cowley, *The Faulkner-Cowley File: Letters and Memories, 1944–1962* (New York, 1966), 153.

17. PS to Richard P. Adams, 1 June 1962.

18. See William R. Ferris, Jr., "William Faulkner and Phil Stone: An Interview with Emily Stone," *South Atlantic Quarterly* 68 (1969): 536–42.

19. Faulkner, "Verse Old and Nascent," in Collins, *Early Prose and Poetry,* 114, 117. Blotner (*Faulkner's Library,* 69) lists three sets of Keats at Rowan Oak.

20. Robert W. Hamblin and Louis Daniel Brodsky, *Selections from the William Faulkner Collection of Louis Daniel Brodsky: A Descriptive Catalogue* (Charlottesville, 1979), 21.

21. Hamblin and Brodsky, *Faulkner Collection*, 20.

22. See "From Imagism to Symbolism: The Crisis in Culture," in Cleanth Brooks, R. W. B. Lewis, and Robert Penn Warren (eds.), *American Literature: The Makers and the Making* (2 vols.; New York, 1973), 2:2050.

23. Interview with Louis Daniel Brodsky, 29 June 1980.

24. Stone's annotations are in a book from his library, *Others for 1919: An Anthology of New Verse*, edited by Alfred Kreymborg. See pages 132, 103, 68.

25. Emily Stone to Carvel Collins, 1 July 1964.

26. Now in the William Boozer Collection.

27. The book is inscribed 8 March 1917 by PS. See Hamblin and Brodsky, *Faulkner Collection*, 20.

28. The extant copy, in the William Boozer Collection, was inscribed for Faulkner by Stone on 25 September 1917. In PS's memo to his children inside the book, dated Christmas Eve, 1953 (?), he explained having requested the return of the book, for the "reasons" mentioned below.

29. PS to Louis Cochran, 28 December 1931, reprinted in James B. Meriwether, "Early Notices of Faulkner by Phil Stone and Louis Cochran," *Mississippi Quarterly* 17 (Winter 1964): 141.

30. Willard Huntington Wright, *The Creative Will: Studies in the Philosophy and the Syntax of Aesthetics* (New York, 1916), 58, 224, 205–6, 183, 199, 77, 199.

31. Ibid., 205, 232, 225, 204, 76, 78, 144.

32. Phil Stone, Preface to *The Marble Faun*, in William Faulkner, *"The Marble Faun" and "A Green Bough"* (1924 and 1933; rpr. New York, 1965), 8.

33. Blotner, *Faulkner*, 126.

34. Collins, *Early Prose and Poetry*, 27.

35. Interview with Judge Richard Thomas, 15 May 1978.

36. Phil Stone, "William Faulkner: The Man and His Work," *Oxford Magazine* 1 (November 1934), reprinted in Meriwether, "Early Notices," 163–64.

37. PS to Carvel Collins, 8 March 1957; Collins to PS, 4 March 1957.

38. *Ole Miss*, 1915.

39. Interview with Emily Whitehurst Stone, 28 June 1973.

40. PS to Harry Boyle, 12 October 1953.

41. Harry Boyle to PS, c. 12 October 1953; interview with Jim Kyle Hudson, Jr.; group photograph, probably for DKE, owned by Hudson, Memphis, Tenn.

42. Interview with D. R. Johnson, 16 March 1976; *Ole Miss*, 1916.

43. Interview with Jim Kyle Hudson, Jr.

44. Interview with Robert J. Farley.

45. Blotner, *Faulkner*, 179. But see Thomas E. Lamar, "Debits and Cred-

its in Faulkner's Hand Found in Old Bank Ledgers," *Faulkner Newsletter and Yoknapatawpha Review*, 1 (July–September 1981), 1, 3. Lamar discovered no evidence of Faulkner's employment in the First National Bank ledgers until January–30 March 1918, although newsletter editor William Boozer notes that some of the earlier documents may have been destroyed.

46. Blotner, *Faulkner*, 277; interview with Jim Kyle Hudson, Jr.

47. Stark Young, "New Year's Craw," *New Republic*, 12 January 1938, p. 283. Oddly, Faulkner's 13 February 1938 note to Young, wherein he enclosed "the autograph" (?), makes no mention of Young's article, according to Mrs. Lois B. Garcia, Research Associate, Humanities Research Center, University of Texas at Austin.

48. Stark Young to Eldon J. Hoar, 25 November 1950, in John Pilkington (ed.), *Stark Young, A Life in the Arts: Letters, 1900–1962* (2 vols.; Baton Rouge, 1975), 1155–56. See also Young to Julian Huxley, 27 November [1950], in Pilkington, *Stark Young*, 1157.

49. Stark Young, *The Pavilion: Of People and Times Remembered, Of Stories and Places* (New York, 1951), 59; PS to Alan R. Frederiksen, 21 June 1962.

50. Pilkington, *Stark Young*, note to 146, 161, xxiv.

51. Pilkington, *Stark Young*, xxiii–iv, note to 60; George Wilson Pierson, *Yale College: An Educational History, 1871–1921* (New Haven, 1952), 346, 361; Kelley, *Yale*, 312.

52. Stark Young to Howard Phelps Putnam [2 September 1915], in Pilkington, *Stark Young*, 63–64.

CHAPTER 5. New Haven and the Great War

1. Brooks Mather Kelley, *Yale: A History* (New Haven, 1974), 312; George Wilson Pierson, *Yale College: An Educational History, 1871–1921* (New Haven, 1952), 282, 355–56, 347.

2. Pierson, *Yale*, 427, 359–60. PS later ordered Tinker's *Boswell* from the Brick Row, according to Joseph Blotner (comp.), *William Faulkner's Library— A Catalogue* (Charlottesville, 1964), 126. Other Brick Row officers were Howell Cheney, '92, M.A. 1909, Roswell P. Angier (later dean of freshmen), and secretary-treasurer Charlton Dowes Cooksey, according to Yale *Banner and Pot Pourri*, 1918.

3. Pierson, 361–65. PS remembered a campus witticism about MacLeish, "the only line-backing poet known to science."

4. Details of PS's curriculum and grades come from his transcript and from *School of Law Bulletin of Yale University, 1917–1918*.

5. PS to *Yale Alumni Weekly*, 7 January 1927; PS to Mrs. James Stone, 11 June 1917.

6. Robert W. Hamblin and Louis Daniel Brodsky, *Selections from the William Faulkner Collection of Louis Daniel Brodsky: A Descriptive Catalogue* (Charlottesville, 1979), 20.

7. Pierson, *Yale*, 449, 465ff., 677; Kelley, *Yale*, 349.

8. Pierson, *Yale*, 465, 464, 458.

9. Ibid., 465–66.

10. Ibid., 449, 466, 467.

11. Hamblin and Brodsky, *Faulkner Collection*, 20–21.

12. Pierson, *Yale*, 467, 468; Minott A. Osborn (ed.), *Life at Yale* (New Haven, 1920), 44; Pierson, *Yale*, 288, 464; Osborn, *Life at Yale*, 3; Kelley, *Yale*, 355.

13. PS to Mrs. James Stone, 11 June 1917.

14. Kelley, *Yale*, 355.

15. *Selective Service Regulations* (2d ed.; Washington, 1918), 349, 353, 356.

16. William F. Holmes, *The White Chief: James Kimble Vardaman* (Baton Rouge, 1970), 347.

17. Frederick Palmer, *Bliss, Peacemaker* (1934; rpr. Freeport, N.Y., 1970), 105, 179.

18. PS to James Stone, Sr., 1918, with Taft's card, and PS memo to his son, January 1944; PS to Mrs. James Stone, later dated by PS, "Feb. 1918."

19. "Phil Stone: An Autobiography," a sixteen-page, third-person narrative penciled at Whitfield, the state mental institution in Jackson, in autumn 1963; Joseph Blotner, *Faulkner: A Biography* (2 vols.; New York, 1974), 192.

20. Dunbar Rowland, *History of Mississippi: The Heart of the South* (4 vols.; Chicago, 1925), 3:170, 173.

21. Interview with Philip Thornton, Jr., 16 March 1976.

22. Blotner, *Faulkner*, 235. See excerpts from PS's correspondence with gambler Lee Brown in chapter 6.

23. *Ole Miss*, 1917; Blotner, *Faulkner*, 180.

24. *Ole Miss*, 1918; Blotner, *Faulkner*, 352.

25. Interview with Jim Kyle Hudson, Jr., 16 May 1976.

26. Hamblin and Brodsky, *Faulkner Collection*, 21.

27. *Ole Miss*, 1918.

28. Pierson, *Yale*, 470; Kelley, *Yale*, 252.

29. PS to James Stone, Sr., 1918, with Taft's card.

30. Yale *Banner and Pot Pourri*, 1918.

31. Pierson, *Yale*, 364; Carl P. Rollins to PS, 14 October 1931, and PS to Rollins, 17 October 1931, Humanities Research Center, University of Texas at Austin.

32. Enclosure with PS to Four Seas, 5 November 1924, HRC.

33. PS to Mrs. James Stone, later dated by PS, "Feb. 1918."

34. "Autobiography."

35. Interview with Alice James Gatchell (Mrs. Kenneth P. Gatchell), 14 August 1975.

36. "Autobiography"; PS to George Thatcher, 8 October 1957.

37. Blotner, *Faulkner*, 196–97. PS never mentioned to his wife having telephoned Maud Falkner, however.

38. "Autobiography." Similar details of Faulkner's grooming eccentricities appear in PS's anecdote of Faulkner's briefly sharing Stark Young's New York apartment in 1921.

39. Carvel Collins (ed.), *William Faulkner: Early Prose and Poetry* (Boston, 1962), 4.

40. "Autobiography"; Emily W. Stone, "The Writings of William Faulkner," taped speech probably delivered in the mid-1960s at All Saints Episcopal School, Vicksburg, Miss.

41. Yale *Daily News*, 9 April, 11 May, 14 April 1918; Kelley, *Yale*, 353.

42. Yale *Daily News*, 4 June, 14 and 17 April 1918.

43. Two almost identical versions of the anecdote appear in PS to William Faulkner, 10 April 1953, and to Carl P. Rollins, 4 March 1959. Discrepancies are noted in the text.

44. The only written version of the elaborate enlistment stories below is PS's autobiography, although his wife checked many details with Stone in a taped interview at Whitfield. Her notes from that interview of 2 November 1963 are among the Phil Stone Papers.

45. Blotner, *Faulkner*, 207.

46. Ibid., 206–7.

47. According to Collins (*Early Prose and Poetry*, 4), Faulkner left on 8 July 1918.

48. Blotner, *Faulkner's Library*, 77.

49. Blotner, *Faulkner*, note page 43.

50. *Selective Service Regulations*, 210.

51. PS memo to his son, 8 March 1945; *Oxford Eagle*, 5 June 1902, and 11 June 1903.

52. Hamblin and Brodsky, *Faulkner Collection*, 21. As was his custom, PS noted the date he completed the novel on the last page.

53. PS to Glenn O. Carey, 5 April and 20 February 1950.

54. Interview with Robert J. Farley.

55. PS to Glenn O. Carey, 5 April 1950. But see Blotner, *Faulkner*, 232. Stone telescopes several events in the Carey letter.

CHAPTER 6. The Lawyer and the Poet

1. Joseph Blotner, *Faulkner: A Biography* (2 vols.; New York, 1974), 248.

2. "Phil Stone: An Autobiography," a sixteen-page, third-person narrative penciled at Whitfield, the state mental institution in Jackson, in autumn 1963.

3. PS to Glenn O. Carey, 21 January 1950; William Faulkner, *Flags in the Dust,* ed. Douglas Day (New York, 1973), 193.

4. "Autobiography."

5. According to his clerk and partner T. H. Freeland III, Phil Stone won twenty-seven reversals on appeals of only one judge's decisions; furthermore, Stone "was successful in the Supreme Court in four out of six cases he took there, a phenomenal record." Freeland to Susan Snell, 26 July 1976.

6. Interviews with Robert J. Farley, February 1976, and W. H. Anderson, 14 July 1976.

7. Interviews with Mr. and Mrs. A. S. Scott, Jr., 9 August 1975, and W. M. Reed, 15 August 1975.

8. Dunbar Rowland, *History of Mississippi: The Heart of the South* (4 vols.; Chicago, 1925), 3:170–73.

9. Ibid.

10. Boyce House, "$500,000 Factory Begins Operations," Lumber Vertical File news clipping, dateline Charleston, 7 September 1919, Special Collections, Mitchell Memorial Library, Mississippi State University.

11. PS to Robert Coughlan, 15 April 1954; interviews with W. E. Stone V, 10 August 1975, and Philip Thornton, Jr., 16 March 1976.

12. "Autobiography"; PS to A. L. Williams, 2 March 1954; interview with Mrs. A. S. Scott, Jr.

13. Boyce House, "$500,000 Factory Begins Operations"; interview with Philip Thornton, Jr.

14. Interview with Philip Thornton, Jr.

15. Ibid.; interview with W. E. Stone V.

16. William Faulkner, "Verse Old and Nascent: A Pilgrimage" (1925), rpr. in Carvel Collins (ed.), *William Faulkner: Early Prose and Poetry* (Boston, 1962), 116.

17. Blotner, *Faulkner,* 245–46.

18. John Pilkington (ed.), *Stark Young, A Life in the Arts: Letters, 1900–1962* (2 vols.; Baton Rouge, 1975), note to 89.

19. PS to Harrison Smith, 2 June 1959, published in *Saturday Review,* 27 June 1959, 23.

20. Collins, *Early Prose and Poetry,* 6; Maud Morrow Brown, "An Old Friend Remembers Fondly," in James W. Webb and A. Wigfall Green (eds.), *William Faulkner of Oxford* (Baton Rouge, 1965), 38.

21. Edith Brown Douds, "Recollections of William Faulkner and the Bunch," in Webb and Green, *Faulkner of Oxford*, 50–51. Although the origin of the name remains obscure, a Drusilla Brahan appears among the 1918 *Ole Miss* beauties.

22. Blotner, *Faulkner*, 252–53.

23. Ibid., 256–57; *Ole Miss*, 1916 and 1917; Mrs. Herbert Ray to Susan Snell, 9 August 1976.

24. See Robert W. Hamblin and Louis Daniel Brodsky, *Selections from the William Faulkner Collection of Louis Daniel Brodsky: A Descriptive Catalogue* (Charlottesville, 1979), 31–34.

25. Blotner, *Faulkner*, 264; Stark Young to Julia Young Robertson [2 May 1949], in Pilkington, *Stark Young*, 1090.

26. PS to James Meriwether, 19 February 1957.

27. William Boozer Collection; Hamblin and Brodsky, *Faulkner Collection*, 21.

28. Blotner, *Faulkner*, 264 passim.

29. Phil Stone, "William Faulkner and His Neighbors," *Saturday Review*, 19 September 1942, 12, reprinted in *The Saturday Review Treasury* (New York, 1957), 230–32.

30. Blotner, *Faulkner*, 283–84; Jack Cofield, *William Faulkner: The Cofield Collection* (Oxford, 1978), 60; PS to R. P. Adams, 14 December 1960.

31. William Faulkner, *The Marionettes*, ed. Noel E. Polk (Charlottesville, 1977), x–xiii; interview with Jim Kyle Hudson, Jr., 16 May 1978; PS's "Burned Papers," Humanities Research Center, University of Texas at Austin. See also Ben Wasson, *A Memory of Marionettes* (Oxford, 1975), iii–viii.

32. Blotner, *Faulkner*, 287.

33. William Boozer Collection.

34. Emily Stone to Carvel Collins, 1 July 1964. Among the forty sheets she describes, two Faulkner poems were dated 24 and 29 October 1924.

35. Interviews with W. E. Stone V and Mrs. A. S. Scott, Jr.

36. "The Order for the Burial of William Robert Boles, April 29, 1954" is among the Stone Papers.

37. Interviews with W. E. Stone V and Mrs. A. S. Scott, Jr.

38. See Ilse Dusoir Lind, "Faulkner's Relationship to Jews: A Beginning," in *New Directions in Faulkner Studies: Faulkner and Yoknapatawpha, 1983*, edited by Doreen Fowler and Ann J. Abadie (Jackon, 1984), 119–42. Lind was among the scholars the Stones talked to at length.

39. See William Faulkner's note to Mrs. W. E. Stone IV (Myrtle Stone) [postmarked 5 September 1922], in Joseph Blotner (ed.), *Selected Letters of William Faulkner* (New York, 1977), 4.

40. John Faulkner, *My Brother Bill: An Affectionate Reminiscence* (New York, 1963), 146. In Myrtle Stone's copy of this memoir, she identified the secretary as Stegbauer, though spelling the name differently from that in the text, which follows PS's mailing list to Four Seas, 5 November 1924, HRC.

41. See Carvel Collins's Introduction to William Faulkner, *Mayday* (Notre Dame, 1978), 17–18: "When she did not respond to Faulkner's affection he felt considerable emotional distress. But he cured himself, he told Stone, by deliberately developing mental pictures of that otherwise idealized person engaged in the least romantic regularly repeated acts of our species."

42. C. P. J. Mooney (ed.), *The Mid-South and Its Builders* (Memphis, 1920), 241.

43. Ibid., 883; Dunbar Rowland, *Military History of Mississippi, 1803–1898* (1908; rpr. Spartanburg, S.C., 1978), 547.

44. Interview with Jim Kyle Hudson, Jr.

45. William Faulkner to Estelle Lake [received 2 September 1919], in Blotner, *Selected Letters*, 4.

46. Interview with Jim Kyle Hudson, Jr.

47. Unless otherwise indicated, Memphis details here derive from the Sesquicentennial Edition of the Memphis *Commercial Appeal*, 25 May 1969.

48. "Autobiography."

49. Harry Abernathy, " 'New World' Scorned by Clarksdale Elite," *Clarksdale Press Register*, 14–15 August 1982. See also Harry Abernathy, "Issaquena Avenue: Colorful Past a Fading Memory," *Clarksdale Press Register*, 11 April 1987.

50. "Autobiography"; T. H. Freeland to Susan Snell, 26 July 1976.

51. Lee [Dolph] Brown (born 1890, according to HRC card) to PS, 3 and 19 February 1922, PS to Brown, 28 February 1922, HRC.

52. Henry James, *The Wings of the Dove* (1902; rpr. Columbus, Ohio, 1970), 42.

53. PS to Robert Coughlan, 15 April 1954; interview with Philip Thornton, Jr.; Malcolm Cowley, *The Faulkner-Cowley File: Letters and Memories, 1944–1962* (New York, 1966), 108; Blotner, *Faulkner*, note to 292, quoting William Faulkner, "Mississippi," *Holiday*, April 1954, 39.

54. Interviews with W. E. Stone V and Mrs. A. S. Scott, Jr.

55. Rowland, *History of Mississippi*, 3:170.

56. William Lincoln Giles, "Agricultural Revolution, 1890–1970," in Richard Aubrey McLemore (gen. ed.), *A History of Mississippi* (2 vols.; Hattiesburg, 1973), 2:197.

57. Blotner, *Faulkner*, 238.

58. Ibid., 305, 313–14; Rowland, *History of Mississippi*, 3:170–73.

59. Emily W. Stone, "The Writings of William Faulkner," taped speech probably delivered in the mid-1960s at All Saints Episcopal School, Vicksburg, Miss.; Phil Stone, "William Faulkner and His Neighbors," 12; Blotner, *Faulkner*, 294.

60. Stark Young to Julian Huxley, 10 October [1921], Young to Mary Williams Goldmann, 25 July [1921], and Young to Julian and Juliette Huxley, 20 December [1921], in Pilkington, *Stark Young*, 158, 157, 163; Blotner, *Faulkner*, 313; Stark Young, *The Pavilion: Of People and Times Remembered, of Stories and Places* (New York, 1951), 59–60; Carvel Collins (ed.), *William Faulkner: New Orleans Sketches* (Rev. ed.; New York, 1968), xii. See Collins, Introduction to *Mayday*, 10–11, and Elizabeth Anderson and Gerald R. Kelly, *Miss Elizabeth: A Memoir* (Boston, 1969), 46, 32.

61. PS to William B. Wisdom, 23 April 1951: "I got Stark Young to put Bill up."

62. Blotner, *Faulkner*, 316; Stark Young to Mary Williams Goldmann, 25 July [1921], and Young to Julian and Juliette Huxley, 20 December [1921], in Pilkington, *Stark Young*, 157, 163; Collins, Introduction to *Mayday*, 10–11; Anderson and Kelly, *Miss Elizabeth*, 27, 39ff.; William Spratling, "Chronicle of a Friendship: William Faulkner in New Orleans," *Texas Quarterly* 9 (Spring 1966), 35. Perhaps PS ordered Katrina Carter's Christmas volumes that year from New York: John Masefield, *King Cole* (1921), and Joseph Hergesheimer, *San Cristóbal de la Habana* (1920). See Hamblin and Brodsky, *Faulkner Collection*, 21–22.

63. Interview with D. R. Johnson, 16 March 1976; Blotner, *Faulkner*, 318; James B. Meriwether, "Early Notices of Faulkner by Phil Stone and Louis Cochran," *Mississippi Quarterly* 17 (Winter 1964): 144, 139; Blotner, *Faulkner*, 325–27.

64. John K. Bettersworth, *Mississippi: A History* (Austin, 1959), 453.

65. B. P. Harrison to PS, 4 May 1922, HRC.

66. *Oxford Eagle*, 12 January 1922; Blotner, *Faulkner*, 257–60; M. P. Sturdivant to James Stone, Sr., 1 February 1931; Ben B. McNew, "Banking, 1890–1970," in McLemore, *History of Mississippi*, 2:318–19.

67. *Eagle*, 26 January 1922; Al DeLacey to PS, 27 January 1922, HRC.

CHAPTER 7. *The Marble Faun*

1. PS to William Faulkner, 10 January 1922, and to Brick Row, 18 February 1922, Humanities Research Center, University of Texas at Austin; Joseph Blotner, *Faulkner: A Biography* (2 vols.; New York, 1974), 307; Carvel Collins

(ed.), *William Faulkner: New Orleans Sketches* (Rev. ed.; New York, 1968), xvi.

2. PS to Van Kincannon, Jr., 10 January 1922, HRC; PS to John McClure, 28 March 1922, HRC; Emily Stone to Carvel Collins, 1 July 1964. See also Robert W. Hamblin and Louis Daniel Brodsky, *Selections from the William Faulkner Collection of Louis Daniel Brodsky: A Descriptive Catalogue* (Charlottesville, 1979), 39.

3. E. A. Robinson to PS, 7 March 1922, found in Stone's single extant issue of *Poetry: A Magazine of Verse* 24 (August 1924), William Boozer Collection. PS's Robinson books burned with the house.

4. Edith Brown Douds, "Recollections of William Faulkner and the Bunch," in James W. Webb and A. Wigfall Green (eds.), *William Faulkner of Oxford* (Baton Rouge, 1965), 50.

5. PS's Brick Row correspondence is now in the HRC. His orders are listed in Appendix, Joseph Blotner (comp.), *William Faulkner's Library—A Catalogue* (Charlottesville, 1964), 123–27.

6. Carvel Collins (ed.), *William Faulkner: Early Prose and Poetry* (Boston, 1962), 101–3. See Hamblin and Brodsky, *Faulkner Collection*, 22.

7. PS to R. P. Adams, 4 October 1961; Blotner, *Faulkner's Library*, 76–77, 125; Richard Ellmann, *James Joyce* (Rev. ed.; New York, 1982), 441–42; R. P. Adams, *Faulkner: Myth and Motion* (Princeton, 1968), 58; PS to Elizabeth Y. Grosch, 19 July 1962. Except for the Greek orders, evidence of Stone's having introduced Faulkner so early to Joyce's " 'mythical method' " is circumstantial. The Frazer book has not survived. Faulkner's *Ulysses* was issued in January 1924, and Stone's extant Joyce orders are dated January 1926. The only confirmation of Stone's anecdotal claims is in the necessarily suspect 1960s letters.

8. PS to John McClure, 28 March 1922, HRC; Blotner, *Faulkner*, 337, 253, 322–23 and notes, 332; Joseph Blotner (ed.), *Uncollected Stories of William Faulkner* (New York, 1979), 495ff. and notes; Collins, *Early Prose and Poetry*, 90–92.

9. PS to Brick Row, 18 February 1922, HRC; PS to Boni & Liveright, 18 November 1926, HRC; O. B. Emerson to PS, 23 October 1956.

10. O. B. Emerson to PS, 23 October 1956; Willard Huntington Wright, *The Creative Will: Studies in the Philosophy and the Syntax of Aesthetics* (New York, 1916), 284, 45, 98–101, 44–45.

11. Phil Stone, Preface to *The Marble Faun*, in William Faulkner, *"The Marble Faun" and "A Green Bough"* (1924 and 1933; rpr. New York, 1965), 6–7; PS to Louis Cochran, 28 December 1931, reprinted in James B. Meriwether, "Early Notices of Faulkner by Phil Stone and Louis Cochran," *Mississippi Quarterly* 17 (Winter 1964): 139–40. Wright's words, syntax, and ideas

also literally recur in Stone's censure of Faulkner's mature prose style. "The highest type of literary style . . . should vary with every thought or fact expressed," according to Wright (p. 153). "What is commonly termed 'style' in literature is little more than an idiosyncrasy of expression—a mannerism. . . . A great stylist can write suavely, simply and delicately, as well as robustly, complexly and brutally" (p. 154). Faulkner's "style which makes wonderful reading sometimes as to sonorous prose is really not a style in the proper sense but merely a personal mannerism," Phil echoed in his Cowley letter (see below). "As Willard Huntington Wright pointed out, the great ones like Shakespeare and Balzac varied their styles and wrote either gently, robustly or dryly as the subject matter dictated, thus adapting the style to the subject."

12. PS to Malcolm Cowley, 30 April 1945.

13. PS to Carl P. Rollins, 17 October 1931, HRC.

14. PS to Brick Row, 30 September 1922, Al DeLacey to PS, 29 March 1922, PS to Brick Row, 18 November 1922, Pauline A. Clark to PS, 7 December 1922, HRC.

15. Blotner, *Faulkner*, 347; Blotner, *Uncollected Stories*, 699; Hamblin and Brodsky, *Faulkner Collection*, 22; Blotner, *Faulkner's Library*, 20, 15. With no Faulkner poetry volume actually written in 1923, one is tempted to interpret a reference to the lost work in Faulkner's comment: "It was 1923 and I wrote a book and discovered that my doom, fate, was to keep on writing books . . ." Foreword to *The Faulkner Reader* (New York, 1959), viii. For details of the Cabell influence on Faulkner, especially John McClure's part in it, see Carvel Collins, Introduction to *Mayday*, 15–23.

16. Phil Stone, "William Faulkner: The Man and His Work," reprinted in Meriwether, "Early Notices," 162–63.

17. Calvin S. Brown, Jr., "Billy Faulkner, My Boyhood Friend," in Webb and Green, *Faulkner of Oxford*, 42–45; Blotner, *Faulkner*, 347.

18. Douds, "Recollections," in Webb and Green, *Faulkner of Oxford*, 49–51.

19. William Faulkner, *The Town* (New York, 1957), 180–81ff.

20. William Boozer, *William Faulkner's First Book: "The Marble Faun," Fifty Years Later* (Memphis, 1974), 26–27; Marian D. Chamberlin to Susan Snell, 25 May 1977.

21. PS to Stark Young and Byrne Hackett, 3 July 1926, PS to Frances S. Starks, 13 July 1926, HRC; PS to Marian Davis, 13 July 1926; Hackett to PS, 7 July 1926; Chamberlin to Snell, 25 May 1977.

22. My interview with W. M. Reed, 15 August 1976, is the principal source for this section.

23. W. M. Reed, " 'I Know William Faulkner,' " *Oxford Eagle*, 16 November 1950.

24. See Emily Whitehurst Stone, "Faulkner Gets Started," *Texas Quarterly* 7 (Winter 1965): 144.

25. Boozer, *"The Marble Faun,"* 9; Blotner, *Faulkner*, 347.

26. Blotner, *Faulkner*, 349–50.

27. Nevertheless, the extant books dating from that spring are still fiction: Katrina Carter's birthday gift to Stone, Elinor Wylie's historical novel *Jennifer Lorn: A Sedate Extravaganza*, and his 3 May gift to her, John Masefield's *The Taking of Helen and Other Prose Selections*. See Hamblin and Brodsky, *Faulkner Collection*, 22–23.

28. PS to R. P. Adams, 1 June 1962.

29. PS to Four Seas, 13 May 1924, Four Seas to PS, 17 May 1924, PS to Four Seas, 24 May 1924, HRC; PS to William Van O'Connor, 15 November 1955. Incidentally, although the Stone "k" stenographer had submitted a "Faulkner" story to the *Double Dealer* in 1922, in PS's 1924 Boston letters "k" and "p" inconsistently type the surname as "Falkner" and "Faulkner."

30. Four Seas to PS, 13 June 1924, HRC.

31. PS to Four Seas, 26 June 1924, HRC. Unlike all other sources, PS's 22 May 1946, resume cites his being "a delegate to four [not three] Democratic Conventions." Except for this 26 June 1924 letter, however, no contemporary reference rules out his going to New York in 1924, although it is doubtful that he was away from Oxford for the entire, protracted convention, 24 June–10 July 1924.

32. Blotner, *Faulkner*, 356, 358; Four Seas to PS, 30 June 1924, and PS to Four Seas, 20 August 1924, HRC.

33. Blotner, *Faulkner*, 359.

34. PS to Four Seas, 20 August 1924, HRC.

35. Emily Whitehurst Stone, "Faulkner Gets Started," 145–46.

36. Four Seas to William Faulkner, 13 September 1924, HRC; Blotner, *Faulkner*, 361; Four Seas to PS, 26 August 1924, PS to Four Seas, 29 August 1924, Four Seas telegram to PS, 10 September 1924, PS telegram to Four Seas, 18 September 1924, HRC.

37. Blotner, *Faulkner*, 362; Emily Whitehurst Stone, "Faulkner Gets Started," 146–47; Blotner, *Faulkner*, 366.

38. Phil Stone, "William Faulkner," reprinted in Meriwether, "Early Notices," 150.

39. PS to Four Seas, 24 September 1924, HRC; Stone, Preface to *The Marble Faun*, 6–8.

40. Stark Young to Ella Somerville, 20 February 1935, and Young to Phil Stone, 20 February 1935, in John Pilkington (ed.), *Stark Young, A Life in the Arts: Letters, 1900–1962* (2 vols.; Baton Rouge, 1975), 581–82 and notes.

41. See Phil Stone to Louis Cochran, 28 December 1931, reprinted in Meriwether, "Early Notices," 140: "Besides, if I have to write what good is Bill to me?"

42. Stone, Preface to *The Marble Faun*, 6–8.

43. PS to Four Seas, 24 September 1924, HRC.

44. Four Seas to William Faulkner, 23 September 1924; Four Seas to PS, 29 September 1924, PS to Four Seas, 29 September 1924, HRC.

45. PS to Four Seas, 29 September 1924, HRC.

46. Four Seas to PS, 3 October 1924, Four Seas to William Faulkner, 6 October 1924, PS to Four Seas with enclosures, 5 and 13 October 1924; Four Seas to William Faulkner, 16 October 1924, HRC.

47. PS to Four Seas, 5 November 1924, HRC.

48. Enclosures with PS to Four Seas, 13 October 1924, HRC.

49. PS to *Yale Alumni Weekly*, 15 October 1924, HRC.

50. PS to Four Seas, 19 October 1924, and undated "Dear friends" longhand note, Four Seas to PS, 23 October 1924. Katrina Carter's son owns one version of "Mississippi Hills: My Epitaph" dated 17 October 1924.

51. Blotner, *Faulkner*, 374.

52. PS to Four Seas with enclosures, 5 November 1924, HRC.

53. Ibid.; Blotner, *Faulkner*, 376.

54. PS to Four Seas, 7 November 1924, Four Seas to PS, 10 November 1924, HRC.

55. Blotner, *Faulkner*, 377–78; PS to *Atlantic Monthly*, 13 November 1924, PS telegram to Four Seas, 13 November 1924, HRC.

56. PS to Four Seas, 17 November 1924, PS telegram to Four Seas, 9 December 1924, Four Seas telegram to PS, 9 December 1924, HRC.

57. Blotner, *Faulkner*, 378.

58. Boozer, "*The Marble Faun*," 28.

59. Boozer, "*The Marble Faun*," 26, 22, 29–30, 23, 35. Interview with Pauline A. Clark, 31 August 1975.

60. Blotner, *Faulkner*, 376–78. With his 7 November 1924 letter to Four Seas, PS reverts to "James Stone & Sons" stationery, discontinuing his use of the "James Stone, Oldham, Stone & Stone" letterhead. L. E. Oldham and James Stone, Sr., had dissolved their law partnership, amicably, by autumn 1924.

CHAPTER 8. Distant Company

1. Phil Stone to Four Seas Publishing Co., 29 December 1924 and 2 January 1925, and Faulkner check, Humanities Research Center, University of Texas at Austin.

2. PS to Four Seas, 3 January 1925, HRC; Sanborn Insurance Map of New

Orleans (1908; rev. through 1934), Special Collections, Howard-Tilton Memorial Library, Tulane University; Elizabeth Anderson and Gerald R. Kelly, *Miss Elizabeth: A Memoir* (Boston, 1969), 85. See Carvel Collins (ed.), *William Faulkner: New Orleans Sketches* (Rev. ed.; New York, 1968), xi–xxxiv.

3. Interview with W. H. Anderson (contemporary campus stringer), 14 July 1976; PS to Glenn O. Carey, 21 January 1950: "I took Faulkner down there and got George and John to let him write stuff for the Times-Picayune so that he could make a living and got him with a crowd that was then publishing The Double Dealer." Healy, Ole Miss class of 1926, could have been in regular contact with the news staff from 1922.

4. PS to Four Seas, 13 January 1925, HRC.

5. William Spratling, "Chronicle of a Friendship: William Faulkner in New Orleans," *Texas Quarterly* 9 (Spring 1966): 35; Stark Young to Gladys Coates Hamilton, 19 November 1922, to Sherwood Anderson, 22 June [1923], to Anderson [August 1924], in John Pilkington (ed.), *Stark Young, A Life in the Arts: Letters, 1900–1962* (2 vols.; Baton Rouge, 1975), 176, 192–93, 212–13; Hamilton Basso quoted in Joseph Blotner, *Faulkner: A Biography* (2 vols.; New York, 1974), 393.

6. See Young to Anderson [9 November 1924], in Pilkington, *Stark Young,* 216–17; Young to Anderson [April–May 1925] and telegram to Anderson, 5 June 1925, in the same source, 225–26 and note.

7. Joseph Blotner (comp.), *William Faulkner's Library—A Catalogue* (Charlottesville, 1964), 15; Collins, *New Orleans Sketches,* xviii.

8. Blotner, *Faulkner,* 396; PS to Four Seas, 31 March 1925, and PS to *New Republic,* 16 August 1927, HRC.

9. PS to Glenn O. Carey, 9 February 1950; William Faulkner, "Verse Old and Nascent: A Pilgrimage" (1925), reprinted in Carvel Collins (ed.), *William Faulkner: Early Prose and Poetry* (Boston, 1962), 114; Collins, *New Orleans Sketches,* 138.

10. PS to Glenn O. Carey, 9 February 1950; James B. Meriwether, "Early Notices of Faulkner by Phil Stone and Louis Cochran," *Mississippi Quarterly* 17 (Winter 1964): 140.

11. Blotner, *Faulkner,* 388–89; Anderson and Kelly, *Miss Elizabeth,* 85.

12. PS to Carvel Collins, 16 August 1954; James K. Feibleman, "Literary New Orleans Between World Wars," *Southern Review* n.s., 1 (1965), 706–7.

13. Collins, *New Orleans Sketches,* xix; Anderson and Kelly, *Miss Elizabeth,* 85; Spratling, "Chronicle," 35.

14. PS to Four Seas, 13 January 1925, HRC.

15. Four Seas to PS, 16 January 1925, and PS to Four Seas, 19 January 1925, HRC.

16. PS check and Four Seas to PS, 10 January 1925, HRC.

17. *Oxford Eagle*, 15 January 1925.

18. Interview with Jim Kyle Hudson, Jr., 16 May 1978; *Eagle*, 22 January 1925.

19. *Eagle*, 15 January 1925; Blotner, *Faulkner*, 390; PS to R. P. Adams, 1 June 1962.

20. Blotner, *Faulkner*, 390.

21. Collins, *New Orleans Sketches*, xix; PS to Carvel Collins, 14 December 1953. Stone remembered a rate of five dollars each. He was amused at the first reprinting of the 1925 sketches: "They are certainly not worth publishing. John McClure and George Healy, at my request, got this work for Bill."

22. PS check and Monte Cooper to PS, 7 February 1925, HRC.

23. Quoted in Blotner, *Faulkner*, 393.

24. Carvel Collins, "To Whom It May Concern," 9 April 1964, for a Stone *Marble Faun* sale; William Boozer, *William Faulkner's First Book: "The Marble Faun," Fifty Years Later* (Memphis, 1974), 26, 21, 19, 25, 28, 35, 36, 14; PS checks, HRC. Stone's "Oxford" inscription to Furr dated 6 January 1925 is suspect in light of the other evidence placing him in New Orleans then.

25. Blotner, *Faulkner*, 397–98; poem fragment in HRC; George W. Healy, Jr., "No Beck and Call for Bill," in James W. Webb and A. Wigfall Green (eds.), *William Faulkner of Oxford* (Baton Rouge, 1965), 59.

26. Blotner, *Faulkner*, 400; Meriwether, "Early Notices," 138.

27. Blotner, *Faulkner*, 400–401; PS to Carvel Collins, 16 August 1954.

28. Blotner, *Faulkner*, 406; PS to Four Seas, 31 March 1925, HRC.

29. Blotner, *Faulkner*, 406, 415; Pilkington, *Stark Young*, 160; Young to Sherwood Anderson [April–May 1925], Young to Maxwell Perkins, 26 December [1922], to Perkins [January 1923], to Perkins, 7 February 1923, in Pilkington, *Stark Young*, 225, 242, 180–83.

30. PS to Four Seas, 18 April 1925, HRC.

31. Blotner, *Faulkner*, 402ff., 430; James B. Meriwether, "Faulkner's Essays on Anderson," in George H. Wolfe (ed.), *Faulkner: Fifty Years After "The Marble Faun"* (University, Ala., 1976), 167.

32. Blotner, *Faulkner*, 430–31; Meriwether, "Anderson," 177; Collins, *New Orleans Sketches*, xxxi.

33. Faulkner, "Verse Old and Nascent," in Collins, *Early Prose and Poetry*, 115; quoted in Blotner, *Faulkner*, 422–23; PS to Four Seas, 18 April 1925, HRC.

34. PS to Judith S. Bond, Curator, Modern Poetry Library, 18 January 1955.

35. PS to Four Seas, 28 April 1925, and Four Seas to PS, 8 May 1925, HRC.

36. Collins, *New Orleans Sketches*, xxi.

37. Blotner, *Faulkner*, 432, 439; Edith Brown Douds, "Recollections of William Faulkner and the Bunch," in Webb and Green, *Faulkner of Oxford*, 51; Blotner, *Faulkner*, 439; PS to Glenn O. Carey, 9 February 1950.

38. Blotner, *Faulkner*, 433, 439.

39. Interviews with Mrs. A. S. Scott, Jr., 9 August 1975, and W. E. Stone V, 10 August 1975; W. E. Stone V to Susan Snell, 31 July 1982.

40. Blotner, *Faulkner*, 435.

41. PS to Robert Coughlan, 15 April 1954. Stone had forgotten Orbrey Street's debunking the W. C. Falkner epitaph story in 1927 (see below) and was incredulous when Collins's visit to the Hindman graveyard proved the Stone anecdote untrue.

42. The correspondence burned with the house.

43. Edwin R. Holmes to PS, 27 October 1953; Boozer, *"The Marble Faun,"* 33, 30, 23.

44. Blotner, *Faulkner*, 439–40, 442.

45. William F. Holmes, *The White Chief: James Kimble Vardaman* (Baton Rouge, 1970), 380; John K. Bettersworth, *Mississippi: A History* (Austin, 1959), 413.

46. See Blotner, *Faulkner*, 346–47.

47. Interview with W. H. Anderson, 14 July 1976; *Eagle*, 16 December 1954, 19 March 1953, and 15 January 1925.

48. Blotner, *Faulkner*, 446ff., 450; Sherwood Anderson to Phil Stone, 17 August 1925, in Howard Mumford Jones, with Walter B. Rideout (eds.), *The Letters of Sherwood Anderson* (Boston, 1953), 145–46; Stark Young to Maxwell Perkins, 7 February 1923, in Pilkington, *Stark Young*, 183.

49. PS to Four Seas, 10 August 1925, and Four Seas to PS, 14 August 1925, HRC; Meriwether, "Early Notices," 163; Phil Stone, Preface to *The Marble Faun*, reprinted in William Faulkner, *"The Marble Faun" and "A Green Bough"* (1924 and 1933; rpr. New York, 1965), 8.

50. Blotner, *Faulkner*, 467; William Faulkner to Mrs. M. C. Falkner, 7 and 15 October 1925, in Joseph Blotner (ed.), *Selected Letters of William Faulkner* (New York, 1977), 28–29, 31.

51. William Faulkner to Mrs. M. C. Falkner [postmarked 10 September 1925] and 15 October 1925, in Blotner, *Letters*, 21, 31; Blotner, *Faulkner*, 448, 452.

52. Blotner, *Faulkner*, 477–78, 481; PS to Four Seas, 6 November 1925, HRC.

53. Two copies of the letter (with only typographical differences) and the poem are among the Phil Stone Papers, HRC. See James B. Meriwether (ed.), *William Faulkner: An Exhibition of Manuscripts* (Austin, 1959), 6.

54. Meriwether, "Early Notices," 139.

55. PS to Alan R. Fredericksen, 21 June 1962.

56. See William Faulkner to Mrs. M. C. Falkner, 3 October 1925, in Blotner, *Letters*, 28.

57. Blotner, *Faulkner*, 492.

58. Blotner, *Faulkner's Library*, 77; PS to Brick Row, 12 January 1926, PS to Brick Row, 13 February 1926, HRC. Although Blotner (*Faulkner*, 352) accepts Faulkner's "Rowan Oak. 1924" inscription to date Faulkner's acquisition of the January 1924 printing of *Ulysses*, a 1925 New Orleans or Paris purchase seems more likely.

59. Blotner, *Faulkner*, 494.

60. Ibid., 503–4; PS to B. G. Lowrey, 9 and 20 March 1926, Lowrey to PS, 24 March 1926, and PS check, marked "Loan," dated 17 March 1926, HRC.

61. Blotner, *Faulkner*, 505–6; PS to Boni & Liveright, 21 April and 15 May 1926, John S. Clapp to PS, 18 May 1926, PS to Boni & Liveright, 21 May 1926, Boni & Liveright to PS, 19 May 1926, PS to Boni & Liveright, 22 May 1926, HRC.

62. [William Faulkner] to Mrs. [sic] Horace Liveright, 4 June 1926, HRC.

63. PS to Glenn O. Carey, 9 February 1950.

64. Blotner, *Faulkner*, 506–7; PS to Byrne Hackett and Stark Young, both 3 July 1926, PS to Frances S. Starks, 13 July 1926, HRC; Stark Young to Julian Huxley, 24 July [1926], in Pilkington, *Stark Young*, 251.

65. William Faulkner to Helen Baird [August 1926], in Blotner, *Letters*, 33; Blotner, *Faulkner*, 523.

66. Blotner, *Faulkner*, 521; William Faulkner to Robert K. Haas [received 22 March 1939], in Blotner, *Letters*, 111.

67. PS to Boni & Liveright, 23 August 1926, John S. Clapp to PS, 27 August 1926, HRC.

68. Blotner, *Faulkner*, 524.

69. Boni & Liveright to PS, 27 September and 8 November 1926, PS to Boni & Liveright, 10 November 1926, Boni & Liveright to PS, 16 November 1926, PS to Boni & Liveright, 26 November 1926, HRC.

70. Blotner, *Faulkner*, 534–36.

71. PS to Brick Row, 11 January 1927, HRC.

72. Brick Row Statement to James Stone, 27 December 1926, Brick Row to James Stone, 23 December 1926, Brick Row to PS, 8 January 1927, PS to Brick Row, 11 January 1927, HRC.

73. PS to Carl Rollins, 27 January 1927, HRC; Yale Alumni Records.

74. PS to Carl Rollins, 27 January 1927, HRC.

75. William Faulkner to Horace Liveright, 18 February 1927, in Blotner, *Letters*, 34–35. Faulkner's references were to *Flags* and stories later incorporated as *These Thirteen*, according to Blotner.

76. William Faulkner to William Stanley Braithwaite [February 1927], in Blotner, *Letters*, 35–36; Robert W. Hamblin and Louis Daniel Brodsky, *Selec-*

tions from the William Faulkner Collection of Louis Daniel Brodsky: A Descriptive Catalogue (Charlottesville, 1979), 20; PS to Robert Daniel, 6 April 1942, in L. D. Brodsky Collection.

CHAPTER 9. The Major Fiction

1. Joseph Blotner, *Faulkner: A Biography* (2 vols.; New York, 1974), 546–47.

2. Four unsigned, undated paragraphs among the Phil Stone Papers, Humanities Research Center, University of Texas at Austin.

3. William D. McCain, "The Triumph of Democracy, 1916–1932," in Richard Aubrey McLemore (gen. ed.), *A History of Mississippi* (2 vols.; Hattiesburg, 1973), 2:84; William Alexander Percy, *Lanterns on the Levee: Recollections of a Planter's Son* (1941; rpr. Baton Rouge, 1973), 249.

4. Ben B. McNew, "Banking, 1890–1970," in McLemore, *History of Mississippi*, 2:320; William Faulkner, "Mississippi," *Holiday*, April 1954, 40.

5. Blotner, *Faulkner*, 531–32, 527–28ff. In a 19 February 1957 letter to James Meriwether, Stone remarked, "Bill once wrote fifteen or twenty pages on the idea of the Snopes trilogy which he entitled 'Father Abraham' but I think that has disappeared."

6. James B. Meriwether, "Early Notices of Faulkner by Phil Stone and Louis Cochran," *Mississippi Quarterly* 17 (Winter 1964): 152.

7. See Louis D. Rubin, Jr., "Southern Literature: The Historical Image," in Louis D. Rubin, Jr., and Robert D. Jacobs (eds.), *South: Modern Southern Literature in Its Cultural Setting* (Garden City, N.J., 1961), 29; Faulkner "Mississippi," 36. PS, claiming to be Faulkner's primary Civil War source, wrote Glenn O. Carey, 5 April 1950: "Bill never in his life saw a Confederate General"; furthermore, "almost all of his relations who had served in the Confederate army were dead before Bill got old enough to take notice."

8. PS to Elizabeth Y. Grosch, 19 July 1962. His letter to O. B. Emerson, 30 August 1957, is more general, "between 1925 and 1930."

9. PS to James Meriwether, 19 February 1957. There he dates the Snopeses only "before *Sartoris.*"

10. Quoted in PS to James Meriwether, 19 February 1957.

11. William Faulkner to Horace Liveright [received 22 July 1927], in Joseph Blotner (ed.), *Selected Letters of William Faulkner* (New York, 1977), 36–37.

12. Blotner, *Faulkner*, 531; William Faulkner to Horace Liveright [16 October 1927], in Blotner, *Letters*, 38.

13. William Faulkner to Horace Liveright [received 22 July 1927]; in Blotner, *Letters*, 37; PS to *New Republic*, 16 August 1927, HRC; William Faulkner to Liveright [late July 1927], in Blotner, *Letters*, 37.

14. Blotner, *Faulkner*, 557; Orbrey Street to PS, 7 and 12 October 1927, HRC; James Meriwether, *The Literary Career of William Faulkner* (Princeton, 1961), 64–65; William Faulkner, *Flags in the Dust*, ed. Douglas Day (New York, 1973), 365.

15. William Faulkner to Horace Liveright [16 October 1927], and 30 November [1927], in Blotner, *Letters*, 38–39; *Sartoris* dedication.

16. William Faulkner to Horace Liveright, 30 November [1927], in Blotner, *Letters*, 39; PS to Carl Rollins, 17 October 1931, HRC.

17. Blotner, *Faulkner*, 560.

18. PS to Carl Rollins, 17 October 1931, HRC.

19. Blotner, *Faulkner*, 560; William Faulkner to Horace Liveright, 30 November [1927], [mid or late February 1928], [early March 1928], in Blotner, *Letters*, 39–40.

20. PS to Elizabeth Y. Grosch, 19 July 1962.

21. William Faulkner to Horace Liveright [mid or late February 1928], in Blotner, *Letters*, 39; Blotner, *Faulkner*, 563, 561; Faulkner, *Flags*, vi; Faulkner to Mrs. Walter B. McLean [probably spring 1928], in Blotner, *Letters*, 40–41; Faulkner, *Flags*, viii; Blotner, *Faulkner*, 570, 563, 590.

22. Blotner, *Faulkner*, 555 and note. See William Faulkner to Horace Liveright, 18 February 1927, in Blotner, *Letters*, 34–35, and Blotner, *Faulkner*, 524, 539, 557, 561, 563.

23. Stone wedding announcement, clipping, 19 October 1935; Meriwether, "Early Notices," 152–53; *Time*, 2 July 1928; interview with W. H. Anderson, 14 July 1976.

24. *New York Times*, 25 June 1928; *Time*, 25 June 1928; *New York Times*, 23 May 1928; "Phil Stone: An Autobiography," a sixteen-page, third-person narrative penciled at Whitfield, the state mental institution in Jackson, in autumn 1963.

25. David Burner, *The Politics of Provincialism* (New York, 1968), 192.

26. *Time*, 2 and 9 July 1928. Mrs. A. S. Scott, Jr., in a 9 August 1975 interview, remembered her father's brown derby, given him by Smith during the campaign, she said.

27. Burner, *Politics of Provincialism*, 202ff., 217–18ff.; interviews with W. H. Anderson and Mrs. A. S. Scott, Jr.; Burner, *Politics of Provincialism*, 187.

28. PS to Carvel Collins, 16 August 1954, and to James Meriwether, 7 July 1960. *The Sound and the Fury* section below, except where indicated, follows the letter to Collins.

29. Emily Whitehurst Stone, "Faulkner Gets Started," *Texas Quarterly* 8 (Winter 1965): 144.

30. PS to Carvel Collins, 17 and 24 August 1954; PS to Howard R. Bartlett, 24 August 1954; Meriwether, "Early Notices," 139.

31. Blotner, *Faulkner*, 580–81, 583.

32. William Faulkner to PS [c. 11 November 1928], HRC; Blotner, *Faulkner*, 581, 583–84, 585, 593, 587, 592, 595, 598; handwritten note at bottom of "Hermaphroditus," HRC; Blotner, *Faulkner*, 584–85.

33. *Bench and Bar of Mississippi: A Pictorial and Biographical Directory* (Jackson, 1938), 4; McCain, "Triumph of Democracy," in McLemore, *History of Mississippi*, 2:88; Blotner, *Faulkner*, 600–602; interview with W. M. Reed, 15 August 1975.

34. Blotner, *Faulkner*, 603–4; William Faulkner to Alfred Harcourt, 18 February 1929, in Blotner, *Letters*, 42–43.

35. PS to Carvel Collins, 16 August 1954; William Faulkner to Mrs. Walter B. McLean [postmarked 10 September 1925], and to Mrs. M. C. Falkner [postmarked 6 September 1925], in Blotner, *Letters*, 20, 17; Meriwether, "Early Notices," 162.

36. PS to Elizabeth Y. Grosch, 19 July 1962.

37. Edith Brown Douds, "Recollections of William Faulkner and the Bunch," in James W. Webb and A. Wigfall Green (eds.), *William Faulkner of Oxford* (Baton Rouge, 1965), 52; Phil Stone, " 'I Know William Faulkner,' " *Oxford Eagle*, 16 November 1950; PS to Elizabeth Y. Grosch, 19 July 1962; Blotner, *Faulkner*, 610–11, 613–14.

38. PS to James Meriwether, 19 February 1957; PS to Robert Coughlan, 30 September 1952. See Blotner, *Faulkner*, 619–20.

39. Blotner, *Faulkner*, 619, 624ff., 629, 627–28, 630.

40. Ibid., 633–34, 641. Stone reiterated that he had worked closely only with the first six novels, but see below. He proofread *Absalom*, at least, as well.

41. PS to Osmar Pimental, 6 November 1954; PS to O. B. Emerson, 30 August 1957.

42. Blotner, *Faulkner*, 632–33, 639, 643–44. Stone told Ed Meek (*Birmingham News*, 7 February 1961): "The only difference is that Stevens is a Harvard graduate. . . . [Faulkner] always likes to take a humorous stab at me when he can."

43. Unsigned lease contract between ____ Mayfield and William Faulkner, January 1930; interview with Judge Richard Thomas, 15 May 1978; Blotner, *Faulkner*, 652–53 (though there W. E. Stone IV and W. I. Stone are confused); PS to Four Seas, 5 November 1924, HRC; *Eagle*, 1 January 1931; Blotner, *Faulkner*, 646, 648, 654–55, 657, 661.

44. John K. Bettersworth, *Mississippi: A History* (Austin, 1959), 419–20;

Thomas D. Clark, "Changes in Transportation," in McLemore, *History of Mississippi*, 2:295–96; McCain, "Triumph of Democracy," in McLemore, *History of Mississippi*, 2:91; interview with Alice James Gatchell (Mrs. Kenneth P. Gatchell), 14 August 1975; *Eagle*, 17 February 1955 and 16 December 1954; PS to his son with 1907 *Eagle* election extra.

45. PS to Hubert Starr, 27 June 1930, HRC.

46. Blotner, *Faulkner*, 667, 669–70; PS to Myrtle Ramey Demarest, 31 October 1930, HRC.

47. Blotner, *Faulkner*, 673, 676; PS to Elizabeth Y. Grosch, 19 July 1962.

48. Emily Whitehurst Stone, "Faulkner Gets Started," 148; Meriwether, "Early Notices," 150.

49. Blotner, *Faulkner*, 681–82; *Eagle*, 1 January 1931.

CHAPTER 10. For Honor and for Love

1. Ben B. McNew, "Banking, 1890–1970," in Richard Aubrey McLemore (gen. ed.), *A History of Mississippi* (2 vols.; Hattiesburg, 1973), 2:321; *Oxford Eagle*, 9 July 1931.

2. *Eagle*, 1 January, 23 April, 24 September, and 10 December 1931.

3. Ibid., 22 January 1931. In an interview in Oxford in February 1976, Robert J. Farley labeled Phil's father "a crook" (while declaring Phil's ethics above reproach). No other sources corroborated the former opinion; several were incredulous at it.

4. Interview with Jim Kyle Hudson, Jr., 16 March 1978 (who corroborates Emily Stone's and the newspaper's details); Joseph Blotner, *Faulkner: A Biography* (2 vols.; New York, 1974), 750; M. P. Sturdivant to James Stone, Sr., 1 February 1931; Phil Stone to Charles D. Patterson, 29 May 1956.

5. Fred H. Montgomery to PS, 16 June 1931; PS to Al DeLacey, 13 July 1931; PS original (7 July) of 15 July 1931 *New Republic* ad; Byrne Hackett to PS, 3 July 1931; DeLacey to PS, 11 July 1931; Carl P. Rollins to PS, 14 October 1931. All of these are in the Humanities Research Center, University of Texas at Austin. Stone's 1931 *Marble Faun* correspondence with the Walden Book Shop, Henry Malcheski, L. L. Crane, Jr., John S. Mayfield, Benjamin Hauser, Raymond Green, Paul Leahy, the Tulsa Book Shop, and F. R. Billingslea is also now in the HRC. In a November 1931 correspondence Ben Wasson and PS bargained over six copies.

6. Benjamin Hauser to PS, 5 November 1931, PS to Hauser, 13 November 1931. See also F. Reed Alsop (Tulsa Book Shop) to PS, 9 July 1931, HRC.

7. Raymond Green to PS, and Benjamin Hauser to PS, 5 November 1931, PS to Carl P. Rollins, 17 October 1931, Cape & Smith to PS, 15 September and

13 October 1931, PS to Cape & Smith, 17 September and 15 October 1931, PS to William Faulkner, 18 November 1931, HRC.

8. *Eagle*, 20 August, 8 and 29 October, 13 August 1931; PS to Henry Hobson, 30 May 1960; PS to Philip, c. 1940s memo.

9. William Faulkner to Alfred Dashiell [probably 16 December 1931], and to Harrison Smith [probably early January 1922], in Joseph Blotner (ed.), *Selected Letters of William Faulkner* (New York, 1977), 54; PS to Lester C. Franklin, 4 April 1932.

10. James B. Meriwether, "Early Notices of Faulkner by Phil Stone and Louis Cochran," *Mississippi Quarterly* 17 (Winter 1964): 136–48, reprints PS's 28 December 1931 letter and Cochran's article. Cochran to PS, 23 December 1931, 15 January 1932, and 12, 14, and 26 April 1932, and PS to Cochran, 28 December 1931, are now in the HRC. See Blotner, *Faulkner*, 751ff.

11. Blotner, "Chronology," *Faulkner*, note p. 219.

12. Mississippi House Bill 318 (balances owed on 1932 State Employees' Salaries), Phil Stone Papers; PS to Barnet J. Beyer, Inc., 14 July 1932, PS to Al DeLacey, 13 July 1931, Bruce Humphries to William Faulkner, 14 May 1932, Byrne Hackett to PS, 28 July 1932, HRC.

13. Interviews with W. E. Stone V, 10 August 1975, and Mrs. A. S. Scott, Jr., 9 August 1975.

14. William Faulkner to Ben Wasson [received 25 September 1932], and to Harrison Smith [probably late October 1932], in Blotner, *Letters*, 65–66; Robert W. Hamblin and Louis Daniel Brodsky, *Selections from the William Faulkner Collection of Louis Daniel Brodsky: A Descriptive Catalogue* (Charlottesville, 1979), 69.

15. Blotner, "Chronology," *Faulkner*, note p. 219, 818.

16. Hubert Creekmore to PS, 24 May 1930, HRC; Emily Whitehurst Stone, "Some Arts of Self-Defense," in James W. Webb and A. Wigfall Green (eds.), *William Faulkner of Oxford* (Baton Rouge, 1965), 95–98.

17. Blotner, *Faulkner*, 876–77.

18. *Eagle*, 22 August 1957, 15 October 1953. PS's essay, "William Faulkner: The Man and His Work," is reprinted in Meriwether, "Early Notices," 148–64.

19. Meriwether, "Early Notices," 140.

20. Blotner, *Faulkner*, 841, 850.

21. Ibid., 849.

22. Unsigned carbon of will dated June _____, 1934, now in L. D. Brodsky Collection. See Hamblin and Brodsky, *Faulkner Collection*, 78.

23. PS to Robert Coughlan, 15 April 1954; William Faulkner to Mrs. William Faulkner [postmarked 7 July 1934], in Blotner, *Letters*, 81. See also Hamblin and Brodsky, *Faulkner Collection*, 77, 80.

24. Interview with Alice James Gatchell (Mrs. Kenneth P. Gatchell), 14 August 1975; PS to Morton Goldman, 20 February 1936. See Alice James's book *Mississippi Verse* (Chapel Hill, 1934), which includes *Green Bough* poems.

25. Interview with D. R. Johnson, 16 March 1976.

26. PS to A. P. Hill, 14 November 1938; PS to Herbert Holmes, 22 November 1938.

27. PS to Morton Goldman, 22 January and 10 February 1936; Goldman to PS, 22 February 1936; PS to Goldman, 26 February 1936.

28. PS to *American Mercury*, 4 March and 3 August 1936; PS to Wesson Oil, 14 August 1936.

29. PS to Harold Guinzburg, 14 August 1936; Guinzburg's secretary to PS, 20 August 1936; PS to Guinzburg, 7 January 1937.

30. See Blotner, *Faulkner*, 879, for Faulkner's 1930s association with Stone Stop.

31. Interview with Mrs. Herbert Ray, 5 March 1980.

32. W. E. Stone V to Susan Snell, 31 July 1982; interviews with W. E. Stone V and Mrs. A. S. Scott, Jr.

33. Interview with Mrs. Herbert Ray; *Record of Sigma Alpha Epsilon* 57 (March 1937): 43.

34. Interviews with W. E. Stone V and Mrs. A. S. Scott, Jr.

35. PS to Harold Guinzburg, 1 January 1937; PS to Edward Aswell, 17 March 1937; PS to Guinzburg, 19 and 23 March 1937; Telegram, Aswell to PS, 20 March 1937; PS to Aswell, 23 March 1937; Aswell to PS, 25 and 26 March 1937; PS to Aswell, 29 March 1937; PS to Guinzburg's secretary, 30 March 1937; Aswell to PS, 31 March 1937; PS to Aswell, 2 April 1937; Guinzburg to PS, 12 April 1937.

36. PS to Mr. and Mrs. Aswell, 4 May 1937; Aswell to Stones, 6 May 1937; PS to Aswell, 10 May 1937; Aswell to PS, 10 May 1937; PS to Aswell, 2 and 7 June 1937; Aswell to Emily Stone, 4 and 11 June 1937; Aswell to PS, 10 June 1937; PS to Simon & Schuster, 8 June 1937.

37. Warren Bower to Emily Stone, 22 June 1937; PS to Editor, *Scribner's Presents*, 14 June 1937; PS to Macmillan, 22 November 1937 and 13 January 1938.

38. Emily W. Stone to Mrs. Mary Hutchinson, 10 February 1938; PS to Dr. Henry Boswell, 28 March 1938; Boswell to Dr. J. R. Simms, 21 April 1938; PS to Investor's Syndicate, 7 July 1937 and 16 August 1938; Blotner, *Faulkner*, 983, 986–88, 991ff.

39. PS to Little, Brown, 22 August 1938; PS to Myra Mason Lindsey, 11 October 1938; PS to Grossett & Dunlap, 9 July 1938; Atlanta *Constitution*,

5 September 1978 (Myrick obituary); PS to W. M. Whitehurst, 13 July 1938; PS to Hawks-Volcke, 22 August 1938, and 9 September 1938; William Faulkner to Hawks-Volcke, 24 August 1938; PS to *Yale Alumni Magazine*, 21 March 1947.

40. PS to Appleton-Century, 1 February 1939; PS to Edward Aswell, 1 February 1939; PS to Director General, Pan American Union, 16 February 1939; PS to Manuel Durande, Argentine Consul General, 16 February 1939.

41. PS to Ferner & Beane, 30 January 1939; PS to R. E. Todd, 31 January 1939.

42. William Faulkner to Robert K. Haas [received 22 March 1939], and 25 March 1939, in Blotner, *Letters*, 111–12. Although Blotner has reason to infer that the second, 25 March letter to Haas was typed at the Stone office, the stenographer's initials, "sp," are not those of the March 1939 office secretary, Estelle Patton, "ekp."

43. PS to Mrs. M. E. Whitehurst, 5 and 18 May 1939.

44. PS to Nona E. Woodward, 5 October 1939; Emily W. Stone check for $25.00 to William Faulkner, 7 October 1939. Another, perhaps the only other repayment, dated 25 August 1941, is now in the L. D. Brodsky Collection.

45. PS to Harrison Kroll, 13 November 1939; PS to Kroll, 8 April 1940; Kroll to PS, 9 April 1940.

46. PS to *Atlantic Monthly*, 27 December 1939; PS to Hawks-Volcke, 4 March 1940.

47. An undated Emily Whitehurst Stone typescript, "Some Aspects of the Uses of Mythology in the Works of William Faulkner," is the source for details on *The Hamlet* composition and dedication.

48. PS to Harry Harrison Kroll, 16 November 1939.

49. Faulkner's 27 March 1940 will is now in the L. D. Brodsky Collection. See Hamblin and Brodsky, *Faulkner Collection*, 87.

50. Blotner, *Faulkner*, 818 (but the name is McCrady, not McCready).

CHAPTER 11. Compensations But No Reprieve

1. For example, Phil Stone to James A. Farley, 3 November 1939; PS to J. A. Latimer, 1 and 14 December 1939. See also Latimer to PS, 18 December 1939.

2. Joseph Blotner, *Faulkner: A Biography* (2 vols.; New York, 1974), 1196.

3. PS's secretary to J. T. Thomas, 13 December 1940, and PS to Thomas, 21 December 1940.

4. Rudolph Field to PS, 4 December 1940; House of Field to Mrs. Phil Stone, postmarked 22 November 1940; PS to House of Field, 14 December 1940.

5. PS to Mrs. Sewell Haggard, 3 and 20 March 1941; Haggard to PS, 19, 28, and 31 March 1941; PS to Major W. Calvin Wells, Sr., 24 April 1941; PS to Haggard, 1 and 16 May 1941.

6. Emily W. Stone to American Committee, 24 March 1941; Blotner, *Faulkner*, 1075 (PS saved the Civil Defense pamphlets for Philip).

7. Blotner, *Faulkner*, 1072, 1083; PS memo to Philip, 13 October 1951; Mrs. Phil Stone's check to William Faulkner, 25 August 1941, now in the L. D. Brodsky Collection. See Robert W. Hamblin and Louis Daniel Brodsky, *Selections from the William Faulkner Collection of Louis Daniel Brodsky: A Descriptive Catalogue* (Charlottesville, 1979), 93. Among the options Faulkner considered to finance a new novel in 1941 was to "collect enough of the loan I made the friend two years ago," (Blotner, *Faulkner*, 1072), so apparently PS's real estate speculation misled Faulkner too about the state of Stone's finances.

8. Harry Kroll to the Stones, 21 and 25 October 1941; another, postmarked 19 November 1941; Alfred W. Sturgis to PS, postmarked 4 December 1941.

9. Interviews with W. E. Stone V, 10 August 1975, and Mrs. A. S. Scott, Jr., 9 August 1975; PS to B. C. Adams, 29 December 1941.

10. PS to Branham Hume, 15 January 1942.

11. The Lee biography and the replacement Faulkner presentation copies are now in the Brodsky Collection.

12. PS to Thurman Arnold, Assistant Attorney General, 27 March 1942; PS to John L. Lewis, 27 March 1942 (research for new Whitehurst novel); Emily W. Stone to Edward Aswell, 10 June 1943; Emily Stone to PS, 15 May 1942.

13. William Faulkner, *Go Down, Moses* (New York, 1942), 305.

14. PS to Robert Daniel, 6 and 25 April 1942, and 12 May 1942, in the Brodsky Collection.

15. Blotner, *Faulkner*, 1113; Phil Stone, "William Faulkner and His Neighbors," *Saturday Review*, 19 September 1942, 12.

16. Carvel Collins to PS, 27 August 1953; PS to James T. Babb, 27 April 1954; Jennie B. Gardiner, "Book Ends," Memphis *Commercial Appeal*, 1 November 1942.

17. PS memo to Philip with club program, 1 March 1943; PS to Simon & Schuster, 2 June 1943.

18. PS to Harry Gorden, 18 March 1943.

19. PS to *Reader's Digest*, 5 March and 14 May 1943. Emily Stone's *Commercial Appeal* reviews resulted in a short correspondence with Ellen Glasgow—e.g., a card from Glasgow, 20 December 1943.

20. PS to Estelle K. Patton, 4 November 1943; *Commercial Appeal*, 22 October 1943.

21. Blotner, "Chronology," *Faulkner*, note p. 219, 1151–52.

22. David Cohn to the Stones, 24 March 1945.

23. James E. Gooch to PS, 23 April 1945.

24. Blotner, *Faulkner*, 1163–64, 1172–73, 1181–82; PS to Malcolm Cowley, 30 April 1945.

25. See Hamblin and Brodsky, *Faulkner Collection*, 87–90, 102. Stone's inscribed 1946 Modern Library volume is now in the William Boozer Collection.

26. Charles E. Merriam, *Systematic Politics* (Chicago, 1945), with PS's commentary in the book; Phil Stone, review of Merriam, *Systematic Politics*, in *American Bar Association Journal* 31 (December 1945): 656–57; Michael de L. Landon, *The Honor and Dignity of the Profession: A History of the Mississippi State Bar, 1906–1976* (Jackson, 1979), 67–68; *Jackson Daily News*, 24 August 1948; PS (resumé) to *American Bar Association Journal*, 22 May 1946; PS to G. W. Armstrong, 4 May 1951.

27. PS to *American Bar Association Journal*, 22 May 1946.

28. Emily Whitehurst Stone, "Faulkner Gets Started," *Texas Quarterly* 7 (Winter 1965): 142–43. See Blotner, *Faulkner*, 1216–18.

29. David Cohn to the Stones, 24 March 1945; Cohn to PS, 8 March 1946; PS memo to Philip, 13 December 1946; PS memo to Philip, c. Christmas 1946.

30. William Faulkner to Harold Ober [received 24 June 1946], in Joseph Blotner (ed.), *Selected Letters of William Faulkner* (New York, 1977), 238.

31. PS memo to Philip; Phil Stone, "What Is the Matter with Our Law Schools?" *American Bar Association Journal* 33 (May 1947): 470.

32. *Commercial Appeal*, 30 May 1948; *Jackson Daily News*, 24 August 1948; *American Bar Association Journal* 34 (August 1948): 736–37; Landon, *Mississippi State Bar*, 120.

33. Landon, *Mississippi State Bar*, 118; Jack Hancock, "Under the Ding-Dong Domes," *Jackson Daily News*, 24 August 1948, p. 3.

34. PS's copy of William Van O'Connor (ed.), *Forms of Modern Fiction* (Minneapolis, 1948), is now in the William Boozer Collection.

35. See Hamblin and Brodsky, *Faulkner Collection*, 107, and Blotner, *Faulkner*, 1275.

36. *Oxford Eagle*, 25 November 1948; Hamblin and Brodsky, *Faulkner Collection*, 105; PS memo to Philip, 18 March 1949.

37. Conference program, 25–26 March 1949.

38. Stark Young to W. Alton Bryant, 4 April 1949, and to Julia Young Robertson [2 May 1949], in John Pilkington (ed.), *Stark Young, A Life in the Arts: Letters, 1900–1962* (2 vols.; Baton Rouge, 1975), 1086 and note, 1090.

39. Stark Young to Ella Somerville [23 May 1951], Young to Somerville [5 May 1952], Young to Somerville, 20 February 1935, Young to Somer-

ville [2 June 1935], in Pilkington, *Stark Young*, 1170–72, 1204, 581–82 and notes, 630.

40. Stark Young to Julia Young Robertson [2 May 1949], to Ella Somerville [3 May 1949], to Somerville [26 April 1949], to Somerville [3 May 1949], in Pilkington, *Stark Young*, 1089, 1093, 1087, 1095; PS memo to Araminta, 9 May 1949; Stark Young to Somerville [16 August 1949], in Pilkington, *Stark Young*, 1111.

41. Phil Stone, "Let Us Turn to Liberalism," President's Annual Address, Mississippi State Bar, *Mississippi Law Journal* 20 (1949): 424–30.

42. PS memo to Philip, June 1949. In the late 1940s or early 1950s PS was also mentioned for a state supreme court vacancy.

43. Hamblin and Brodsky, *Faulkner Collection*, 105; PS to Stark Young, 9 April 1951; PS memo to Araminta, 13 October 1949.

44. PS to Bank of Batesville, 30 November 1949.

45. Hamblin and Brodsky, *Faulkner Collection*, 109.

CHAPTER 12. The Embittered Friend

1. Phil Stone to Glenn O. Carey, 30 December 1949; 21 January, 9 February, 20 March, and 5 April 1950.

2. PS to Carvel Collins, 20 April 1950.

3. Carvel Collins to PS, 28 April 1950; PS to Collins, 28 April 1950; Collins to PS, 1 May 1950; PS to Collins, 3 May 1950; PS to Collins, 8 May 1950; Telegram, Collins to PS, 15 May 1950.

4. PS to Carvel Collins, 8 and 18 August 1950; Robert W. Hamblin and Louis Daniel Brodsky, *Selections from the William Faulkner Collection of Louis Daniel Brodsky: A Descriptive Catalogue* (Charlottesville, 1979), 111.

5. PS to R. O. Gerow, 25, 28, 29, and 30 August, 4 and 7 September 1950; Gerow to PS, 26 August, 5 and 9 September 1950.

6. PS to Editor, Memphis *Commercial Appeal*, c. 10 November 1950; *Commercial Appeal*, 15 October 1950, p. 4, with PS memo to Philip; PS to Paul H. Bowdre, 10 November 1950; Bowdre to PS, 18 November 1950.

7. Joseph Blotner, *Faulkner: A Biography* (2 vols.; New York, 1974), 1337–43.

8. Phil Stone, "'I Know William Faulkner,'" *Oxford Eagle*, 16 November 1950.

9. Blotner, *Faulkner*, 1346–52; typescript draft (?), Robert Coughlan, "William Faulkner Close Up—Part II, vi, 9–10," in Phil Stone Papers; PS to Stark Young, 20 March 1951; PS 1950 Christmas memo to Philip.

10. Hamblin and Brodsky, *Faulkner Collection*, 116. See Blotner, *Faulkner*, 1374.

11. Hamblin and Brodsky, *Faulkner Collection*, 112.

12. PS to William Faulkner, 12 February 1951.

13. James T. Babb to PS, 22 February 1951; PS to William Wisdom, 13 March 1951.

14. PS to Stark Young, 2 March 1951; Young to PS, "Monday," c. March or May 1951; Young to PS, "Saturday," late March 1951; PS to Young, 30 March 1951; PS to Judge George W. Armstrong, 4 and 10 May 1951; Armstrong to PS, 8 May 1951.

15. PS to Niles Campbell, 16 March 1951 (one of several dozen); PS to Professor M. W. Weems, 6 July 1951.

16. PS to Ross Barnett, 4 and 10 May 1951; Barnett to PS, 7 May 1951.

17. PS to Stark Young, 9 April 1951.

18. PS memos to Philip, 28 May 1951, with Jill Faulkner note to Emily Stone, 8 June 1951.

19. PS memos to Philip, 7 and 15 June 1951.

20. Blotner, *Faulkner*, 1390–93.

21. Stark Young to PS, 4, 12, 20 October and c. December 1951.

22. Hamblin and Brodsky, *Faulkner Collection*, 117–18; PS's 24 October 1951, note in his copy of *The Pavilion*, p. 194ff., in the William Boozer Collection; PS to Stark Young, 16 and 29 October 1951; PS to Carvel Collins, 26 October and 17 November 1951.

23. Madeleine Kilpatrick to Emily Stone, 28 December 1951; PS to Stark Young, 17 March 1952.

24. PS to Jerrold Nedwick, 17 March 1952; Charles D. Johnson to the Stones, 9 July 1952; PS to Hudson Strode, 23 April 1951; Strode to the Stones, n.d., on Robert E. Lee Hotel (Jackson) stationery; PS June 1952 memo; PS to Paul Flowers, 27 May 1952.

25. Interview with Arthur and Zoe Kreutz, 21 July 1976; *Eagle*, 11 September 1952.

26. William Van O'Connor to PS, 16 February 1952; PS to Ward L. Miner, 29 September and 27 October 1952.

27. PS to Robert Coughlan, 30 September 1952.

28. Ibid.; PS to Robert Coughlan, 10 October 1952.

29. PS to Carvel Collins, 13 November 1952; Collins to PS, 2 April 1952.

30. PS to Howard Magwood, 14 November and 27 December 1952, 12 and 22 January and 3 February 1953; PS to Boris Kaplan, 3 and 17 February 1953.

31. Hamblin and Brodsky, *Faulkner Collection*, 121.

32. PS to William Faulkner, 10 April 1953; PS to Robert Coughlan, 6 May 1953; PS to Carvel Collins, 20 April 1953; Blotner, *Faulkner*, 1452–54, 1456–57.

33. *Eagle*, 24 September and 29 October 1953; PS to FHA, 28 April and

7 May 1953; *Eagle*, 21 and 28 May 1953; *Commercial Appeal*, 15 September 1953.

34. PS to Robert Coughlan, 6 May 1953; Emily Stone to Harold Latham, 15 May 1953; Macmillan to Emily Stone, 15 and 22 July 1953; Emily Stone to Macmillan, 25 July 1953; Macmillan to Emily Stone, 15 August 1953; PS to Robert Coughlan, 16 September 1953; PS to Carvel Collins, 1 and 18 September 1953; Emily Stone to Macmillan, 21 September 1953; Coughlan to Emily Stone, 28 September 1953; Harold Latham to Emily Stone [late September 1953]; PS to Macmillan [early October 1953].

35. Robert Coughlan, "The Private World of William Faulkner," *Life*, 28 September 1953, 118–36; PS to Coughlan, 30 September, 1 October, and 24 September 1953; Blotner, *Faulkner*, 1468–69; Malcolm Cowley, *The Faulkner-Cowley File: Letters and Memories, 1944–1962* (New York, 1966), 131; Coughlan to PS, 27 October 1953; Blotner, *Faulkner*, 1469; PS to Coughlan, 1 October 1953; Robert Coughlan, "The Man Behind the Faulkner Myth," *Life*, 5 October 1953, pp. 55–68; PS to Editors, *Life*, 1 October 1953 (published in the issue of 26 October, pp. 19–20).

36. Whitney North Seymour to PS, 2 October 1953; Joe C. Barrett to PS, 6 October 1953; PS to Barrett, 7 October 1953; PS to Coughlan, 5 October 1953.

37. PS to Robert Coughlan, 30 October 1953; PS to Whitney North Seymour, Sr., 5 October 1953; unsigned letter, Mildred Spurrier Topp to Houghton Mifflin (for Emily Stone), n.d.; *Eagle*, 5 November 1953; Elizabeth Spencer to Emily Stone [September 1953]; Edward Dodd to Emily Stone, 24 September 1953; William Raney to Emily Stone, 30 September 1953.

38. PS to Safety Responsibility Bureau, 6 October 1953; Robert Coughlan to PS, 27 November 1953; PS to Coughlan, 30 November 1953; PS to Carvel Collins, 14 December 1953.

39. PS to Carvel Collins, 14 December 1953; *Eagle*, 3 December 1953; PS to Susan Myrick [October 1953].

40. PS to Robert Coughlan, 27 April 1954; assorted 1953 PS memos to Philip; PS to James Meriwether, 18 May 1957; PS to Robert S. Hotz, 15 November 1954; Hotz to PS, 7 December 1954.

41. *Eagle*, 4 March and 18 February 1954, 10 December 1953.

42. PS to Harold Latham, 11 February 1954; PS to Robert Coughlan, 15 January 1954; PS to Annie Laurie Williams, Inc., 20 February 1954; Williams to PS [February 1954] and 6 April 1954; Coughlan to the Stones, 4 April 1954; Emily Stone to Shirley Fisher, 10 April 1954.

43. Robert Coughlan to PS, 13 April 1954; PS to Coughlan, 15 April 1954; PS to Coughlan, 16 and 27 April 1954.

44. Shirley Fisher to Emily Stone, 12 May 1954; Elizabeth Otis to Stones, 15 May 1954; Otis to Emily Stone [late May 1954]; PS to Otis, 31 May 1954;

PS to Robert Coughlan, 31 May 1954; Emily Stone to Otis, 31 May 1954; PS to Otis, 3 June 1954; Otis to PS, 4 June 1954.

45. Hamblin and Brodsky, *Faulkner Collection*, 122–23, 117, 131. PS's 12 April 1954 letter, his single lapse, reported his part in Faulkner's career, but also Emily's purposely not reading Faulkner in the last two years.

46. PS to Elizabeth Otis, 3 June 1954; PS to Otis, 22 July 1954.

47. Hamblin and Brodsky, *Faulkner Collection*, 123–24; PS to Carvel Collins, 12 January 1953 ("a good girl [whom] we think very highly of"); *Eagle*, 2 September 1954.

48. PS to Carvel Collins, 16 August (copy to Howard R. Bartlett), 17, 24, 1 August 1954; PS to Bartlett, 24 August 1954.

49. PS to Whitney North Seymour, Sr., 4 September 1954; Seymour to PS, 2 September 1954; PS to Robert Coughlan, 4 October 1954; Emily Stone to Elizabeth Otis, 28 September 1954.

50. PS to Robert Coughlan, 4 and 6 October 1954; PS to Osmar Pimental, 6 November 1954; Pimental to PS, 30 October 1954.

51. PS to Robert Coughlan, 4 October 1954; PS to Elizabeth Otis, 24 November 1954 (reiterating his wife's wish "to [have] quit" a decade before); Emily Stone to Otis, 19 October 1954 and 3 January 1955.

52. *Eagle*, 16 December 1954.

53. Emily Stone to Elizabeth Otis, 3 January 1955.

54. PS to Frances Craighead Dwyer, 15 March 1955; Emily Stone to Elizabeth Otis [April 1955].

55. Dave Womack, Letter to Editors, *Commercial Appeal*, 27 March 1955; PS to Womack, 28 March 1955; PS to Susan Myrick, 31 March 1955; Hamblin and Brodsky, *Faulkner Collection*, 125; PS to William Van O'Connor, 15 November 1955; Samuel Blazer to PS, 28 March 1955; PS to Blazer, 4 April 1955.

56. PS to Samuel Blazer, 4 April 1955; *Chicago Review* to Emily Stone, 31 July 1955; Emily Stone to Elizabeth Otis [September 1955?]; Emily Stone to Otis, 8 December 1955; *Chicago Review* to Emily Stone, 5 March 1956; Emily Whitehurst Stone, "Feet of Clay," *Chicago Review* 10 (Spring 1956): 10–35.

57. *Eagle*, 19 May 1955; PS memo to Philip with Stork Club photograph; Emily Stone to Elizabeth Otis, 18 January 1956; PS to Carvel Collins, 18 June 1956; PS to Allen Hoey, 30 July 1956.

CHAPTER 13. Cataclysm

1. Phil Stone to Robert Nichols, Jr., 24 March 1956; PS to Joe T. Patterson, 28 May 1956; PS to Clarence Morgan, Sr., 4 June 1956; PS to Nichols, 24 March 1956.

2. PS to D. R. Johnson, 16 August 1956; PS to C. E. Morgan, 11 June 1956; Morgan to PS, 15 August and 8 September 1956.

3. PS to Patterson, 14 September 1956; Patterson to PS, 15 September 1956.

4. PS to Donald P. Duclos, 9 February 1956; drafts and corrected typescript, Emily Stone to Annie Laurie [Williams], blind copy to James Meriwether, 25 September 1956.

5. PS to Robert Nichols, 6 April 1956.

6. PS to Joe T. Patterson, 14 September 1956; interview with D. R. Johnson, 16 March 1976; PS to C. E. Morgan, 9 August and 9 July 1957; Morgan to PS, 29 July 1957; D. R. Johnson to Morgan, 31 July and 8 August 1957; PS to Robert Nichols, 5 October 1957.

7. PS to Carvel Collins, 7 December 1956 (repeated almost verbatim to James Meriwether, 19 February 1957).

8. PS to Richard Crocker Gurney, 19 January 1957; James Meriwether to PS, 13 November 1956 and 11 February 1957; Joseph Blotner, *Faulkner: A Biography* (2 vols.; New York, 1974), 1619.

9. PS to James Meriwether, 19 February 1957.

10. PS to William S. Dix, 18 April 1957; PS to James Meriwether, 17, 18, 25, and 28 May 1957; PS to Robert Holland, 1 June 1957 (with Emily Stone postscript).

11. Zoe Kreutz to George Savage, 23 June 1957.

12. PS to William S. Dix, 18 April 1957; Dix to PS, 24 April 1957; PS to Carvel Collins, 17 May 1957.

13. James Meriwether to PS, 3 November 1957; PS to James Meriwether, 16 September 1957; PS to Carvel Collins, 19 July 1957; PS to Carvel Collins, 16 September 1957. See Blotner, *Faulkner*, 1675–76. Stone did not know that Faulkner soon reworked and expanded a canceled paragraph from the Memphis letter to send to the *New York Times*.

14. PS to Carvel Collins, 4 October 1957; PS to James Meriwether, 6 November 1957; PS to Henry Tetlow, 23 January 1958.

15. PS to Henry Tetlow, 23 January 1958; PS to Maud Falkner, 14 February 1958; *Oxford Eagle*, 13 March 1958.

16. PS to Harold Ober, 15 May and 10 October 1958. See Robert W. Hamblin and Louis Daniel Brodsky, *Selections from the William Faulkner Collection of Louis Daniel Brodsky: A Descriptive Catalogue* (Charlottesville, 1979), 133–34, for a summary of the full correspondence.

17. T. H. Freeland III to Susan Snell, 26 July 1976; PS to D. R. Johnson, 11 January and 3 September 1958.

18. *Hotchkiss Record*, 16 May 1958; PS to Carvel Collins, Robert Coughlan, Nelson Levings, Katherine Compton, 22 April 1958; PS to Elizabeth Otis,

2 May 1958; PS to Allen Hoey, 14 May 1958; Hoey to PS, 20 May 1958; PS to Philip C. Hynson, 15 May 1958.

19. PS to Jeff Davis, 18 September 1958; Robert Ballou to PS, 25 November 1958; Philip Alston Stone to Araminta Stone, c. 23 November 1958.

20. Elizabeth Otis to the Stones [September–October], 1958; PS to Otis, 27 September and 3 November 1958.

21. James Meriwether to PS, 3 November 1957; Meriwether to PS, 11 November 1957; PS to Meriwether, 6 November 1957; Meriwether to PS, 3 December 1958; PS to Meriwether, 6 December 1958; PS to Meriwether, 9 January and 7 January 1959; Elizabeth Otis to PS, 30 December 1958.

22. PS to James Meriwether, 7 and 9 January 1959; PS to Elizabeth Otis, 2 January 1959; PS to Meriwether, 2 January 1959; Meriwether to PS, 10 January 1959; PS to Meriwether, 12 January 1959; Meriwether to PS, 14 January 1959; PS to Meriwether, 16 January 1959; Meriwether to PS, 19 January 1959. The sale was for about eighty pages of manuscript and typed sheets.

23. William Faulkner to Harold Ober, 4 February 1959, in Joseph Blotner (ed.), *Selected Letters of William Faulkner* (New York, 1977), 421.

24. PS to D. R. Johnson, 9 February 1959.

25. Rollene W. Saal, "Four New Faces in Fiction," *Saturday Review*, 11 April 1959, 38.

26. PS to D. R. Johnson, 2 April 1959; PS to American Air Lines, 23 March 1959; interview with Evans Harrington, 21 July 1976. Harrington, an older fellow writer, and Philip's closest Oxford confidant, believes, however, that the brilliance of the boy postponed—and deepened—Philip's inevitable rebellion against his parents and that, especially after reading Freud at Harvard that year, he "retroactively developed a sense of bitterness" toward them, one that Philip would not work through until long after his father's collapse.

27. Joseph Blotner (comp.), *William Faulkner's Library—A Catalogue* (Charlottesville, 1964), 53; Blotner, *Faulkner*, 1728; John Faulkner to Philip Stone, 23 March 1959; PS to W. E. Stone V, 15 April 1959; interview with W. E. Stone V, 10 August 1975; PS to Erle Howry (bookshop partner of Walter Armstrong), 9 April 1959; Robert Coughlan to PS, 15 September 1959; PS to Aaron Condon, 21 October 1959; PS to Elizabeth Otis, 9 March 1959; PS to James Meriwether, 23 May 1959.

28. Albert M. Parillo, "Young Writers," *Cosmopolitan*, August 1959, 62; "Briefly Noted," *New Yorker*, 18 April 1959, 164; Frank H. Lyell, "Life and Death of a Demagogue," *New York Times Book Review*, 17 May 1959, section 7, p. 28; Shirley Ann Grau, "Mississippi Is Their Mystique," *Saturday Review*, 2 May 1959, 24. Sales by 30 April were 2,165.

29. PS to Robert Ballou, 19 May 1959; PS to Book Review Editor, *New York*

Times (for Frank Lyell), 16 May 1959; Parillo, "Young Writers," 62; PS to James Meriwether, 24 August 1959.

30. *Eagle*, 11 June 1959; PS to Charles D. Johnson, 2 September 1959; Hubert Starr to PS, 16 April 1959.

31. PS to D. R. Johnson, 24 and 29 June, 29 July, 24 August, 8 and 18 September 1959.

32. PS to Harrison Smith, 2 June 1959, published in *Saturday Review*, 27 June 1959, 23; PS to William Faulkner, 9 December 1959 (PS did not keep copies of the enclosures); Elizabeth Otis to PS, "Wednesday," [October] 1959; PS to Otis, 9 October 1959.

33. Telephone interview, Herbert Fant, 10 July 1976.

34. PS to Elizabeth Otis, 1 March 1960; Otis to PS, "Thursday," [early March] 1960.

35. Interview with Robert J. Farley, February 1976; PS to Nelson Levings, 1 May 1959.

36. PS to Mrs. J. C. Jourdan, 5 June 1961; PS memo to Araminta, 10 June 1960; PS to James Meriwether, 7 July 1960; PS to R. P. Adams, 31 October 1960; Kraig Klosson to PS, 17 October 1960; Blotner, *Faulkner*, 1764–65; PS to Klosson, 21 October 1960.

37. William Rossky to PS, 10 November 1960; PS to D. R. Johnson, 19 January 1961 and 12 December 1960; PS to T. H. Freeland III, 30 January 1961.

38. For example, PS to D. R. Johnson, 26 August 1960: "I told Hal it just does me good to look at you. I know that's silly, but that's just the way it is."

39. Jean A. Adams to Emily Stone, 29 July 1961; PS to R. P. Adams, 3 August 1961.

40. James Meriwether to PS, 23 July 1961; *Jackson Daily News*, 27 April 1961, p. 2.

41. PS memo to Philip, 31 August 1961.

42. Ewing L. Hurdle to Philip Stone, 18 September 1961; PS to D. R. Johnson, 13 and 21 September 1961; R. P. Adams to PS, 3 October 1961; PS to Adams, 4 October 1961.

43. Partnership agreement, October 1961; PS to D. R. Johnson, 17 June and 18 July 1961.

44. PS to James Meriwether, 27 November 1961; Meriwether to PS, 22 November 1961; Alan R. Frederiksen to PS, 5 May 1962; PS to Fredericksen, 14 May 1962.

45. PS to D. R. Johnson, 15 May 1961; telephone interview with Herbert Fant, 10 July 1976; interview with Evans Harrington, 21 July 1976; 16 January 1962, Codicil to Phil Stone will.

46. PS to Harvard Student Agencies, 18 May 1962; telegram, Philip Stone to PS, 31 May 1962.

47. R. P. Adams to PS, 18 May 1962; PS to Adams, 1 and 8 June 1962; James Meriwether to PS, 26 May 1962; PS to Meriwether, 1 June 1962; Adams to PS, 4 and 14 June 1962; PS to Adams, 18 June 1962; Meriwether to PS, 10 June 1962.

48. Hamblin and Brodsky, *Faulkner Collection*, 144; PS to William Falkner [sic], 13 June 1962; an undated Emily Whitehurst Stone typescript, "Some Aspects of the Uses of Mythology in the Works of William Faulkner."

49. PS to William Falkner [sic], 13 June 1962; PS to James Meriwether, 15 June 1962.

50. Hubert Starr to PS, 6 July 1962; Blotner, *Faulkner*, 1835–38. PS confessed to Starr, 11 July 1962: "I had no idea that Bill's death would hit me as hard as it did but I have not gotten over it yet."

51. Hamblin and Brodsky, *Faulkner Collection*, 145–47; Blotner, *Faulkner*, 1844–46.

52. PS to R. P. Adams, 9 July 1962; PS to Paul D. Summers, 12 July 1962.

53. McGraw-Hill to PS, 17 July 1962; PS to McGraw-Hill, and to Paul D. Summers, 12 July 1962; R. P. Adams to PS, 17 July 1962; James Meriwether to PS, 13 and 17 July 1962; Paul D. Summers, Jr., to PS, 18 July 1962; PS to Summers, 21 July 1962; H. E. Richardson to PS, 15 July 1962; PS to Richardson, 19 July 1962.

54. PS to John Starr, 20 August and 21 July 1962.

55. Philip A. Stone to Phil and Emily Stone, 5 August 1962; PS to James Meriwether, 14 August 1962. Many of the details of Stone's breakdown are recorded in commitment affidavits by Emily Stone, T. H. Freeland III, Gerry Gafford, and attorney Glenn Fant.

56. T. H. Freeland III to Susan Snell, 26 July 1976; telegram, PS to "Dr. McCool," 21 September 1962.

57. Principal facts for the Meredith section derive from the Stones' copies of *Time*, 5 October 1962, pp. 15–17, and 12 October 1962, pp. 19–22. In addition to the bulky, exhaustive Ole Miss Riots file that Emily Stone compiled (comprising court records, propaganda, newspapers, magazines, etc.), she composed a diary (1–3 October) and a short draft essay "Good Lord, Deliver Us" on which I rely as well.

58. Carvel Collins to PS, 5 October 1962; PS to Collins, 11 and 29 October 1962.

Index

Index